Instructor's Manual (Chapters 1-17)

Accounting
TWENTY-FIRST EDITION

OR

Financial Accounting
NINTH EDITION

CARL S. WARREN • JAMES M. REEVE • PHILIP E. FESS

Prepared by

Donna Chadwick
Sinclair Community College

THOMSON

SOUTH-WESTERN

Australia · Canada · Mexico · Singapore · Spain · United Kingdom · United States

Instructor's Manual to accompany Accounting, 21e Ch. 1-17 or Financial Accounting, 9e

Carl S. Warren, James M. Reeve, Philip E. Fess
Prepared by Donna Chadwick

VP/Editorial Director:
Jack W. Calhoun

VP/Editor-in-Chief:
George Werthman

Publisher:
Rob Dewey

Executive Editor:
Sharon Oblinger

Developmental Editor:
Erin Joyner

Marketing Manager:
Keith Chassé

Production Editor:
Heather Mann

Manufacturing Coordinator:
Doug Wilke

Technology Project Editor:
Sally Neiman

Media Editors:
Robin Browning & Kelly Reid

Design Project Manager:
Michelle Kunkler

Illustrator:
Matsu

Cover Designer:
Michael H. Stratton

Printer:
Globus Printing, Inc.
Minster, OH

COPYRIGHT © 2005
by South-Western, part of the Thomson Corporation. South-Western, Thomson, and the Thomson logo are trademarks used herein under license.

Printed in the United States of America
1 2 3 4 5   06 05 04 03

ISBN: 0-324-20414-0

The text of this publication, or any part thereof, may be reproduced for use in classes for which Accounting, 21e or Financial Accounting, 9e by Warren, Reeve, and Fess is the adopted textbook. It may not be reproduced in any manner whatsoever for any other purpose without written permission from the publisher.

For permission to use material from this text or product, contact us by
Tel (800) 730-2214
Fax (800) 730-2215
http://www.thomsonrights.com

For more information
contact South-Western,
5191 Natorp Boulevard,
Mason, Ohio, 45040.
Or you can visit our Internet site at:
http://www.swlearning.com

Contents

	Introduction	v
Section I	**Description of Problems**	vii
Section II	**Instructor's Resource Materials**	

Chapter 1 Introduction to Accounting and Business
    Teaching Suggestions 1
    Transparency Masters 16

Chapter 2 Analyzing Transactions
    Teaching Suggestions 35
    Transparency Masters 45

Chapter 3 The Matching Concept and the Adjusting Process
    Teaching Suggestions 63
    Transparency Masters 78

Chapter 4 Completing the Accounting Cycle
    Teaching Suggestions 89
    Transparency Masters 101

Chapter 5 Accounting Systems and Internal Controls
    Teaching Suggestions 119
    Transparency Masters 130

Chapter 6 Accounting for Merchandising Businesses
    Teaching Suggestions 141
    Transparency Masters 156

Chapter 7 Cash
    Teaching Suggestions 185
    Transparency Masters 196

Chapter 8 Receivables
    Teaching Suggestions 209
    Transparency Masters 227

Chapter 9 Inventories
    Teaching Suggestions 239
    Transparency Masters 253

Chapter 10 Fixed Assets and Intangible Assets
    Teaching Suggestions 275
    Transparency Masters 291

Chapter 11 Current Liabilities
    Teaching Suggestions 315
    Transparency Masters 326

Chapter 12 Corporations: Organization, Capital Stock Transactions, and Dividends
    Teaching Suggestions 341

	Transparency Masters	359
	Chapter 13 Partnerships and Limited Liability Corporations	
	Teaching Suggestions	373
	Transparency Masters	387
	Chapter 14 Income Taxes, Unusual Income Items, and Investments in Stocks	
	Teaching Suggestions	403
	Transparency Masters	416
	Chapter 15 Bonds Payable and Investments in Bonds	
	Teaching Suggestions	431
	Transparency Masters	450
	Chapter 16 Statement of Cash Flows	
	Teaching Suggestions	467
	Transparency Masters	478
	Chapter 17 Financial Statement Analysis	
	Teaching Suggestions	487
	Transparency Masters...	493
Section III	**Using the Power Accounting System Software (P.A.S.S)**	
	How to Use the P.A.S.S. Inspector CD	505
	Power Accounting System Software Setup	513

Introduction

The resources contained in this Instructor's Manual are provided for your use in preparing for and conducting your class, using the 21st edition of *ACCOUNTING*, Chapters 1-17, or the 9th edition of *FINANCIAL ACCOUNTING*, by Warren, Reeve, and Fess. These resources are: (1) a Description of Problems, which identifies the topic(s) covered by each problem and the estimated time required for students to solve each problem; (2) for each chapter, a manual of teaching suggestions and transparency masters; (3) instructions for using the Inspector Disk to check problems that students solve with the Power Accounting System Software (P.A.S.S.) that is available with the text; and (4) instructions for adding your own problems to the P.A.S.S.

Section I
Description of Problems

Description of Problems

Chapter	Problem	Description	Software*	Estimated Time (Hours)
1	1A(B)	Effect of transactions on accounting equation		1/2
1	2A(B)	Financial statements	S	1/2
1	3A(B)	Financial statements	S	3/4
1	4A(B)	Effect of transactions on accounting equation; financial statements	S	1
1	5A(B)	Effect of transactions on accounting equation; financial statements	P, S	1 1/2
1	6A(B)	Financial statements	S	1 1/2
2	1A(B)	Enter transactions in T accounts; trial balance		1 1/2
2	2A(B)	Enter transactions in journal and post to ledger; trial balance	P, S	1 1/2
2	3A(B)	Enter transactions in journal and post to ledger; trial balance	P, S	1 1/2
2	4A(B)	Enter transactions in journal and post to ledger; trial balance	P, S	2
2	5A(B)	Locate errors and prepare corrected trial balance (WP**)		2
2	6A(B)	Corrected trial balance	S	1 1/2
3	1A(B)	Adjusting entries		1/2
3	2A(B)	Adjusting entries		3/4
3	3A(B)	Adjusting entries	P	1
3	4A(B)	Adjusting entries	P	3/4
3	5A(B)	Adjusting entries and adjusted trial balance	P, S	1
3	6A(B)	Adjusting entries; effect of omitted adjustments	S	1
4	1A(B)	Work sheet; statements; adjusting and closing entries	P, S	2 1/4
4	2A(B)	Adjusting and closing entries; statement of owner's equity	S	1
4	3A(B)	Ledger accounts; work sheet; statements; adjusting and closing entries (WP**)		2 1/4
4	4A(B)	Work sheet; statements; determine relationship of net income to revenue	P, S	2 1/4
4	5A(B)	Ledger accounts; work sheet; statements; adjusting and closing entries	P, S	2 1/2

*P = Power Accounting Systems Software
S = Spreadsheet Template
**Problem data are included in the Working Papers that accompany the text

Chapter	Problem	Description	Software*	Estimated Time (Hours)
5	1A(B)	Revenue journal; accounts receivable and general ledgers	S	1
5	2A(B)	Revenue and cash receipts journals; general and accounts receivable ledgers	P	1 3/4
5	3A(B)	Purchases journal; accounts payable and general ledgers	P	1
5	4A(B)	Purchases and cash payments journals; accounts payable and general ledgers	P	1 3/4
5	5A(B)	All ledgers and journals, trial balance	P	2 1/4
6	1A(B)	Multiple-step income statement, statement of owner's equity, and report form balance sheet	P	1 1/2
6	2A(B)	Single-step income statement, statement of owner's equity, and account form of balance sheet	S	1
6	3A(B)	Sales-related transactions	P, S	3/4
6	4A(B)	Purchase related transactions	P	1/2
6	5A(B)	Sales-related and purchase-related transactions	P	1 1/4
6	6A(B)	Sales-related and purchase-related transactions		1
6	7A(B)	Work sheet, financial statements, and adjusting and closing entries		2 1/2
7	1A(B)	Internal control of cash		1/2
7	2A(B)	Transactions for petty cash and cash short and over	S	3/4
7	3A(B)	Bank reconciliation and related entries	P, S	3/4
7	4A(B)	Bank reconciliation and related entries	P	3/4
7	5A(B)	Bank reconciliation, determined from records and bank statement; related entries		1 3/4
8	1A(B)	Entries for transactions, adjusting and closing related to uncollectible accounts	P	1
8	2A(B)	Aging of receivables; estimating allowance for doubtful accounts	S	1
8	3A(B)	Comparison of direct write-off and allowance methods of accounting for receivables	S	1
8	4A(B)	Calculations and transactions for notes receivable	S	1/2
8	5A(B)	Transactions for notes receivable		1
8	6A(B)	Transactions for sales and notes receivable	P	1
9	1A(B)	Perpetual inventory record by fifo and entries for sales and cost of merchandise sold	S	3/4
9	2A(B)	Perpetual inventory record by lifo	S	3/4
9	3A(B)	Cost of inventory by three cost methods	S	1 1/2
9	4A(B)	Lower of cost (fifo) or market for physical inventory count (WP**)		1 1/2
9	5A(B)	Retail method; gross profit method		1 1/4

Chapter	Problem	Description	Software*	Estimated Time (Hours)
10	1A(B)	Allocation of payments and receipts to fixed asset accounts	S	1
10	2A(B)	Depreciation by three methods	S	1
10	3A(B)	Depreciation by three methods – partial years	S	1
10	4A(B)	Depreciation by two methods; trade including entries and cost basis of new equipment	P	1 1/4
10	5A(B)	Transactions and ledger accounts related to delivery equipment, including trade and sale	P	1 1/2
10	6A(B)	Amortization and depletion entries		3/4
11	1A(B)	Transactions for notes payable and product warranty	P	3/4
11	2A(B)	Entries for payroll and payroll taxes	P	1
11	3A(B)	Wage and Tax Statement data; employer FICA tax	S	1 1/4
11	4A(B)	Payroll register and entries (WP**)		1
11	5A(B)	Payroll register	S	1 1/4
11	6A(B)	Payroll-related accounts and entries	P	2
12	1A(B)	Dividends on preferred and common stock	S	1
12	2A(B)	Entries for corporate expansion	P	3/4
12	3A(B)	Entries for stock transactions including treasury stock	P	1
12	4A(B)	Entries for selected corporate transactions, including stock dividends, and treasury stock; general ledger accounts	P, S	1
12	5A(B)	Entries for selected corporate transactions, including treasury stock, stock dividends, and stock split	P, S	1
13	1A(B)	Entries for partnership investment, balance sheet, and closing entries	P, S	1
13	2A(B)	Dividing partnership income	S	1
13	3A(B)	Financial statements for a partnership	S	1 1/2
13	4A(B)	Admitting a partner: entries and balance sheet	P	1 1/2
13	5A(B)	Statement of partnership liquidation	S	1
13	6A(B)	Statement of partnership liquidation	S	1
14	1A(B)	Income tax allocation	S	3/4
14	2A(B)	Income statement including loss from disposal of a segment, fixed asset impairment, extraordinary item, and appropriate earnings per share amounts	S	1
14	3A(B)	Income statement, retained earnings statement, and balance sheet	S	1 1/2
14	4A(B)	Entries for investments in stock	P	3/4
15	1A(B)	Effect of financing on earnings per share	S	1 1/2
15	2A(B)	Entries for sale of bonds; interest payments and amortization of premium by the straight-line method	P	1

Chapter	Problem	Description	Software*	Estimated Time (Hours)
15	3A(B)	Entries for sale of bonds; interest payments and amortization of discount by the straight-line method	P	1
15	4A(B)	Entries for bond transactions; determine amount of interest expense and bond carrying amount	P, S	1
15	5A(B)	Entries for long-term investments in bonds	P, S	1 1/4
15	6A(B)	Entries for interest payments and amortization of premium by the interest method		3/4
15	7A(B)	Entries for interest payments and amortization of discount by the interest method		3/4
16	1A(B)	Statement of cash flows – indirect method		1 1/4
16	2A(B)	Statement of cash flows – indirect method	S	1 1/2
16	3A(B)	Statement of cash flows – indirect method	S	1 1/2
16	4A(B)	Statement of cash flows – direct method	P, S	1 1/4
16	5A(B)	Statement of cash flows – direct method	S	1 1/4
17	1A(B)	Comparative income statement, using horizontal analysis	P, S	1
17	2A(B)	Comparative income statement, using vertical analysis	P, S	1
17	3A(B)	Current position ratios and effect of transactions on them	S	1
17	4A(B)	Nineteen ratios	S	2
17	5A(B)	Solvency and profitability trend analysis		1 1/2
C	1	Sales-related and purchase-related transactions in a periodic inventory system		1
C	2	Sales-related and purchase-related transactions in a periodic inventory system		1
C	3	Sales-related and purchase-related transactions in a periodic inventory system	P	1 1/4
C	4	Work sheet, financial statements, and adjusting and closing entries in a periodic inventory system	P	2
D	1	Entries for transactions made in foreign currency	P	1 1/4

Section II
Instructor's Resource Materials

INSTRUCTOR'S RESOURCE MATERIALS

The Instructor's Resource Materials are designed to provide you with fresh ideas for teaching accounting. These materials should minimize your classroom preparation time by providing lecture aids and practical teaching suggestions that are easy to carry directly into the classroom.

The teaching suggestions emulate many of the teaching initiatives being stressed in higher education today, including active learning, collaborative learning, critical thinking, and writing across the curriculum. These initiatives are integrated into the lecture notes, overhead transparency masters, demonstration problems, group learning activities, and writing exercises that accompany each chapter. The following notes will assist you in using these features effectively in your classes.

Demonstration Problems

You can use the demonstration problems to illustrate accounting practices in a classroom setting. Most students like to see accounting methods demonstrated in the classroom prior to attempting homework problems. Working through an accounting problem gives the instructor an opportunity to point out pitfalls that students should avoid. It also provides the opportunity to stress the underlying concepts and practical applications of an accounting practice.

Demonstration problems can be presented by using the traditional lecture mode of instruction. However, with only slight modifications in teaching style, they can be used to move students from passive note takers to active learners.

Rather than working through an entire problem for your students, ask them to participate by performing simple steps or calculations on their own. For example, assume you are working a problem in class that illustrates the process of recording business transactions. Complete a few entries for your students and then instruct them to record the next entry on their own. After giving them a minute to think and record their answer, present the correct solution. This method forces students into an active role and also gives them immediate feedback on their understanding of the techniques being presented.

Also consider asking students to perform all formula-based calculations that accompany demonstration problems. For example, give students the formula to calculate straight-line depreciation and the data to be applied to this formula, and then ask them to calculate the answer. This methodology forces students to match the raw data with a formula. As students become more comfortable with performing calculations in class, you can also work to wean them from a formula-based approach to accounting in favor of a conceptual-based approach. For example, rather than showing your students a formula to calculate straight-line depreciation, describe the concept, present example data, and ask them to decipher the calculation.

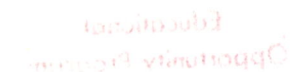

Group Learning Activities

Group learning activities provide another opportunity to actively involve students in the learning process. These activities ask students to apply accounting topics by completing an assigned task in small groups of three to five students. This process involves students in collaborative learning. They learn to ask questions and help each other master course content.

Small group work is an excellent way to introduce variety into the accounting classroom. It also encourages questions, since many students are more comfortable with admitting what they don't know in a small group than in front of the entire class. Group work allows students to discover solutions, rather than being shown a solution. It also frees the instructor to move through the class and work with small groups of students.

In many classes, you will find that group learning activities are more productive if you do not allow students to choose their own groups. When students do so, they usually work with friends or students with similar academic abilities. Groups provide the best learning environment if top students are mixed with average and poor students.

You may want to assign groups randomly at the beginning of the term. After the first test results are in, you may want to reassign groups so that each group contains a student who excelled on the first exam, as well as students who earned average and poor grades.

One easy way to break the class into groups is to distribute cards. At the beginning of the term, ask each student to pick one card from a deck of ordinary playing cards. Ask students to form groups of four, based on the card they choose (i.e., all kings are a group or all queens are a group).

Cards also make it easy to assign roles to individual group members. For example, you may want to assign the following roles for each activity:

1. Leader—makes sure that the task is completed in the allocated time.
2. Reporter—records and reports results to the class.
3. Socializer—makes sure that all group members are involved in the assignment. For example, if one member is not participating, the socializer should make it a point to ask for his or her input.
4. E.P.A. (Environmental Protection Agent)—makes sure that all desks and chairs are back in the proper place at the end of the activity.

By distributing the playing cards, you assign these roles by choosing a suit (e.g., the leader will be the spade, the reporter will be the heart). The cards also give you the flexibility to rotate roles daily.

Writing Exercises

Good written communication skills are essential to any businessperson. The textbook includes writing exercises designed to help students sharpen their communication skills. This Instructor's Resource Materials also include writing exercises. However, these exercises concentrate on writing as a learning tool, rather than writing as a means to a finished document.

If students can express a concept in writing, they understand that concept. By asking students to write about an accounting concept, both you and the students can determine exactly what they do and do not understand. Writing can make students vividly aware of gaps in their knowledge.

The writing assignments will ask students to respond to specific questions that probe their knowledge of conceptual issues related to accounting. They are designed to be completed in one to three minutes.

As the instructor, you have several options on how to use these writing exercises. You may want to collect your students' responses to gauge how well the class is grasping the course material. By reading even a sample from the responses, you can usually assess students' overall understanding of the material.

As an alternative, you could ask students to share their responses in small groups. This allows students who do understand course material to share their ideas with students who are struggling with course concepts.

Chapter 1
Introduction to Accounting and Business

OPENING COMMENTS

For many students, Chapter 1 of ACCOUNTING is their first taste of the accounting discipline. The teaching challenge is to get students to understand and accept the importance of learning accounting. This will make the course more than just another requirement that students must complete to graduate. Because this chapter will set the tone for the entire course, avoid the temptation to rush through the material.

Chapter 1 begins with a discussion of the three different types of businesses (manufacturing, merchandising, and service) and types of business organization (proprietorship, partnership, and corporation). Next, the chapter describes accounting as an information system, introduces business ethics, and provides a description of the accounting profession. Following this introductory information, the text explains the accounting equation and begins the discussion of recording business transactions in accounts. When transactions are recorded, changes in assets, liabilities, and owner's equity are stated as "increases" or "decreases"—the terms debit and credit are not introduced until Chapter 2. The chapter ends with examples of how to prepare financial statements and how to analyze a balance sheet using the ratio of liabilities to owner's equity.

After studying the chapter, your students should be able to:

1. Describe the nature of a business.
2. Describe the role of accounting in business.
3. Describe the importance of business ethics and the basic principles of proper ethical conduct.
4. Describe the profession of accounting.
5. Summarize the development of accounting principles and relate them to practice.
6. State the accounting equation and define each element of the equation.
7. Explain how business transactions can be stated in terms of the resulting changes in the basic elements of the accounting equation.
8. Describe the financial statements of a proprietorship and explain how they interrelate.
9. Use the ratio of liabilities to owner's equity to analyze the ability of a business to withstand poor business conditions.

OBJECTIVE 1 — Describe the nature of a business.

KEY TERMS:
- Business
- Business Strategy
- Combination Strategy
- Corporation
- Differentiation Strategy
- Limited Liability Corporation
- Low-Cost Strategy
- Manufacturing Business
- Merchandising Business
- Partnership
- Profit
- Proprietorship
- Service Business
- Stakeholder
- Value Chain

SUGGESTED APPROACH

The first class of your semester/quarter often sets the tone for the rest of the term. Many instructors believe it is easier to spark classroom discussion if you can get each student to speak on the first day of class. Objective 1 provides a good opportunity to encourage early class participation. Your students will be familiar with most of the terms introduced in this learning objective. Use the following writing exercise and classroom discussion suggestions to get students talking about business and accounting.

WRITING EXERCISE — Definition of Business

Everyone has heard the term "business." Ask your students to write short sentences/phrases that describe a business. After giving them a couple of minutes, ask your students to share their ideas as you make a list of their key phrases. Next, ask your students to use these ideas to write a definition of "business." You may want to compare their definitions to the one provided in the text, which defines a business as "an organization in which basic resources (inputs), such as materials and labor, are assembled and processed to provide goods or services (outputs) to customers."

CLASS DISCUSSION — Types of Businesses and Types of Business Organizations

List the three types of businesses:

      Manufacturing Businesses
      Merchandising Businesses
      Service Businesses

Ask for students to name examples of each type of business. Next, list the three types of business organizations:

      Proprietorship
      Partnership
      Corporation

Again, ask students to name examples of businesses in each category. Explain that in the early chapters of the text, they will be learning about accounting concepts related to service businesses organized as proprietorships.

You may also want to emphasize the following key facts about business organizations:

1. More than 70% of the businesses in the United States are organized as proprietorships.
2. About 10% of businesses are organized as partnerships.
3. About 20% of businesses are organized as corporations; however, they generate over 90% of the total dollars of business receipts.

GROUP LEARNING ACTIVITY – Business Strategies

Ask your students, working in a small group of 3 to 5, to decide on a business they would like to start (such as a coffee shop, a web page design service, a kitchen remodeling business, etc.) Once they have their business idea, instruct them to prepare a newspaper advertisement announcing the opening of their business. Give a tight time limit (5 – 7 minutes) and assure them that any ad art can be at the "stick people" level of artistry. After the working time, ask each group to share their business idea and ad with the class.

Briefly explain the following business strategies: low-cost, differentiation, and combination. Quickly review the ads and ask students to identify which strategy (if any) was implied in each advertisement.

LECTURE AIDS — Business Stakeholder

A business stakeholder is "a person or entity that has an interest in the economic performance of the business." Explain that stakeholders include owners, managers, employees, customers, creditors, and various government agencies. These stakeholders use accounting data to gauge the economic performance of businesses. Their information needs will be discussed in more detail under Objective 2.

EXERCISES & PROBLEMS FOR REINFORCEMENT:
    Exercise 1-1
    Exercise 1-2

OBJECTIVE 2 — Describe the role of accounting in business.

KEY TERMS:
    Accounting

SUGGESTED APPROACH

The text defines accounting as "an information system that provides reports to stakeholders about the economic activities and condition of a business." The goal of Objective 2 is to make this definition meaningful and to make students aware of the uses of accounting data.

To spark discussion, you may want to ask students what they think of when they hear the term "accounting." You could also ask what accounting information they or their families need in managing their finances (such as information for preparing income tax returns, budgeting everyday expenses, applying for college loans, etc.).

LECTURE AIDS — Accounting as an Information System

The goal of accounting can be illustrated using the following equation:

Goal of Accounting = Record + Report + Interpret
economic data for use by decision makers

Ask your students to name those who would be interested in the economic results of a business. List their responses on the board. When complete, the list should contain many of the following:

1. Owner
2. Investors/Stockholders
3. Bankers
4. Governmental Agencies (i.e., IRS)
5. Managers
6. Employees
7. Customers
8. Competitors

After compiling this list, you may want to ask students to state what economic data each of those listed previously would be interested in seeing and why. Examples follow.

	Interested In	Reason
1. Owner	Sales	Is advertising effective?
	Profit	Can I take home more money each week?
	Cash	Can I afford to buy more equipment?
2. Investors/Stockholders	Profit	Is my investment making money?
	Dividends	What dividends are being paid?
3. Bankers	Debts	Can this business repay a loan?
4. IRS	Profit	What taxes does this business owe?
5. Managers	Expenses	Am I keeping expenses within my budget?
	Sales	Will I be eligible for a bonus this year?
6. Employees	Profit	Can my company afford raises?
		Is my job secure?
7. Customers	Amount spent on warranty claims	How dependable is this product? How responsive is the service department?
8. Competitors	Amount spent on ads	How do I compare to my competitor?

You may want to emphasize that different accounting data are needed by different people and organizations. For example, a banker evaluating an application for a short-term loan and a public utility commission considering a rate increase would not consider the same types of accounting information.

GROUP LEARNING ACTIVITY — Accounting as an Information System

Handout 1-1 is a group exercise that has proven to be an excellent attention getter for a first class session. The exercise gives students information about the operations of an upholstery shop for a period of one year. The students are asked to calculate the shop's profit.

The upholstery shop exercise contains many accounting twists that the beginning student will not know how to handle, such as credit customers who have not yet paid, supplies that have been purchased but not used, and assets that will last more than one year. These twists will generally spur considerable student discussion. They also allow the instructor to illustrate the need for standardized accounting procedures.

Begin this exercise by asking the class to define the word profit. Next, break the students into small groups (two to five students). Ask them to read the upholstery shop exercise and determine the shop's profit. It is best to put the students at ease by announcing that, for today, there will be no "incorrect" answers. Give the students 10 or 15 minutes to work. Ask for each group's answer, and record it on the board.

The groups typically will provide a wide range of answers. This will allow you to emphasize that there must be standards for recording business transactions and rules on how to determine profit if that information is going to be useful to decision makers.

This exercise is a good icebreaker at the beginning of the course. It prompts the students to meet each other and to actively participate in the class. Because the goal of this exercise is to show the diversity in financial reporting that would occur without accounting standards, I usually do not announce the correct answer to this exercise. However, for your information, the shop's net income for its first year of operations is $18,580.

You may also want to use this exercise again at the end of the course. By that time, it is hoped that the groups will be able to come to a consensus on the "correct" answer.

OBJECTIVE 3 — Describe the importance of business ethics and the basic principles of proper ethical conduct.

KEY TERMS:
   Ethics

SUGGESTED APPROACH

This objective introduces ethical conduct as it applies in the business setting. You may want to supplement text material by discussing the codes of professional ethics for accountants.

Transparencies 1-1 and 1-2 present summaries of the Institute of Management Accountants and the American Institute of Certified Public Accountants codes of ethics. It is important to illustrate how these codes can be used to help accountants make difficult decisions. Four cases, which should stimulate a class discussion on ethics, follow.

You may want to refer to your college or university "Student Code of Conduct" as an example of an ethical code for students. To spark discussion, ask your students to develop a "Student Code of Conduct" for your course. Controversial issues you could ask them to consider is whether or not their code of conduct should include a policy on attending classes or the proper use of the textbook's solutions manual.

CLASS DISCUSSION —— Ethics in Accounting

Read one or more of the following cases to the class and discuss whether or not the accountant acted ethically. You can stimulate discussion by playing "devil's advocate"——arguing an opposing view to whatever opinion is first offered. (You may want to use Transparencies 1-3 through 1-6 in presenting these cases.)

1. Lauren Smith is the controller for Sports Central, a chain of sporting goods stores. She has been asked to recommend a site for a new store. Lauren has an uncle who owns a shopping plaza in the area of town where the new store is to be located, so she decides to contact her uncle about leasing space in his plaza. Lauren also contacted several other shopping plazas and malls, but her uncle's store turned out to be the most economical place to lease. Therefore, Lauren recommended locating the new store in her uncle's shopping plaza. In making her recommendation to management, she did not disclose that her uncle owns the shopping plaza.

    DISCUSSION NOTES: Lauren has a conflict of interest in recommending her uncle's shopping plaza as a site for the new store. After reviewing the data, management at Sports Central may agree with Lauren that her uncle's plaza is the most economical place to lease; however, Lauren should not make that recommendation without disclosing the family relationship. By hiding the conflict of interest, Lauren appears to lack integrity.

2. John Jones is the chief accountant for the Southwest district office of Security Life Insurance Company. While preparing the fourth-quarter sales report, John overheard the company president say that he would close Security's Phoenix office if it did not meet its fourth-quarter sales quota. John's best friend from college works at the Phoenix office.

    Anxious to find out whether the office was in jeopardy, John immediately finished the Phoenix office's report, only to find that it showed sales 25% below the quota. Later that afternoon, the company president called John for Phoenix's sales results. John told the president that he had not finished preparing the sales report for the Phoenix office. John wanted time to compile data that might convince the president to continue operations in Phoenix, despite lagging sales.

    DISCUSSION NOTES: Management accountants must communicate all information, both good and bad, fairly and objectively. It is not ethical to mislead management by withholding available information.

3. Tech-Smart Computer Company recently discovered a defect in the hard disks installed in its model R24 computer. The hard disk head in these units retracts too violently whenever the computers are turned off. As a result, the hard disks are destroyed after the computer is turned

on and off approximately 500 times. Tech-Smart has sold 4,000 model R24 computers nationwide.

The marketing department at Tech-Smart contacted most of the 4,000 owners of the model R24 computer and discovered that 20% (or 800) use their computers in businesses that operate 24 hours per day. These customers never turn their computers off; therefore, the defect should not damage their hard disk units.

Judy Govan, Tech-Smart's controller, has been asked to determine the cost to correct the hard disk problem and recommend a course of action. After studying the marketing department's report, Judy decides to recommend that Tech-Smart replace the hard drives only in the 3,200 units used by customers who actually turn their computers off.

DISCUSSION NOTES: In the real world, accountants must be good stewards of company funds. For example, although it may be socially responsible to donate a portion of the company's profits to a well-deserved charity, it is financially irresponsible to donate funds needed to meet payroll or loan obligations. In this case, the 800 customers who do not turn off their computers will not experience any problem with the R24. Replacing the drives will be costly, but it will add no benefit. Therefore, it is ethical to replace only the drives at risk because of the defect.

4. Tom Brown, the controller for MicroTech Software Company, is responsible for preparing the company's financial statements. He learns that sales for the first quarter of the year have dropped so dramatically that the company is in danger of bankruptcy. As a result, he applies for an accounting position with another software company that competes with MicroTech. During his job interview, Tom is asked why he wants to leave MicroTech. He replies truthfully, "The company's sales are down another 10% this quarter. I fear they will go out of business." At that time, MicroTech had not released its sales results to the public.

DISCUSSION NOTES: Tom may not disclose any confidential information. He is expressly forbidden from providing non-public sales information to anyone.

EXERCISES & PROBLEMS FOR REINFORCEMENT:
    Exercise 1-3

OBJECTIVE 4 — Describe the profession of accounting.

KEY TERMS:
    Certified Internal Auditor (CIA)   Financial Accounting
    Certified Management Accountant (CMA)   Managerial Accounting
    Certified Public Accountant (CPA)   Private Accounting
    Controller   Public Accounting

SUGGESTED APPROACH

This learning objective provides the opportunity to stress that accountants do more than just prepare tax forms!

You may want to begin by describing the differences between public and private accounting and then discussing specialized fields in accounting. Transparencies 1-7 through 1-9 present information to assist you with this presentation.

To emphasize the many employment alternatives available in accounting, ask students to bring in examples of advertisements for accounting positions from a local newspaper. If you know of an accounting professional with an especially interesting or unusual job, you may want to invite that individual to speak to your class. Even if this speaker must be scheduled later in the term, it will help emphasize the diversity in the accounting profession and dispel the "bean-counter" image.

You may also want to research the requirements for becoming a CPA in your state and share those with your students.

INTERNET ACTIVITY – Accounting Careers

Ask your students to do some research on some nontraditional accounting careers. Two government organizations who hire accountants to help with investigations of fraud and criminal activities are the FBI and the IRS. Websites for these organizations are:
      http://www.jobs.irs.gov/
      https://www.fbijobs.com

Please note: since websites are frequently changed, it is always a good idea to try these web sites at the beginning of each term to check the accuracy of the web address.

OBJECTIVE 5 —— Summarize the development of accounting principles and relate them to practice.

KEY TERMS:
    Business Entity Concept   Objectivity Concept
    Cost Concept   Unit of Measure Concept
    Financial Accounting Standards Board (FASB)
    Generally Accepted Accounting Principles (GAAP)

SUGGESTED APPROACH

This objective introduces students to the business entity concept, the cost concept, the objectivity concept, and the unit of measure concept——four principles that govern how accounting data are accumulated. Remind students that accounting data would be inconsistent from company to company if standardized procedures were not followed, as the class demonstrated in the Classic Upholstery Shop exercise from Objective 2 (Handout 1-1).

The following example may help in illustrating the business entity concept: If an individual owned a dry cleaner, a video store, and a gas station, how would the owner know the profitability of each? Answer: by keeping separate accounting records.

To emphasize the benefits of recording transactions at historical cost, ask your students to write down what their car (or other asset) cost and what it is currently worth. For many students, it will be easier to remember what their car cost than to estimate what it is worth. Next ask them to identify which value is more objective. The objectivity concept requires that accounting records be based on objective (verifiable) evidence. By writing amounts in terms of dollars, your students were using the unit of measure concept. This concept prescribes that all economic data should be recorded in dollars.

The writing exercise included below will help you determine whether your students can apply the business entity and cost concepts. This exercise can be assigned either (1) after you have briefly reviewed these two concepts in class or (2) before any in-class review as a test to see whether or not students have completed their reading assignment.

WRITING EXERCISE —— Business Entity and Cost Concept

Ask students to write an answer to the following questions (Transparency 1-10).

1. Sally Vertrees purchased a personal computer for use at home. Sally owns a dental practice. She occasionally uses the computer for a task related to her dental practice; however, the computer is used primarily by Sally's children. Can the computer be recorded as an asset in the accounting records of Sally's dental office? Why or why not?

2. Jason Thompson purchased an office building 10 years ago for $780,000. The building was just appraised at $1.25 million. What value should be used for the building in Jason's accounting records? Support your answer.

EXERCISES & PROBLEMS FOR REINFORCEMENT:
    Exercise 1-4

OBJECTIVE 6 —— State the accounting equation and define each element of the equation.

KEY TERMS:
    Accounting Equation   Liabilities
    Assets   Owner's Equity

SUGGESTED APPROACH

This objective asks the student to state the accounting equation: Assets = Liabilities + Owner's Equity. Transparency 1-11, which presents an alternative way to describe this accounting equation, is an effective lecture aid.

This objective also asks the student to define each element of the equation. Most students easily grasp the meaning of the terms assets (resources owned by a business) and liabilities (debts). Owner's equity, however, is not a simple concept.

One way to explain owner's equity is to compare it to the "equity" that a homeowner has in his or her home. Most students understand this usage of the term equity. A homeowner's equity is that portion of his or her home's value that would be received if the home were sold—it's what would be left after paying off the mortgage. In the same way, the owner's equity in a business is that owner's residual interest—what would be left if the assets were used to pay off all the business's debts.

To emphasize these new terms, ask your students to list their assets and liabilities on a sheet of paper and place a value on each item. Next ask them to calculate their equity, which for individuals is often called "net worth."

EXERCISES & PROBLEMS FOR REINFORCEMENT:
 Exercise 1-5
 Exercise 1-6

OBJECTIVE 7 — Explain how business transactions can be stated in terms of the resulting changes in the basic elements of the accounting equation.

KEY TERMS:
Account Payable	Expenses
Account Receivable	Prepaid Expenses
Business Transaction	Revenue

SUGGESTED APPROACH

This objective illustrates recording business transactions within the framework of the accounting equation. The text defines a business transaction as "an economic event or condition that directly changes the entity's financial position or directly affects its results of operations." Transparency 1-12 describes some of the economic events that are recorded as business transactions. This list can assist your students in determining what events/conditions to record. For practice, ask students to list transactions that they recently entered into with a business entity.

The basics of recording transactions can be effectively illustrated by working a sample problem for the students. Transparency 1-13 provides several example transactions for Jim's Lawn Care, which you can use to demonstrate how transactions are recorded. The following accounts will be needed to record these transactions:

Cash	Accounts Receivable	Supplies	Lawn Equipment	Accounts Payable	Jim Hamilton, Capital

You will probably need to emphasize the following points as you demonstrate transactions:

1. The accounting equation must always stay in balance. Transactions may require additions to both sides, subtractions from both sides, or an addition and subtraction on the same side, but the equation must always balance.
2. Revenue represents the receipt of assets for goods sold or services rendered. The receipt of assets from the owner is an investment.
3. Revenues are recognized when services are rendered, not when the cash is received.
4. Expenses are costs incurred in generating revenues. Purchases of assets, payments of liabilities, and owner's withdrawals are not recorded as expenses.

GROUP LEARNING ACTIVITY —— Recording Business Transactions

Rather than working through all of the transactions in Transparency 1-13 for your students, consider working only the first six. Divide the class into small groups (two to five students) and ask them to complete the exercise. Transparency 1-14 provides the solution. Give your students the opportunity to check their work and ask questions after they have completed their assignment.

EXERCISES & PROBLEMS FOR REINFORCEMENT:
    Exercise 1-9   Problem 1-1A   Problem 1-1B
    Exercise 1-10
    Exercise 1-11
    Exercise 1-12
    Exercise 1-13
    Exercise 1-14

OBJECTIVE 8 —— Describe the financial statements of a proprietorship and explain how they interrelate.

KEY TERMS:
Account Form	Net Income
Balance Sheet	Net Loss
Financial Statements	Report Form
Income Statement	Statement of Cash Flows
Matching Concept	Statement of Owner's Equity

SUGGESTED APPROACH

This objective introduces the concept of "matching." It is helpful to emphasize that matching is one of the most important concepts in accounting. If revenues and expenses are not properly matched, then the amount reported for net income is incorrect.

Transparency 1-15 provides a blank shell for preparing an income statement, balance sheet, and statement of owner's equity for Jim's Lawn Care. Review these formats with your class, emphasizing the following:

1. The date portion of the heading varies among the financial statements. The income statement and statement of owner's equity summarize transactions for a period of time, while the balance sheet shows a "snapshot" of the business on a particular date.
2. Net income from the income statement is used in calculating the ending capital balance on the statement of owner's equity.
3. The ending capital balance from the statement of owner's equity is the amount shown as "Capital" on the balance sheet. As a result, the balance sheet "balances."

Next, ask your students to build on the transactions recorded for Jim's Lawn Care under Objective 7 in the following group learning activity.

After covering the income statement, statement of owner's equity, and balance sheet, you may want to describe the statement of cash flows. Transparency 1-17 provides the highlights of this statement. Coverage of the cash flow statement also may be completely omitted at this point.

Appendix F contains examples of actual financial statements. You may want to refer students to these statements while covering this objective.

GROUP LEARNING ACTIVITY — Preparing Financial Statements

With Transparency 1-15 displayed on the overhead projector, divide the class into small groups. Ask students to use the balances from Jim's Lawn Care (Objective 7) to prepare financial statements for the month of May. Transparency 1-16 provides completed financial statements to share with the class after they have completed this assignment.

EXERCISES & PROBLEMS FOR REINFORCEMENT:

Exercise 1-8	Problem 1-2A	Problem 1-2B
Exercise 1-15	Problem 1-3A	Problem 1-3B
Exercise 1-16	Problem 1-4A	Problem 1-4B
Exercise 1-17	Problem 1-5A	Problem 1-5B
Exercise 1-18	Problem 1-6A	Problem 1-6B
Exercise 1-19		
Exercise 1-20		
Exercise 1-21		
Exercise 1-22		
Exercise 1-23		
Exercise 1-24		
Exercise 1-25		

OBJECTIVE 9 — Use the ratio of liabilities to owner's equity to analyze the ability of a business to withstand poor business conditions.

KEY TERMS:
Ratio of Liabilities to Owner's Equity

SUGGESTED APPROACH

To emphasize the importance of interpreting financial statements, financial ratios and other analytical tools are introduced throughout the text. Chapter 1 presents the ratio of liabilities to owner's equity. The following activities will assist you in explaining the importance of this ratio and illustrating its calculation.

LECTURE AIDS —— Relationship Between Debt and Risk

Recording business transactions within the framework of the accounting equation (assets = liabilities + owner's equity) allows the financial statement reader to quickly assess how much of a business' assets are financed with debt. Transparency 1-18 presents the accounting equation for two theoretical companies:

	Assets	=	Liabilities	+	Owner's Equity
Company A:	100,000		95,000		5,000
Company B:	100,000		10,000		90,000

Ask your students which company they would rather own and why. Next, ask which business has more risk—which will suffer first in an economic downturn? Point out that, just as a person with a high amount of debt will be in financial trouble very quickly after losing a job, Company A would probably suffer first because of high debt payments. You may also want to remind students that having some debt is not necessarily bad. Just as most individuals would never be able to buy a home without taking on debt, businesses often must borrow money to grow.

Next, present the formula used to calculate the ratio of liabilities to owner's equity:

$$\text{Ratio of Liabilities to Owner's Equity} = \frac{\text{Total Liabilities}}{\text{Total Owner's Equity}}$$

Ask your students to calculate the ratio of liabilities to owner's equity for the two companies on Transparency 1-18.

Company A: 95,000/5,000 = 19
Company B: 10,000/90,000 = .11

Point out that a higher ratio represents a higher level of debt. The following summary may also be helpful.

If Ratio of Liab. to OE > 1, debts exceed equity (business is financed mostly with debt)
If Ratio of Liab. to OE < 1, equity exceeds debts (business is financed mostly with equity)
If Ratio of Liab. to OE = 1, the business has equal amounts of debt and equity

GROUP LEARNING ACTIVITY —— Calculating the Ratio of Liabilities to Owner's Equity

Bring the annual reports for several companies to class. Divide students into groups, giving each group an annual report. Instruct students to locate the balance sheet in their annual report. You may want to warn students that another common name for the balance sheet is a "Statement of Financial Position." Once students have located the balance sheet, ask them to calculate the ratio of liabilities to owner's equity. It will be helpful if you explain that corporations use the term "total stockholder's equity" instead of total owner's equity. After students have finished calculating the ratio, have them report on their answer. This will allow students to see the range of values investors see in typical corporations.

EXERCISES & PROBLEMS FOR REINFORCEMENT:
    Exercise 1-26
    Exercise 1-27

Handout 1-1

CLASSIC UPHOLSTERY SHOP

Tyler Smith has worked in an upholstery shop for 10 years. Last year, Tyler's wages were $20,000. Lately, Tyler has been unhappy with the shop's owner. Convinced that he could run an upholstery shop that did better work at a lower cost, Tyler decided to go into business for himself and opened CLASSIC UPHOLSTERY SHOP.

To get the business going, Tyler decided to invest heavily in advertising. He spent $6,000 on advertising aimed at consumers and another $2,000 on advertising aimed at getting work from interior decorators and interior design stores. Tyler also purchased industrial sewing machines costing $4,000 and other tools and equipment costing $3,000. He estimated that the sewing machines can be used for about 5 years, before maintenance costs will be too high and the machines will need to be replaced. The other tools and equipment are not as durable and will have to be replaced in 3 years.

At the end of the first year of business, Tyler had received $80,000 in cash from customers for upholstery work. Tyler was owed another $2,500 from customers who are not required to pay cash, but are billed every 30 days.

A review of Tyler's checkbook shows he paid the following expenses (in addition to those mentioned previously) during the first year of business:

Upholstery fabric	$40,000
Other supplies	10,000
Wages—part-time assistant	9,500
Rent	4,800
Insurance (2-year policy)	3,200
Utilities	2,500
Miscellaneous expenses	1,700

Tyler's utility bill for the last month of the year has not arrived. He estimated that the bill will be approximately $320.

Tyler keeps some stock of upholstery fabric in popular colors on hand for customers who do not want to wait for special-order fabric to arrive. At the end of the year, about $14,000 of the fabric purchased during the year was in his store stock. In addition, $2,300 in supplies had not been used.

HOW MUCH PROFIT DID TYLER MAKE IN HIS FIRST YEAR OF BUSINESS? DO YOU THINK IT WAS A GOOD IDEA TO OPEN THE UPHOLSTERY SHOP, OR WOULD TYLER BE BETTER OFF WITH HIS OLD JOB?

Transparency Master 1-1

Institute of Management Accountants Standards of Ethical Conduct

1. Maintain an appropriate level of professional competence.

2. Refrain from disclosing confidential information.

3. Avoid conflicts of interest.

4. Communicate information fairly and objectively.

American Institute of Certified Public Accountants
Codes of Professional Conduct

1. Exercise sensitive professional and moral judgment.

2. Act in a way that will serve the public interest, honor the public trust, and demonstrate commitment to professionalism.

3. Perform all professional responsibilities with the highest sense of integrity.

4. Maintain objectivity and be free of conflicts of interest.

5. Observe the profession's technical and ethical standards and continually improve competency and quality of services.

6. Use ethical standards when determining the scope and nature of services to be provided.

ETHICS CASE

Lauren Smith is the controller for Sports Central, a chain of sporting goods stores. She has been asked to recommend a site for a new store. Lauren has an uncle who owns a shopping plaza in the area of town where the new store is to be located, so she decides to contact her uncle about leasing space in his plaza. Lauren also contacted several other shopping plazas and malls, but her uncle's store turned out to be the most economical place to lease. Therefore, Lauren recommended locating the new store in her uncle's shopping plaza. In making her recommendation to management, she did not disclose that her uncle owns the shopping plaza.

ETHICS CASE

John Jones is the chief accountant for the Southwest district office of Security Life Insurance Company. While preparing the fourth-quarter sales report, John overheard the company president say that he would close Security's Phoenix office if it did not meet its fourth-quarter sales quota. John's best friend from college works at the Phoenix office.

Anxious to find out whether the office was in jeopardy, John immediately finished the Phoenix office's report, only to find that it showed sales 25% below the quota. Later that afternoon, the company president called John for Phoenix's sales results. John told the president that he had not finished preparing the sales report for the Phoenix office. John wanted time to compile data that might convince the president to continue operations in Phoenix, despite lagging sales.

Transparency Master 1-5

ETHICS CASE

Tech-Smart Computer Company recently discovered a defect in the hard disks installed in its model R24 computer. The hard disk head in these units retracts too violently whenever the computers are turned off. As a result, the hard disks are destroyed after the computer is turned on and off approximately 500 times. Tech-Smart has sold 4,000 model R24 computers nationwide.

The marketing department at Tech-Smart contacted most of the 4,000 owners of the model R24 computer and discovered that 20% (or 800) use their computers in businesses that operate 24 hours per day. These customers never turn their computers off; therefore, the defect should not damage their hard disk units.

Judy Govan, Tech-Smart's controller, has been asked to determine the cost to correct the hard disk problem and recommend a course of action. After studying the marketing department's report, Judy decides to recommend that Tech-Smart replace the hard drives only in the 3,200 units used by customers who actually turn their computers off.

ETHICS CASE

Tom Brown, the controller for MicroTech Software Company, is responsible for preparing the company's financial statements. He learns that sales for the first quarter of the year have dropped so dramatically that the company is in danger of bankruptcy. As a result, he applies for an accounting position with another software company that competes with MicroTech. During his job interview, Tom is asked why he wants to leave MicroTech. He replies truthfully, "The company's sales are down another 10% this quarter. I fear they will go out of business." At that time, MicroTech had not released its sales results to the public.

SPECIALIZED FIELDS IN ACCOUNTING

Financial Accounting — preparing reports that show the profits and financial health of the company using the rules of accounting, known as generally accepted accounting principles (GAAP)

Auditing — evaluating financial records and reports to determine whether they present the results of a company's operations fairly

Management Accounting — providing data to management to assist in running day-to-day operations

SPECIALIZED FIELDS IN ACCOUNTING

Cost Accounting —— tracking costs, particularly those to manufacture a product

Tax Accounting —— preparing tax returns and helping companies and individuals reduce the amount of taxes paid by carefully planning their business activities

Accounting Systems —— designing accounting systems that collect accurate data and protect a company's assets (cash, inventory, etc.) from misuse or theft; since most accounting systems today are maintained on a computer, this area requires computer hardware and software knowledge

Transparency Master 1-9

SPECIALIZED FIELDS IN ACCOUNTING

International Accounting —— focusing on issues related to international trade; for example, buying or selling goods in a foreign currency

Not-for-Profit Accounting —— reporting on the operations of nonprofit organizations (such as churches, charities, educational institutions, and governmental agencies)

Social Accounting —— measuring the social costs and benefits of various actions

Accounting Instruction —— teaching accounting to students

WRITING EXERCISE

1. Sally Vertrees purchased a personal computer for use at home. Sally owns a dental practice. She occasionally uses the computer for a task related to her dental practice; however, the computer is used primarily by Sally's children. Can the computer be recorded as an asset in the accounting records of Sally's dental office? Why or why not?

2. Jason Thompson purchased an office building 10 years ago for $780,000. The building was just appraised at $1.25 million. What value should be used for the building in Jason's accounting records? Support your answer.

THE ACCOUNTING EQUATION

Assets   =   Liabilities + Owner's Equity

OR

| The Cost of the Items Used in Running a Business | = | Where the Funds to Buy Those Items Came From, Either Creditors or the Owner |

Example: A business buys a $20,000 delivery van by using $5,000 of the owner's money as a down payment and financing the rest.

Assets = Liabilities + Owner's Equity
$20,000 = $15,000 + 5,000

Transparency Master 1-12

EVENTS/CONDITIONS RECORDED IN ACCOUNTING RECORDS

1. Receipt of cash

2. Payment of cash

3. Events that create a legal obligation to pay out cash (or other assets) in the future

4. Events that obligate another party to pay you cash (or other assets) in the future

5. Sale of a product or completion of a service for a customer—this is known as earning revenue

6. The use of products or services in running your business—this is known as incurring an expense

Transparency Master 1-13

RECORDING BUSINESS TRANSACTIONS
Jim's Lawn Care

1. Jim Hamilton began a lawn care business in May by depositing $800 in a business bank account.
2. Purchased lawnmowers and other lawn equipment on account, $1,000.
3. Paid cash for supplies, $50.
4. Performed lawn care services for credit customers and billed them $700.
5. Received $700 cash from the customers billed in #4.
6. Paid $1,000 cash for the lawn equipment purchased in #2.
7. Paid for an advertisement in a local newspaper, $150.
8. Performed lawn care services for cash customers and immediately received $420.
9. Paid wages to a part-time assistant, $85.
10. Performed lawn care services for credit customers and billed them $600.
11. Received an invoice from Gas-n-Go for gasoline purchased on account during May, $110. The invoice will not be paid until next month.
12. At the end of May, Jim withdrew $100 from the business for personal use.

Transparency Master 1-14

RECORDING BUSINESS TRANSACTIONS
Jim's Lawn Care — Solution

	Cash	Accounts Receivable	Supplies	Lawn Equipment	Accounts Payable	J. Hamilton, Capital	
1.	+800					+800	Investment
Bal.	800					800	
2.				+1,000	+1,000		
Bal.	800			1,000	1,000	800	
3.	-50		+50				
Bal.	750		50	1,000	1,000	800	
4.		+700				+700	Revenue
Bal.	750	700	50	1,000	1,000	1,500	
5.	+700	-700					
Bal.	1,450	0	50	1,000	1000	1,500	
6.	-1,000				-1,000		
Bal.	450		50	1,000	0	1,500	
7.	-150					-150	Adv. Exp.
Bal.	300		50	1,000		1,350	
8.	+420					+420	Revenue
Bal.	720		50	1,000		1,770	
9.	-85					-85	Wage Exp.
Bal.	635		50	1,000		1,685	
10.		+600				+600	Revenue
Bal.	635	600	50	1,000		2,285	
11.					+110	-110	Gas Exp.
Bal.	635	600	50	1,000	110	2,175	
12.	-100					-100	Withdrawal
Bal.	535	600	50	1,000	110	2,075	

Transparency Master 1-15

FINANCIAL STATEMENTS
Jim's Lawn Care
Income Statement
For the Month Ended May 31, 20——

Fees earned		$
Operating expenses:		
Advertising expense	$	
Gasoline expense	$	
Wages expense	$	
Total operating expenses		$
Net income		$

Jim's Lawn Care
Statement of Owner's Equity
For the Month Ended May 31, 20——

Jim Hamilton, capital, May 1		$
Investment	$	
Net income for May	$	
Less withdrawals	$	
Increase in owner's equity		$
Jim Hamilton, capital, May 31		$

Jim's Lawn Care
Balance Sheet
May 31, 20——

Assets		Liabilities	
Cash	$	Accounts payable	$
Accounts receivable	$		
Supplies	$	**Owner's Equity**	
Lawn equipment	$	Jim Hamilton, capital	$
Total assets	$	Total liabilities and owner's equity	$

Transparency Master 1-16

FINANCIAL STATEMENTS——SOLUTIONS
Jim's Lawn Care
Income Statement
For the Month Ended May 31, 20——

Fees earned		$1,720
Operating expenses:		
Advertising expense	$150	
Gasoline expense	110	
Wages expense	85	
Total operating exp.		345
Net income		$1,375

Jim's Lawn Care
Statement of Owner's Equity
For the Month Ended May 31, 20——

Jim Hamilton, Capital		$ 0
Investment	$ 800	
Net income for May	1,375	
	$2,175	
Less withdrawals	100	
Increase in owner's equity		2,075
Jim Hamilton, capital, May 31		$2,075

Jim's Lawn Care
Balance Sheet
May 31, 20——

Assets		Liabilities	
Cash	$ 535	Accounts payable	$ 110
Accounts receivable	600		
Supplies	50	**Owner's equity**	
Lawn equipment	1,000	Jim Hamilton, capital	2,075
Total assets	$2,185	Total liabilities and owner's equity	$2,185

STATEMENT OF CASH FLOWS

PURPOSE: Report cash received and cash paid in the course of doing business.

Cash flows are divided into the following categories:

1. Cash flows from operating activities
   OPERATING ACTIVITIES: Cash received or paid in
   * Providing services to a customer
   * Buying and selling a product

2. Cash flows from investing activities
   INVESTING ACTIVITIES: Cash received or paid in
   * Buying or selling long-term assets

3. Cash flows from financing activities
   FINANCING ACTIVITIES: Cash received or paid due to
   * Investments and withdrawals by owner
   * Borrowing and repaying cash

Relationship Between Liabilities and Owner's Equity

	Assets	=	Liabilities	+	Owner's Equity
Company A	100,000	=	95,000	+	5,000
Company B	100,000	=	90,000	+	10,000

Chapter 2
Analyzing Transactions

OPENING COMMENTS

Chapter 2 introduces students to the rules of debit and credit, two-column journals, four-column ledgers, the chart of accounts, the trial balance, and horizontal analysis. And, quite frankly, if students fail to grasp the concepts in this chapter, the first seeds of destruction will be sown for those students who will ultimately withdraw from or fail the course.

Emphasize that Chapter 2 builds the foundation for all that will be learned about accounting principles. Unlike many other college courses, it is impossible to understand Chapter 3 and beyond if the principles of Chapter 2 are not mastered. You need to dispel the false belief that "maybe I'll get the next chapter—even though I'm totally lost now."

Also encourage your students to seek help immediately if they begin to struggle with course content. Make them aware of the resources available at your institution: tutorial services, peer assistance, your office hours, etc. Too frequently, students wait until after they have failed their first examination to seek help. For those who heed them, these simple warnings will help students avoid failure.

After studying the chapter, your students should be able to:

1. Explain why accounts are used to record and summarize the effects of transactions on financial statements.
2. Describe the characteristics of an account.
3. List the rules of debit and credit and the normal balances of accounts.
4. Analyze and summarize the financial statement effects of transactions.
5. Prepare a trial balance and explain how it can be used to discover errors.
6. Discover errors in recording transactions and correct them.
7. Use horizontal analysis to compare financial statements from different periods.

OBJECTIVE 1 — Explain why accounts are used to record and summarize the effects of transactions on financial statements.

KEY TERMS:
- Account
- Assets
- Chart of Accounts
- Drawing
- Expenses
- Ledger
- Liabilities
- Owner's Equity
- Revenues

SUGGESTED APPROACH

Remind students that accounts are used to record business transactions. An account is simply a record of all the increases and decreases in a financial statement item (such as cash, supplies, and accounts payable). A group of accounts is called a ledger.

Point out that only a very small enterprise with very few transactions (such as a lawn mowing service run by students) could use the accounting system illustrated in Chapter 1. For most businesses, this system would be inefficient. For example, in the prior chapter all business transactions affecting owner's equity were recorded in the capital account. In Chapter 2, the different types of owner's equity transactions will be separated and recorded in the following accounts: capital, drawing, revenue, and expense accounts. This separation will make it easier to prepare financial statements. Transparency 2-1 can be used to highlight this change.

GROUP LEARNING ACTIVITY — Chart of Accounts

Objective 1 also introduces a chart of accounts and a flexible system of numbering accounts. Under the text's indexing system, accounts are assigned a two-digit number. The first digit indicates the account's classification (1=assets, 2=liabilities, 3=owner's equity, 4=revenue, and 5=expenses.) Stress that all enterprises will have the same categories of accounts; however, the account titles used and number of accounts will vary. You can emphasize this variety by asking students to bring in charts of accounts from businesses where they or a relative work.

Transparency 2-2 presents information related to the business transactions of Larry Sharp, M.D. Divide students into small groups and ask them to use the information to develop a chart of accounts for Dr. Sharp. Also ask them to assign a number to each account.

This activity will test whether your students can identify the accounts needed to record Dr. Sharp's typical business transactions and apply the concept of a flexible numbering system. The group activity may be assigned before discussing the information related to charts of accounts presented in the text. This will force students to recall some information from their reading assignment and reinforce your expectation that all reading assignments are to be completed prior to classroom discussion

Transparency 2-3 presents a suggested chart of accounts that you may want to share with the class after they have completed their group work. Remind them that the chart of accounts is different for every company, reflecting each company's typical business transactions.

You will notice that the suggested solution in Transparency 2-3 does not include insurance expense or depreciation expense accounts. These accounts, although necessary for preparing adjusting entries, have been omitted since that step in the accounting cycle will not be introduced until Chapter 3.

INTERNET ACTIVITY – Chart of Accounts

There are organizations that post recommended charts of accounts on the internet so your students can see some real-world examples. For example, the American Booksellers

Association provides a suggested chart of accounts for its members. They also provide an extensive explanation of why a standard chart of accounts is helpful. The web address is:
> http://www.ambook.org/misc/member/scoatext.html

Another standard chart of accounts is provided by North Carolina Schools. Of course, this chart of accounts is set up to facilitate governmental fund accounting, so it may require some explanation. The web address is:
> http://www.ncpublicshools.org/fbs/coa

You might also want to encourage your students to search for other suggested charts of accounts.

EXERCISES & PROBLEMS FOR REINFORCEMENT:
> Exercise 2-1
> Exercise 2-2
> Exercise 2-3

OBJECTIVE 2 — Describe the characteristics of an account.

KEY TERMS:
Balance of the Account	Debits
Credits	T Account

SUGGESTED APPROACH

The first account form introduced in Chapter 2 is the T account. Draw a T account on the board and remind students that the left side will be called the debit side and the right side will be called the credit side.

OBJECTIVE 3 — List the rules of debit and credit and the normal balances of accounts.

KEY TERMS:
Double-Entry Accounting	Journal Entry
Journal	Journalizing

SUGGESTED APPROACH

Learning the rules of debit and credit is one of the first major hurdles for students in accounting principles. Remind students that debit and credit simply represent the left and right sides of an account. The trick is remembering which accounts are increased with debits and which are increased with credits.

Two approaches to explain the rules of debit and credit follow. You may want to present both methods to your class and encourage each student to use the approach that he or she understands best.

LECTURE AIDS — Rules of Debit and Credit

"Mirror Image" Approach: One way to explain the rules of debit and credit is to draw the following equation on the board.

Assets	=	Liabilities	+	Owner's Equity
+ | −		− | +		− | +

Point out that the rules for increasing and decreasing liabilities and owner's equity accounts are the mirror image of the rules for assets. Therefore, if students can remember the rules for assets, they can deduce the rules for the remaining accounts.

Although this is the most simplistic approach, some students become very confused by the treatment of the drawings and expense accounts. Increases to these accounts are debits, since they reduce owner's equity. However, some students want to record expenses and drawings as credits because the schematic has a + sign on the credit side of owner's equity accounts.

Alternative Approach: The rules of debit and credit can also be explained with the following saying: After eating dinner, let's read the comics.

Here's how it works.

After Eating Dinner,	Let's Read the Comics
Accounts increased with a debit:	Accounts increased with a credit:
Assets	Liabilities
Expenses	Revenues
Drawings	Capital

GROUP LEARNING ACTIVITY — Rules of Debit and Credit

After explaining the rules of debit and credit, it is important to reinforce those concepts with an example.

Remind students that business transactions are initially recorded in a record called a journal. After each entry is journalized, it is posted to the proper account in the ledger. In this group exercise, students will post entries into a T account.

Ask your students to draw the following T accounts on a sheet of paper:

    Cash   M. Gordon, Capital
    Accounts Receivable   M. Gordon, Drawing

38

Supplies   Fees Earned
Stereo Equipment   Wages Expense
Accounts Payable   Advertising Expense

Transparency 2-4 lists several business transactions. Illustrate the process by recording the first two or three transactions in a journal format and posting them to the appropriate T account. As you work these examples, emphasize that there is a 3-step process in analyzing each entry: (1) determine which accounts are affected, (2) decide whether each account should be increased or decreased, and (3) translate the increase or decrease into a debit or a credit.

After completing your examples, ask your students to work in small groups to complete the transactions. Transparency 2-5 presents the solution to this exercise.

EXERCISES & PROBLEMS FOR REINFORCEMENT:
    Exercise 2-4   Exercise 2-11
    Exercise 2-7   Exercise 2-12
    Exercise 2-8
    Exercise 2-9
    Exercise 2-10

OBJECTIVE 4 — Analyze and summarize the financial statement effects of transactions.

KEY TERMS:
    Posting
    Two-Column Journal
    Unearned Revenue

SUGGESTED APPROACH

At this point, it is time to introduce your students to the standard journal and four-column ledger formats. It is interesting to point out that while T accounts are not actually used to record business transactions, accountants frequently use them to analyze complex transactions. In the same way, students will find the T account a useful tool throughout this and future accounting courses.

Transparency 2-6 shows a series of transactions recorded in a two-column journal. Use this exhibit to review the two-column journal format with your students. You may want to stress the following format issues:

1. Dates: The year is entered only at the top of the date column. The month is entered on the first line of the date column on each page; it is also entered for the first transaction whenever changing to a new month. The date is entered for each transaction.
2. Explanations: A brief description of the transaction should be written below the debit and credit account titles. This description may be omitted if the transaction is a normal business occurrence and its nature is obvious from the entry.
3. Blank Lines: A blank line should separate all transactions to make them easier to read.

It is also helpful to emphasize the importance of using correct journal entry format by writing the following entry on the board and asking students to identify what is wrong:

    Supplies   500
    Cash   500

Since the credit in the entry is not indented, it is difficult to identify the debit and the credit. Were supplies purchased using cash or were they sold for cash?

DEMONSTRATION PROBLEM — The Ledger

Transparency 2-7 is a series of four-column ledger accounts. Use these blank accounts to demonstrate posting of the first three transactions from Transparency 2-6. As you post the transactions, remind students that a posting reference must be entered in the appropriate columns of both the journal and the ledger. Also emphasize that transactions should be posted carefully to avoid errors. Careless posting may result in a lot of time being wasted trying to find errors.

WRITING EXERCISE — The Journal and The Ledger

It is important for students to understand the reason that business transactions are recorded in a journal as the book of original entry and later posted to a ledger. To check their understanding of these concepts, ask them to write a response to the following questions. These questions are also found on Transparency 2-8.

1. Why are business transactions initially recorded in a journal?
2. Why are business transactions posted from the journal to a ledger?

GROUP LEARNING ACTIVITY — The Journal and The Ledger

This activity presents another method to emphasize the purpose of the journal and the ledger in the accounting process. Transparency 2-9 lists questions a business owner might ask that can be answered by examining the company's accounting records. Your students' task is to determine which accounting record holds the answer: the journal or the ledger. Answers to this activity are provided on Transparency 2-10.

EXERCISES & PROBLEMS FOR REINFORCEMENT:
    Exercise 2-5
    Exercise 2-13
    Exercise 2-14
    Exercise 2-15

OBJECTIVE 5 — Prepare a trial balance and explain how it can be used to discover errors.

KEY TERMS:
    Trial Balance

SUGGESTED APPROACH

Remind students that a trial balance is simply a listing of accounts and their balances. It is used to check the accuracy of posting by testing to see that total debits equal total credits. At this point, students have learned two controls over recording entries in a double-entry accounting system: (1) Debits = Credits and (2) Assets = Liabilities + Owner's Equity.

DEMONSTRATION PROBLEM — Preparing a Trial Balance

To demonstrate how to prepare a trial balance, place Transparency 2-5 (the T accounts from the group learning activity under Objective 3) on your overhead projector. Ask your students to work in small groups to complete a trial balance using these account balances. Transparency 2-11 shows the completed trial balance.

GROUP LEARNING ACTIVITY — Errors in a Trial Balance

The goal of this activity is to demonstrate the use of a trial balance in detecting errors made while recording journal entries, posting, and computing account balances. Transparency 2-12 presents journal entries, T accounts, and a trial balance. Several errors have been made in posting the journal entries and, as a result, the trial balance does not balance. Ask your students to work in small groups to uncover the errors and correct the trial balance. Transparency 2-13 shows the corrected trial balance.

You may want to give your students the following hints to help them detect the errors:

1. Re-add the columns of the trial balance to check for math errors.
2. Look for accounts with abnormal balances on the trial balance. This usually points to an error.
3. Compare account balances on the trial balance with those in the ledger. Watch for omitted accounts or transposition errors.
4. Recompute the balance of each account to check for math errors.
5. Trace each posting back to the journal entry to make sure the proper amount was posted. Watch for transposition errors.

You will also want to point out that the trial balance does not catch every possible accounting error. The following errors will not be discovered simply by preparing a trial balance (page 72 of the text).

1. Failing to record a transaction or to post a transaction.
2. Recording the same erroneous amount for both the debit and the credit parts of a transaction.
3. Recording the same transaction more than once.
4. Posting part of a transaction correctly as a debit or credit but to the wrong account.

As an example, ask your class the following question: Would recording an $800 sale on account as a debit to Cash and credit to Fees Earned cause the columns of a trial balance to be unequal? Answer: No.

EXERCISES & PROBLEMS FOR REINFORCEMENT:

Exercise 2-6	Problem 2-1A	Problem 2-1B
Exercise 2-16	Problem 2-2A	Problem 2-2B
Exercise 2-17	Problem 2-3A	Problem 2-3B
Exercise 2-18	Problem 2-4A	Problem 2-4B
Exercise 2-19		
Exercise 2-20		

OBJECTIVE 6 — Discover errors in recording transactions and correct them.

KEY TERMS:
- Materiality Concept
- Slide
- Transposition

SUGGESTED APPROACH

Briefly introduce your students to transpositions and slides by giving an example of each of these errors. For example, recording an entry for $678 as $687 is a transposition; recording an entry for $120 as $1200 is a slide. Remind students that if either of these errors have occurred and there are no other errors, the difference between the two columns of a trial balance can be evenly divided by 9.

Exhibit 7 in the text summarizes the procedures for correcting errors. Review these procedures with the class.

You can demonstrate the process used to correct improper postings by using Transparency 2-12 from Objective 5. For example, draw a line through the incorrect postings to the capital and fees earned accounts and write in the correct amounts.

The following group learning activity will give students the opportunity to practice correcting journal entries.

GROUP LEARNING ACTIVITY — Correcting Journal Entries

Transparency 2-14 presents several errors in recording journal entries. These incorrect journal entries have been posted. Divide the class into small groups and ask your students to prepare journal entries to correct these errors.

If your students are having trouble with these entries, suggest the following steps:

1. In T accounts, record the debit and credit for the incorrect journal entry.
2. In T accounts, record what the debit and credit should have been to journalize the entry correctly.

3. Determine what entry must be made to bring the accounts from #1 in line with what they should be according to #2.

The solution to this exercise is presented in Transparency 2-15.

WRITING EXERCISE — Correcting Errors

The following exercise will allow your students to practice both their communication and critical thinking skills.

The text emphasizes that all errors are corrected either through a correcting journal entry or by drawing a line through the incorrect title or amount. The text does not address why accountants do not simply erase mistakes.

Pose the following question to your class and ask them to write their response. (This question also appears on Transparency 2-16.)

> Errors may be corrected either by (1) preparing a correcting journal entry or (2) drawing a line through the incorrect account title or amount and writing in the correct information above the error. Why do you think it is not acceptable to simply erase the error and write in the correction?

EXERCISES & PROBLEMS FOR REINFORCEMENT:
    Exercise 2-21   Problem 2-5A   Problem 2-5B
    Exercise 2-22   Problem 2-6A   Problem 2-6B

OBJECTIVE 7 — Use horizontal analysis to compare financial statements from different periods.

KEY TERMS:
    Horizontal Analysis

SUGGESTED APPROACH

Financial statements are prepared to communicate information to owners, managers, and others interested in a business' performance. One technique used to assess trends of the items on financial statements is horizontal analysis. By discussing this analytical technique in Chapter 2, the text emphasizes that both preparation and interpretation of financial statements are essential in the field of accounting.

DEMONSTRATION PROBLEM — Horizontal Analysis

Transparency 2-17 presents comparative Income Statements for Bazan Company. Use these simple financial statements to illustrate horizontal analysis.

To begin this illustration, ask your students to compute the increase in fees earned between 2003 and 2004. Next, ask them to compute the percentage change in fees earned. The correct answer (rounded to the nearest whole percentage) is 17%, which is computed as follows:

$$\frac{\text{Increase in Fees Earned between 2003 \& 2004}}{\text{Fees Earned in 2003 (base year)}} = \frac{\$20,000}{\$120,000} = 17\%$$

Most likely, a few students will have 14% as an answer. These students have compared the $20,000 increase in fees earned to fees earned in 2004. Remind them that a percentage change in a financial statement item is computed by comparing the change in dollars to the base year amount. The base year is the starting point—2003 in this case.

Ask your students to compute the increase/decrease in each of the expenses, total operating expenses, and net income. Also instruct them to compute the percentage change in each item. Fill in this information as your students compute the answers, or show them the completed solution on Transparency 2-18. Emphasize that applying horizontal analysis to an income statement helps assess trends in revenues and expenses. Also mention that this same technique can be used to examine trends in balance sheet accounts.

WRITING EXERCISE — Horizontal Analysis

Ask your students to comment, in writing, on any significant changes revealed by applying horizontal analysis to Bazan Company's Income Statement. After allowing time for students to make comments in writing, engage them in a class discussion.

EXERCISES & PROBLEMS FOR REINFORCEMENT:
　　Exercise 2-23
　　Exercise 2-24

Assets = Liabilities + Owner's Equity

OWNER'S EQUITY ACCOUNTS

Account	Used to Record
Capital	Owner's Investments
Drawing	Owner's Withdrawals
Revenue	Revenues from Customers
Expense	Expenses Incurred in Running the Business

Transparency Master 2-2

CHART OF ACCOUNTS
Larry Sharp, M. D.

The following information pertains to the medical practice of Larry Sharp, M. D. Using the information, develop a chart of accounts for Dr. Sharp. Remember to number the accounts using a flexible system of indexing, as described in your textbook.

1. Dr. Sharp is the sole owner of his medical practice.
2. Dr. Sharp has the following assets that are used in the business: $15,000 in cash, $1,200 worth of supplies, and medical equipment that cost $8,900.
3. Dr. Sharp buys all of his medical supplies on account and pays for them within 30 days of the purchase.
4. In payment for his services, Dr. Sharp will accept cash or will bill his patients.
5. Dr. Sharp rents his office space. His lease agreement requires him to pay his own utilities.
6. Dr. Sharp is required to carry malpractice insurance, which is paid at the beginning of each year.
7. Dr. Sharp has one receptionist and one medical assistant who work for him full-time. Each year, he buys the receptionist and assistant flowers on their birthdays.
8. To keep current on medical advances, Dr. Sharp frequently attends medical seminars. These seminars can cost as much as $10,000 each year.

SAMPLE CHART OF ACCOUNTS
Larry Sharp, M. D.

Assets

- 10 Cash
- 11 Accounts Receivable
- 12 Supplies
- 13 Prepaid Insurance
- 14 Medical Equipment

Liabilities

- 21 Accounts Payable

Owner's Equity

- 31 Larry Sharp, Capital
- 32 Larry Sharp, Drawing

Revenues

- 41 Fees Earned

Expenses

- 51 Wages Expense
- 52 Rent Expense
- 53 Utilities Expense
- 54 Medical Seminar Expense
- 55 Supplies Expense
- 56 Miscellaneous Expense

Transparency Master 2-4

POSTING ENTRIES INTO T ACCOUNTS

Mark Gordon decided to start a business as a disc jockey for wedding receptions, reunions, and other parties. His business is called Music Express. Record the following journal entries for Music Express and post these entries to the appropriate T accounts.

a. Mark transferred $7,000 from a personal bank account to an account to be used for his business.
b. Purchased $5,700 of stereo equipment on account.
c. Paid for an advertisement in local newspapers, $500.
d. Paid cash for supplies, $75.
e. Received $1,000 cash from customers for music provided at class reunions.
f. Paid for stereo equipment purchased in (b).
g. Provided music at a wedding reception; the bride's father was billed $300. Payment is due in 30 days.
h. Paid wages of an assistant, $150.
i. Received cash from the customer billed in (g).
j. Mark withdrew $575 cash for personal use.

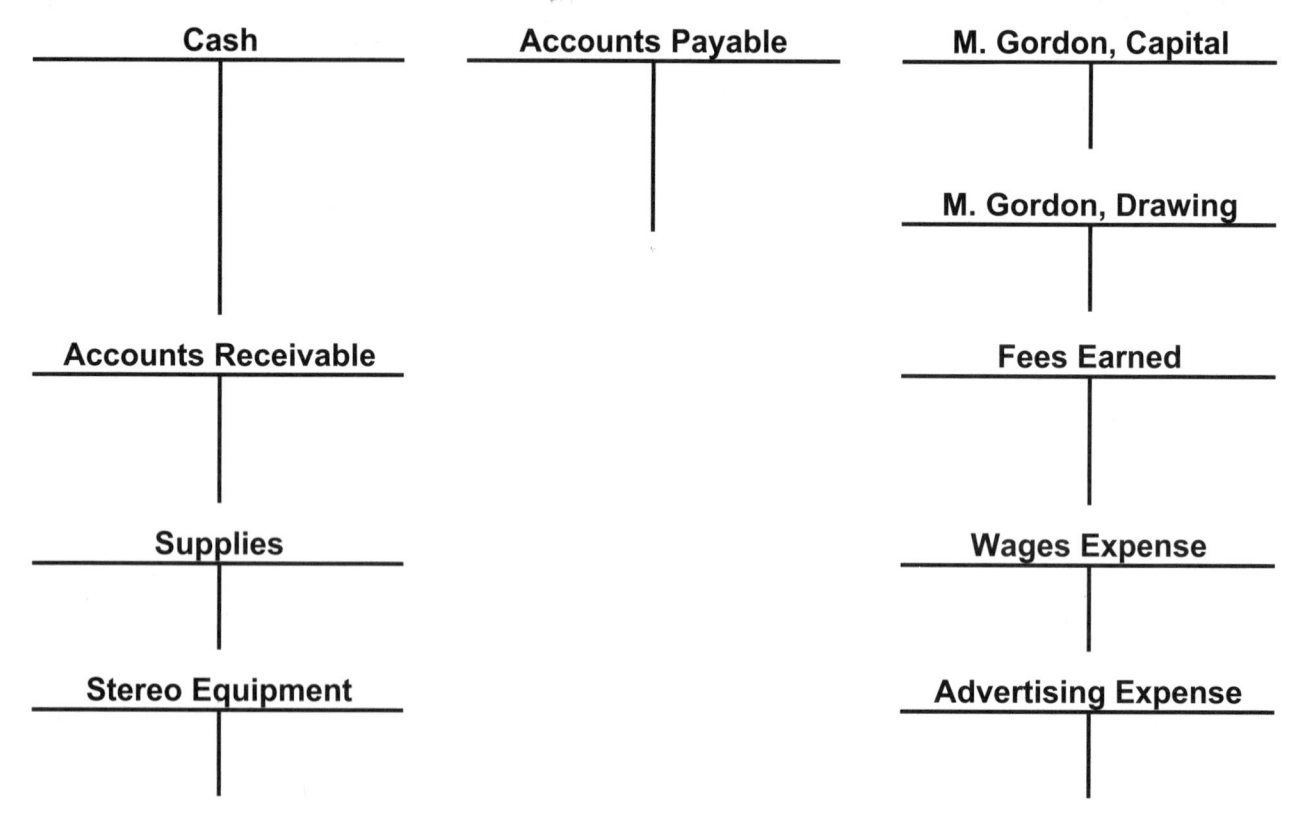

Cash	Accounts Payable	M. Gordon, Capital

		M. Gordon, Drawing

Accounts Receivable		Fees Earned

Supplies		Wages Expense

Stereo Equipment		Advertising Expense

Transparency Master 2-5

POSTING ENTRIES INTO T ACCOUNTS
Solution

Mark Gordon decided to start a business as a disc jockey for wedding receptions, reunions, and other parties. His business is called Music Express. Record the following journal entries for Music Express and post these entries to the appropriate T accounts.

a. Mark transferred $7,000 from a personal bank account to an account to be used for his business.
b. Purchased $5,700 of stereo equipment on account.
c. Paid for an advertisement in local newspapers, $500.
d. Paid cash for supplies, $75.
e. Received $1,000 cash from customers for music provided at class reunions.
f. Paid for stereo equipment purchased in (b).
g. Provided music at a wedding reception; the bride's father was billed $300. Payment is due in 30 days.
h. Paid wages of an assistant, $150.
i. Received cash from the customer billed in (g).
j. Mark withdrew $575 cash for personal use.

Cash				Accounts Payable				M. Gordon, Capital		
a.	7,000	c.	500			b.	5,700		a.	7,000
e.	1,000	d.	75	f.	5,700					
i.	300	f.	5,700					M. Gordon, Drawing		
		h.	150				0	j.	575	
		j.	575							
	1,300							Fees Earned		

Accounts Receivable							
g.	300	i.	300			e.	1,000
						g.	300
	0						1,300

Supplies			Wages Expense		
d.	75		h.	150	

Stereo Equipment			Advertising Expense		
b.	5,700		c.	500	

49

Transparency Master 2-6

JOURNAL

Page 1

DATE	DESCRIPTION	POST. REF.	DEBIT	CREDIT

1998 Sept. 1	Cash
	    S. Morgan, Capital
	        Owner's initial investment.
			8,000	8,000

3	Supplies
	    Cash
	        Purchased supplies.
			200	200

7	Cash
	    Fees Earned
	        Received from cash customers.
			500	500

12	Wages Expense
	    Cash
	        Paid wages of assistant.
			100	100

15	Office Equipment
	    Accounts Payable
	        Purchased fax machine.
			275	275

20	Accounts Receivable
	    Fees Earned
	        Billed credit customers.
			1,310	1,310

Transparency Master 2-7

ACCOUNT Cash　　　　　　　　　　　　　　　　　　　　　ACCOUNT NO. 10

DATE	ITEM	POST. REF.	DEBIT	CREDIT	BALANCE DEBIT	BALANCE CREDIT

ACCOUNT Supplies　　　　　　　　　　　　　　　　　　　ACCOUNT NO. 12

DATE	ITEM	POST. REF.	DEBIT	CREDIT	BALANCE DEBIT	BALANCE CREDIT

ACCOUNT S. Morgan, Capital　　　　　　　　　　　　　　ACCOUNT NO. 31

DATE	ITEM	POST. REF.	DEBIT	CREDIT	BALANCE DEBIT	BALANCE CREDIT

ACCOUNT Fees Earned　　　　　　　　　　　　　　　　　ACCOUNT NO. 41

DATE	ITEM	POST. REF.	DEBIT	CREDIT	BALANCE DEBIT	BALANCE CREDIT

Transparency Master 2-8

WRITING EXERCISE

1. Why are business transactions initially recorded in a journal?

2. Why are business transactions posted from the journal to a ledger?

Transparency Master 2-9

Where Is the Answer—The Journal or the Ledger?

The answers to the following business questions can be determined by examining accounting records. For each question, state whether the answer can be found in the journal or the ledger.

1. A business owner has decided to purchase a piece of equipment costing $1,500. He wants to know whether the business has enough cash to pay for the equipment.

2. The company checkbook shows that a $750 check was written on March 28. The owner wants to know why that check was written.

3. A personnel manager wants to know the total her company has spent on employee wages so far this month.

4. The marketing manager of a company wants to know the cost of a special full-page ad placed in the *Wall Street Journal* during the first week of December last year. The company frequently advertises in a variety of newspapers and magazines.

Transparency Master 2-10

Where Is the Answer—The Journal or the Ledger?

Solution

1. A business owner has decided to purchase a piece of equipment costing $1,500. He wants to know whether the business has enough cash to pay for the equipment.

   The ledger will show the current balance in the cash account.

2. The company checkbook shows that a $750 check was written on March 28. The owner wants to know why that check was written.

   The journal will show the account debited when the check was written and a brief description of the transaction.

3. A personnel manager wants to know the total her company has spent on employee wages so far this month.

   The ledger will show the current balance in the wages expense account.

4. The marketing manager of a company wants to know the cost of a special full-page ad placed in the *Wall Street Journal* during the first week of December last year. The company frequently advertises in a variety of newspapers and magazines.

   The journal entries around the first week of December will need to be searched for the cost of this ad. The description accompanying the entry should identify the Wall Street Journal ad.

TRIAL BALANCE

Music Express
Trial Balance
May 31, 20—

Cash	1,300	
Supplies	75	
Stereo Equipment	5,700	
M. Gordon, Capital		7,000
M. Gordon, Drawing	575	
Fees Earned		1,300
Wages Expense	150	
Advertising Expense	500	
	8,300	8,300

Transparency Master 2-12

WHAT'S WRONG WITH THIS?

Journal Entries:

a. Cash 8,000
    J. Day, Capital   8,000

b. Supplies 200
    Cash   200

c. Cash 550
    Fees Earned   550

d. Wages Expense 1,340
    Cash   1,340

e. Accounts Receivable 810
    Fees Earned   810

T Accounts:

Cash	
a. 8,000	b. 200
c. 550	d. 1,340
6,970	

J. Day, Capital	
	a. 8,000
	e. 810
	8,810

Accounts Receivable	
e. 810	

Fees Earned	
	c. 500

Supplies	
b. 200	

Wages Expense	
d. 1,340	

Trial Balance

Cash	6,970	
Accounts Receivable	810	
Supplies	200	
J. Day, Capital		8,810
Fees Earned		500
Wages Expense	1,340	
	9,810	8,810

Transparency Master 2-13

WHAT'S WRONG WITH THIS?

Solution

Trial Balance

Cash	7,010	
Accounts Receivable	810	
Supplies	200	
J. Day, Capital		8,000
Fees Earned		1,360
Wages Expense	1,340	
	9,360	9,360

CORRECTING JOURNAL ENTRIES

During the year-end audit for Posey Company, the following errors were discovered. Since these errors have been posted, they must be corrected by preparing a correcting journal entry.

Record the entry necessary to correct each error.

1. Posey purchased $100 of office supplies on credit. The entry to record the purchase debited Store Equipment and credited Accounts Payable for $100.

2. Posey received $300 from a credit customer as payment on an account receivable. The entry to record the cash received debited Cash and credited Fees Earned for $300.

3. Posey paid a $75 utility bill. The entry to record this payment debited Cash and credited Utility Expense for $75.

4. Posey received $152 from a cash customer. The entry to record the cash received debited Cash and credited Fees Earned for $125.

Transparency Master 2-15

CORRECTING JOURNAL ENTRIES

Solution

1. Office Supplies 100
       Store Equipment   100

2. Fees Earned 300
       Accounts Receivable   300

3. Utility Expense 150
       Cash   150

4. Cash 27
       Fees Earned   27

WRITING EXERCISE

Errors may be corrected either by (1) preparing a correcting journal entry or (2) drawing a line through the incorrect account title or amount and writing in the correct information above the error. Why do you think it is not acceptable to simply erase the error and write in the correction?

Bazan Company
Income Statement
For the Years Ended Dec. 31, 2003 and 2004

	2004	2003	Increase/(Decrease) Amount	Percent
Fees earned	$140,000	$120,000		
Expenses:				
Wages expense	38,000	32,000		
Advertising expense	10,000	3,000		
Rent expense	6,000	5,700		
Utilities expense	4,000	3,900		
Misc. expense	2,000	3,500		
Total oper. exp.	$60,000	$48,100		
Net income	$80,000	$71,900		

Transparency Master 2-18

Bazan Company
Income Statement
For the Years Ended Dec. 31, 2003 and 2004

	2004	2003	Increase/(Decrease) Amount	Percent
Fees earned	$140,000	$120,000	$20,000	17%
Expenses:				
Wages expense	38,000	32,000	6,000	19%
Advertising expense	10,000	3,000	7,000	233%
Rent expense	6,000	5,700	300	5%
Utilities expense	4,000	3,900	100	3%
Misc. expense	2,000	3,500	(1,500)	(43%)
Total oper. exp.	$ 60,000	$ 48,100	11,900	25%
Net income	$ 80,000	$ 71,900	8,100	11%

Chapter 3
The Matching Concept and the Adjusting Process

OPENING COMMENTS

Chapter 3 introduces students to the adjusting process. The basic idea of the matching concept was presented in Chapter 1, where expenses incurred were matched against revenues. Now in Chapter 3, matching is introduced formally and as a stand-alone concept. The matching concept is defined and discussed, and the chapter includes full coverage of the accrual basis and cash basis of accounting. Of all the accounting concepts and principles introduced in the early chapters of the text, matching is the most important.

The chapter's main emphasis is on the preparation of adjusting entries. Definitions, calculations where pertinent, and examples of the four basic types of deferrals and accruals are included. The chapter then covers the adjustment of fixed assets (depreciation). The financial statement analysis concept introduced in Chapter 3 is vertical analysis.

After studying the chapter, your students should be able to:

1. Explain how the matching concept relates to the accrual basis of accounting.
2. Explain why adjustments are necessary and list the characteristics of adjusting entries.
3. Journalize entries for accounts requiring adjustment.
4. Summarize the adjustment process and prepare an adjusted trial balance.
5. Use vertical analysis to compare financial statement items with each other and with industry averages.

OBJECTIVE 1 — Explain how the matching concept relates to the accrual basis of accounting.

KEY TERMS:
- Accounting Period Concept
- Accrual Basis
- Adjusting Process
- Cash Basis
- Matching Concept
- Revenue Recognition Concept

SUGGESTED APPROACH

Under this objective, you will need to illustrate and explain the matching concept. Two short, group learning activities follow. One will help introduce the matching concept; the other will review it after a thorough explanation of the concept.

This objective also explains the difference between the cash and accrual basis of accounting. To check your students' understanding of these concepts, pose the following questions:

If rent for May is paid on June 1, in which month will it be reported as an expense under (a) the cash basis and (b) the accrual basis? Answer: (a) June, (b) May.

If a university received cash in August for football season tickets, when should this be reported as revenue under (a) the cash basis and (b) the accrual basis? Answer: (a) August, (b) throughout football season as games are played.

You may also want to point out that the cash basis of accounting is used by most individuals for income tax purposes.

GROUP LEARNING ACTIVITY — Introduction to the Matching Concept

Transparency 3-1 provides financial information about an individual filling out a loan application. The loan application asks for total monthly expenses. The person applying for the loan has a few expenses that are paid annually or semiannually. Therefore, your students must "match" expenses to the time period requested by the loan application: a month. The expenses paid annually and semiannually must be divided into monthly amounts to properly determine the applicant's total monthly expenses.

The solution to this exercise is provided in Transparency 3-2.

LECTURE AIDS — Matching Concept

Remind your students that, similar to personal expenses, not all business expenses are paid monthly. If a business wants to know its true expenses for the month, it must consider all expenses incurred, not just the expenses paid that month.

Likewise, payment for services provided to customers is not always received in the same month that the service is completed. If a business wants to know how much revenue it has earned, it must determine the value of services provided, not just the cash received in payment for services rendered.

The accrual basis of accounting dictates that all revenues be recorded in the accounting records when they are earned, instead of when the cash payment is received from customers. All expenses are to be recorded in the accounting records when they are incurred, not when they are paid.

Finally, if a business wants to determine whether the pricing of its services results in an adequate profit, it must compare the revenues earned from providing services to all the expenses incurred in providing those services.

The matching concept in accounting states that all the expenses incurred in providing a service or selling a product must be recorded in the same period that the revenue from the service or sale is recorded. Expenses are matched against the revenue they generate.

The matching concept and accrual basis of accounting go hand in hand. Because of these concepts, some accounts must be updated at the end of an accounting period to show the correct revenues and expenses. This process of updating the accounts is accomplished through adjusting entries.

GROUP LEARNING ACTIVITY — Reviewing the Matching Concept

Transparency 3-3 asks students to apply the matching concept by determining the profit on a stone patio laid by Artisan Stone and Brick. Transparency 3-4 provides the solution to this exercise.

OBJECTIVE 2 — Explain why adjustments are necessary and list the characteristics of adjusting entries.

KEY TERMS:
- Accruals
- Accrued Expenses
- Accrued Revenues
- Adjusting Entries
- Deferrals
- Deferred Expenses
- Deferred Revenues
- Prepaid Expenses
- Unearned Expenses

SUGGESTED APPROACH

This learning objective reviews the purpose of adjusting entries. Remind students that adjusting entries are necessary to update the accounting records to include all revenues earned and all expenses incurred. Making adjusting entries is a requirement of the accrual basis of accounting.

After reviewing the purpose of adjusting entries, you will need to distinguish between deferrals and accruals. The lecture aids and the group learning activity that follow will help you explain the difference.

LECTURE AIDS — Accruals and Deferrals

Deferrals adjust accounts that are already a part of a company's accounting records.

Deferred expenses occur when an asset that will be used up or will expire is purchased. As this asset is used, its cost must be recorded as an expense. Therefore, you defer recording the cost of the asset as an expense until it is used. An example of a deferred expense for a student is tuition paid at the beginning of each term. Business examples of deferred expenses include the following:

1. Supplies — recorded as an asset when they are purchased. As the supplies are used, an adjusting entry is made to transfer the cost of the supplies to an expense account. This adjusting entry was demonstrated in Chapter 1.
2. Prepaid insurance — when an insurance policy is paid in advance of the period covered, its cost is recorded as an asset. An adjusting entry must be made to transfer the cost of the insurance policy to an expense account as the policy expires.

Revenues are deferred when cash is received from a customer before a business completes its service for the customer or delivers its product. When cash is received under these circumstances, it cannot be recorded as revenue, since it has not been earned. Instead, it is recorded as a liability, reflecting the company's obligation to provide its service or to deliver its product to the customer. Once this obligation has been fulfilled, the liability is removed and revenue is recognized. Therefore, you defer recording revenue until it is earned. A student would have deferred revenue if they received cash in advance from a neighbor to mow a lawn.

Unearned revenues is the liability account used to record cash received from customers in advance. If any portion of the goods or services paid for has been delivered to the customer by the end of the accounting period, an adjusting entry must be made to transfer the revenue earned to a revenue account.

Accruals record expenses that have been incurred or revenues that have been earned that have not been recorded in the accounting records. A student has an accrued expense when he/she uses utilities (such as water or electricity) before receiving the monthly bill. Other examples of accruals follow:

1. Accrued expenses — salaries/wages owed to employees at the end of an accounting period that have not been paid; interest owed on loans that have not been paid.
2. Accrued revenues — fees earned by an attorney or real estate agent that have not been received; interest on a savings account or other investment that has been earned but not received.

GROUP LEARNING ACTIVITY — Deferrals and Accruals

Transparency 3-5 prompts students to personalize the concepts of deferrals and accruals, rather than view them strictly as business terms. The transparency defines a deferral and an accrual as they relate to your students. It also instructs them to list examples of deferrals and accruals from their own lives.

Ask your students to work in small groups to complete this exercise. After all groups have finished, ask them to share their answers with the class.

OBJECTIVE 3 — Journalize entries for accounts requiring adjustment.

KEY TERMS:
    Accumulated Depreciation   Depreciation
    Book Value of the Asset   Depreciation Expense
    Contra Accounts   Fixed Assets

SUGGESTED APPROACH

Adjusting entries can be effectively presented to your class by working through an example of each adjusting entry covered in the text. A series of demonstration problems and sample explanations follow.

DEMONSTRATION PROBLEM — Adjusting Entry for Prepaid Insurance

An example of an expense that is typically paid in advance is insurance. Insurance policies are paid at the beginning of a policy period. This outlay of cash is recorded in Prepaid Insurance—an asset account. The portion of the insurance coverage that has expired by the end of the accounting period must be transferred to an expense account.

Graphically, this can be illustrated as follows:

```
                     New Data
Asset: Prepaid     ─────────────────▶    Expense: Insurance
       Insurance    Amount of Insurance            Expense
                    Coverage Expired
```

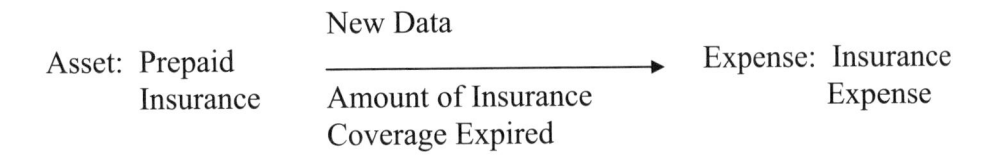

For example, on December 1, Atherton Plumbing purchased a 6-month insurance policy for $600. As of December 31, one month (or $100) of that coverage had expired.

Original Entry:	Prepaid Insurance.........	600	
	Cash...............		600
Adjusting Entry:	Insurance Expense.........	100	
	Prepaid Insurance		100

The T-accounts follow.

```
         Prepaid Insurance              Insurance Expense
12/1   600  |                          |
            |   Adj.  100     Adj. 100 |
            |                          |
Bal.   500  |                          |
```

The T-accounts show that the $500 (or 5 months) of insurance coverage that has not expired is carried as the balance in the prepaid insurance account.

DEMONSTRATION PROBLEM — Adjusting Entry for Supplies

Another asset that must be adjusted at the end of the accounting period is the supplies account. All supplies are recorded in the supplies account as they are purchased. By the end of the accounting period, some of the supplies will have been used. The supplies used must be taken out of the supplies account and transferred to an expense account.

Graphically, this can be illustrated as follows:

```
                     New Data
Asset: Supplies    ─────────────────▶    Expense: Supplies
                    Amount of Supplies             Expense
                    that Have Been Used
```

For example, on December 5, Atherton Plumbing purchased $250 in supplies. As of December 31, only $50 worth of those supplies were left.

Original Entry:	Supplies...............	250	
	Cash............		250
Adjusting Entry:	Supplies Expense......	200	
	Supplies.........		200

(NOTE: $200 represents the supplies used)

The T-accounts follow.

```
          Supplies                          Supplies Expense
    ─────────────────                    ─────────────────
    12/5  250 | Adj. 200                  Adj. 200 |
    ─────────────────
    Bal.   50 |
```

The T-accounts show that the balance of the supplies account is $50—the amount of supplies left.

To illustrate why businesses typically count the amount of supplies left at the end of the month and use that information to determine the cost of supplies used, ask your students the following question:

> What is the easiest way to determine how many miles you have driven your car this month? Answer: record the beginning and ending odometer readings. This is easier than writing down the miles driven each time the car is used.

DEMONSTRATION PROBLEM — Adjusting Entry for Unearned Revenue

If payment for goods or services is received before the goods are delivered or the service is performed, it cannot be recognized as revenue. Revenue can be recorded only after it is earned. Therefore, when payment is received in advance, it is recorded in an unearned revenue account. This is a liability account. By receiving payment, the company has obligated itself to deliver the goods or provide the services for which it was paid. This obligation is expressed in the accounting records as a liability. If a portion (or all) of the revenue has been earned by the end of the accounting period, some (or all) of the unearned revenue is transferred to a revenue account.

Graphically, this can be illustrated as follows:

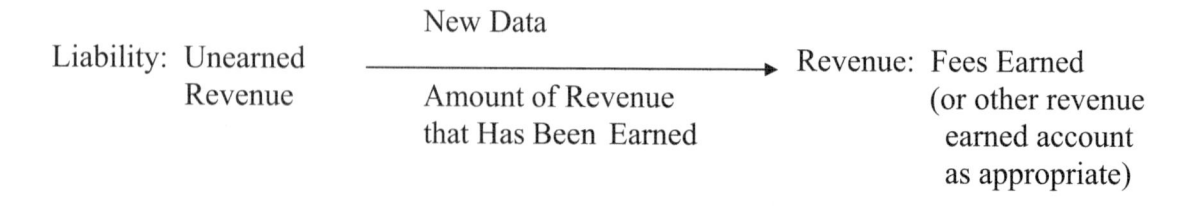

```
                          New Data
   Liability: Unearned   ─────────────────→   Revenue: Fees Earned
              Revenue     Amount of Revenue             (or other revenue
                          that Has Been Earned          earned account
                                                        as appropriate)
```

For example, on November 2, Huber Rental Properties received 3 months' rent, totaling $2,400, in advance for one of its commercial properties. As of December 31, 2 months' worth of this rent had been earned.

Original Entry:	Cash..........................	2,400	
	Unearned Rent....		2,400
Adjusting Entry:	Unearned Rent.............	1,600	
	Rent Income.......		1,600

The T-accounts follow.

Unearned Rent		Rent Income
Adj. 1,600	11/2 2,400		Adj. 1,600
	Bal. 800	

The T-accounts show that the balance of the unearned rent is equal to the one month's rent that has not been earned—$800.

You will probably need to stress that "unearned" rent is a liability on the balance sheet; "earned" rent is revenue on the income statement.

DEMONSTRATION PROBLEM — Adjusting Entry for Accrued Expenses

Any expenses that a business has incurred must be recorded before preparing financial statements, in order to get a true measure of profitability. The act of recording expenses that have not been paid is called accruing expenses.

One common example is wages paid to employees. Many organizations pay their employees on Friday. Wages expense is generally recorded only when wages are paid. Therefore, if the accounting period ends on a day other than payday, the employees will have earned wages that have not been recorded as an expense. These wages must be accrued.

Graphically, this can be illustrated as follows:

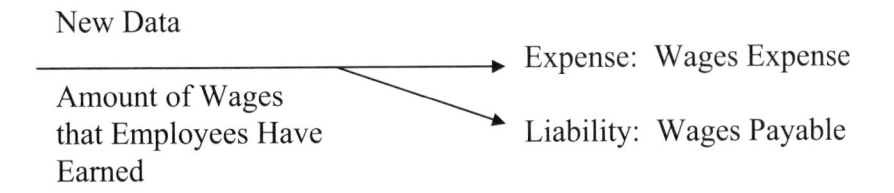

```
New Data
─────────────────────────────→ Expense: Wages Expense
Amount of Wages
that Employees Have   ────────→ Liability: Wages Payable
Earned
```

For example, assume that December 31 is a Wednesday. On that date, Huber Rental Properties owes $500 in wages to employees. These wages will be paid on Friday, the usual payday.

Original
Entry: None

Adjusting   Wages Expense............   500
Entry: Wages Payable.....   500

The T-accounts follow.

```
       Wages Expense              Wages Payable
      ─────────────              ─────────────
      Adj.  500                          │ Adj.  500
                │                        │
```

DEMONSTRATION PROBLEM — Adjusting Entry for Accrued Revenues

Any revenue that a business has earned must be recorded before preparing financial statements in order to get a true measure of profitability. The act of recording revenues that have not been received is called accruing revenues.

One example of accrued revenue is interest. Assume that a company charges its customers interest whenever they ask for more than 30 days to pay for a credit purchase. The interest is paid at the same time as the receivable. At the end of an accounting period, that company may have earned interest that it has not received, since the customer has not paid the account. That interest must be recorded in a revenue account (to show it has been earned) and a receivable account (to show it will be received in the future).

Graphically, this can be illustrated:

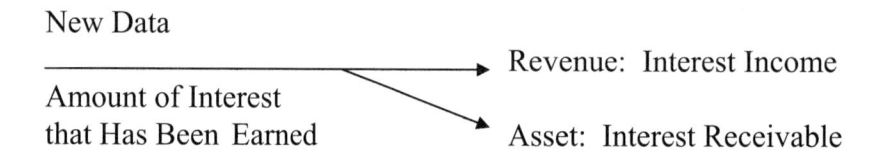

New Data
──────────────────────────→ Revenue: Interest Income
Amount of Interest
that Has Been Earned ──────→ Asset: Interest Receivable

For example, Atherton Plumbing granted a customer additional time to pay an invoice; however, the customer must pay interest at a rate of 10% annually. At the end of the accounting period, the interest that has accumulated totals $80.

Original
Entry: None

Adjusting   Interest Receivable.............   80
Entry: Interest Income.........   80

The T-accounts follow.

Interest Receivable	Interest Income
Adj. 80	Adj. 80

Other examples of accrued revenues would be commissions earned by a travel agent but not billed or fees earned by an attorney but not billed. You could also illustrate the concept of accrued revenue by asking your students to estimate any wages they have earned that have not been paid as of today.

DEMONSTRATION PROBLEM — Adjusting Entry for Depreciation

Read the following scenario to your class:

> Assume that your car needs four new tires. One set of tires you are considering costs $200. The manufacturer estimates that these tires will last 20,000 miles. Since you drive about 10,000 miles per year, that equates to 2 years.
>
> Another set of tires costs $300. These tires should last 40,000 miles or 4 years.
>
> Assuming that you plan to keep your car at least another 4 years, which set of tires is the best deal? Why?
>
> The $200 set of tires will cost the driver $100 per year. The $300 set will cost only $75 per year. Therefore, the $300 set is a better value in the long run.

It is common to break the cost of a long-term asset into a cost per year or a cost per month when evaluating whether or not to purchase the asset. Allocating the cost of an asset (such as the tires) to the years it is used makes it easier to determine the yearly expense of owning the asset. The cost of owning the $300 set of tires is $75 per year.

The accrual basis of accounting requires business owners to allocate the cost of long-term assets to the years they are used. This process is called depreciation.

Consider the following example. A florist purchases a delivery van for $12,000. The van will last 3 years. What is the florist's cost per year for this van? (Answer: $4,000.)

When the florist purchases the van, he will record it in an asset account. Does that van remain an asset forever? No, after 3 years, the van's usefulness will be gone. Therefore, the van's cost must be transferred from the asset account to an expense account over the 3 years it is used. In other words, the van must be depreciated over the 3 years it is used.

The florist's accountant is required to record depreciation on the delivery van for the following two reasons:

1. Whenever an asset is used up in running a business, it must be recorded as an expense. Similar to supplies or prepaid insurance, the florist's van will not last forever. Its usefulness will eventually expire. Therefore, a portion of the van will be recorded as an expense in each year the van is used.
2. The matching principle dictates that all costs incurred in running a business must be matched against the revenues they generate. The van will allow the florist to sell flowers and make deliveries for 3 years. Therefore, a portion of the cost of the van must be matched against the revenue earned in each of those 3 years.

Graphically, this can be illustrated as follows:

```
                        New Data
  Asset: Delivery    ─────────────────────→    Expense: Depreciation
         Van         Portion of the Van's                Expense
                     Usefulness that Has
                     Expired
```

The journal entries to record the purchase of the van and the first year's depreciation are as follows:

Original Entry:	Delivery Van............................	12,000	
	Cash............................		12,000
Adjusting Entry:	Depreciation Expense—Delivery Van	4,000	
	Accumulated Depreciation —Delivery Van.............		4,000

Note that the account credited by the adjusting entry is Accumulated Depreciation—Delivery Van. This is a contra-asset account—an account that works "against" another asset account to reduce it. The accumulated depreciation—delivery van account works against the delivery van account.

The T-accounts follow.

```
         Delivery Van                    Depreciation Expense—Delivery Van

         12,000                          Adj.  4,000


Bal.     12,000                          Bal.  4,000
```

```
Accumulated Depreciation—
     Delivery Van
─────────────┬─────────────
             │  Adj. 4,000
─────────────┼─────────────
             │  Bal. 4,000
             │
```

The asset and contra-asset accounts are reported on the balance sheet as follows:

Delivery van	$12,000
Less: Accum. deprec.	4,000
Net book value of van	$ 8,000

Why use a contra-account to record the adjusting entry for depreciation? Why not just reduce the delivery van account directly?

1. Both the original cost and the amount of depreciation recorded on a fixed asset should be reported on the balance sheet. Therefore, the amounts are kept in separate accounts.
2. Any depreciation recorded on a fixed asset is just an estimate of the asset's usefulness that has expired. This estimate is maintained in a separate account.

As you cover the adjusting entries for depreciation, you will probably need to emphasize the following points:

1. A fixed asset must be owned and used by the business.
2. Depreciation expense is a noncash expense.
3. Depreciation is not related to the value of the asset.
4. The normal balance of the accumulated depreciation account is a credit.

TEACHING SUGGESTION — Use of an Accumulated Depreciation Account

To help students understand the purpose of accumulated depreciation contra-accounts, show the following example:

	Company 1	Company 2
Net book value of Equipment	$10,000	$10,000

Without using a contra-account, both companies look identical. Now show the following:

	Company 1	Company 2
Equipment	$100,000	$11,000
Accumulated Depreciation	90,000	1,000
Net book value of Equipment	$ 10,000	$10,000

What information does the contra-account provide? First, the equipment is 90% depreciated in Company 1 and only about 9% depreciated in Company 2. Second, Company 1 originally invested nearly 10 times as much into its equipment as Company 2. Therefore, Company 1 is probably a much larger operation. Since Company 2 has recorded a smaller percentage of depreciation, it may be a younger organization. Conclusion: Companies 1 and 2 are quite different, and reporting only book values does not reveal the differences.

WRITING EXERCISE — Adjusting Entry for Depreciation

To see how well your students have grasped the concept of depreciation, ask them to write an answer to the following question (also on Transparency 3-6):

> Assume that you are the accountant for Computer Consultants. Prior to this year, Computer Consultants operated out of a leased office. However, the company purchased its own office building this year. The building is in an area where real estate values have been increasing an average of 6% per year.
>
> The owner of Computer Consultants has asked why you recorded depreciation on the building if real estate values are appreciating. Write a response to the owner explaining why depreciation must be recorded on the company's accounting records.

EXERCISES & PROBLEMS FOR REINFORCEMENT:

Exercise 3-1	Exercise 3-14	Problem 3-1A	Problem 3-1B
Exercise 3-2	Exercise 3-15	Problem 3-2A	Problem 3-2B
Exercise 3-3	Exercise 3-16	Problem 3-3A	Problem 3-3B
Exercise 3-4	Exercise 3-17	Problem 3-6A	Problem 3-6B
Exercise 3-5	Exercise 3-18		
Exercise 3-6	Exercise 3-19		
Exercise 3-7	Exercise 3-20		
Exercise 3-8	Exercise 3-21		
Exercise 3-9	Exercise 3-22		
Exercise 3-10	Exercise 3-23		
Exercise 3-11	Exercise 3-24		
Exercise 3-12	Exercise 3-25		
Exercise 3-13			

OBJECTIVE 4 — Summarize the adjustment process and prepare an adjusted trial balance.

KEY TERMS:
Adjusted Trial Balance

SUGGESTED APPROACH

This objective illustrates the posting of adjusting entries and introduces the adjusted trial balance. Exhibit 8 in the text illustrates a work sheet which can be used to show the effect of adjusting entries and compute account balances to be included on an adjusted trial balance. Please note that this work sheet is not the traditional ten-column work sheet (which is presented in Chapter 4), but rather a modified work sheet used only to summarize adjusting entries.

Handout 3-1 presents two exercises to assess your students' understanding of adjusting entries. Part 1 of the handout asks students to complete a worksheet similar to Exhibit 8. In order to be successful with this exercise, students must understand which accounts are increased and decreased as the result of the adjustment process. Part 2 of the handout presents a trial balance and an adjusted trial balance. From this information, students are asked to deduce the adjusting entries that were recorded. This exercise is similar to several of the end-of-chapter exercises and problems. After students have journalized the adjusting entries, you may want to ask them to write a brief explanation for each entry, such as "Insurance expired equals $190." Many students will find it requires a higher level of understanding for them to work backwards through a problem.

The solution to Part 1 of Handout 3-1 is presented below. The journal entries for Part 2 of the handout are listed on Transparency 3-7.

Zeller Company Unadjusted Trial Balance Dec. 31	DR	CR	Effect of Adjusting Entry	Zeller Company Adjusted Trial Balance Dec. 31	DR	CR
Cash	300			Cash	300	
Accounts Receivable	20		+ 55	Accounts Receivable	75	
Supplies	80		− 70	Supplies	10	
Equipment	600			Equipment	600	
Accumulated Depreciation		30	+ 20	Accumulated Depreciation		50
Accounts Payable		240		Accounts Payable		240
P. Zeller, Capital		120		P. Zeller, Capital		120
Fees Earned		800	+ 55	Fees Earned		855
Wages Expense	150			Wages Expense	150	
Supplies Expense			+ 70	Supplies Expense	70	
Depreciation Expense			+ 20	Depreciation Expense	20	
Miscellaneous Expense	40			Miscellaneous Expense	40	
	1,190	1,190			1,265	1,265

EXERCISES & PROBLEMS FOR REINFORCEMENT:
    Exercise 3-26   Problem 3-4A   Problem 3-4B
    Exercise 3-27   Problem 3-5A   Problem 3-5B

OBJECTIVE 5 — Use vertical analysis to compare financial statement items with each other and with industry averages.

KEY TERMS:
    Vertical Analysis

SUGGESTED APPROACH

Under vertical analysis, all financial statement items are shown as a percentage of a significant total on the statement. On an income statement, all items are shown as a percentage of revenues. On a balance sheet, all items are shown as a percentage of total assets. The following group activity can be used to present vertical analysis.

GROUP LEARNING ACTIVITY — Vertical Analysis - Income Statement

Transparency 3-8 presents a simple income statement which can be used to illustrate vertical analysis. Remind students that vertical analysis shows all income statement amounts as a percentage of revenues. Therefore, the percentage is determined by dividing each amount on the income statement by the revenue amount.

On Transparency 3-8, fill in 100% for the Fees Earned account. Next, demonstrate that Wages Expense is 40% of Fees Earned ($800/$2,000 = 0.40). Ask your students to compute percentages for the remaining income statement items. Transparency 3-9 shows the completed income statement. An income statement which shows percentages calculated using vertical analysis is also called a *common-size income statement*.

You may want to refer students to Exhibit 9 in the text, which shows common-size income statements for two years. Use this exhibit to stress the importance of comparing trends from year-to-year.

GROUP LEARNING ACTIVITY — Vertical Analysis - Balance Sheet

Transparency 3-10 presents a balance sheet for illustrating vertical analysis. Remind students that all balance sheet amounts are stated as a percentage of total assets. Ask them to compute the percentages for the balance sheet on Transparency 3-10. The solution is found on Transparency 3-11.

INTERNET ACTIVITY – Vertical Analysis and Industry Averages

The text reminds students that comparing percentages computed under vertical analysis with industry averages can provide valuable information in assessing a company's performance. One web site where students can find some data on industry averages without paying a subscription is http://www.MarketGuide.com. After reaching this web site, students will need to click on the "Industries" tab and select the industry they wish to view. Under the profitability section of the industry statistics, they will find the Net Profit Margin %. This number compares to the percentage computed for Net Income on a common-size income statement.

EXERCISES & PROBLEMS FOR REINFORCEMENT:
    Exercise 3-28
    Exercise 3-29

Handout 3-1

Part 1: Zeller Company needs to record the following adjusting entries:
  a) Supplies on hand on Dec. 31 were $10.
  b) Fees earned but not billed on Dec. 31 were $55.
  c) Depreciation of equipment was estimated to be $20 for the year.

Use the form below to record the effect of each adjusting entry and the determine the balances on Zeller's adjusted trial balance. You may want to refer to Exhibit 8 in your text.

	Zeller Company Unadjusted Trial Balance Dec. 31		Effect of Adjusting Entry	Zeller Company Adjusted Trial Balance Dec. 31		
	DR	CR			DR	CR
Cash	300			Cash		
Accounts Receivable	20			Accounts Receivable		
Supplies	80			Supplies		
Equipment	600			Equipment		
Accumulated Depreciation		30		Accumulated Depreciation		
Accounts Payable		240		Accounts Payable		
P. Zeller, Capital		120		P. Zeller, Capital		
Fees Earned		800		Fees Earned		
Wages Expense	150			Wages Expense		
Supplies Expense				Supplies Expense		
Depreciation Expense				Depreciation Expense		
Miscellaneous Expense	40			Miscellaneous Expense		
	1,190	1,190				

Part 2: The trial balance and the adjusted trial balance for Matrix Company are presented below. Compare the numbers on these trial balances to determine what adjusting entries were prepared by Matrix's accountant. Journalize the four adjusting entries on a separate sheet of paper. You may assume none of the accounts were effected by more than one adjusting entry.

Matrix Company
Trial Balance
Dec. 31

	Unadjusted		Adjusted	
Cash	1,500		1,500	
Accounts Receivable	700		700	
Supplies	200		140	
Prepaid Insurance	400		210	
Accounts Payable		600		600
Wages Payable		---		130
Unearned Revenue		100		30
J. Morgan, Capital		500		500
Fees Earned		10,000		10,070
Wages Expense	7,200		7,330	
Rent Expense	1,200		1,200	
Supplies Expense	---		60	
Insurance Expense	---		190	
Total	11,200	11,200	11,330	11,330

Transparency Master 3-1

MONTHLY EXPENSES— LOAN APPLICATION

Assume that you are filling out a loan application. The application asks you for your total monthly committed expenses for housing, transportation, insurance, and debt repayment. After reviewing your checkbook, you compile the following list:

Rent..........................	$375	each month
Utilities.......................	110	each month–level billing
Car payment	200	each month
Car insurance	480	every 6 months
Life insurance...........	120	paid once per year
VISA..........................	20	each month (to pay off Florida vacation taken last year)

What is the total amount to be included on the loan application?

Transparency Master 3-2

MONTHLY EXPENSES— LOAN APPLICATION

Solution

Rent	**$375**
Utilities	110
Car payment	200
Car insurance	80
Life insurance	10
VISA	20
Total	**$795**

NOTE: The car and life insurance payments must be broken into a monthly amount. If the entire 6-month car insurance and 12-month life insurance payment were included on the application, the monthly expenses would be overstated. Therefore, a monthly amount is computed and "matched" against the other expenses.

Transparency Master 3-3

ARTISAN STONE AND BRICK

During May, Artisan Stone and Brick laid a stone patio for Louise McCowan for a fee of $1,200. The job took one full week. Artisan's expenses associated with the job are as follows:

1. Decorative stones, $400. These stones were purchased on account. They will be paid for in June.

2. Cement, two $10 bags. The bags were purchased and paid for in April.

3. Wages paid to assistants, $200. These wages were paid at the end of the week.

In addition, Artisan spends approximately $600 per month on rent, utilities, and insurance for its office.

Compute Artisan's profit on the job, using the matching concept.

ARTISAN STONE AND BRICK

Solution

Revenue		$1,200
Expenses:		
Stones	$400	
Cement	20	
Wages	200	
Office Expenses		
(1/4 of monthly total)	<u>150</u>	<u>770</u>
Profit		<u>$ 430</u>

DEFERRALS AND ACCRUALS

1. A deferred expense occurs when you pay for an item or a service before it is actually used. List four expenses that you typically pay in advance.

2. A deferred revenue occurs when you receive a payment before you have actually earned it. List two times that you have been paid for a service or merchandise in advance.

3. An accrued expense occurs when you use an item or a service before you have paid for it. List four expenses that you typically pay "after the fact."

4. An accrued revenue occurs when you have earned revenue, but you have not yet received payment. List two examples of revenues that you earn before you receive payment.

Transparency Master 3-6

WRITING EXERCISE

Assume that you are the accountant for Computer Consultants. Prior to this year, Computer Consultants operated out of a leased office. However, the company purchased its own office building this year. The building is in an area where real estate values have been increasing an average of 6% per year.

The owner of Computer Consultants has asked why you recorded depreciation on the building if real estate values are appreciating. Write a response to the owner explaining why depreciation must be recorded on the company's accounting records.

Matrix Company
Adjusting Entries

1. **Supplies Expense** **60**
    Supplies **60**

    Explanation: Supplies on hand on Dec. 31, $140 or...Supplies used during the year, $60.

2. **Insurance Expense** **190**
    Prepaid Insurance **190**

    Explanation: Insurance expired during year, $190.

3. **Wages Expense** **130**
    Wages Payable **130**

    Explanation: Wages accrued but not paid at Dec. 31, $130.

4. **Unearned Revenue** **70**
    Fees Earned **70**

    Explanation: Unearned fees at Dec. 31, $30.

Vertical Analysis
Income Statement

	Amount	Percent
Fees Earned	$2,000	
Operating Expenses:		
Wages Expense	$ 800	
Rent Expense	500	
Utilities Expense	250	
Supplies Expense	100	
Total Operating Exp.	$1,650	
Net Income	$ 350	

Vertical Analysis
Income Statement

	Amount	Percent
Fees Earned	$2,000	100.0%
Operating Expenses:		
Wages Expense	$ 800	40.0%
Rent Expense	500	25.0%
Utilities Expense	250	12.5%
Supplies Expense	100	5.0%
Total Operating Exp.	$1,650	82.5%
Net Income	$ 350	17.5%

Balance Sheet
Vertical Analysis

Assets	Amount	Percent
Cash	$ 1,300	
Accts. Receivable	3,700	
Supplies	7,000	
Fixed Assets	12,000	
Total Assets	**$24,000**	

Liabilities		
Accounts Payable	$ 6,000	

Owner's Equity		
J. Cox, Capital	18,000	
Total Liab. & Owner's Equity	**$24,000**	

Balance Sheet
Vertical Analysis

Assets	Amount	Percent
Cash	$ 1,300	5.4%
Accts. Receivable	3,700	15.4%
Supplies	7,000	29.2%
Fixed Assets	12,000	50.0%
Total Assets	**$24,000**	**100.0%**
Liabilities		
Accounts Payable	$ 6,000	25.0%
Owner's Equity		
J. Cox, Capital	18,000	75.0%
Total Liab. & Owner's Equity	$24,000	100.0%

Chapter 4
Completing the Accounting Cycle

OPENING COMMENTS

Chapter 4 opens with a listing of the seven steps in the accounting cycle and explains that the work sheet and closing process will be explained in this chapter. The text then proceeds to illustrate the preparation of the work sheet. The work sheet becomes the source of information used to prepare formal financial statements. Chapter 4 introduces the classified balance sheet. The discussion of working capital and the current ratio, found at the end of the chapter, shows the need for classifying assets and liabilities on the balance sheet.

Chapter 4 reminds students that it is not sufficient to record adjusting entries only on the work sheet. These entries must be journalized and posted to make them a part of a company's accounting records. Next, the accounting cycle is completed by explaining closing entries and the post-closing trial balance. The chapter also discusses the fiscal year and the natural business year.

After studying the chapter, your students should be able to:

1. Review the seven basic steps of the accounting cycle.
2. Prepare a work sheet.
3. Prepare financial statements from a work sheet.
4. Prepare the adjusting and closing entries from a work sheet.
5. Explain what is meant by the fiscal year and the natural business year.
6. Analyze and interpret the financial solvency of a business by computing working capital and the current ratio.

OBJECTIVE 1 — Review the seven basic steps of the accounting cycle.

KEY TERMS:
 Accounting Cycle

SUGGESTED APPROACH

This learning objective lists the seven steps in the accounting cycle. It provides a good review of the first three chapters plus an overview of the material covered in chapter 4 (the work sheet and closing entries.) You may want to briefly review Exhibit 1 as an introduction to the chapter.

Rather than simply memorizing the seven steps in their proper order, it is helpful if students understand the relationships between the steps in the accounting cycle. Students will not make the mistake of listing "Financial statements prepared" before completing the work sheet if they understand that the work sheet provides the data necessary to prepare financial statements.

Therefore, you may want to use the activities described below after covering the worksheet and closing entries (learning objectives 2 through 4.)

Emphasize that the accounting cycle is the same for all businesses, no matter how complex or how simple. The accounting cycle is repeated each period in which financial statements are prepared.

GROUP LEARNING ACTIVITY — Accounting Cycle

Show your class Transparency 4-1, which lists the steps in the accounting cycle in random order. Ask students to put the steps in the proper order. You can ask them to work individually or in small groups.

WRITING EXERCISE — Accounting Cycle

Write the seven steps of the accounting cycle on the board. Ask your students to record what information is needed as an input to each step in the accounting cycle. For example, source documents are needed in order to analyze transactions and record them in journals (Step 1). Completed journal entries are needed to post transactions to the ledger (Step 2).

After giving the students a few minutes to write, review the inputs needed for each step. Show students that knowing what information is needed to complete each step in the accounting cycle will make it easy to put the steps in the proper order.

EXERCISES & PROBLEMS FOR REINFORCEMENT:
    Exercise 4-1

OBJECTIVE 2 — Prepare a work sheet.

KEY TERMS:
    Work Sheet

SUGGESTED APPROACH

Transparency 4-2 presents information that can be used in explaining the purpose of the work sheet. After reviewing this material, use Transparency 4-3 to explain how to complete the columns of the work sheet. You may want to instruct your students to turn to the work sheet illustrated in the text while you review this information. Point out that it is not necessary to prepare a separate trial balance if a work sheet is used. You may also want to emphasize that the adjusted trial balance columns are a check on the mathematical accuracy of the work sheet.

It is helpful to allow your students to practice completing a work sheet. The following group learning activity will assist in accomplishing this goal.

GROUP LEARNING ACTIVITY — Preparing a Work Sheet

Handout 4-1 is a work sheet for Dixie Machinery. The Trial Balance columns have been completed using account balances from the company's ledger. Make copies of this handout for each of your students. Divide the class into small groups and instruct them to enter the adjusting entries from Transparency 4-4 on the work sheet. Also ask them to complete the Adjusted Trial Balance columns.

At this point, display Transparency 4-5, which shows the first three columns of the completed work sheet. After your students have checked their work, instruct them to complete the income statement and balance sheet columns by sorting the account balances to the proper financial statement. Transparency 4-6 shows the adjusted trial balance, income statement, and balance sheet columns. The net income is not illustrated on this transparency. This gives you the opportunity to complete that step for your students on the transparency. Fill in these columns as follows:

	Income Statement		Balance Sheet	
	Debit	Credit	Debit	Credit
Total of Accounts	11,290	15,140	7,400	3,550
Net Income	3,850			3,850
	15,140	15,140	7,400	7,400

Check your students' understanding of using the work sheet to compute net income by asking the following questions:

1. If the totals of the Income Statement columns of a work sheet are Debit, $2,800 and Credit, $2,500, what is the net income or net loss? Answer: Net loss, $300.

2. If the totals of the Balance Sheet columns of a work sheet are Debit, $1,250 and Credit, $1,110, what is the net income or net loss? Answer: Net income, $140.

EXERCISES & PROBLEMS FOR REINFORCEMENT:
    Exercise 4-2   Exercise 4-5
    Exercise 4-3   Exercise 4-6
    Exercise 4-4

OBJECTIVE 3 — Prepare financial statements from a work sheet.

KEY TERMS:
    Current Assets   Long-Term Liabilities
    Current Liabilities   Notes Receivable
    Fixed Assets   Plant Assets

SUGGESTED APPROACH

The group learning activity used to explain Objective 2 will yield a completed work sheet. Use that work sheet to prepare financial statements. Before preparing financial statements, however, you will need to explain account classifications.

GROUP LEARNING ACTIVITY — Preparing Financial Statements

To complete this activity, you can either break the class into small groups or ask each student to work individually. Ask the students to list all the asset and liability accounts they can think of. Give the students 2 to 3 minutes to complete their lists.

Ask the students to call out the accounts on their lists as you write them on the board.

Next, explain the following account classifications:

> Current Assets
> Property, Plant, and Equipment
> Current Liabilities
> Long-Term Liabilities

Instruct your students to go back to the accounts on their lists and indicate where each account would be classified on a balance sheet: current assets; property, plant, and equipment; current liabilities; or long-term liabilities. After giving the students a minute or two to work, list the proper classification for each account on the board.

Next, using the work sheet from Objective 2, ask the students to prepare formal financial statements. You may want to show your students Transparency 4-7 to guide them through the process of preparing financial statements. The completed financial statements are displayed on Transparencies 4-8 and 4-9. If time allows, compare these financial statements to the real-world financial statements for Home Depot in Appendix F of the text.

It is helpful to emphasize the following points regarding the statement of owner's equity.

1. In preparing the statement of owner's equity, it is necessary to examine the owner's capital account to determine whether any additional investments have been made during the period.

2. The ending capital balance of the owner's capital account does not appear on the work sheet. The ending capital balance is determined by preparing the statement of owner's equity.

EXERCISES & PROBLEMS FOR REINFORCEMENT:
> Exercise 4-7   Exercise 4-14
> Exercise 4-10   Exercise 4-15
> Exercise 4-11   Exercise 4-16
> Exercise 4-12   Exercise 4-17
> Exercise 4-13   Exercise 4-18

OBJECTIVE 4 — Prepare the adjusting and closing entries from a work sheet.

KEY TERMS:
- Clearing Account
- Closing Entries
- Income Summary
- Nominal Accounts
- Post-Closing Trial Balance
- Real Accounts
- Temporary Accounts

SUGGESTED APPROACH

Students need to be reminded that writing adjusting entries on the work sheet does not make the entries a part of the company's accounting records. The only way to get adjustments "on the books" is to journalize and post these entries.

Understanding closing entries tends to be a real struggle for students. All too frequently, students resort to memorizing the mechanics of closing entries without understanding the purpose of this step in the accounting cycle. As a result, the instructor may want to introduce this topic with a few attention-getting exercises that attempt to explain why closing entries are prepared. As a next step, try a group learning activity that allows students to discover the mechanics of preparing closing entries. End the class with a short writing exercise to summarize why and how closing entries are prepared.

GROUP LEARNING ACTIVITY — Journalizing Adjusting Entries

From Objective 2, the students will have a completed work sheet. Ask the students to break into groups and record the adjusting entries in journal format.

WRITING EXERCISE — Benefits of the Work Sheet

Ask your students to read and answer the following case (Transparency 4-10).

> Keith Martin is the controller for Daniels Printing Service. Keith has been putting in a lot of overtime; therefore, Mr. Daniels has allowed Keith to hire an assistant. Keith's assistant is a bright, high school graduate, but he has never taken an accounting class. Keith is trying to decide which accounting activities could be delegated to his assistant. Keith is willing to give the assistant a few simple instructions on how to complete each task, but he doesn't have the time to teach the assistant to be an accountant.
>
> For each task listed, state whether Keith should continue to do the work or delegate the task to his assistant. Explain each answer.
>
> 1. List the account balances from the general ledger in the Trial Balance columns of the work sheet.
> 2. Add the Debit and Credit columns of the trial balance.
> 3. Make the adjusting entries on the work sheet.
> 4. Complete the work sheet.

5. Type the formal financial statements using the data from the Income Statement and Balance Sheet columns of the work sheet.
6. Journalize and post the adjusting entries.

LECTURE AIDS — Purpose of Closing Entries

Bring a stopwatch to class. Ask for a student volunteer who knows how to run a stopwatch. Instruct your volunteer to time a few students completing a simple activity. For example, you may want to time how long it takes the first row in your classroom to pass out Handout 4-2 (which will be used in the next group learning activity) to all the students in that row. Then time the next row in your class. Ask the student volunteer to write the time for each row on the board.

Next, ask the student volunteer to explain how he or she timed each row. As part of that student's explanation, he or she should mention that after timing each row, the stopwatch had to be reset to zero. Discuss the problems that would have resulted if the student had neglected to reset the stopwatch to zero.

Because the information we wanted from the exercise was how long it took each row to distribute the papers, it was important to time each row separately and reset the stopwatch after each row performed the task. In business, we want to know how much income a business earns during the course of one year. Therefore, we record revenues and expenses for the year and prepare an income statement. Before we begin recording revenues and expenses for the second year, however, we must reset each of the revenue and expense accounts to a zero balance, just as the stopwatch was reset. The drawing account is also reset to a zero balance. The process of getting these accounts to a zero balance is accomplished through closing entries.

GROUP LEARNING ACTIVITY— Closing Entries

Before beginning this exercise, review the purpose of closing entries. One primary concern in closing entries is to reset the revenue, expense, and drawing accounts (the temporary accounts) to a zero balance.

The second purpose of closing entries is to move the balance of all revenue, expense, and drawing accounts to the owner's capital account. Remind students that in Chapter 1, all revenue, expense, and withdrawal transactions were recorded in the owner's capital account, because they affect owner's equity. In Chapter 2, students began recording these transactions in separate accounts to make it easier to prepare financial statements. Now it is time to move those transactions back to the capital account.

Be sure your students can identify temporary and real accounts. Ask them to turn to the completed work sheet (Exhibit 5) in the textbook. From that exhibit, quiz students on which accounts will be closed at the end of the accounting period and which will be left open.

Ask your students to break into groups of three or four and, using Handout 4-2, Part A, prepare entries that will zero-out the revenue, expense, and drawing accounts and move their balances to the capital account. Remind students that they must keep debits and credits equal in all entries. If some groups finish early, ask them to practice preparing financial statements by constructing an income statement and a statement of owner's equity for this company.

Review the exercise with the class, using Transparency 4-11. Next, compute the balance of the J. Jones, capital account. Show your students that the account balance equals the ending capital balance shown on a statement of owner's equity (Transparency 4-12).

At this time, explain the purpose of Income Summary. When preparing closing entries, accountants first move the balances of all revenue and expense accounts to Income Summary. If all revenue and expense accounts are correctly transferred to Income Summary, the account's balance should equal net income. After verifying that the account balance does equal net income, Income Summary is closed to the owner's capital account. Therefore, the income summary account is used simply to check the accuracy of the closing entries, similar to a trial balance being used to check the equality of debits and credits after preparing journal entries and posting. Emphasize that the income summary account does not appear on financial statements.

Instruct the class to use Part B of Handout 4-2 to prepare the closing entries in the actual format used by accountants. The following instructions will guide them in the proper order to prepare the entries.

a) Close the revenue account to Income Summary.
b) Close the expense accounts to Income Summary.
c) Make sure that the balance in Income Summary equals net income. If it doesn't, correct entries from (a) or (b).
d) Close Income Summary to Capital.
e) Close the drawing account to Capital.

Review these entries using Transparency 4-13. Stress that the drawing account is not closed to Income Summary, since it is not included when calculating net income. Instead, the drawing account is closed directly to Capital. After completing T account entries, you may want to ask your students to prepare these same entries in journal entry format.

LECTURE AIDS – Closing Entries

You can also illustrate closing entries with a visual example using five cups and paper clips. Label each of the five cups with one of the following titles: Revenues, Expenses, Income Summary, Drawings, and Capital. Styrofoam cups work great because you write on them with an ink pen. Next, place a few paper clips in each cup.

Illustrate closing entries by pouring the paper clips from the Revenue cup into the Income Summary cup. Emphasize that the Revenue cup is now closed (empty) because its contents were transferred to the Income Summary cup. Repeat the same process for the Expenses cup. Now, explain to your students that the analogy is not perfect because the revenue paper clips are "positive" clips and the expense paper clips are "negative." But, in effect, the Income Summary cup now holds the net income.

Pour the contents of the Income Summary cup into the Capital cup, illustrating the transfer of net income to the Owner's Capital account. Finally, pour the paper clips from the Drawings cup into the Capital cup. Emphasize that all the cups except Capital are now empty (closed). You can also reinforce that the Capital account is not closed—the contents of all the other cups were transferred there.

WRITING EXERCISE — Closing Entries

After discussing closing entries, ask your students to write answers to the following questions (also on Transparency 4-14).

1. Why are closing entries prepared?
2. Why do we use Income Summary when preparing closing entries?
3. Why are closing entries prepared after financial statements?
4. What are some examples of temporary accounts that would be closed for a physician?

LECTURE AIDS — Post-Closing Trial Balance

Remind your students that a post-closing trial balance is a trial balance prepared after closing entries. The post-closing trial balance is prepared to make sure that the ledger is in balance to start the next accounting period. You may want to refer your students to an example of a post-closing trial balance by turning to Exhibit 12 in the text.

Pose the following questions to stimulate class discussion:

1. What three classes of accounts will not appear on a post-closing trial balance? Answer: revenues, expenses, and drawings.
2. What accounts will appear on a post-closing trial balance? Answer: assets, liabilities, and capital.
3. If a temporary account was overlooked in the closing process, would the post-closing trial balance still balance? Answer: Yes, but the balance of the owner's capital account would not agree with the amount shown on the balance sheet.

EXERCISES & PROBLEMS FOR REINFORCEMENT:

Exercise 4-8	Problem 4-1A	Problem 4-1B
Exercise 4-9	Problem 4-2A	Problem 4-2B
Exercise 4-19	Problem 4-3A	Problem 4-3B
Exercise 4-20	Problem 4-4A	Problem 4-4B
Exercise 4-21	Problem 4-5A	Problem 4-5B
Exercise 4-22		
Exercise 4-23		
Exercise 4-24		
Exercise 4-25		

OBJECTIVE 5 — Explain what is meant by the fiscal year and the natural business year.

KEY TERMS:
    Fiscal Year
    Natural Business Year

SUGGESTED APPROACH

Objective 5 asks the student to understand the definitions of fiscal year and natural business year, not just memorize these definitions. Therefore, the instructor must get the student to internalize these concepts.

LECTURE AID — Fiscal Year

To begin this exercise, explain the definitions of fiscal year and natural business year. Then ask students who work either full- or part-time to raise their hands. Call on one of these students and ask where he or she works.

Next, ask the student at what time of the year the company is at the end of its natural business year (i.e., when stocks are lowest, prices are normal, the company is not buying heavily). Ask the student whether he or she knows when the company closes its fiscal year. If the student doesn't know, ask when the company takes a physical inventory count. That may provide a clue. Repeat the same exercise with several other students.

TEACHING SUGGESTION — Financial History of a Business

On page 159 of the text, the authors illustrate how a series of balance sheets and income statements show the financial history of a business. You can emphasize this point with the following analogy. For a football game, the yardage and other game statistics are similar to income statement revenue and expense data for a business. The final score of the game is similar to net income for a business. The team's record for each game is similar to a balance sheet for a business. The team's success is measured by its record at the end of the season, similar to measuring the success of a business at the end of its life.

OBJECTIVE 6 — Analyze and interpret the financial solvency of a business by computing working capital and the current ratio.

KEY TERMS:
    Current Ratio
    Solvency
    Working Capital

SUGGESTED APPROACH

The following group learning activity will explain solvency and allow your students to compute and interpret working capital and the current ratio.

GROUP LEARNING ACTIVITY — Working Capital and the Current Ratio

Transparency 4-15 presents the formulas for working capital and the current ratio. It also gives current assets and current liabilities amounts for two companies. The instructions ask your students to compute these ratios and state which company is more solvent. Ask your students to complete this activity in small groups.

As you review the solution to this activity (Transparency 4-16), emphasize that the current ratio is helpful when comparing two companies of unequal size. The current ratio compares the relative size of current assets and current liabilities, rather than looking at absolute dollar figures.

INTERNET ACTIVITY – Current Ratio

A web site which provides a variety of information on financial ratios is www.investopedia.com. If your students visit http://www.investopedia.com/university/ratios/workingcapital.asp, they will find a tutorial on the current ratio which explains the purpose of the ratio and gives an example of how to calculate the ratio. From the home page of this web site, the information on financial ratios can be accessed by selecting the "tutorials" tab.

The current ratio is listed as one of the industry statistics provided by www.MarketGuide.com. This web site provides some information on industry averages without requiring a subscription. After reaching this web site, students will need to click on the "Industries" tab and select the industry they wish to view. Remind students that to have an accurate picture of a company's solvency, it is important to compare the current ratio with other companies in the same line of business and look at trends in the current ratio over several years.

EXERCISES & PROBLEMS FOR REINFORCEMENT:
    Exercise 4-26
    Exercise 4-27

APPENDIX — Reversing Entries

SUGGESTED APPROACH

Remind students that reversing entries may be used for accrual-type adjusting entries. When covering this topic, it is a good idea to contrast the payment of an accrued expense or receipt of an accrued revenue both with and without the use of reversing entries. This will demonstrate how reversing entries simplify the accounting for accruals.

It is essential to show reversing entries both in journal format and in T accounts. Without T accounts, students cannot see the effect of reversing entries on account balances.

Reversing entries are optional, both in practice and in academia. Coverage of this topic may be omitted without disrupting the flow of the course.

DEMONSTRATION PROBLEM — Reversing Entries

Ask students to record the following transactions in their notes:

1. On Friday, December 26, $500 was paid to employees for one week's (5 days) salaries.

   Dec. 26   Salaries Expense.........   500
                   Cash..............   500

2. Assume that December 31 is on a Tuesday. Make the adjusting entry to record the 2 days of salaries owed to employees.

   Dec. 31   Salaries Expense.........   200
                   Salaries Payable   200

3. On Friday, January 3, $500 was paid to employees for one week's salaries. (This $500 includes the $200 accrued on December 31.)

   Jan. 3   Salaries Expense.........   300
             Salaries Payable..........   200
                   Cash..............   500

Why are the entries on December 26 and January 3 different when the same event occurred on both days? Answer: because of the adjusting entry made on December 31.

Reversing entries allows the payment of salaries on January 3 to be recorded with a debit to Salaries Expense and a credit to Cash—as if there had not been an adjusting entry. As a result, the entry to pay salaries is always the same. This reduces the chance of errors.

Illustrate the same transactions, this time using reversing entries. After each journal entry, post entries to Salaries Expense and Salaries Payable T accounts.

1. Entry to accrue $200 of salaries on December 31.

   Dec. 31   Salaries Expense.........   200
                   Salaries Payable   200

2. On December 31, closing entries are made. The salaries expense account (along with the other expenses) would be closed to Income Summary.

   Dec. 31   Income Summary.........   200
                   Salaries Expense   200

3. On January 1, a reversing entry is recorded. This entry reverses the adjustment made on December 31.

Jan. 1   Salaries Payable..........   200
                Salaries Expense   200

4. On January 3, $500 in salaries are paid.

Jan. 3   Salaries Expense..........   500
                Cash...............   500

Salaries Expense		Salaries Payable	
Adj. 200			Adj. 200
	Clos. 200		
Bal. 0			Bal. 200
	Rev. 200	Rev. 200	
Payday 500			
Bal. 300			Bal. 0

Emphasize that even though Salaries Expense was debited for $500 on January 3, the account balance is only $300—representing the 3 days of salaries earned by employees in January. The account balance is $300 because the reversing entry subtracted the $200 of Salaries Expense that had been recognized in December.

EXERCISES & PROBLEMS FOR REINFORCEMENT:
    Exercise 4-28
    Exercise 4-29

Handout 4-1

Dixie Machinery
Work Sheet
For the Year Ended December 31, 20—

ACCOUNT TITLE	TRIAL BALANCE DEBIT	TRIAL BALANCE CREDIT	ADJUSTMENTS DEBIT	ADJUSTMENTS CREDIT	ADJUSTED TRIAL BALANCE DEBIT	ADJUSTED TRIAL BALANCE CREDIT	INCOME STATEMENT DEBIT	INCOME STATEMENT CREDIT	BALANCE SHEET DEBIT	BALANCE SHEET CREDIT
Cash	825									
Accounts Receivable	300									
Prepaid Insurance	500									
Office Equipment	5,050									
Accumulated Depr.—Office Equipment		180								
Accounts Payable		250								
Salaries Payable										
Bill McCowan, Capital		2,370								
Bill McCowan, Drawing	1,100									
Repair Revenue		15,140								
Salaries Expense	8,025									
Rent Expense	1,500									
Utilities Expense	640									
Insurance Expense										
Depreciation Expense—Office Equipment										
	17,940	17,940								

101

Handout 4-2

CLOSING ENTRIES

Part A—Make entries that will bring the revenue, expense, and drawing accounts to a zero balance. Do this by moving the balance of each account to the capital account. After you have completed your entries, compute the balance of the capital account.

Service Revenue	Salaries Expense	Rent Expense
3,500	1,400	600

J. Jones, Drawing		J. Jones, Capital
1,200		10,000

Part B—Prepare closing entries in the format used by accountants. To do this, close the revenue, expense, and drawing accounts in the following order:

(a) Close the revenue account to Income Summary.
(b) Close the expense accounts to Income Summary.
(c) Make sure that the balance in Income Summary equals net income. If it doesn't, correct entries from (a) or (b).
(d) Close Income Summary to Capital.
(e) Close the drawing account to Capital.

After you have completed all the entries, compute the balance in the capital account.

Service Revenue	Salaries Expense	Rent Expense
3,500	1,400	600

J. Jones, Drawing	Income Summary	J. Jones, Capital
1,200		10,000

Transparency Master 4-1

STEPS IN THE ACCOUNTING CYCLE

Instructions: List the following steps in the correct order.

- Financial statements prepared.

- Transactions posted to the ledger.

- Closing entries journalized & posted to ledger.

- Transactions analyzed and recorded in journal.

- Trial balance prepared, adjustment data assembled, and work sheet completed.

- Post-closing trial balance prepared.

- Adjusting entries journalized & posted to ledger.

PURPOSE OF WORK SHEET

1. Tool to assist with end-of-accounting-period work

2. Information to prepare adjusting entries and financial statements on one continuous form

3. Format that is easily adapted to a computer spreadsheet program

Transparency Master 4-3

WORK SHEET

To complete the columns of a work sheet:

1. List all account balances from the ledger in the Trial Balance columns. Total the Debit and Credit columns; they should be equal.

2. Record the adjusting entries in the Adjustments columns. Total the Debit and Credit columns; they should be equal.

3. Enter the balance of each account, after computing any changes due to adjusting entries, in the Adjusted Trial Balance columns. Total the Debit and Credit columns; they should be equal.

4. Enter the balance of all revenue and expense accounts in the Income Statement columns. Total the debit and credit columns; the difference between these columns is Net Income.

5. Enter the balance of assets, liabilities, capital, and drawings in the Balance Sheet columns. Total the debit and credit columns. Net income must be added to the credit column to make the balance sheet columns balance.

Transparency Master 4-4

WORK SHEET

Enter the following adjusting entries on the work sheet for Dixie Machinery:

1. **$375 of the prepaid insurance has expired.**

3. **Depreciation to be recorded on the office equipment is $400.**

4. **$350 of salaries are owed to Dixie Machinery's employees.**

Dixie Machinery
Work Sheet
For the Year Ended December 31, 20—

ACCOUNT TITLE	TRIAL BALANCE DEBIT	TRIAL BALANCE CREDIT	ADJUSTMENTS DEBIT	ADJUSTMENTS CREDIT	ADJUSTED TRIAL BALANCE DEBIT	ADJUSTED TRIAL BALANCE CREDIT
Cash	825				825	
Accounts Receivable	300				300	
Prepaid Insurance	500			375	125	
Office Equipment	5,050				5,050	
Accum. Depr.—Off. Equip.		180		400		580
Accounts Payable		250				250
Salaries Payable				350		350
Bill McCowan, Capital		2,370				2,370
Bill McCowan, Drawing	1,100				1,100	
Repair Revenue		15,140				15,140
Salaries Expense	8,025		350		8,375	
Rent Expense	1,500				1,500	
Utilities Expense	640				640	
Insurance Expense			375		375	
Depreciation Expense —Office Equipment			400		400	
	17,940	17,940	1,125	1,125	18,690	18,690

Dixie Machinery
Work Sheet
For the Year Ended December 31, 20—

ACCOUNT TITLE	ADJUSTED TRIAL BALANCE DEBIT	ADJUSTED TRIAL BALANCE CREDIT	INCOME STATEMENT DEBIT	INCOME STATEMENT CREDIT	BALANCE SHEET DEBIT	BALANCE SHEET CREDIT
Cash	825				825	
Accounts Receivable	300				300	
Prepaid Insurance	125				125	
Office Equipment	5,050				5,050	
Accum. Depr.—Off. Equip.		580				580
Accounts Payable		250				250
Salaries Payable		350				350
Bill McCowan, Capital		2,370				2,370
Bill McCowan, Drawing	1,100				1,100	
Repair Revenue		15,140		15,140		
Salaries Expense	8,375		8,375			
Rent Expense	1,500		1,500			
Utilities Expense	640		640			
Insurance Expense	375		375			
Depreciation Expense—Office Equipment	400		400			
	18,690	18,690	11,290	15,140	7,400	3,550
Net Income						

Transparency Master 4-6

FINANCIAL STATEMENTS

Income Statement

Revenues	(from the work sheet)
− **Expenses**	(from the work sheet)
Net Income	

Statement of Owner's Equity

Beginning Capital Balance	(from the work sheet or owner's capital account in the ledger)
+ Investments	(from the owner's capital account in the ledger)
+ Net Income	(from the income statement)
− **Drawing**	(from the work sheet)
Ending Capital Balance	

Balance Sheet

Current Assets	(from the work sheet)
+ **Property, Plant & Equip.**	(from the work sheet)
Total Assets	

Current Liabilities	(from the work sheet)
+ **Long-Term Liabilities**	(from the work sheet)
Total Liabilities	
+ **Capital Balance**	(from statement of owner's equity)
Total Liabilities and Owner's Equity	.

Transparency Master 4-8

FINANCIAL STATEMENTS

Dixie Machinery
Income Statement
For the Year Ended December 31, 20—

Revenues:		
Repair revenue		$15,140
Expenses:		
Salaries expense	$8,375	
Rent expense	1,500	
Utilities expense	640	
Depreciation expense—office equipment	400	
Insurance expense	375	
Total expenses		11,290
Net income.......................................		$ 3,850

Dixie Machinery
Statement of Owner's Equity
For the Year Ended December 31, 20—

Bill McCowan, capital, January 1		$2,370
Net income..	$3,850	
Less withdrawals	1,100	
Increase in owner's equity		2,750
Bill McCowan, capital, December 31 ...		$5,120

FINANCIAL STATEMENTS

Dixie Machinery
Balance Sheet
December 31, 20—

Assets

Current assets:
Cash	$ 825	
Accounts receivable	300	
Prepaid insurance	125	
Total current assets		$1,250

Property, plant, and equipment:
Office equipment	$5,050	
Less accumulated depreciation	580	
Total property, plant, and equipment		4,470
Total assets		$5,720

Liabilities

Current liabilities:
Accounts payable	$ 250	
Salaries payable	350	
Total liabilities		$ 600

Owner's Equity

Bill McCowan, capital	5,120
Total liabilities and owner's equity	$5,720

Transparency Master 4-10

WRITING EXERCISE

Keith Martin is the controller for Daniels Printing Service. Keith has been putting in a lot of overtime; therefore, Mr. Daniels has allowed Keith to hire an assistant. Keith's assistant is a bright, high school graduate, but he has never taken an accounting class. Keith is trying to decide which accounting activities could be delegated to his assistant. Keith is willing to give the assistant a few simple instructions on how to complete each task, but he doesn't have the time to teach the assistant to be an accountant.

For each task listed, state whether Keith should continue to do the work or delegate the task to his assistant. Explain each answer.

1. List the account balances from the general ledger in the Trial Balance columns of the work sheet.

2. Add the Debit and Credit columns of the trial balance.

3. Make the adjusting entries on the work sheet.

4. Complete the work sheet.

5. Type the formal financial statements using the data from the Income Statement and Balance Sheet columns of the work sheet.

6. Journalize and post the adjusting entries.

CLOSING ENTRIES

Part A

Service Revenue

	3,500	Bal.	3,500
		Bal.	0

Salaries Expense

Bal.	1,400	1,400
Bal.	0	

Rent Expense

Bal.	600	600
Bal.	0	

J. Jones, Drawing

Bal.	1,200	1,200
Bal.	0	

J. Jones, Capital

	1,400	Bal.	10,000
	600		3,500
	1,200		
		Bal.	10,300

J. Jones Company
Income Statement
For the Year Ended December 31, 20—

Service revenue		$3,500
Expenses:		
Salaries expense	$1,400	
Rent expense	600	
Total expenses		2,000
Net income		$1,500

J. Jones Company
Statement of Owner's Equity
For the Year Ended December 31, 20—

J. Jones, capital, January 1		$10,000
Net income	$1,500	
Less withdrawals	1,200	
Increase in owner's equity		300
J. Jones, capital, December 31		$10,300

CLOSING ENTRIES
Part B

Service Revenue			
		Bal.	3,500
a.	3,500		
		Bal.	0

Salaries Expense			
Bal.	1,400		
		b.	1,400
Bal.	0		

Rent Expense			
Bal.	600		
		b.	600
Bal.	0		

J. Jones, Drawing			
Bal.	1,200		
		d.	1,200
Bal.	0		

Income Summary			
		a.	3,500
b.	2,000		
		Bal.	1,500*
c.	1,500		
		Bal.	0

J. Jones, Capital			
		Bal.	10,000
		c.	1,500
d.	1,200		
		Bal.	10,300

*$1,500 Balance = Net Income

WRITING EXERCISE

1. Why are closing entries prepared?

2. Why do we use Income Summary when preparing closing entries?

3. Why are closing entries prepared after financial statements?

4. What are some examples of temporary accounts that would be closed for a physician?

Transparency Master 4-15

Financial Analysis and Interpretation

Working Capital = Current Assets - Current Liabilities

Current Ratio = $\dfrac{\text{Current Assets}}{\text{Current Liabilities}}$

	Wilson Company	Menedez Company
Current Assets	$1,600,000	$230,000
Current Liabilities	$1,450,000	$100,000

INSTRUCTIONS:

1. Compute Working Capital for both companies.
2. Compute the Current Ratio for both companies.
3. Which company is more solvent? Why? (Solvency is a business's ability to pay its debts.)

Transparency Master 4-16

Financial Analysis and Interpretation Solution

	Wilson Company	**Menedez Company**
Working Capital	$150,000	$130,000
Current Ratio	1.1	2.3

Chapter 5
Accounting Systems and Internal Controls

OPENING COMMENTS

Chapter 5 introduces new concepts and new forms. The new concepts relate to accounting system design, developing an internal control framework, computerized accounting, e-commerce and subsidiary ledgers. The new forms introduced are the special journals for a service business: revenue journal, cash receipts journal, purchases journal, and cash payments journal.

The transactions that will be recorded in special journals are the same as those that were covered in Chapters 1-4; only the journal format has changed. But beware—students frequently get lost in the barrage of new forms.

In this chapter, it is especially obvious that there is no substitute for practice. Students need the opportunity to try recording and posting transactions in a setting where they can ask questions. Group learning activities are very effective.

After studying the chapter, your students should be able to:

1. Define an accounting system and describe its implementation.
2. List the three objectives of internal control, and define and give examples of the five elements of internal control.
3. Journalize and post transactions in a manual accounting system that uses subsidiary ledgers and special journals.
4. Describe and give examples of additional subsidiary ledgers and modified special journals.
5. Apply computerized accounting to the revenue and collection cycle.
6. Describe the basic features of e-commerce.

OBJECTIVE 1 — Define an accounting system and describe its implementation.

KEY TERMS:
- Accounting System
- Internal Controls

SUGGESTED APPROACH

An accounting system is the methods and procedures used to collect, classify, summarize, and report financial data. This objective presents the basic principles that should be considered when designing an accounting system. The following brainstorming exercise will help stimulate interest in the topic.

BRAINSTORMING EXERCISE — Accounting Systems

Pose the following scenario to your class (Transparency 5-1): You have decided to open a bookstore that sells textbooks and competes with the campus bookstore. You have chosen a location and have received a list of textbooks used by the college. What other decisions will you have to make regarding the operations of your business?

As your students call out operational concerns, list them on the board. While they will come up with many decisions to be made (e.g., operating hours, personnel requirements, advertising strategy), they may not mention the design of an accounting system.

This will give you the opportunity to remind them that an owner must consider how information needed to prepare financial statements and tax returns will be collected and processed. An entrepreneur cannot simply operate a business by throwing every receipt in a box and hoping that at the end of the year, his or her accountant can figure out what happened.

Likewise, whenever information must be changed within a company, management must review how the new information will be recorded and reported. For example, when the accounting pronouncement requiring companies to prepare a statement of cash flows was issued, one of the first concerns that many companies addressed was how to collect the information needed to prepare this financial statement.

Management must design an accounting system that:

1. Balances costs with benefits
2. Produces effective (useful) reports
3. Is able to adapt to future needs
4. Has adequate internal controls

Ask your students to identify information that would be useful in running the day-to-day operations of the bookstore described above. List these on the board. Much of this information (such as which merchandise is selling best, which merchandise customers are returning, and which merchandise is still on hand) can be obtained from a well-planned accounting system.

OBJECTIVE 2 — List the three objectives of internal control, and define and give examples of the five elements of internal control.

KEY TERMS:
  Elements of Internal Control
  Employee Fraud

SUGGESTED APPROACH

The text lists the three objectives of internal control as reasonable assurance that: (1) assets are safeguarded and used for business purposes, (2) business information is accurate, and (3) employees comply with laws and regulations. The five elements of internal control are: (1) the control environment, (2) risk assessment, (3) control procedures, (4) monitoring, and (5) information and communication. To stimulate interest in these topics, use the following lecture aid.

LECTURE AIDS — Internal Control

Ask the following questions (Transparency 5-2):

If you owned a business, would you expect your employees...

1. To work to achieve the business goals and objectives you establish?
2. To use business assets (such as machinery or automobiles) only for legitimate business purposes and avoid wasting business resources?
3. To record accurate data regarding business transactions so you could accurately judge how well your business is doing?
4. To refrain from stealing your cash or inventory?

In theory, you should be able to expect these things. In practice, however, you must establish an internal control framework to make sure your business objectives are achieved, assets are protected from theft and misuse, and financial data are recorded accurately.

Transparencies 5-3 through 5-5 include information to use in reviewing the elements of internal control.

When reviewing the control environment, give an illustration of a poor control environment and a good control environment. For example, in a poor control environment, you have a dominating management staff that pressures employees to meet budgets and projections at all costs, regardless of circumstances. A good control environment is established by a management that encourages employees to adhere to control policies and procedures and an employee code of conduct.

Under proofs and security measures, you may want to emphasize that businesses should protect their accounting records by using backup computer files and fireproof file cabinets. Companies have gone out of business because fire or theft destroyed their accounting records. For example, the destruction of accounts receivable files could result in significant losses to a business.

Exhibit 3 in the text presents a good list of the "red flags" which may indicate employee fraud or embezzlement. Refer your students to this list for helpful tips in monitoring internal controls.

GROUP LEARNING ACTIVITY — Internal Control Structure

Ask your students to assume that they have decided to open a bookstore that sells textbooks and competes with the campus bookstore (Transparency 5-6). With students in small groups, instruct them to list the internal control procedures they would implement in their store. After giving the groups a few minutes to work, ask each group to share a couple of their ideas.

EXERCISES & PROBLEMS FOR REINFORCEMENT:
> Exercise 5-1   Exercise 5-6
> Exercise 5-2   Exercise 5-7
> Exercise 5-3
> Exercise 5-4
> Exercise 5-5

OBJECTIVE 3 — Journalize and post transactions in a manual accounting system that uses subsidiary ledgers and special journals.

KEY TERMS:
> Accounts Payable Subsidiary Ledger   General Ledger
> Accounts Receivable Subsidiary Ledger   Purchases Journal
> Cash Payments Journal   Revenue Journal
> Cash Receipts Journal   Special Journals
> Controlling Account   Subsidiary Ledger
> General Journal

SUGGESTED APPROACH

Under this learning objective, you need to introduce students to subsidiary ledgers and special journals. Although these topics are traditionally presented as one package, your students' comprehension may be increased by explaining subsidiary ledgers in a two-column journal environment before moving on to the special multicolumn journals.

GROUP LEARNING ACTIVITY — Subsidiary Ledgers

As an attention-getter, pose the following scenario to your class:

> Let's say that you called _____ (name of a local service business) and purchased $200 of their services on account. You knew that the business kept track of the fact that someone owed $200 as an account receivable, but it didn't record who owed the $200. Therefore, the business couldn't send out bills at the end of the month; it simply relied on its customers to remember how much they owed and send in their payment on time. Do you think most people would pay the amount of money they owed on time?

In reality, this is the type of accounting system that your students have been using. In the first four chapters of the text, they recorded that someone owes money to a business by making entries to an accounts receivable account for all services performed on account. But they have not formally recorded who owed money. This is accomplished by using a subsidiary ledger.

Transactions to illustrate the accounts receivable subsidiary ledger are presented in Transparency 5-7. Handout 5-1 is a journal page to be distributed to your students for use in recording these transactions. There are also a few general ledger and accounts receivable subsidiary ledger accounts in T account format.

Divide the class into small groups and ask your students to record the transactions from Transparency 5-7 in the journal provided. After each transaction is recorded, instruct them to post the entry both to the general ledger accounts and the appropriate subsidiary ledger account. Each entry to Accounts Receivable will be posted to two different accounts: Accounts Receivable in the general ledger and the appropriate customer account in the subsidiary ledger. As a result, the Posting Reference column in the journal will have two markings for each entry to Accounts Receivable—an account number to show that the entry was posted to the general ledger and a check mark to show that the entry was posted to the subsidiary ledger.

You may want to record and post the first entry as an example before asking your students to work on their own.

After your students have finished recording and posting these transactions, ask them to add the balances of the customer accounts in the accounts receivable subsidiary ledger. Stress that the total of the customer accounts in the subsidiary ledger must equal the total of Accounts Receivable in the general ledger. Also point out that the individual accounts in the accounts receivable ledger provide a complete credit history for each customer. The solution to this exercise is shown on Transparency 5-8.

Remind your students that it is also necessary to maintain an accounts payable subsidiary ledger. This allows a company to keep track of those who are owed money.

WRITING EXERCISE — Subsidiary Ledgers

Ask your students to write answers to the following questions (Transparency 5-9):

1. What is the purpose of an accounts receivable subsidiary ledger?
2. What information would be included in a subsidiary ledger for a company's fixed asset account? Do you think it would be helpful to keep a fixed asset subsidiary ledger? Explain your answer.

GROUP LEARNING ACTIVITY — Special Journals

Begin coverage of special journals by discussing their purpose and the transactions recorded in each of the four types of special journals.

The goal of special journals is to process data in a manual accounting system more efficiently. Efficiency is gained because account titles do not have to be written out for every transaction, and postings to the general ledger are reduced by posting column totals. Special journals also make it easier to divide the work of journalizing and posting entries among a number of accounting clerks. Assigning the task of recording purchases and/or sales to employees who do not record cash payments and/or receipts also enhances internal controls.

The four special journals and the transactions recorded in each are as follows:

1. Revenue journal — fees earned on account

2. Cash receipts journal — any transaction where cash is received (including services performed for cash customers)
3. Purchases journal — all items purchased on account
4. Cash payments journal — any transaction where cash is paid (including cash purchases of supplies or other items)

It is also useful to point out that any transaction that does not "fit" in a special journal is recorded in the general journal. These transactions include adjusting entries and closing entries.

At this point, refer your students to the revenue journal shown in the text's Exhibit 6. Explain that only a single column is needed in this journal because it is used to record fees earned on account. The accountant knows that all entries in this journal will be posted to Accounts Receivable and Fees Earned. Explain how the journal is posted to the general and subsidiary ledgers and the meaning of all posting reference markings.

Next, refer your students to the cash receipts journal in Exhibit 7. Explain the use of the Other Accounts column in this journal. Emphasize that whenever an entry is made in the Other Accounts column, the title of the ledger account to be credited must be written in the Account Credited column. Explain how this journal is posted to the general and subsidiary ledgers and the meaning of all posting reference markings.

You may also want to review the purchases journal (Exhibit 8) and the cash payments journal (Exhibit 9). However, it will probably suffice to explain that entries to the purchases journal and the cash payments journal are recorded and posted using the same process as the cash receipts journal.

After introducing the special journals, it is helpful to instruct your class to work through a special journal problem as a group learning activity. Although the concepts associated with special journals are relatively easy, these problems require several pages of forms, which can overwhelm students. It is a good idea to get them started in a setting where they can ask questions of their group members or the instructor.

Because special journal problems do require a variety of forms, you will probably want to use a textbook problem and the accompanying working papers for an in-class active learning activity. This will save the duplication of several sheets of paper.

If you take this approach, choose a problem one or two class sessions ahead of time, and instruct students to bring their working papers for that problem with them to class. You may even want to include this instruction in your syllabus.

The following textbook problems are relatively short, making them useful for this purpose:
    Revenue and cash receipts journals   Problems 5-2A or 2B
    Purchases journal   Problems 5-3A or 3B

When it is time to work through the chosen problem, divide the class into small groups. Remind them that entries are posted to the subsidiary ledgers daily; however, postings to the general ledger are made only at the end of the month. You may want to demonstrate a few transactions for the class before they begin working on their own.

WRITING EXERCISE — Special Journals and Subsidiary Ledgers

Ask your students to write answers to the following questions (Transparency 5-10):

1. Why is the revenue journal posted to the accounts receivable subsidiary ledger periodically throughout the month, while it is posted to the general ledger only at the end of the month?

2. Will the balance of the accounts receivable controlling account agree with the balance of the accounts receivable ledger at all times during a month? Why or why not?

EXERCISES & PROBLEMS FOR REINFORCEMENT:

Exercise 5-8	Exercise 5-16	Problem 5-1A	Problem 5-1B
Exercise 5-9	Exercise 5-17	Problem 5-2A	Problem 5-2B
Exercise 5-10	Exercise 5-18	Problem 5-3A	Problem 5-3B
Exercise 5-11	Exercise 5-19	Problem 5-4A	Problem 5-4B
Exercise 5-12	Exercise 5-20	Problem 5-5A	Problem 5-5B
Exercise 5-13	Exercise 5-21		
Exercise 5-14	Exercise 5-22		
Exercise 5-15			

OBJECTIVE 4 — Describe and give examples of additional subsidiary ledgers and modified special journals.

SUGGESTED APPROACH

The text does a good job of pointing out that subsidiary ledgers and special journals can be adapted to fit the needs of different businesses. Several examples of additional subsidiary ledgers and possible modifications to special journals are provided.

The nature of this learning objective provides an excellent opportunity to encourage creative thinking. Ask your students to design a special-purpose journal.

GROUP LEARNING ACTIVITY — Designing a Special Journal

Transparency 5-11 lists businesses with unique accounting needs. Divide your students into small groups and assign each group one of the businesses. Their task will be to design the special journal indicated on Transparency 5-11. You may want to give each group a blank overhead transparency and pen for recording their design. This will make it easier to share their results with the class.

The businesses and special journals listed on Transparency 5-11 are as follows:

Business	Special Journal To Be Designed	Include Columns For *
Dentist	Revenue journal	Checkups, X rays, fillings, dentures
Building Contractor	Revenue journal	New construction, remodeling
Symphony orchestra	Cash receipts journal	Season ticket sales, single ticket sales, cash contributions
College	Cash receipts journal	Application fees, in-state tuition, out-of-state tuition
Landscape company	Purchases journal	Topsoil, mulch, sod, shrubs, trees
McDonald's	Purchases journal	Hamburger meat, buns, cheese, chicken, paper products

* NOTE: This information is for instructor use only.

EXERCISES & PROBLEMS FOR REINFORCEMENT:
    Exercise 5-23

OBJECTIVE 5 —Apply computerized accounting to the revenue and collection cycle.

SUGGESTED APPROACH

Ask your students to give examples of errors they have made while completing homework assignments from the first four chapters of this course and list these errors on the board. To get this list started, you may have to prompt your students by asking if they have posted any entries to the wrong account or incorrectly added an account balance. After you have a few errors listed, ask students to identify which errors would have been avoided if a computer had processed the accounting data in the homework problems. This will allow you to emphasize one of the main advantages of a computerized accounting system: elimination of many of the math, posting, and journal recording errors made in a manual system.

Objective 5 illustrates the revenue and collection cycle in a computerized environment. Use the lecture aids below to simulate how the computer processes revenue and collection information.

LECTURE AIDS — Revenue and Collection Cycle in a Computerized Environment

Ask your student to turn to Exhibit 10 in their textbooks. Refer them to the illustration of the electronic invoice at the top of the page. Ask them to write in their notes the journal entry (two-column journal format) needed when MyMusicClub.com, a customer, is billed for $2,200 for services completed on account. The answer is:

Mar. 2   Accounts Receivable—MyMusicClub.com......... 2,200
              Fees Earned................................... 2,200

Explain that the computer software generates this entry and posts it to the accounts in the general ledger. The software also tracks the balances owed by each customer. MyMusicClub.com's account balance is automatically updated by the invoice.

Next, refer your students to the "receive payment" form in the middle of the page. Ask them to write in their notes the journal entry needed when payment is received from the customer previously billed on account. The answer is:

Mar. 28   Cash... 2,200
              Accounts Receivable— MyMusicClub.com   2,200

Once again, the computer software generates this entry and posts it to the accounts in the general ledger. MyMusicClub.com's accounts receivable balance is also updated.

Ask your students how the software determined the amounts to be reported on the "Customer Balance Summary." Answer: by adding the invoices sent to each customer and subtracting the payments received. Also ask how the software determined the amounts to be reported on the "Income by Customer Summary." Answer: by summing the invoices sent to each customer.

Point out that the total shown on the "Customer Balance Summary" is the total for Accounts Receivable in the general ledger. The total shown on the "Income by Customer Summary" is the balance of Fees Earned in the general ledger.

EXERCISES & PROBLEMS FOR REINFORCEMENT:
    Exercise 5-24

OBJECTIVE 6 — Describe the basic features of e-commerce.

SUGGESTED APPROACH

The text defines e-commerce as "using the internet to perform business transactions." Many of your students will have already engaged in business-to-consumer (B2C) e-commerce. You may want to ask your students for examples of merchandise they purchased using the internet.

As the text mentions, fraud is a definite concern for both businesses and consumers engaging in e-commerce. Use the Internet Activity below to introduce students to WebTrust.

INTERNET ACTIVITY – WebTrust

WebTrust is a service developed by the American Institute of Certified Public Accountants that is provided by CPA's with special training. When a company's web site receives the WebTrust seal, it means the site has
- Been certified by a specially trained and licensed public accounting firm
- Disclosed its business practices
- Been audited to prove the site actually follows those practices
- Met international WebTrust Standards for e-Commerce

The WebTrust seal should provide consumers with some confidence that they are dealing with a reputable company who clearly describes how it does business and delivers on its promises.

Direct your students to visit the following website for more information on the WebTrust program:

http://www.cpawebtrust.org

Handout 5-1

ACCOUNTS RECEIVABLE TRANSACTIONS
Ryan's Computer Consulting Group
JOURNAL

DATE	DESCRIPTION	POST. REF.	DEBIT	CREDIT

GENERAL LEDGER

Acct. No. 101 — Cash

Acct. No. 105 — Accts. Receivable

Acct. No. 401 — Fees Earned

ACCOUNTS RECEIVABLE SUBSIDIARY LEDGER

Milford Tool Co.

Rahn Hills Medical Group

Transparency Master 5-1

BRAINSTORMING EXERCISE

You have decided to open a bookstore that sells textbooks and competes with the campus bookstore. You have chosen a location and have received a list of textbooks used by the college. What other decisions will you have to make regarding the operations of your business?

Transparency Master 5-2

If you owned a business, would you expect your employees...

1. To work to achieve the business goals and objectives you establish?

2. To use business assets (such as machinery or automobiles) only for legitimate business purposes and avoid wasting business resources?

3. To record accurate data regarding business transactions so you could accurately judge how well your business is doing?

4. To refrain from stealing your cash or inventory?

FIVE ELEMENTS OF INTERNAL CONTROL

1. **Control environment:**
   Management attitude should be committed to ethical business practices and to following established control procedures.

2. **Risk assessment:**
   Identify and minimize internal control risks.

3. **Control procedures:**
   Employees should be adequately trained and supervised.
   Rotate job duties or require mandatory vacations.
   Clearly define job responsibilities and keep employees accountable.
   Separate responsibilities for related operations.
   Separate operations, custody of assets, and accounting.
   Use proofs and security measures:
   - Immediately deposit all cash in a bank account.
   - Use cash registers to record sales.
   - Have employees bonded.
   - Install security cameras or hire security guards.

4. **Monitoring:**
   Watch for warning signals indicating dishonesty or fraud.

5. **Information and communication:**
   Gather and communicate appropriate information to assess and monitor internal controls.

SEPARATING DUTIES FOR RELATED OPERATIONS

What risk do you have if the following occur?

1. Salesperson (paid on a commission basis) is responsible for granting credit.

2. Purchasing agent orders supplies, inspects supplies to verify that the correct items and quantity were received, and authorizes payment of the vendor's invoice.

3. Worker in a donut shop takes a customer's order, packs his or her donuts in a bag or box, rings the order on a cash register, and takes the customer's money.

SEPARATING OPERATIONS, CUSTODY OF ASSETS, AND ACCOUNTING

What risk do you have if the following occur?

1. A department store allows its credit customers to pay their bills in person at the store's credit department. Duties of the credit department's clerk include accepting cash payments, giving customers credit for their payments in the store's accounting records, and following up on any overdue accounts.

2. An accounts payable clerk for a hospital reviews all vendor invoices to make sure the hospital has been billed accurately, prepares checks to pay the invoices, mails the checks, and makes the entries necessary to record the payments in the hospital's accounting records.

INTERNAL CONTROL PROCEDURES

You have decided to open a bookstore that sells textbooks and competes with the campus bookstore. List the internal control procedures you would implement in running the store.

Transparency Master 5-7

ACCOUNTS RECEIVABLE TRANSACTIONS

The following transactions relate to fees earned by Ryan's Computer Consulting Group. All consulting services are performed on account and billed to the customer, who must pay within 30 days.

June 1 Assisted Milford Tool Co. in upgrading two office computers and making repairs to a printer. Milford Tool Co. was billed $800 for these services.

5 Installed a networked computer system in the offices of Rahn Hills Medical Group and trained employees to use the network. Rahn Hills Medical Group was billed $2,500 for these services.

24 Installed a modem and software in a home computer for one of the doctors at Rahn Hills Medical Group. This will allow the doctor to access the office network from home. Rahn Hills Medical Group was billed $500 for this service.

26 Received $2,500 payment from Rahn Hills Medical Group.

Transparency Master 5-8

Solution–ACCOUNTS RECEIVABLE TRANSACTIONS
Ryan's Computer Consulting Group
JOURNAL

DATE		DESCRIPTION	POST. REF.	DEBIT	CREDIT
June	1	Accts. Rec.—Milford Tool Co.	105/√	800	
		Fees Earned	401		800
	5	Accts. Rec.—Rahn Hills Med. Gr.	105/√	2,500	
		Fees Earned	401		2,500
	24	Accts. Rec.—Rahn Hills Med. Gr.	105/√	500	
		Fees Earned	401		500
	26	Cash	101	2,500	
		Accts. Rec.—Rahn Hills Med.	105/√		2,500

GENERAL LEDGER

```
    Acct. No. 101                Acct. No. 105                    Acct. No. 401
        Cash                    Accts. Receivable                  Fees Earned
6/26  2,500            6/1      800 | 6/26  2,500            6/1      800
                       6/5    2,500                          6/5    2,500
                       6/24     500                          6/24     500
                              1,300                                 3,800
```

ACCOUNTS RECEIVABLE
SUBSIDIARY LEDGER

```
                                      Rahn Hills
     Milford Tool Co.                Medical Group
6/1    800                    6/5   2,500 | 6/26  2,500
                              6/24    500
                                      500
```

137

WRITING EXERCISE

1. What is the purpose of an accounts receivable subsidiary ledger?

2. What information would be included in a subsidiary ledger for a company's fixed asset account? Do you think it would be helpful to keep a fixed asset subsidiary ledger? Explain your answer.

WRITING EXERCISE

1. Why is the revenue journal posted to the accounts receivable subsidiary ledger periodically throughout the month, while it is posted to the general ledger only at the end of the month?

2. Will the balance of the accounts receivable controlling account agree with the balance of the accounts receivable ledger at all times during a month? Why or why not?

DESIGN A SPECIAL JOURNAL

Business	Special Journal To Be Designed
Dentist	Revenue journal
Building contractor	Revenue journal
Symphony orchestra	Cash receipts journal
College	Cash receipts journal
Landscape company	Purchases journal
McDonald's	Purchases journal

Chapter 6
Accounting for Merchandising Businesses

OPENING COMMENTS

Chapter 6 introduces the merchandising form of business. It opens by contrasting the income statements of service and merchandising businesses. The chapter then presents the financial statements for a merchandising business and summarizes the essential differences between the periodic and perpetual inventory systems.

After a brief description of the periodic inventory system, the chapter focuses solely on the perpetual system. The text illustrates how to record transactions related to the sale and purchase of merchandise under the perpetual inventory system. It also presents a chart of accounts and an overview of the accounting cycle for a merchandiser using a perpetual inventory system.

The 21st edition of ACCOUNTING focuses on the perpetual inventory method, since computerized accounting and inventory systems have made it feasible for even small merchandisers to track each purchase and sale of inventory. In a computerized accounting system, the need for a work sheet is virtually eliminated, and closing entries are performed automatically. Therefore, discussion of these topics is covered in Appendix 2 at the end of this chapter. You may choose to omit coverage of this appendix. This action will not hinder your students' work in future chapters. Appendix 1 illustrates recording merchandising transactions using a manual accounting system with special journals and a computerized accounting system using QuickBooks.

The mechanics of the periodic inventory system for merchandisers are covered in Appendix D at the end of the text.

After studying the chapter, your students should be able to:

1. Distinguish the activities of a service business from those of a merchandising business.
2. Describe and illustrate the financial statements of a merchandising business
3. Describe the accounting for the sale of merchandise.
4. Describe the accounting for the purchase of merchandise.
5. Describe the accounting for transportation costs, sales taxes, and trade discounts.
6. Illustrate the dual nature of merchandising transactions.
7. Prepare a chart of accounts for a merchandising business.
8. Describe the accounting cycle for a merchandising business.
9. Compute the ratio of net sales to assets as a measure of how effectively a business is using its assets.

OBJECTIVE 1 — Distinguish the activities of a service business from those of a merchandising business.

KEY TERMS:
    Cost of Merchandise Sold
    Gross Profit
    Merchandise Inventory

SUGGESTED APPROACH

The goal of Objective 1 is to introduce the student to the basic skeleton of the income statement for the merchandiser.

        Sales
      - <u>Cost of Merchandise Sold</u>
        Gross Profit
      - <u>Operating Expenses</u>
        Net Income

To demonstrate the need for this new format, ask your students the following question: What is the largest expense incurred by a retail store, such as Target or Old Navy? Answer: the cost of the merchandise that is sold to the customer.

Because this cost is the retailer's major expense, it is shown separately from the operating expenses when preparing the income statement. The cost of merchandise sold is deducted from sales to get the subtotal gross profit. This amount is the profit left after "paying for" the merchandise that was sold to the customer. It must be used to "pay" the retailer's operating expenses, such as salaries, rent, utilities, and advertising.

Objective 1 also introduces Merchandise Inventory, explaining that this account is reported as a current asset on the balance sheet.

EXERCISES & PROBLEMS FOR REINFORCEMENT:
    Exercise 6-1
    Exercise 6-2

OBJECTIVE 2 — Describe and illustrate the financial statements of a merchandising business.

KEY TERMS:

Account Form	Periodic Method	Sales
Administrative Expenses	Perpetual Method	Sales Discount
Income from Operations	Purchase Allowance	Sales Returns & Allowances
Multiple-Step Income Statement	Purchase Discount	Selling Expenses
Other Expense	Purchase Return	Single-Step Income Statement
Other Income	Report Form	

SUGGESTED APPROACH

Chapter 6 introduces the multiple-step income statement. This income statement format contains various sections, subsections, and subtotals, which increases the length and complexity of the income statement. Point out that the benefit of this more detailed format is greater flexibility in analyzing a company's performance. For example, the gross profit percentage (gross profit divided by net sales) is used to analyze the mark-up above cost charged by retailers.

The trap that many students fall into is blindly attempting to memorize the multiple-step income statement line by line. Instead, they need to approach it as a series of pieces (sections) that must be fit together to provide a total picture of a company—similar to fitting together pieces of a jigsaw puzzle.

GROUP LEARNING ACTIVITY — Multiple-Step Income Statement

Before digging into the Multiple-Step Income Statement, you will need to define the new terms for your students.

> Sales: the amount charged customers for merchandise. (This is a revenue account.)
> Sales Returns: the amount refunded to customers who return merchandise.
> Sales Allowances: a reduction in price given to a customer to compensate for a problem, such as damaged merchandise
> Sales Discount: a reduction in price given to a customer for paying early, such as giving a 2% discount on the price of merchandise if the customer pays in 10 days.
> Selling Expenses: costs incurred in selling the merchandise, such as the cost of advertising or commissions paid to salespersons
> Administrative Expenses: costs incurred in the administration or general operations of the business, such as the cost of office supplies or the salary paid to an accountant.
> Income from Operations: profit earned by the conducting the company's primary business of buying and selling merchandise
> Other Income: income earned from activities other than the company's primary business, such as interest revenue on a checking account or rent revenue from leasing unused space.
> Other Expense: costs incurred from activities other than the company's primary business of buying and selling it's product, such as interest expense on business loans.

You may want to demonstrate how intuitive the calculations are on the income statement by asking the following question.

> Assume a retailer sold $100 in merchandise to a customer on account. That customer returned $10 of the merchandise. The customer also paid for the remaining merchandise early entitling him to a $5 discount. What amount of revenue was really earned on the sale? (Answer: $85.)

This is essentially the calculation of net sales:

        Sales
     - Sales Returns & Allowances
     - <u>Sales Discounts</u>
        Net Sales

Transparency 6-1 shows the individual sections of the multiple-step income statement and how they interrelate. Review this transparency with the class, explaining each section and its placement in the statement.

Transparency 6-2 lists an adjusted trial balance for Gem City Music. Divide students into small groups and ask them to prepare an income statement for this retailer. A completed income statement is shown on Transparency 6-3.

GROUP LEARNING ACTIVITY – Statement of Owner's Equity and Balance Sheet

This learning objective contrasts the account form of balance sheet (assets on the left-hand side and liabilities and owner's equity on the right-hand side) with the report form (assets at the top of the page with liabilities and owner's equity at the bottom). The report form is illustrated in Exhibit 5 in this chapter. An account form of balance sheet can be found back in Chapter 4 Exhibit 6. A quick reference to these illustrations should be sufficient to explain these two balance sheet formats. You may want to check your students' comprehension of these formats by asking them to identify whether the balance sheet for Home Depot in Appendix F is in report form or account form.

Point out that there are no differences between the Statements of Owner's Equity for a service business and a merchandiser. Remind students that the only difference on the Balance Sheet is that a merchandising company will show Merchandise Inventory as a current asset on its Balance Sheet. If time permits, your students can review these financial statements by preparing a statement of owner's equity and balance sheet from the adjusted trial balance for Gem City Music on Transparency 6-2. See Transparencies 6-4 and 6-5 for the completed financial statements.

LECTURE AIDS – Calculating Cost of Merchandise Sold using the Periodic Inventory system

This objective presents a brief comparison of the perpetual and periodic inventory systems. Transparencies 6-6 through 6-8 contrast the two inventory systems, show the costs and benefits of a perpetual inventory system, and offer insight on how businesses choose an inventory system. To illustrate the essence of a perpetual inventory system, relate it to a checkbook. Maintaining a checkbook register for a bank account is a type of perpetual inventory system. By tracking increases (deposits) and decreases (withdrawals or checks written) in the checkbook register, you can keep a running balance of your cash.

A merchandiser who uses the periodic inventory system must compute the Cost of Merchandise Sold when preparing an income statement. This calculation is based on the amount of inventory purchased and the amount in inventory at the beginning and the end of the period. The following story will illustrate this calculation.

> Assume that you are a "Twinkies junkie." Whenever you study, you eat Twinkies. One evening, before a big accounting test, you go to your cupboard and find that you have only 3 Twinkies left. You know that 3 Twinkies will never get you through the night, so you head off to the grocery to buy another box. The box contains 12 Twinkies. You then to proceed to study and eat, study and eat, and study and eat. The next morning, you decide to figure out how many Twinkies you ate while studying. You didn't count the Twinkies as you ate them, but you know the old box is empty and the new box has only 5 Twinkies left. How many Twinkies did you eat? (After waiting for a response, continue the illustration.)
>
> Let's review your calculation using accounting terminology. You started with a beginning inventory of 3 Twinkies. You then purchased 12 Twinkies. This gave you 15 Twinkies available for consumption. Since 5 Twinkies were left in ending inventory, you must have eaten 10.

This is essentially the calculation of Cost of Merchandise Sold under a periodic inventory system:

>   Merchandise Inventory on hand at the beginning of the year
>   + Cost of Merchandise Purchased
>   Merchandise Available for Sale
>   − Merchandise Inventory left at the end of the year
>   Cost of Merchandise Sold

When purchasing merchandise inventory, a business may be required to pay transportation costs to have the merchandise delivered from the supplier. The purchaser may also receive early payment discounts or make returns of unwanted merchandise. Therefore, the Cost of Merchandise Purchased must be calculated as follows:

>   Purchases
>   − Purchase Returns and Allowances
>   Purchase Discounts
>   Net Purchases
>   Transportation In
>   Cost of Merchandise Purchased

Transparency 6-9 shows these calculations and how they fit together.

Transparency 6-10 provides a practice problem related to the calculation of Cost of Merchandise Sold in the periodic system. Ask your students to calculate the Cost of Merchandise Purchased (answer = $975) and the Cost of Merchandise Sold (answer = $905).

EXERCISES & PROBLEMS FOR REINFORCEMENT:

| Exercise 6-3 | Exercise 6-8 | Problem 6-1A | Problem 6-1B |
| Exercise 6-4 | Exercise 6-9 | Problem 6-2A | Problem 6-2B |

Exercise 6-5   Exercise 6-10
Exercise 6-6   Exercise 6-11
Exercise 6-7

OBJECTIVE 3 – Describe the accounting for the sale of merchandise.

KEY TERMS:
Credit Memorandum
Invoice

SUGGESTED APPROACH

This objective covers the entries to record sales in a perpetual inventory system. Begin by stressing that selling merchandise to a customer requires two entries—one to record the sales revenue and another to remove the item sold from merchandise inventory.

DEMONSTRATION PROBLEM — Entries To Record Merchandise Sales

Transparencies 6-11 and 6-12 present a matrix that explains the new accounts related to sales. Review these transparencies with your class.

Transparencies 6-13 and 6-14 list several sales-related transactions for S & V Office Supply Company. One method to present this material is to give the students examples of the entries to record the sale of inventory items in lecture format. Another is to allow students to decipher the entries on their own. Try reading the first transaction to your students and ask them to journalize it in their notes. After giving them a minute to work, show them the correct journal entry. Proceed with the other transactions listed on the transparency. The correct journal entries are listed on Transparencies 6-15 and 6-16.

The transactions on Transparency 6-13 do include references to credit terms (for example, 2/10, n/30). You may want to explain these credit terms before beginning this exercise.

WRITING EXERCISE — Recording Merchandise Sales

To emphasize some of the operational considerations in recording sales, ask your students to write answers to one or more of the following questions (Transparency 6-17).

1. Why would a retailer offer customers sales discounts?
2. How is using a separate account for sales returns and allowances useful to management?
3. If you owned a merchandising business, how would you decide which credit cards, if any, to accept?
4. Which of the following credit terms would be more generous to your customers: n/30 or n/eom?

EXERCISES & PROBLEMS FOR REINFORCEMENT:
Exercise 6-12
Exercise 6-13

Exercise 6-14
Exercise 6-15
Exercise 6-16

OBJECTIVE 4 – Describe the accounting for the purchase of merchandise.

KEY TERMS:
　　Debit Memorandum

SUGGESTED APPROACH

This objective covers journal entries for purchases under the perpetual inventory system. The following demonstration problem will introduce these new entries to your class.

DEMONSTRATION PROBLEM — Entries for Merchandise Purchases

Purchases of merchandise for resale to a customer are recorded in the merchandise inventory account. Point out that this account is an asset. Therefore, it is debited whenever inventory is increased and credited whenever inventory is decreased.

Transparency 6-18 lists purchase-related transactions for S & V Office Supply Company. Read the first transaction to your students and ask them to journalize it in their notes. After giving them a minute to work, show them the correct journal entry. Proceed with the other transactions listed on the transparency. The correct journal entries are listed on Transparency 6-19.

The transactions on Transparency 6-18 do include references to credit terms (for example, 2/10, n/30). Remind students that all merchandise purchases are recorded at invoice price; discounts are shown as a reduction to the cost recorded for the inventory only if they are taken. The amount of the discount is credited to the merchandise inventory account at the time of payment.

LECTURE AIDS — Discounts

For many students, a 2% discount doesn't sound very impressive. They may need a little help understanding the true financial impact of taking discounts on purchases. The following questions will stress the savings of taking discounts:

1. What is the net savings from borrowing at a 12% interest rate in order to take the discount on a $10,000 purchase, terms 1/10, n/30? Answer: $34 ($100 - {$9,900 x 20/360 x 12%}).

2. What is the interest rate earned on taking a discount with terms 3/15, n/60? Answer: 24% (3% x 360/45).

EXERCISES & PROBLEMS FOR REINFORCEMENT:
　　Exercise 6-17　　Exercise 6-20
　　Exercise 6-18　　Exercise 6-21
　　Exercise 6-19

OBJECTIVE 5 — Describe the accounting for transportation costs, sales taxes and trade discounts.

KEY TERMS:
    FOB Destination
    FOB Shipping Point
    Trade Discounts

SUGGESTED APPROACH

To introduce trade discounts to your students, you need only to define the term and give a quick example. A trade discount is a discount off the normal (or list) price of merchandise given to a certain class of buyers, such as customers buying wholesale, not-for-profits or governmental agencies, etc. If merchandise with a list price of $700 is sold to a customer entitled to a 25% trade discount, the selling price is reduced to $525. ($700 x 25% = $175. $700 - $175 = $525.) Remind students that trade discounts are not shown separately in journal entries. The amount credited to sales (and debited to cash or accounts receivable) is simply the discounted price.

Unless your students have lived exclusively in a state that does not charge sale tax, they will already be familiar with this concept. Remind students that when sales tax is collected by a merchandiser at the time of a sale, it is recorded in a liability account (sales tax payable); the merchandiser is obligated to remit the sales tax collected to the appropriate government authority. You may want to refer to the journal entries related to sales tax on page 249 of the text.

FOB (free on board) terms identify (1) when legal title to goods passes from seller to buyer and (2) who is responsible for paying transportation costs. Transparency 6-20 lists the operational implications of FOB terms.

Notice that Transparency 6-20 points out that the buyer bears the risk of loss during transportation when merchandise is shipped FOB Shipping Point. Therefore, the buyer should make sure that the merchandise is insured against loss during shipment.

A couple of points related to shipping terms usually need special emphasis. First, when merchandise is shipped FOB shipping point, the seller frequently prepays the transportation costs and adds this amount to the buyer's invoice. Second, remind students that transportation costs are not eligible for early payment discounts. Those discounts apply only to the cost of the merchandise purchased. To test their understanding of these concepts, ask them to compute the cash to be paid in the following problem (Transparency 6-21.)

    Logan Appliances purchased $8,000 of merchandise, 2/10, n/30, FOB shipping point. The seller prepaid the shipping charges of $200. If Logan pays for this merchandise within the discount period, how much should Logan remit to the seller? (Answer: $8,040.)

DEMONSTRATION PROBLEM — Transportation Costs on Purchases

Ask your students to record the transactions related to the purchase of merchandise and transportation costs on Transparency 6-22. The correct entries are listed on Transparency 6-23.

LECTURE AIDS — Transportation Costs on Sales

If merchandise is sold FOB destination, the seller is responsible for paying the shipping cost. The cost is debited to Transportation Out. For example, assume goods costing $100 are sold to a customer on account for $250, terms FOB Destination. The freight cost paid to have these goods delivered is $25. The following entries are needed to record this sale and the transportation costs:

Accounts Receivable............	250	
Sales.....................		250
Cost of Merchandise Sold......	100	
Merchandise Inventory		100
Transportation Out..............	25	
Cash.....................		25

EXERCISES & PROBLEMS FOR REINFORCEMENT:
    Exercise 6-22   Problem 6-3A   Problem 6-3B
    Exercise 6-23   Problem 6-4A   Problem 6-4B
    Exercise 6-24   Problem 6-5A   Problem 6-5B
    Exercise 6-27

OBJECTIVE 6 — Illustrate the dual nature of merchandising transactions.

SUGGESTED APPROACH

Just as one person's pay increase is another person's price increase, one person's sale is another person's purchase. This learning objective illustrates a series of transactions from both the seller's and buyer's points of view. In reality, this simply reinforces material already covered in the earlier sections of the chapter.

If you wish to give your students additional practice, you could ask them to work textbook Problem 6-6A or 6-6B in class or assign one of these problems as homework.

EXERCISES & PROBLEMS FOR REINFORCEMENT:
    Exercise 6-25   Problem 6-6A   Problem 6-6B
    Exercise 6-26

OBJECTIVE 7 — Prepare a chart of accounts for a merchandising business.

SUGGESTED APPROACH

In discussing the chart of accounts for a merchandising firm, the text uses a 3-digit account number. This reflects the growing number of accounts required by the increased complexity of a merchandiser's accounting transactions.

Under the 3-digit chart of accounts, the first digit represents the account classification (1 for assets, 2 for liabilities, etc.). The second represents the subclassification (11 for current assets and 21 for current liabilities). The third digit identifies the specific account.

TEACHING SUGGESTION — Chart of Accounts

After explaining the text's system, it is interesting to point out the variety in charts of accounts and their numbering systems by providing some real-world examples. Ask students to bring in copies of charts of accounts for merchandising businesses. Students may have access to charts of accounts through their job or the job of a relative. As an alternative, you may want to describe the chart of accounts for a local company you are familiar with.

EXERCISES & PROBLEMS FOR REINFORCEMENT:
    Exercise 6-30

OBJECTIVE 8 — Describe the accounting cycle for a merchandising business.

KEY TERMS:
    Inventory Shrinkage

SUGGESTED APPROACH

Transparency 6-20 presents the year-end procedures used by a merchandising company in a manual accounting system. Emphasize that merchandising companies use the same basic year-end procedures as service businesses.

Accounting work at year-end can be greatly reduced by implementing a computerized accounting system. In a computerized system, it is not necessary to prepare a work sheet—a good software package can prepare financial statements immediately after adjusting entries have been input. Computerized accounting packages also prepare closing entries automatically. Since personal computers have made it financially feasible for even small businesses to computerize their accounting systems, work sheets and closing entries for merchandisers are covered in the appendix to this chapter.

However, the accountant still must input adjusting entries, even in a computerized accounting system. This objective introduces the adjusting entry for inventory shrinkage. Remind students that merchandisers also record any of the adjusting entries introduced in Chapter 3 which are applicable (for example, supplies used, insurance expired, wages owed to employees, fees earned, etc.).

LECTURE AIDS — Adjusting Entry for Inventory Shrinkage

Unfortunately, inventory shrinkage is considered a normal cost of operations for a retailer. Theft of inventory (shoplifting), damaged inventory, and mistakes in recording inventory can never be totally eliminated. Therefore, the inventory account must be adjusted prior to preparing financial statements. Any shrinkage is recorded as an expense.

For example, assume a company's perpetual inventory records show that there should be $89,500 of inventory on hand. (Emphasize that the perpetual records show what should be in inventory based on merchandise purchased and sold during the year.) However, a physical inventory count reveals that only $87,000 is actually on hand at year end. Ask your students to determine the amount of shrinkage. (Answer: $2,500.)

This shrinkage is recorded as following:

    Cost of Merchandise Sold……….   2,500
        Merchandise Inventory…..   2,500

You may want to point out that if the amount of shrinkage is unusually large, it is better to record it in a separate account, such as Loss from Merchandise Inventory Shrinkage. Stress that all companies must do a physical inventory count at least once per year to verify the information in the perpetual inventory records.

EXERCISES & PROBLEMS FOR REINFORCEMENT:
    Exercise 6-28
    Exercise 6-29

OBJECTIVE 9 — Compute the ratio of net sales to assets as a measure of how effectively a business is using its assets.

SUGGESTED APPROACH

The ratio of net sales to assets is used to measure how efficiently a business is using its assets to generate sales. The formula for this ratio is:

$$\text{Ratio of Net Sales to Assets} = \frac{\text{Net Sales}}{\text{Average Total Assets}}$$

It is important to explain the meaning of this ratio and illustrate its calculation.

LECTURE AIDS — Ratio of Net Sales to Assets

The following examples can be used to help students interpret the ratio of net sales to assets:

If a business has $1,000 in assets and $2,000 of sales, the ratio of net sales to assets is 2.0 ($2,000/$1,000). Every dollar invested in assets generates two dollars of sales.

If a business with a ratio of net sales to assets of 1.5 has $1,000 in assets, what amount of sales revenue did the business generate? (Answer: $1,500.)

The actual formula for computing the ratio of net sales to assets uses "Average Total Assets." Transparency 6-25 can be used to explain this calculation. A business' sales are earned across an entire year. As a result, annual sales needs to be compared to the average amount of assets used during the year. While it would be better to average total assets at the end of each month, as a short-cut, the beginning and end of year amounts can be averaged.

EXERCISES & PROBLEMS FOR REINFORCEMENT:
    Exercise 6-31   Exercise 6-32

APPENDIX 1 — Accounting Systems for Merchandisers

SUGGESTED APPROACH

This objective discusses the processing of accounting entries for merchandisers under manual and computerized accounting systems. The manual system looks at changes that would be needed to adapt the special journals, introduced in Chapter 5, for a merchandiser. The computerized system illustrates recording inventory purchases and sales using QuickBooks.

LECTURE AIDS — Manual Accounting System

Make an overhead transparency of a revenue journal form from the working papers for Chapter 5. Ask your students to sketch the form that would be used by a merchandiser to record sales to customers on account. After allowing a few minutes for students to put their ideas on paper, refer them to the Sales Journal in Exhibit 12. You may want to poll your students to see how many added a column to record the cost of merchandise sold.

Point out the following differences in the remaining special journals:

- Exhibit 13 - Purchases Journal includes a Merchandise Inventory Dr. column.
- Exhibit 14 - Cash Receipts Journal has two modifications to accommodate cash sales: (1) includes a Sales Cr. column, (2) includes a Cost of Merchandise Sold Dr./Merchandise Inventory Cr. column to record the cost of inventory sold to cash customers. The journal also has a Sales Discounts Dr. column to record discounts taken by customers paying within the discount period.
- Exhibit 15 - Cash Payments Journal includes a Merchandise Inventory Cr. column to record discounts taken on inventory purchases.

GROUP LEARNING ACTIVITY - Computerized Accounting Systems

The text illustrates the screens used to input inventory purchases and sales using QuickBooks. These illustrations are found in Exhibits 17 and 18. Exhibit 16 shows the information needed to initially set up inventory items.

Ask your students to review Exhibits 17 and 18 and identify the accounting entries QuickBooks creates to record these transactions. The solution is found on Transparency 6-26.

EXERCISES & PROBLEMS FOR REINFORCEMENT:
    Exercise 6-33

APPENDIX 2 — Work Sheet & Adjusting & Closing Entries for a Merchandising Business

SUGGESTED APPROACH

So that your students understand (and appreciate) the work performed by a computer at year-end, this appendix covers the manual steps in preparing financial statements and closing the books of a merchandiser. This material can be covered quite effectively as a group learning activity, since it is essentially a review of processes introduced in Chapters 3 and 4.

GROUP LEARNING ACTIVITY — Preparing the Work Sheet of a Merchandiser

Handout 6-1 is a sample work sheet that may be copied and distributed to your students. Divide the class into small groups and ask them to complete the Adjustments column of the work sheet. They will need to record the following adjustments:

1. A physical inventory count revealed that only $9,600 of merchandise is on hand.
2. Salaries owed to office employees equal $550; salaries owed to sales employees equal $700.
3. $2,800 in depreciation should be recorded on the office equipment.

After your students have prepared the adjusting entries, they should be instructed to complete the remaining columns. To save class time, the balances for all accounts not affected by adjusting entries have been entered into the Adjusted Trial Balance and Financial Statement columns. Your students will need to fill in balances only for accounts that were adjusted. Transparency 6-27 shows the completed work sheet.

Remind students that the adjustments recorded on the work sheet must be journalized and posted to make them part of a company's accounting records. It will probably suffice to simply remind students of this fact. If you wish to give your students additional practice in this area, you could ask them to record the adjustments from Handout 6-1 in journal entry format. The adjusting journal entries can be taken directly from the Adjustments column of the work sheet.

GROUP LEARNING ACTIVITY — Closing Entries for a Merchandiser

The process of closing entries has not changed from Chapter 4; there are simply more accounts to close. In a perpetual inventory system, the sales discounts, sales returns and allowances, and cost of merchandise sold accounts are closed to Income Summary, along with the other debit balance accounts shown in the Income Statement column of the work sheet.

Transparency 6-28 reviews the basics of the closing process. Remind students that closing entries can be taken directly from the Income Statement columns of the work sheet. Also stress that the balance of the Income Summary account after the first two closing entries must equal the net income or net loss for the period. After a brief review of these concepts, ask your students to prepare closing entries for Gem City Music, using the work sheet on Handout 6-1. These closing entries are displayed on Transparency 6-29.

EXERCISES & PROBLEMS FOR REINFORCEMENT:
    Exercise 6-34   Problem 6-7A   Problem 6-7B

Handout 6-1

Gem City Music
Work Sheet
For the Year Ended December 31, 20—

ACCOUNT TITLE	TRIAL BALANCE DEBIT	TRIAL BALANCE CREDIT	ADJUSTMENTS DEBIT	ADJUSTMENTS CREDIT	ADJUSTED TRIAL BALANCE DEBIT	ADJUSTED TRIAL BALANCE CREDIT	INCOME STATEMENT DEBIT	INCOME STATEMENT CREDIT	BALANCE SHEET DEBIT	BALANCE SHEET CREDIT
Cash	11,000				11,000				11,000	
Accounts Receivable	15,800				15,800				15,800	
Merchandise Inventory	10,400									
Office Equipment	23,000				23,000				23,000	
Accumulated Depreciation —Office Equipment		6,400								
Accounts Payable		16,000				16,000				16,000
Salaries Payable										
M. Marx, Capital		11,500				11,500				11,500
M. Marx, Drawing	12,800				12,800				12,800	
Sales		189,300				189,300		189,300		
Sales Returns and Allowances	1,700				1,700		1,700			
Sales Discounts	500				500		500			
Cost of Merchandise Sold	99,200									
Rent Expense	7,800				7,800		7,800			
Sales Salaries Expense	17,000									
Office Salaries Expense	22,000									
Depreciation Expense —Office Equipment										
Interest Expense	2,000				2,000		2,000			
	223,200	223,200								

155

Transparency Master 6-1

The Income Statement— An Expanded View

Single-Step Income Statement (Chapters 1–4)	Multiple-Step Income Statement (Chapter 6)
Revenues	Revenue from Sales { **Revenue from Sales:** Sales − Sales Returns & Allowances − Sales Discounts **Net Sales**
− Expenses	− Cost of Merchandise Sold Gross Profit
	− Operating Expenses { **Operating Expenses:** Selling Expenses + Administrative Expenses Total Operating Expenses
	Income from Operations + Other Income (i.e., Interest, Rent) − Other Expenses (i.e., Interest)
Net Income	**Net Income**

ADJUSTED TRIAL BALANCE

Gem City Music
Adjusted Trial Balance
December 31, 20—

Cash	11,000	
Accounts Receivable	15,800	
Merchandise Inventory	9,600	
Office Equipment	23,000	
Accumulated Depreciation—Office Equipment		9,200
Accounts Payable		16,000
Salaries Payable		1,250
M. Marx, Capital		11,500
M. Marx, Drawing	12,800	
Sales		189,300
Sales Returns and Allowances	1,700	
Sales Discounts	500	
Cost of Merchandise Sold	100,000	
Rent Expense	7,800	
Sales Salaries Expense	17,700	
Office Salaries Expense	22,550	
Depreciation Expense—Office Equipment	2,800	
Interest Expense	2,000	
Total	227,250	227,250

Transparency Master 6-2

INCOME STATEMENT

Gem City Music
Income Statement
For the Year Ended December 31, 20—

Revenue from sales:			
Sales			$189,300
Less: Sales returns and allowances		$ 1,700	
Sales discounts		500	2,200
Net sales			$187,100
Cost of merchandise sold			100,000
Gross profit			$ 87,100
Operating expenses:			
Selling expenses:			
Sales salaries expense		$17,700	
Administrative expenses:			
Rent expense	$ 7,800		
Office salaries expense	22,550		
Depreciation expense—office equipment	2,800	33,150	
Total operating expenses			50,850
Income from operations			$ 36,250
Other expense:			
Interest expense			2,000
Net income			$ 34,250

STATEMENT OF OWNER'S EQUITY

Gem City Music
Statement of Owner's Equity
For the Year Ended December 31, 20—

M. Marx, Capital, January 1, 20--.		$11,500
Net income for the year	$34,250	
Less withdrawals	12,800	
Increase in owner's equity		21,450
M. Marx, Capital, December 31, 20--		$32,950

BALANCE SHEET

Gem City Music
Balance Sheet
December 31, 20—

ASSETS

Current Assets:
Cash	$11,000
Accounts Receivables	15,800
Merchandise Inventory	9,600
Total Current Assets	$36,400

Property, Plant & Equipment:
Office Equipment	$23,000	
Less Accumulated Depreciation	9,200	
Total Property, Plant & Equipment		13,800
Total Assets		$50,200

LIABILITIES

Current Liabilities:
Accounts Payable	$16,000
Salaries Payable	1,250
Total Liabilities	$17,250

OWNER'S EQUITY

M. Marx, Capital	32,950
Total Liabilities & Owner's Equity	$50,200

TWO INVENTORY SYSTEMS

PERPETUAL:

- The Merchandise Inventory account is increased when inventory is purchased.
- The Merchandise Inventory account is decreased when inventory is sold to a customer.
- Therefore, the Merchandise Inventory account always (perpetually) shows the amount of inventory on hand.

PERIODIC:

- Purchases of inventory are recorded in a Purchases account.
- Inventory is not removed from the accounting records when it is sold.
- Therefore, the amount of inventory on hand must be determined by taking a physical inventory count.

SUMMARY:

The perpetual inventory system requires more accounting entries, but it provides more up-to-date information for managing inventory.

COST-BENEFIT ANALYSIS IMPLEMENTING A PERPETUAL INVENTORY SYSTEM

Benefits:

1. Accounting records always show the amount of inventory on hand. This will assist in:
   a. determining when to reorder inventory.
   b. determining how much inventory to reorder.
   c. analyzing whether an item of inventory is a "hot seller" or "slow mover."
   d. making decisions on markdowns or special promotions.

2. A physical inventory count is necessary only at year-end. This count validates the perpetual inventory records.

Costs:

1. Hiring extra accounting personnel or increased fees paid to an accounting service as the result of a greater number of transactions that must be recorded and processed.

OR

2. Purchasing optical scanners and computerized equipment to track purchases and sales of inventory items.

Transparency Master 6-8

CHOOSING AN INVENTORY SYSTEM

Size of Retailer	Unit Cost of Inventory Items	Probable Choice	Reason
Small	Low	Periodic	Perpetual inventory systems may be too costly for a small retailer who sells many low-priced inventory items.
Small	High	Perpetual	Because the cost of inventory items is high, a smaller number of the items would be sold during the year. This keeps the cost of a perpetual system affordable. In addition, tight control over the high-cost inventory items is essential.
Large	Low	Perpetual	A large retailer will have sufficient sales volume to cover the cost of a perpetual system even if the cost of inventory items is relatively low. The sales volume and number of inventory items make it difficult to manage the business without inventory records that are updated daily.
Large	High	Perpetual	The sales volume and need for tight inventory control of high-priced items will dictate the use of a perpetual inventory system.

CALCULATING COST OF MERCHANDISE SOLD UNDER A PERIODIC INVENTORY SYSTEM

Merchandise Inventory, Beg. of Year

+ Cost of Merchandise Purchased

Merchandise Available for Sale

− Merchandise Inventory, End of Year

Cost of Merchandise Sold

{
Purchases
- Purchase Returns & Allowances
- Purchase Discounts
Net Purchases
+ Transportation In
Cost of Merchandise Purchased
}

CALCULATING COST OF MERCHANDISE SOLD UNDER A PERIODIC INVENTORY SYSTEM

Christopher's Gourmet Chocolates is a small retail store which uses a periodic inventory system. Compute Christopher's Cost of Merchandise Sold for November based on the following information:

Inventory on November 1	$280
Merchandise purchased	1,000
Merchandise returned due to quality problems	50
Discounts on Merchandise purchased	20
Delivery costs for merchandise purchased	45
Inventory on November 30	350

Transparency Master 6-11

MERCHANDISE SALES

The following new accounts are used to record sales of merchandise to customers.

Account	Purpose	Account Classification	Normal Balance
Sales	Used to record sales revenue whenever a sale is made to a cash or credit customer.	Revenue	Credit
Sales Returns & Allowances	Used to record cash or credit refund given to a customer who returns merchandise.	Contra-Revenue	Debit
Sales Discounts	Used to record discounts granted to a customer for paying an account receivable within a discount period. (for example: 2/10, n/30)	Contra-Revenue	Debit

(Continued)

MERCHANDISE SALES
(Concluded)

The following new accounts are used to record sales of merchandise to customers.

Account	Purpose	Account Classification	Normal Balance
Cost of Merchandise Sold	Used to record the cost of inventory items sold to customers. The inventory items sold must be removed from the merchandise inventory account.	Expense	Debit
Credit Card Expense	Used to record the service fee charged by credit card companies.	Expense	Debit
Sales Tax Payable	Used to record sales tax collected by the seller; these taxes must be paid to the appropriate tax authority (example: state or county).	Liability	Credit

Transparency Master 6-13

SALES TRANSACTIONS FOR S & V OFFICE SUPPLY COMPANY

1. Sold $500 in merchandise to a cash customer. The cost of the merchandise sold was $280.

2. Sold $1,200 worth of merchandise to a customer who charged the merchandise to her VISA card. The cost of the merchandise sold was $950. [Hint: Bank card sales (VISA and MasterCard) are treated the same as cash sales because the retailer may deposit the credit card slips directly into his or her bank account.]

3. Sold $2,000 in merchandise to a credit customer on a store account. The terms of the sale are 2/10, n/30. The cost of the merchandise sold was $1,600.

(Continued)

Transparency Master 6-14

SALES TRANSACTIONS FOR S & V OFFICE SUPPLY COMPANY
(Concluded)

4. Accepted a return of $50 worth of merchandise from the cash customer in #1. The cost of the merchandise returned was $30. The customer received a cash refund.

5. Received payment from the credit customer in #3 within the discount period. (Hint: Since the customer did pay within the discount period, you must show that discount in your journal entry.)

6. Paid the service fee on VISA and Master Card sales to Third National Bank, $75.

Transparency Master 6-15

SALES TRANSACTIONS FOR S & V OFFICE SUPPLY COMPANY

Solution

1. Sold $500 in merchandise to a cash customer. The cost of the merchandise sold was $280.

Cash..	500	
Sales..		500
Cost of Merchandise Sold	280	
Merchandise Inventory..................		280

2. Sold $1,200 worth of merchandise to a customer who charged the merchandise to her VISA card. The cost of the merchandise sold was $950.

Cash..	1,200	
Sales..		1,200
Cost of Merchandise Sold	950	
Merchandise Inventory..................		950

3. Sold $2,000 in merchandise to a credit customer on a store account. The terms of the sale are 2/10, n/30. The cost of the merchandise sold was $1,600.

Accounts Receivable	2,000	
Sales..		2,000
Cost of Merchandise Sold	1,600	
Merchandise Inventory..................		1,600

(Continued)

Transparency Master 6-16

SALES TRANSACTIONS FOR S & V OFFICE SUPPLY COMPANY

Solution (Concluded)

4. Accepted a return of $50 worth of merchandise from the cash customer in #1. The cost of the merchandise returned was $30. The customer received a cash refund.

Sales Returns and Allowances	50	
Cash		50
Merchandise Inventory	30	
Cost of Merchandise Sold..............		30

5. Received payment from the credit customer in #3 within the discount period.

Cash..	1,960	
Sales Discounts.....................................	40	
Accounts Receivable.......................		2,000

6. Paid the service fee on VISA and MasterCard sales to Third National Bank, $75.

Credit Card Expense	75	
Cash		75

WRITING EXERCISE

1. Why would a retailer offer customers sales discounts?

2. How is using a separate account for sales returns and allowances useful to management?

3. If you owned a merchandising business, how would you decide which credit cards, if any, to accept?

4. Which of the following credit terms would be more generous to your customers: n/30 or n/eom?

PURCHASE TRANSACTIONS FOR S & V OFFICE SUPPLY COMPANY

1. S & V purchased $500 worth of merchandise for cash.

2. S & V purchased $4,000 of merchandise on account; terms n/30.

3. S & V paid for the merchandise purchased in #2.

4. S & V purchased $2,000 of merchandise from its supplier on account; terms 3/15, n/45.

5. S & V returned $100 worth of the merchandise purchased in #4 because it was damaged.

6. S & V paid for the merchandise purchased in #4, less the amount returned in #5. This invoice was paid within the discount period.

Transparency Master 6-19

PURCHASE TRANSACTIONS FOR S & V OFFICE SUPPLY COMPANY - Solution

1. S & V purchased $500 worth of merchandise for cash.
   Merchandise Inventory 500
      Cash 500

2. S & V purchased $4,000 of merchandise on account; terms n/30.
   Merchandise Inventory 4,000
      Accounts Payable 4,000

3. S & V paid for the merchandise purchased in #2.
   Accounts Payable 4,000
      Cash 4,000

4. S & V purchased $2,000 of merchandise from its supplier on account; terms 3/15, n/45.
   Merchandise Inventory 2,000
      Accounts Payable 2.000

5. S & V returned $100 worth of the merchandise purchased in #4 because it was damaged.
   Accounts Payable 100
      Merchandise Inventory 100

6. S & V paid for the merchandise purchased in #4 less the amount returned in #5. This invoice was paid within the discount period.
   Accounts Payable 1,900
      Cash 1,843
      Merchandise Inventory 57

FREIGHT TERMS

	FOB Shipping Point	FOB Destination
Ownership (title) passes to buyer when merchandise is..........................	Delivered to freight carrier	Received by buyer
Transportation costs are paid by	Buyer	Seller
Risk of loss during transportation belongs to..............	Buyer	Seller

Transparency Master 6-21

Freight Terms and Discounts

Logan Appliances purchased $8,000 of merchandise, 2/10, n/30, FOB shipping point. The seller prepaid the shipping charges of $200. If Logan pays for this merchandise within the discount period, how much should Logan remit to the seller?

PURCHASE TRANSACTIONS FOR S & V OFFICE SUPPLY COMPANY

FREIGHT TERMS

1. S & V purchased $1,000 worth of merchandise on account; terms 2/10, n/30, FOB Shipping Point. The freight costs of $50 were prepaid by the seller and added to the invoice.

2. S & V paid for the merchandise purchased in #1 within the discount period. (Hint: The discount does not apply to the transportation costs.)

PURCHASE TRANSACTIONS FOR S & V OFFICE SUPPLY COMPANY

FREIGHT TERMS

Solution

1. S & V purchased $1,000 worth of merchandise on account; terms 2/10, n/30, FOB Shipping Point. The freight costs of $50 were prepaid by the seller and added to the invoice.

   Merchandise Inventory 1,050
       Accounts Payable   1,050

2. S & V paid for the merchandise purchased in #1 within the discount period.

   Accounts Payable 1,050
       Cash   1,030
       Merchandise Inventory ...   20

END-OF-PERIOD PROCEDURES— MERCHANDISING COMPANIES
(Manual Accounting System)

1. Prepare a trial balance of the ledger on a work sheet.

2. Review the accounts and gather the data required for the adjustments.

3. Insert the adjustments and complete the work sheet.

4. Prepare financial statements from the data in the work sheet.

5. Journalize the adjusting entries and post to the ledger.

6. Journalize the closing entries and post to the ledger.

7. Prepare a post-closing trial balance of the ledger.

Transparency Master 6-25

Ratio of Net Sales to Assets

Net Sales $700,000

Net Sales were earned throughout the year

Average Assets:
$$\frac{\$3,654,000}{12} = 304,500$$

Ratio of Net Sales to Assets:
$$\frac{\$700,000}{\$304,500} = 2.30$$

Total Assets:
Jan.	$302,000
Feb.	$310,000
Mar.	$295,000
Apr.	$298,000
May	$292,000
Jun.	$303,000
Jul.	$315,000
Aug.	$307,000
Sept.	$299,000
Oct.	$310,000
Nov.	$312,000
Dec.	$311,000
Total	$3,654,000

Or...as a shortcut

Average Assets:
$$\frac{\$611,000}{2} = \$305,500$$

Ratio of Net Sales to Assets:
$$\frac{\$700,000}{\$305,500} = 2.29$$

Total Assets:
Beg. of Year
(12/31/x1 bal.) $300,000
End of Year
(12/31/x2 bal.) $311,000
$611,000

Transparency Master 6-26

Computerized Accounting Systems

Exhibit 17 - Entry to record inventory purchase

Mar. 4   Merchandise Inventory…   13,880
               Accounts Payable…..   13,880

Exhibit 18 - Entries to record sale

Mar. 14 Accounts Receivable……   4,260
               Sales…………………..   4,260

Mar. 14 Cost of Merchandise Sold 3,470
               Merchandise Inventory   3,470

Gem City Music
Work Sheet
For the Year Ended December 31, 20—

ACCOUNT TITLE	TRIAL BALANCE DEBIT	TRIAL BALANCE CREDIT	ADJUSTMENTS DEBIT	ADJUSTMENTS CREDIT	ADJUSTED TRIAL BALANCE DEBIT	ADJUSTED TRIAL BALANCE CREDIT	INCOME STATEMENT DEBIT	INCOME STATEMENT CREDIT	BALANCE SHEET DEBIT	BALANCE SHEET CREDIT
Cash	11,000				11,000				11,000	
Accounts Receivable	15,800				15,800				15,800	
Merchandise Inventory	10,400			800	9,600				9,600	
Office Equipment	23,000				23,000				23,000	
Accumulated Depr.—Office Equipment		6,400		2,800		9,200				9,200
Accounts Payable		16,000				16,000				16,000
Salaries Payable				1,250		1,250				1,250
M. Marx, Capital		11,500				11,500				11,500
M. Marx, Drawing	12,800				12,800				12,800	
Sales		189,300				189,300		189,300		
Sales Returns and Allowances	1,700				1,700		1,700			
Sales Discounts	500				500		500			
Cost of Merchandise Sold	99,200		800		100,000		100,000			
Rent Expense	7,800				7,800		7,800			
Sales Salaries Expense	17,000		700		17,700		17,700			
Office Salaries Expense	22,000		550		22,550		22,550			
Depreciation Expense—Office Equipment			2,800		2,800		2,800			
Interest Expense	2,000				2,000		2,000			
	223,200	223,200	4,850	4,850	227,250	227,250	155,050	189,300	72,200	37,950
Net Income							34,250			34,250
							189,300	189,300	72,200	72,200

Transparency Master 6-27

REVIEW—CLOSING ENTRIES

1. Close all income statement accounts with credit balances to Income Summary.

2. Close all income statement accounts with debit balances to Income Summary.

3. Verify that the balance in Income Summary equals the net income or net loss for the period. Close Income Summary to the capital account.

4. Close the drawing account to the capital account.

CLOSING ENTRIES

Gem City Music

1. Sales 189,300
     Income Summary 189,300

2. Income Summary 155,050
     Sales Returns and Allowances.. 1,700
     Sales Discounts 500
     Cost of Merchandise Sold........... 100,000
     Rent Expense 7,800
     Sales Salaries Expense.............. 17,700
     Office Salaries Expense 22,550
     Depreciation Expense—
         Office Equipment 2,800
     Interest Expense 2,000

3. Income Summary 34,250
     M. Marx, Capital 34,250

4. M. Marx, Capital 12,800
     M. Marx, Drawing 12,800

Income Summary

Closing	155,050	Closing	189,300
		Balance	34,250
Closing	24,250		
		Balance	0

Chapter 7
Cash

OPENING COMMENTS

This chapter applies the principle of internal controls introduced in Chapter 5 to cash. In discussing the internal controls over cash receipts, the chapter presents the use of cash change funds and the cash short and over account. The discussion of internal controls over cash payments includes the voucher system, the discounts lost account, and petty cash funds. The chapter also shows the use of a bank reconciliation to detect errors and irregularities. The chapter ends by explaining how cash is presented in the balance sheet and by discussing electronic funds transfers.

After studying the chapter, your students should be able to:

1. Describe the nature of cash and the importance of internal control over cash.
2. Summarize basic procedures for achieving internal control over cash receipts.
3. Summarize basic procedures for achieving internal control over cash payments, including the use of a voucher system.
4. Describe the nature of a bank account and its use in controlling cash.
5. Prepare a bank reconciliation and journalize any necessary entries.
6. Account for small cash transactions using a petty cash fund.
7. Summarize how cash is presented on the balance sheet.
8. Compute and interpret the ratio of cash to current liabilities.

OBJECTIVE 1 — Describe the nature of cash and the importance of internal control over cash.

KEY TERMS:
    Cash

SUGGESTED APPROACH

Remind your students that cash includes anything a bank would accept for deposit in your account. This includes coins, currency, checks, and money orders. A good system of internal controls is necessary to protect all of these forms of cash.

OBJECTIVE 2 — Summarize basic procedures for achieving internal control over cash receipts.

KEY TERMS:
    Cash short and over
    Change fund
    Detective controls
    Preventive controls
    Remittance advice

SUGGESTED APPROACH

The topic of internal controls can be used to stimulate a lively class discussion. Suggestions for leading that discussion follow.

The cash change fund and cash short and over account are simple topics that can be covered appropriately in a lecture format.

CLASS DISCUSSION — Internal Controls

Protecting business assets is an important concern for any manager or owner. Transparency 7-1 reviews the typical controls for protecting cash received at the cash register. Review these controls with your class. Point out how the principle of separation of accounting, custody of assets, and operations is applied in this scenario.

Next, ask your class to identify the people who have the opportunity to steal cash. The candidates are the clerk and the cashier, because they are the only ones who actually handle cash. Ask your students to identify ways in which these individuals can steal cash and, more important, what procedures can be instituted to prevent theft by these means.

Because many of your students will have worked in businesses that use a cash register, they probably will have heard stories about employees who discovered a way to steal cash from a register. Therefore, your class discussion will probably focus on the clerk. It should point out the internal control reason for many of the policies and procedures your students have experienced in their clerk positions. To summarize the discussion, remind your students that business owners/managers must constantly be alert for ways in which employees and customers could steal cash, and establish controls to prevent theft before it occurs.

The following lists some of the ways for the clerk in Transparency 7-1 to steal cash, and procedures to prevent/detect this theft.

Means to Steal Cash	Way to Prevent/Detect Theft
1. Don't ring the sale on the cash register, and pocket the cash.	1. Odd pricing—clerk must make change. Require receipts for refunds. Put coupons on backs of receipts so the customer will ask for a receipt. Offer customers a bonus if they are not handed a receipt (e.g., a free beverage). Have one employee ring up customer orders and another fill orders from a receipt. Proper supervision—watch for employees who do not ring up orders.
2. Enter the sale on the register, then void the sale and pocket the cash.	2. Only managers can ring voids. Use cash registers that require a key to void a sale. Require all voids to be documented and authorized by a manager.
3. Enter a cash refund on the register and pocket the cash.	3. Require a manager to authorize all refunds in the presence of the customer. Only managers can issue refunds.
4. If more than one clerk uses the register, simply take the cash when no one is looking and hope that someone else will be blamed.	4. Have a separate register for each clerk. Each clerk must balance register at the end of each shift.

Transparency 7-2 presents procedures related to the receipt of cash through the mail. Use this illustration to point out how good internal controls (mainly separation of accounting, custody of assets, and operations) will reduce theft and errors. For example, pose the following questions to the class:

1. Assume that the employee who opens the mail steals a customer payment. How will this theft be detected?
2. Assume that the accounting clerk posts the payment to the wrong customer's account. How will this error be detected?
3. Assume that the accounting clerk posts a customer's payment for the wrong amount, giving the customer credit for less than he or she actually paid. How will this error be detected?
4. Assume that an employee in the cashier's department loses a check. (Maybe it was placed in the customer's file rather than deposited in the bank.) How will this error be detected?

Transparency 7-2 can also be used to explain collusion. Collusion occurs when two or more employees work together to embezzle cash or conceal errors. For example, if the accounting clerk and the employee who opens the mail decide to work together, one can steal customer payments and the other can "doctor" the accounting records. To prevent collusion, companies will institute nepotism policies, job rotation, and mandatory vacations.

LECTURE AIDS — Cash Change Fund and Cash Short and Over Account

Objective 2 also presents the cash change fund and the cash short and over account. Ask students who have worked as cashiers to share what amount of cash was in their cash register at the beginning and end of the day. This represents a cash change fund.

Remind students that a cash fund is required for any business that receives cash from its customers. Someone must be accountable for that change fund at all times. It should be locked in a company vault when not in use.

The cash short and over account is used when the cash on hand at the end of the day does not equal the amount in the beginning cash change fund plus the day's cash sales. It is used to record discrepancies due to errors in recording sales or making change. The cash short and over account is needed because employees will not be accurate 100% of the time.

As long as the cash short and over account shows only small discrepancies, management should not be concerned. If the account shows large discrepancies or continuous shortages, however, management should investigate these differences. Ask your students who have worked as cashiers to describe their employers' policies regarding cash overages and shortages. Point out that deducting cash shortages from a cashier's paycheck may encourage the cashier to overcharge customers, eliminating any chance of a shortage at the end of the day.

You may want to review the journal entry illustrated on page 288 of the text with your class and remind them that a debit balance in the cash short and over account is treated as a miscellaneous administrative expense. A credit balance is included in the Other Income section of the income statement.

INTERNET ACTIVITY – Internal Controls over Cash

Instruct your students to search the web using "Internal Controls" and "Cash Management" as their search criteria. At the time this manual was written, the following sites offered some interesting information:

    www.casbo.org/develop/internal.html
        This site, operated by the California Association of School Business Officials, presents a story about a bookkeeper who stole $80,000 in 3 years by handling the entire cash function.

    www.securitymanagement.com/library/000304.html
        This site discusses the importance of establishing internal controls over petty cash and many other areas.

EXERCISES & PROBLEMS FOR REINFORCEMENT:
    Exercise 7-1   Exercise 7-4
    Exercise 7-2   Exercise 7-5
    Exercise 7-3

OBJECTIVE 3 — Summarize basic procedures for achieving internal control over cash payments, including the use of a voucher system.

KEY TERMS:
    Electronic funds transfer (EFT)
    Voucher
    Voucher system

SUGGESTED APPROACH

The voucher system will require a detailed explanation in lecture format. Transparency 7-3 will help you present this topic. After discussing the voucher system, use a writing exercise to test your students' comprehension of the system.

Objective 3 also addresses electronic funds transfers. Most students will be familiar with electronic funds transfers (EFT) through direct experience with automated teller machines (ATMs), payroll direct deposit, or point-of-sale systems. Use this opportunity to point out the control risks of EFTs and make students aware of the internal control procedures that must be implemented when EFTs are used. To achieve this goal, stimulate a class discussion on control issues related to point-of-sale systems. Next, assign a group learning activity that requires your students to implement EFT control procedures.

LECTURE AIDS — The Voucher System

Transparency 7-3 is a flowchart-style illustration of the voucher system, putting the textbook description in picture format. Review this exhibit with your class, stressing the control aspects of the voucher system. A writing exercise to reinforce your coverage of this topic follows.

WRITING EXERCISE — The Voucher System

After reviewing the voucher system, ask your class to write answers to the following questions (Transparency 7-4):

1. How does the voucher system ensure that management is paying only valid obligations?
2. How does the voucher system help a company maintain a favorable credit standing by aiding management in paying all invoices on time?
3. How would a company using a voucher system investigate a supplier's complaint that an invoice has not been paid?

CLASS DISCUSSION — Control of Point-of-Sale Systems

The following two scenarios (Transparency 7-5) relate to point-of-sale systems. In a classroom discussion, ask your students to identify the control risk associated with each system and name procedures that can be implemented to counterbalance the risk.

1. A grocery store decides to install a point-of-sale system that will allow the customer to use his or her ATM card to pay for merchandise at the checkout line. Previously, the grocery store has accepted only cash and checks as payment.

   Control Risk: In the past, the clerks would have reconciled their cash registers by comparing the sales on the register tape to the total of the cash and checks in the register drawer. Under the new system, a clerk could steal the cash taken for a customer's order and claim that the customer paid by EFT. The clerk also could allow friends and family to leave the store without paying for their merchandise and claim they paid with an EFT. In addition, a customer might mistakenly (or intentionally) authorize the wrong payment amount when using the point-of-sale device.

   Solution: A receipt from the point-of-sale device must be placed in the cash register drawer as evidence of the customer's payment. In reconciling the cash drawer, sales on the register tape would be verified against the total of cash, checks, and point-of-sale receipts. In addition, the point-of-sale receipts must be used to verify actual bank deposits from the EFT system.

2. A self-service gas station decides to install a point-of-sale device at the gasoline pump. This will speed the time it takes a customer to fill his or her gas tank, since payment can be made right at the pump, eliminating the time spent waiting in line for a clerk to accept payment.

   Control Risk: Whenever a customer puts gasoline in the car and drives off, the clerk will assume that the customer paid with the point-of-sale device. In reality, the customer may not have paid at all.

   Solution: The clerk must have a device that clearly indicates which customers have chosen to pay with the point-of-sale device. This will immediately alert the clerk to any customers who simply drive off. Installing cameras to capture the license plate number of cars with drivers who did not pay is also an important control.

GROUP LEARNING ACTIVITY — Electronic Funds Transfers

Transparency 7-6 presents information regarding a company that has decided to use EFT to pay vendor invoices. Divide the class into small groups and ask them to define procedures for paying vendor invoices via EFT. Their procedures should include any documentation, authorization, or reconciliation required and who should be made responsible for those tasks. Transparency 7-7 presents a suggested solution.

EXERCISES & PROBLEMS FOR REINFORCEMENT:
    Exercise 7-6   Problem 7-1A   Problem 7-1B
    Exercise 7-7

OBJECTIVE 4 — Describe the nature of a bank account and its use in controlling cash.

KEY TERMS:
- Check
- Deposit ticket
- Drawee
- Drawer
- Payee
- Remittance advice
- Signature card
- Statement of account
- Transactions register

SUGGESTED APPROACH

Objective 4 presents several terms related to bank accounts. These terms are listed on Transparency 7-8. It is essential that students understand these terms. You can use Transparency 7-8 to either review definitions in lecture format or ask students to write their own definitions for these terms.

Immediately depositing all cash receipts in a bank account and making all cash payments by check are important components in a good system of internal controls. For control purposes, a check which is written in error should not be destroyed. It should be marked "Void" and retained, so that all check numbers are accounted for.

OBJECTIVE 5 — Prepare a bank reconciliation and journalize any necessary entries.

KEY TERMS:
- Bank Reconciliation

SUGGESTED APPROACH

The bank reconciliation is usually an easy task for students who have their own checking accounts. Depending on your student body, you may discover that many of your students do not have a checking account.

Begin this topic with a class discussion that establishes the relevance of the bank reconciliation. Next, give your students the opportunity to practice a bank reconciliation using the group learning activity. Finally, demonstrate the journal entries required by a bank reconciliation.

CLASS DISCUSSION— Establishing Relevance of the Bank Reconciliation

An interesting way to begin your coverage of the bank reconciliation is to ask your class to indicate (by a show of hands) whether they have a checking account. Next, ask if their bank has ever made an error in their checking account. You will probably find that your students will volunteer to describe the bank's error and the wrong they suffered. After listening to these details, ask your students how they discovered the bank's error. The usual responses are either through a bank reconciliation or notification that they were bouncing checks. If the response is bouncing checks, pose this question: What if you had an extra $1,000 (or more) in your account so that your checks would not have bounced as a result of the error? How could you have discovered the error in this case? Now the answer must be: through some sort of reconciliation process.

BRAINSTORMING ACTIVITY — Developing the Format for a Bank Reconciliation

After establishing the relevance of a bank reconciliation, you can discuss how one is prepared. One approach is to direct your students to the form and content of the bank reconciliation on page 295 of the text and discuss the contents of that illustration. Another approach is to ask your class to use brainstorming to determine the items that must be included on the bank reconciliation, thereby allowing them to discover how to prepare a reconciliation. Write "Cash Balance on Bank Statement" and "Cash Balance on Depositor's Records" on opposing sides of the board. Ask your class what items can cause these two totals to disagree when the bank statement is received. As they call out reconciling items, ask whether these items are adjustments to the bank statement balance or the depositor's balance, and whether they are additions or deductions. You may need to fill in a few gaps at the end, but collectively your class should derive a format similar to the one shown in Transparency 7-9.

Many students find the following hint helpful in completing a bank reconciliation successfully. If a bank reconciliation does not balance, check any bank errors and/or depositor's errors first. Students frequently add items that should be deducted, and vice versa.

It is interesting to point out that the amount of cash on deposit in a bank represents a liability to the bank. As a result, customers' accounts have credit balances. A bank credit memo is issued for items that increase a customer's balance. Debit memorandums are issued for service charges or other items that decrease the customer's account balance.

GROUP LEARNING ACTIVITY — Preparing a Bank Reconciliation

Transparency 7-10 presents the information for a bank reconciliation. Ask your students to work in small groups to prepare that bank reconciliation. Transparency 7-11 is the solution, which you can share after the groups have finished. Emphasize that the adjusted balance on the bank reconciliation is the amount that is reported on the balance sheet.

DEMONSTRATION PROBLEM — Journal Entries Required by a Bank Reconciliation

Using Transparency 7-11, demonstrate the following journal entries required as a result of the bank reconciliation. Remind your students that any adjustments made to the depositor's records must be journalized.

To record the note collected by bank:
Cash............................	1,260	
Notes Receivable......		1,200
Interest Revenue.......		60

To record the NSF check:
Accounts Receivable—J. Lane	100	
Cash.....................		100

To correct the error on Check No. 548:
        Utility Expense.................   27
             Cash....................   27

EXERCISES & PROBLEMS FOR REINFORCEMENT:

Exercise 7-8	Exercise 7-12	Problem 7-3A	Problem 7-3B
Exercise 7-9	Exercise 7-13	Problem 7-4A	Problem 7-4B
Exercise 7-10	Exercise 7-14	Problem 7-5A	Problem 7-5B
Exercise 7-11	Exercise 7-15		

OBJECTIVE 6 — Account for small cash transactions using a petty cash fund.

KEY TERMS:
    Petty cash fund

DEMONSTRATION PROBLEM — Petty Cash

In some cases, it is impractical to pay an expense by check, either because the expense is very small or payment is required sooner than a check can be processed. Petty cash is used to cover these types of expenses. When discussing petty cash in class, you will want to address both the journal entries and internal controls related to the fund.

The following example can be used to illustrate the journal entries for petty cash (Transparency 7-12). Emphasize that expenses paid from a petty cash fund are recorded when the fund is replenished, not when the cash is disbursed. Therefore, the petty cash fund should be replenished at the end of the accounting period to bring the accounts up to date.

    Allied Plumbing Supply decides to establish a petty cash fund of $150 on January 1. The petty cash fund will be replenished whenever the fund reaches a balance of $20 or less. On February 10, the fund is replenished and the following receipts for items paid out of the petty cash fund are recorded: office supplies, $34; postage, $28; store supplies, $12; a minor repair on office equipment, $52; and the cost paid to Federal Express to send an urgent letter, $10.

Entry to establish the petty cash fund:
    Jan. 1   Petty Cash..................... 150
                        Cash..................   150

Entry to replenish the petty cash fund:
    Feb. 10   Office Supplies............... 34
                 Postage Expense ($28 + $10) 38
                 Store Supplies 12
                 Repairs Expense............... 52
                        Cash...................   136

In reviewing the internal controls related to petty cash, you will want to mention the following:

1. A trusted employee must be named custodian of the petty cash fund. That employee is responsible for disbursements from the fund.
2. Guidelines should be established for the types of expenses that may be paid from petty cash. In addition, restrictions should be placed on the maximum amount that can be withdrawn from the fund in any one transaction.
3. Whenever a disbursement is made from the fund, a receipt should be prepared that states the details of the expense and has the signatures of both the fund custodian and the person receiving the funds.
4. The fund custodian should submit receipts documenting all fund expenditures before receiving money to replenish the fund.

CLASS DISCUSSION — Internal Controls Over Petty Cash

Ask your students how the custodian of a petty cash fund could steal cash. Answer: by forging a signature on a petty cash receipt.

Next, ask them how this theft could be detected. Your students' ideas may include the following: (1) a periodic audit of the petty cash fund, (2) randomly checking signatures on receipts, or (3) comparing petty cash expenditures with normal or expected amounts. Point out that the small amounts of cash in a petty cash fund normally do not justify elaborate control procedures.

EXERCISES & PROBLEMS FOR REINFORCEMENT:
    Exercise 7-16   Problem 7-2A   Problem 7-2B

OBJECTIVE 7 — Summarize how cash is presented on the balance sheet.

KEY TERMS:
    Cash equivalents
    Compensating balance

SUGGESTED APPROACH

This topic can be covered quickly, but thoroughly, through a brief lecture.

LECTURE AIDS — Cash on the Balance Sheet

To cover this objective, you need only remind students of the following points:

1. Cash is the first asset listed on the balance sheet because it is the most liquid.
2. Funds placed in highly liquid investments such as Treasury bills, money market funds, and commercial paper are called cash equivalents. Since these investments can be sold quickly

and easily, funds in these investments can be accessed as easily as cash held in a bank. Therefore, they are considered "equivalent" to cash.
3. Readers of the financial statements normally assume that a company may use its cash at any time for any purpose. If this is not true, the amount of funds not available for withdrawal must be disclosed in the notes to the financial statements. For example, any compensating balance required by a bank as part of a loan agreement or line of credit must be disclosed. Likewise, multinational companies must disclose any limits that foreign governments set on the amount of cash that may be taken out of deposit in foreign banks.

EXERCISES & PROBLEMS FOR REINFORCEMENT:
> Exercise 7-17

OBJECTIVE 8 — Compute and interpret the ratio of cash to current liabilities.

KEY TERMS:
> Doomsday ratio

SUGGESTED APPROACH

The doomsday ratio compares a business' cash to its current liabilities. This ratio is calculated as follows:

$$\text{Doomsday ratio} = \frac{\text{Cash and Cash Equivalents}}{\text{Current Liabilities}}$$

You may want to ask your students if they would expect this ratio to be greater than or less than one for most businesses.

Next, ask your students to write down an estimate of how much cash they have in the bank. Also ask them to compute the debts they have that will be paid in the next year. With this information, instruct them to compute their own doomsday ratio.

Point out that, like most individuals, most businesses' current liabilities are substantially higher than the cash on hand. Businesses expect to be able to sell their inventory and collect their receivables in order to pay current liabilities. Therefore, the doomsday ratio is generally less than one. However, when comparing doomsday ratios, a higher ratio indicates less risk to creditors.

EXERCISES & PROBLEMS FOR REINFORCEMENT:
> Exercise 7-18

Transparency Master 7-1

Internal Controls—Cash Receipts Cash Register

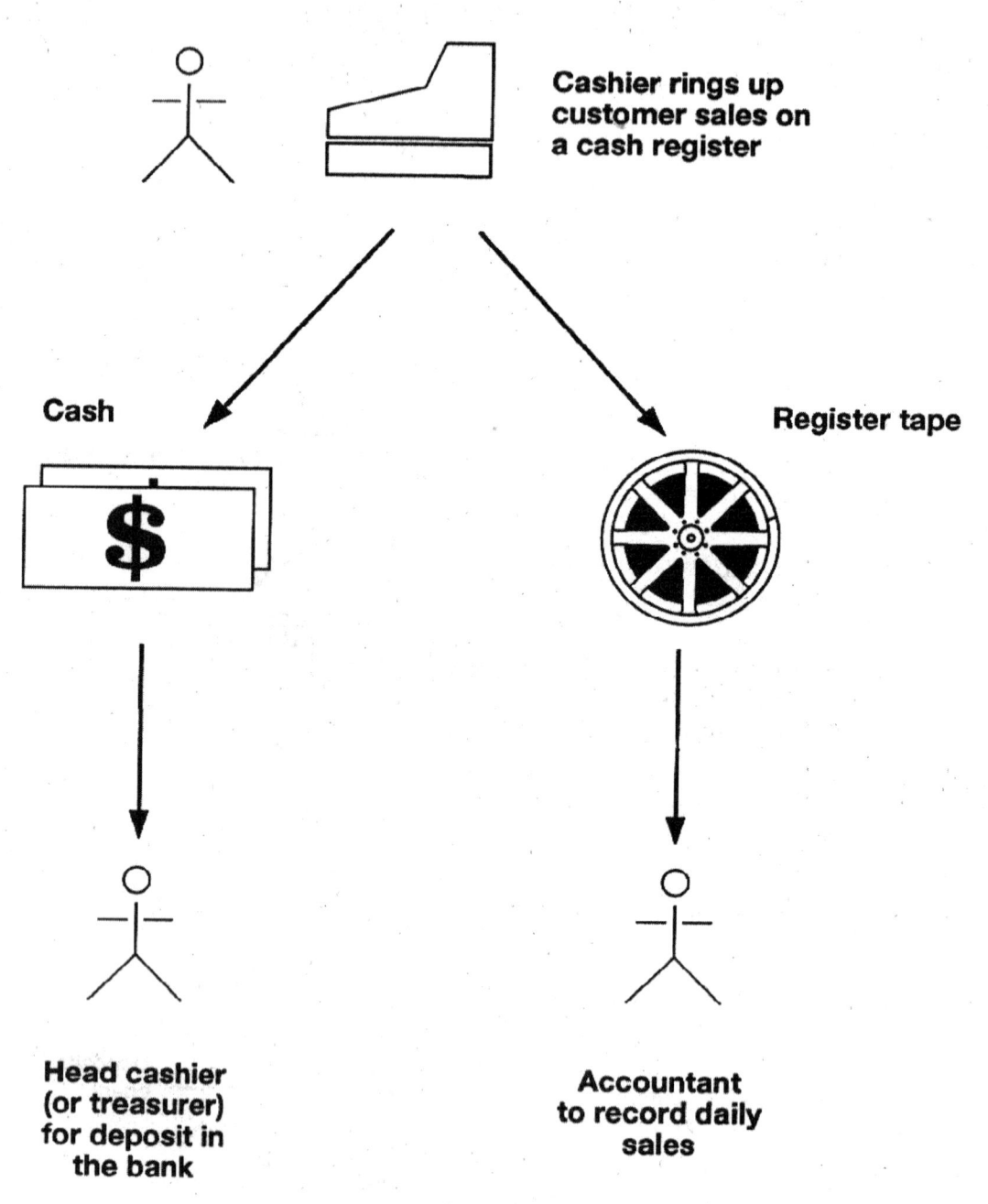

Cashier rings up customer sales on a cash register

Cash

Register tape

Head cashier (or treasurer) for deposit in the bank

Accountant to record daily sales

TM 7-1

Transparency Master 7-2

INTERNAL CONTROLS—CASH RECEIPTS

CUSTOMER PAYMENTS RECEIVED THROUGH MAIL

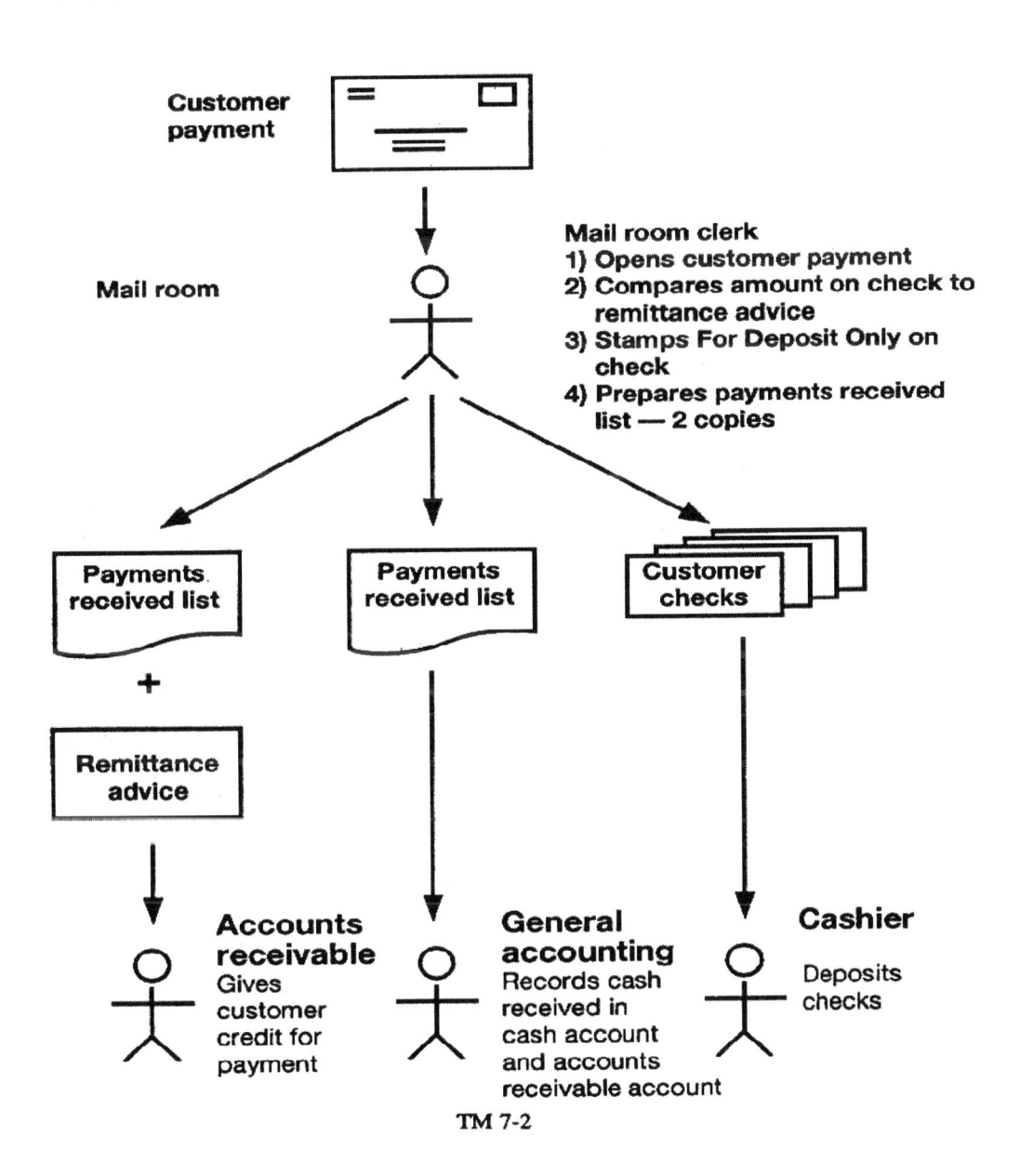

Customer payment

Mail room

Mail room clerk
1) Opens customer payment
2) Compares amount on check to remittance advice
3) Stamps For Deposit Only on check
4) Prepares payments received list — 2 copies

Payments received list + **Remittance advice**

Payments received list

Customer checks

Accounts receivable
Gives customer credit for payment

General accounting
Records cash received in cash account and accounts receivable account

Cashier
Deposits checks

TM 7-2

Transparency Master 7-3

INTERNAL CONTROLS — CASH PAYMENTS

VOUCHER SYSTEM

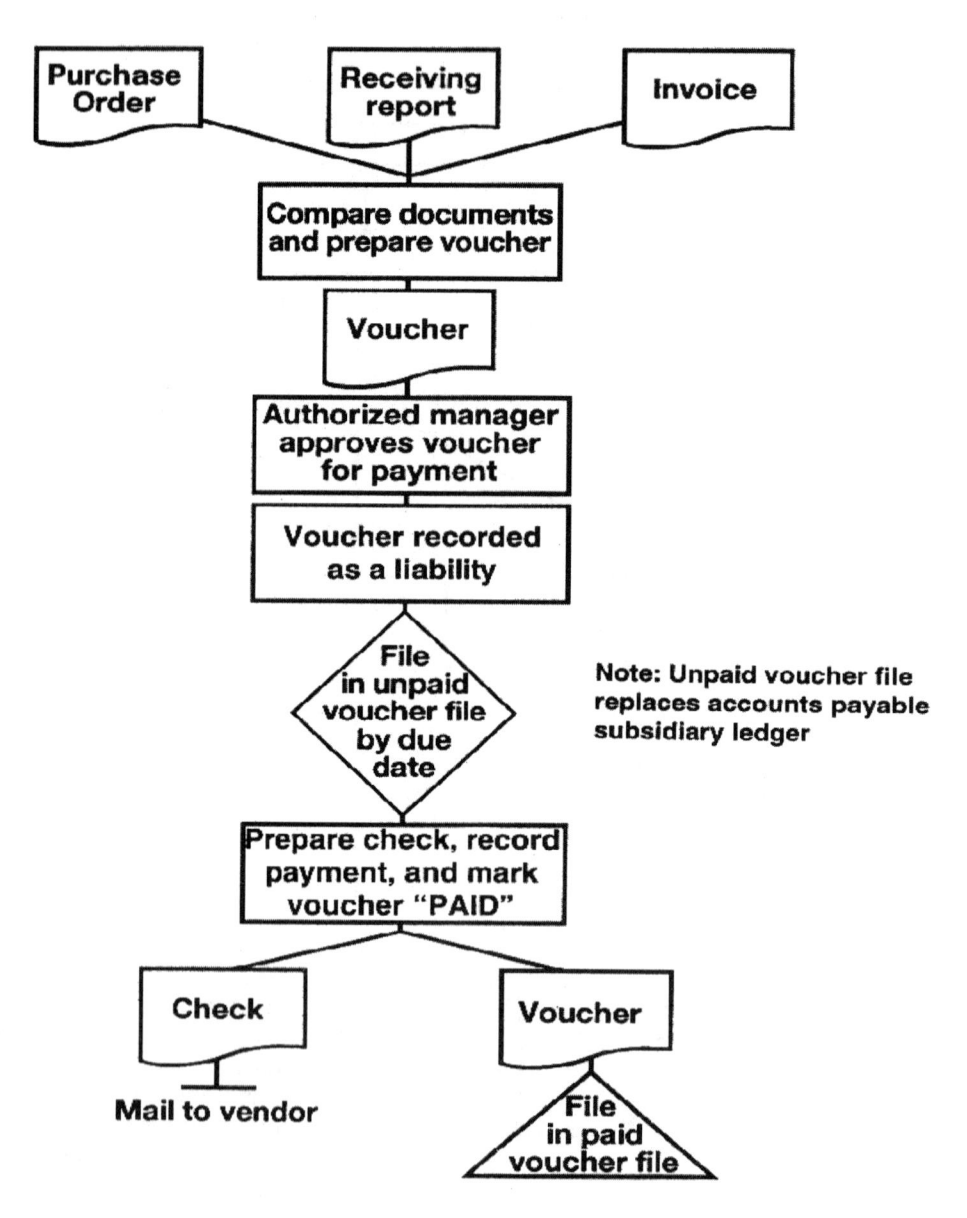

```
   Purchase      Receiving       Invoice
    Order          report
       \             |             /
        \            |            /
         Compare documents
         and prepare voucher
                  |
               Voucher
                  |
         Authorized manager
          approves voucher
             for payment
                  |
          Voucher recorded
            as a liability
                  |
              File
           in unpaid
          voucher file
            by due
              date
                  |
         Prepare check, record
          payment, and mark
           voucher "PAID"
            /           \
          Check        Voucher
            |             |
       Mail to vendor    File
                      in paid
                     voucher file
```

Note: Unpaid voucher file replaces accounts payable subsidiary ledger

TM 7-3

WRITING EXERCISE

1. How does the voucher system ensure that management is paying only valid obligations?

2. How does the voucher system help a company maintain a favorable credit standing by aiding management in paying all invoices on time?

3. How would a company using a voucher system investigate a supplier's complaint that an invoice has not been paid?

ELECTRONIC FUNDS TRANSFERS—CONTROL RISKS

Identify the control risk in implementing each of the following EFT systems. Also identify procedures to overcome the control risk.

1. A grocery store decides to install a point-of-sale system that will allow the customer to use his or her ATM card to pay for merchandise at the checkout line. Previously, the grocery store has accepted only cash and checks as payment.

2. A self-service gas station decides to install a point-of-sale device at the gasoline pump. This will speed the time it takes a customer to fill his or her gas tank, since payment can be made right at the pump, eliminating the time spent waiting in line for a clerk to accept payment.

PAYMENT OF VENDOR INVOICES THROUGH ELECTRONIC FUNDS TRANSFER

Ted's Appliance Store has decided to pay its vendors (General Electric, Maytag, Whirlpool, etc.) via electronic funds transfer.

Ted's currently uses a voucher system to pay invoices by check. Under this system, an accounts payable clerk is responsible for preparing a voucher and attaching the purchase order and receiving report documenting the order. The controller authorizes vouchers for payment. After receiving authorization, the accounts payable clerk records the vouchers.

On the date that payment is due, vouchers are sent to the cash manager, who prepares the checks. The checks are signed by the treasurer, and the vouchers and all supporting documentation are marked paid. The cash manager records payment of the vouchers. The voucher is returned to the accounts payable department where it is filed in the paid vouchers file by number.

Transparency Master 7-7

PAYMENT OF VENDOR INVOICES THROUGH ELECTRONIC FUNDS TRANSFER

Solution

The accounts payable clerk should continue to prepare a voucher for each invoice and attach the purchase order and receiving report as documentation. In addition, vouchers should continue to be authorized by the controller and recorded.

On the date of payment, vouchers should be sent to the cash manager, who calls the bank and, after giving the bank an established password, authorizes an EFT to the appropriate vendor accounts. Since funds are being electronically transferred to outside accounts, the treasurer should also authorize the transactions. The voucher and all supporting documentation should be marked paid.

The voucher should be returned to the accounts payable department, where it is held until an EFT transaction advice is received from the bank. This transaction advice should be compared to the voucher. If they agree, the voucher should be filed in the paid vouchers file by number.

Transparency Master 7-8

BANK ACCOUNTS

Terms

1. Signature Card
2. Deposit Ticket
3. Check
4. Drawer
5. Drawee
6. Payee
7. Transactions Register
8. Bank Statement
9. Canceled Check
10. Remittance Advice

BANK RECONCILIATION

Cash Balance on Bank Statement

+ Deposits not recorded by bank
− Checks that have not cleared

+/− Bank errors
Adjusted balance*

Cash Balance on Depositor's Records

+ Collections made by bank
− NSF checks

− Service charges
−\+ Depositor's errors
Adjusted balance*

*These should agree.

Transparency Master 7-10

BANK RECONCILIATION

Prepare a bank reconciliation for Cartwright Company as of October 31, using the following information:

Cash balance on October 31 bank statement	$10,410
Cash account balance in general ledger	9,890
Deposit made on October 31, not recorded on bank statement	1,865
Note collected by bank ($1,200 plus $60 in interest)	1,260
Outstanding checks: No. 567, $800; No. 569, $452	1,252
Debit memorandum from bank for a NSF check written by J. Lane in payment of his account	100

In addition, Cartwright recorded Check No. 548 written for $152 in payment of the October utility bill as $125 in the cash payments journal.

Transparency Master 7-11

BANK RECONCILIATION

Solution

Cash balance on bank statement		$10,410
Add Oct. 31 deposit..............................		1,865
		$12,275
Deduct outstanding checks:		
No. 567	$800	
No. 569	452	1,252
Adjusted balance		$11,023
Cash balance on depositor's records..		$ 9,890
Add note collected by bank		1,260
		$11,150
Deduct: NSF check	$100	
Error—Check No. 548...	27	127
Adjusted balance.......................		$11,023

PETTY CASH

Allied Plumbing Supply decides to establish a petty cash fund of $150 on January 1. The petty cash fund will be replenished whenever the fund reaches a balance of $20 or less. On February 10, the fund is replenished and the following receipts for items paid out of the petty cash fund are recorded: office supplies, $34; postage, $28; store supplies, $12; a minor repair on office equipment, $52; and the cost to Federal Express to send an urgent letter, $10.

Chapter 8
Receivables

OPENING COMMENTS

Chapter 8 presents the accounting issues related to accounts receivable and notes receivable. The chapter opens with the common classifications of receivables. While presenting those classifications, you will need to make a clear distinction between accounts receivable and notes receivable.

The chapter applies the internal control principles introduced in Chapter 5 to receivables, focusing on the need for separation of duties.

Accounting issues related to uncollectible receivables are covered next. Both the allowance and direct write-off methods are presented. If class time is scarce at this point, coverage of the direct write-off method (theoretically unacceptable because it violates the matching concept) may be omitted without disrupting the flow of the text. Simply omit coverage of Objective 5.

After addressing uncollectible accounts, the text discusses notes receivable transactions. The text presents how to calculate the due date, interest, and maturity value of a note. The journal entries to record the acceptance of a note, receipt of payment on a note, and dishonoring of a note are discussed in detail. Discounting notes receivables is covered in a chapter appendix.

The chapter ends with a discussion of financial ratios related to receivables: the accounts receivable turnover and the number of days' sales in receivables.

After studying the chapter, your students should be able to:

1. List the common classifications of receivables.
2. Summarize and provide examples of internal control procedures that apply to receivables.
3. Describe the nature of and the accounting for uncollectible receivables.
4. Journalize the entries for the allowance method of accounting for uncollectibles, and estimate uncollectible receivables based on sales and on an analysis of receivables.
5. Journalize the entries for the direct write-off of uncollectible receivables.
6. Describe the nature and characteristics of promissory notes.
7. Journalize the entries for notes receivable transactions.
8. Prepare the Current Assets presentation of receivables on the balance sheet.
9. Compute and interpret the accounts receivable turnover and the number of days' sales in receivables.

OBJECTIVE 1 — List the common classifications of receivables.

KEY TERMS:
    Accounts Receivable   Other Receivables
    Notes Receivable   Trade Receivables

SUGGESTED APPROACH

The purpose of this objective is to familiarize students with terms related to receivables. Hints for your review of those terms follow.

LECTURE AIDS — Classification of Receivables

The common classifications of receivables are the following:

1. Accounts Receivable — credit granted to customers for sales of merchandise or services on account. These receivables are usually collected within 30 to 60 days.
2. Notes Receivable — credit granted through a formal credit instrument known as a promissory note. Notes are often used for credit periods of more than 60 days.
3. Other Receivables — such as interest receivable or receivables resulting from loans to officers or employees.

Trade receivables are receivables resulting from the sale of merchandise or services on credit. Both accounts receivable and notes receivable can be classified as trade receivables.

Ask your students to turn to the balance sheet for Home Depot in Appendix F and describe how receivables are presented in this financial statement.

Students generally have the most difficulty distinguishing between accounts receivable and notes receivable. Remind them that an account receivable results from a credit sale on an open account, such as a store charge. These receivables usually require no more than a customer's signature on a receipt or order form. In some cases, the customer's verbal agreement is accepted in lieu of a signature.

A note receivable is evidenced by a signed promissory note. This note is a written promise to pay a specified amount of money. It includes the date that payment is due, to whom payment will be made, and what interest (if any) will accompany the payment.

One advantage of a note receivable is that it represents a stronger legal claim than an accounts receivable. Because the debt and repayment terms are acknowledged by the debtor's signature, a note will hold up better in court if disputed. Since notes are a stronger legal document, it is a good idea to ask a credit customer to sign a note receivable (rather than allowing him or her to buy on an open account) if the following conditions exist.

1. The credit period is longer than 60 days.
2. The purchase involves a large sum of money.

3. The customer has no credit history or a questionable credit history with your firm.
4. The customer is asking for a time extension on an account receivable.

OBJECTIVE 2 — Summarize and provide examples of internal control procedures that apply to receivables.

SUGGESTED APPROACH

The key to internal control with receivables is separation of duties. Transparency 8-1 presents duties related to receivables that must be separated. Review these with your class. A writing exercise can be used to test your students' comprehension of this topic.

Transparency 8-1 points out internal control issues related to granting credit. To stimulate class discussion, ask your students if it is possible for a company's credit approval procedures to be too strict. Answer: Yes, a company may adversely affect income by denying credit and thereby losing potential sales that would be collected.

WRITING EXERCISE — Internal Control of Receivables

Read the following case (or use Transparency 8-2). Ask your students to identify any internal control weaknesses related to accounts receivable.

> Hartwick's of New England is a small custom clothier, specializing in men's and women's career apparel. A customer may apply for an account at Hartwick's by filling out a brief credit application and leaving it with a sales clerk. The store's owner, Jason Hartwick, reviews these applications and approves all new accounts.
>
> Shirley Singleton is responsible for receiving and processing accounts receivable. She opens the mail, records all receipts in the appropriate customer's account, and prepares the deposit slip for the checks received. Mr. Hartwick actually makes the bank deposit in order to keep close tabs on the cash coming into the business. Whenever a customer has a question about his or her account, the customer is referred to Mrs. Singleton, because she is most familiar with the customer accounts.
>
> Are there any internal control weaknesses in the assignment of responsibilities related to accounts receivable? If so, please describe them.

EXERCISES & PROBLEMS FOR REINFORCEMENT:
   Exercise 8-1

OBJECTIVE 3 — Describe the nature of and the accounting for uncollectible receivables.

KEY TERMS:
   Allowance Method   Uncollectible Accounts Expense
   Direct Write-Off Method

SUGGESTED APPROACH

Objective 3 reminds students that a business incurs an expense when customers fail to pay. Three common account titles used to record this expense are (1) uncollectible accounts expense, (2) bad debts expense, and (3) doubtful accounts expense.

When introducing the two methods of recording uncollectible accounts, you will want to stress why the allowance method is the preferred method and when the direct write-off method can be used as an acceptable substitute.

LECTURE AIDS — Allowance and Direct Write-Off Methods

The allowance method of accounting for uncollectible receivables asks the accountant to estimate the accounts that will not be collected and to record this expense before customers actually fail to pay. This method adheres to the matching concept by recognizing the expense of uncollectible accounts in the same period that the sales revenue is recorded. As a result, it is the theoretically correct method.

Under the direct write-off method, the expense of an uncollectible account is recognized when the company decides that further collection efforts on a delinquent account are useless. This method does violate the matching concept, since the sales revenue and the expense related to an uncollectible account may be recognized in different accounting periods. Therefore, it can be used only if it is impossible to estimate a company's bad debts or the amount of bad debts is immaterial.

EXERCISES & PROBLEMS FOR REINFORCEMENT:
    Exercise 8-2

OBJECTIVE 4 — Journalize the entries for the allowance method of accounting for uncollectibles, and estimate uncollectible receivables based on sales and on an analysis of receivables.

KEY TERMS:
    Aging the Receivables
    Contra Asset
    Net Realizable Value

SUGGESTED APPROACH

It is helpful to open your discussion of the allowance method by proving the need to estimate uncollectible accounts. The following lecture notes will assist you in relating the allowance method to the matching concept (introduced in Chapter 3).

The entries required under the allowance method can be presented effectively by using a demonstration problem. When presenting journal entries, point out how each entry affects the net realizable value of accounts receivable reported on the balance sheet.

Demonstration problems to show the estimate of uncollectible accounts based on sales and accounts receivable are also included. These topics can be reviewed at the end of your presentation by asking students to complete a group learning activity.

LECTURE AIDS — Uncollectible Accounts and the Matching Concept

The following explanation may help you present the need to estimate and record uncollectible accounts.

The matching concept dictates that all expenses incurred in making a sale or providing a service are to be recorded in the same accounting period as the revenue from the sale or service. Losses that result from selling to a credit customer who does not pay are an expense. Therefore, when selling to a credit customer who does not pay for his or her merchandise, the sales revenue and the loss must be recorded in the same accounting period.

In most cases, however, you don't find out that an account receivable is uncollectible until several months after the sale is made. Therefore, at the end of each accounting period, you must estimate your losses resulting from sales to customers who will not pay, and record this expense.

The journal entry to record uncollectible accounts:
    Uncollectible Accounts Expense.................. XXX
        Allowance for Doubtful Accounts.......   XXX

Remind students that the Allowance for Doubtful Accounts is a contra asset account. It is used to reduce the value of accounts receivable reported on the balance sheet. Uncollectible Accounts Expense is normally reported as an administrative expense on the income statement.

DEMONSTRATION PROBLEM — Entries for Uncollectible Accounts

Kids-At-Play is a toy store that began operations this year. At the end of its first year of operations, Kids-At-Play had accounts receivable totaling $50,000. The store's manager estimates that $1,500 of those receivables will not be collected.

Journal entry to record uncollectible accounts at the end of the year:
    Uncollectible Accounts Expense.................. 1,500
        Allowance for Doubtful Accounts.......   1,500

The year-end balance sheet will report the following balances under the Current Assets section:
Accounts receivable	$50,000
Less allowance for doubtful accounts	1,500
Net realizable value of accounts receivable	$48,500

Remind your students that $48,500 is the amount of receivables that Kids-At-Play actually expects to collect.

Assume that early in the second year of operations, Kids-At-Play decides to write off as uncollectible a $500 receivable owed by Shirley Smith. Emphasize that once an account has been determined to be uncollectible, it should be written off immediately. This keeps the subsidiary ledger current for references on the credit standing of customers.

Journal entry to write off the uncollectible account:
    Allowance for Doubtful Accounts................ 500
        Accounts Receivable — S. Smith........   500

Many students will want to debit Uncollectible Accounts Expense when writing off an account. Explain that Shirley Smith's $500 account was included in the $1,500 uncollectible accounts expense recorded at the end of last year. Therefore, debiting the expense account now would record the expense twice.

After writing off the uncollectible account, the T accounts and balance sheet would appear as follows:

Accounts Receivable		Allowance for Doubtful Accounts
Bal. 50,000	500 ← Entry to Write-off Account → 500	Bal. 1,500
Bal. 49,500		Bal. 1,000

Balance Sheet Presentation:
    Accounts receivable $49,500
    Less allowance for doubtful accounts   1,000
    Net realizable value of accounts receivable $48,500

Point out that the net realizable value of accounts receivable did not change. Kids-At-Play still expects to collect $48,500 of its receivables. All that has changed is that the company now knows that Shirley Smith, who owes $500, is one credit customer who will probably not pay. There still is approximately $1,000 in bad debts left to be discovered.

Ask your students to record the following journal entry in their notes: Kids-At-Play received notice that another customer, George Jackson, will not be able to pay his $100 account receivable.
    Allowance for Doubtful Accounts................ 100
        Accounts Receivable—G. Jackson.......   100

After demonstrating the write-off of uncollectible accounts under the allowance method, you will need to address how to record collection of an account that has been written off. Assume that after Kids-At-Play has written off George Jackson's account, he does pay the $100 he owes.

Step 1: The account must be reinstated.
    Accounts Receivable—G. Jackson............... 100
        Allowance for Doubtful Accounts.......   100

Step 2: The cash received is recorded.

Cash..	100	
Accounts Receivable—G. Jackson......		100

DEMONSTRATION PROBLEM — Estimating Uncollectible Accounts Based on Sales

When accountants estimate uncollectible accounts based on sales, they determine the amount of expense to be recorded.

Assume that a business sold $750,000 worth of merchandise on credit. The business estimates that 2% of all credit sales are uncollectible.

    Expense to be recorded = $750,000 x 2% = $15,000

The adjusting entry to record uncollectible accounts is:

Uncollectible Accounts Expense.................	15,000	
Allowance for Doubtful Accounts...........		15,000

DEMONSTRATION PROBLEM — Estimating Uncollectible Accounts Based on Receivables

When accountants estimate uncollectible accounts based on receivables, they determine what the balance of the allowance for doubtful accounts should be.

Assume that an accountant determines that $2,000 of the current accounts receivable will probably not be collected. Also assume that the Allowance for Doubtful Accounts currently shows a $200 credit balance.

Allowance for Doubtful Accounts

	200	Current Balance
	1,800	Amount that must be added to the account to get the correct balance
	2,000	Amount that should be in the account based on the estimate of bad debts

The adjusting entry to record uncollectible accounts is:

Uncollectible Accounts Expense.................	1,800	
Allowance for Doubtful Accounts........		1,800

Assume that the accountant determines that $2,000 of the current accounts receivable will probably not be collected and that the Allowance for Doubtful Accounts currently shows a $200 debit balance.

```
                Allowance for Doubtful Accounts
    ─────────────────────────────┬─────────────────────────────
     Current Balance    200      │
                                 │
                                 │   2,200    Amount that must be added to the
                                 │            account to get the correct balance
    ─────────────────────────────┼─────────────────────────────
                                 │   2,000    Amount that should be in the
                                 │            account based on the estimate of bad
                                 │            debts
```

Now, the adjusting entry to record uncollectible accounts is:
    Uncollectible Accounts Expense................   2,200
        Allowance for Doubtful Accounts.......   2,200

Your students may question why the Allowance for Doubtful Accounts would have a debit balance. The following T-account explaining the entries which effect the Allowance will show that a debit balance occurs when the amount of bad debts are underestimated and there are more actual write-offs than expected. In the above example, bad debts from the previous period were underestimated by $200. Since the allowance came up short, the entry to record bad debts in the current period is $2,200—the current expense of $2,000 plus an extra $200 to catch-up for the amount underestimated last accounting period.

```
                Allowance for Doubtful Accounts
    ─────────────────────────────┬─────────────────────────────
         Actual Write-Off        │   Adjusting Entry to
         of Uncollectible        │   Record Estimate of
         Accounts                │   Uncollectible Accounts
                                 │
```

A credit balance occurs when the amount of bad debts are overestimated. The account would have a zero balance if a business perfectly estimated the amount of bad debts.

Remind students that accountants use an aging analysis to determine the amount of accounts receivable that will probably not be collected. You may want to review Exhibits 2 and 3 in the text as an illustration of how to prepare an aging schedule.

Emphasize that the analysis of receivables method emphasizes the accuracy of the expected net realizable value of the receivables reported on the balance sheet. The method of estimating uncollectibles based on sales emphasizes the accuracy of the uncollectible accounts expense reported on the income statement.

GROUP LEARNING ACTIVITY — Entries for Uncollectible Accounts

Transparency 8-3 presents entries for your students to prepare in small groups. This exercise asks them to estimate uncollectible accounts based on receivables, make the adjusting entry for uncollectible accounts, and write off bad accounts. The solution to this exercise is shown on Transparency 8-4.

EXERCISES & PROBLEMS FOR REINFORCEMENT:

Exercise 8-3	Problem 8-1A	Problem 8-1B
Exercise 8-4	Problem 8-2A	Problem 8-2B
Exercise 8-5		
Exercise 8-6		
Exercise 8-7		
Exercise 8-8		
Exercise 8-9		
Exercise 8-11		

OBJECTIVE 5 — Journalize the entries for the direct write-off of uncollectible receivables.

SUGGESTED APPROACH

Compared to the allowance method, the journal entries for the direct write-off method of recording uncollectible accounts are very straight forward. Use the lecture aids that follow to quickly review the basics of the direct write-off method, and ask your students to practice the journal entries using the group learning activity.

LECTURE AIDS — Direct Write-Off of Uncollectible Receivables

Under the direct write-off method, the following occur:

1. Uncollectible Accounts Expense is recorded when an account is written off.
    NOTE: No attempt is made to estimate the amount of uncollectible accounts in advance. An Allowance for Uncollectible Accounts is not established.
2. If an account that has been written off is collected, the account is reinstated before recording the payment received.

Point out that the direct write-off method does not require an adjusting entry at the end of the accounting period.

Remember to emphasize that the direct write-off method is theoretically unacceptable, because the expense resulting from uncollectible accounts may be recognized in a different accounting period from the sales revenue from those accounts. Expenses are not matched against revenues. Therefore, the direct write-off method should be used only when the following two conditions exist:

1. It is impossible to estimate uncollectible accounts with any reasonable accuracy.
2. The amount of uncollectible accounts is immaterial.

GROUP LEARNING ACTIVITY — Direct Write-Off of Uncollectible Receivables

Transparency 8-5 presents five transactions to be recorded under the direct write-off method. Ask your students to work in small groups to journalize these transactions. Transparency 8-6 shows the solution to this exercise.

EXERCISES & PROBLEMS FOR REINFORCEMENT:
    Exercise 8-10   Problem 8-3A   Problem 8-3B
    Exercise 8-12
    Exercise 8-13
    Exercise 8-14

OBJECTIVE 6 — Describe the nature and characteristics of promissory notes.

KEY TERMS:
    Maturity Value
    Promissory Note

SUGGESTED APPROACH

The accounting implications of a promissory note referenced by this learning objective are determining (1) the due date of a note, (2) the interest on a note, and (3) the maturity value of a note. These objectives can be covered effectively by demonstrating each calculation and asking your students to practice the same technique through a group learning activity.

DEMONSTRATION PROBLEM — Determining the Due Date of a Note

To determine the due date of a note, start with the number of days in the term of the note. Next, subtract the number of days in each month that pass until you reach 30 or less. That number represents the due date of the note.

For example, assume that a 120-day note is signed on March 11. The due date of that note is calculated as follows:

Term of the note		120	
Days that pass in March:			
Number of days in March	31		
Date of the note	11	20	
Number of days left		100	
Days that pass in April		30	
Number of days left		70	
Days that pass in May		31	
Number of days left		39	
Days that pass in June		30	
Number of days left		9	9 < 31; therefore, the due date is July 9

Usually, the only aspect of this calculation that troubles students is determining the number of days that pass in the month the note is signed. Remind students that interest is not charged on the date the note is signed. Therefore, you should begin counting on the day after the date on the note to determine the due date.

For example, in the preceding problem, the note was signed on March 11. Therefore, count the number of days in the month of March, starting with March 12. Some students will argue that there are 19 days between March 12 and March 31 (31 - 12 = 19 days). However, if you want to begin with March 12, you subtract only the first 11 days (31 - 11 = 20 days). If your doubting students don't agree with that argument, tell them to count the days on their fingers, beginning with March 12—that will convince them.

After you convince them that there really are 20 days between March 12 and March 31, your students may ask if it really matters whether you collect the note on July 9 or July 10. Remind them that accepting payment on a note one day late without charging interest or a penalty may set a precedent that will make it difficult to collect a note on time in the future.

DEMONSTRATION PROBLEM — Calculating Interest and Maturity Value of a Note

The formula for calculating interest is as follows:
    Interest = Face Amount (or Principal) x Rate x Time

Because interest rates are stated in annual percentages, the formula must include a time period if a note is outstanding for less than one year. The time period is stated either in terms of months (e.g., 9/12 for 9 months) or days (e.g., 60/360), depending on how the time period on the note is stated. Remind students that 360 days is assumed to be the number of days in a year for all their interest calculations.

To demonstrate this concept, calculate the interest on a $10,000, 120-day, 12% note.
    $10,000 x 12% x 120/360 = $400 interest

The interest on any amount for 60 days at 6% can be determined by moving the decimal point in the principal two places to the left. For example, the interest on $1,500 for 60 days at 6% is $15. This is called the 60-day, 6% method. This method is useful for checking the "reasonableness" of computations when a calculator is used.

You will also need to demonstrate the calculation of maturity value. The maturity value of a note is the amount that is due to be paid on the maturity date. The formula is:
    Maturity Value = Face Amount + Interest

The maturity value on the $10,000, 120-day, 12% note is calculated as follows:
    $10,000 + $400 = $10,400

GROUP LEARNING ACTIVITY — Determining Due date, Interest & Maturity value of a note

Transparency 8-7 provides information on two promissory notes. Divide the class into small groups and ask your students to determine the due date, interest, and maturity value for each. Transparency 8-8 shows the solution to this exercise.

EXERCISES & PROBLEMS FOR REINFORCEMENT:
Exercise 8-15

OBJECTIVE 7 — Journalize the entries for notes receivable transactions.

KEY TERMS:
Dishonored Note Receivable

SUGGESTED APPROACH

You will want to begin coverage of this objective with the entries to record acceptance and collection of notes. A demonstration problem for that purpose follows.

Your students should find the entries to record the acceptance and collection of notes to be relatively simple. Therefore, as an alternative to showing students how to do these entries, you may want to ask them to try the entries on their own. Give the class the transactions and ask them to record the correct journal entries. Ask them to work individually on this assignment. After allowing a couple of minutes to work, write the correct entries on the board. This approach helps develop critical thinking skills. It also sends a subtle message to your students that you don't have to tell them every answer. Transactions for dishonored notes and accruing interest earned on notes will be more difficult for your students. You will probably need to demonstrate those entries.

DEMONSTRATION PROBLEM — Journal Entries for Notes Receivable Transactions

Two reasons for accepting a note from a customer are (1) as a promise of payment on a credit purchase, and (2) to grant a time extension on an amount owed on an open account. In both cases, the customer's note is recorded in a notes receivable account.

Use the following transactions for Joy's TV and Electronics to demonstrate journal entries for your class.

1. June 1: Sold a $2,000 big-screen TV to a customer. The customer was asked to sign a 120-day, 12% note. (Hint: the interest is not recorded until it is earned.)

    June 1 Notes Receivable........................ 2,000
           Sales...........................   2,000

1. Sept. 29: Received payment on the $2,000, 120-day, 12% note.

    Sept. 29 Cash...................................... 2,080
          Notes Receivable................   2,000
          Interest Revenue................   80

2. Oct. 1: Granted a 60-day time extension to S. Greene, who owed $1,000 on account. Ms. Green signed a 60-day, 15% note for the amount owed.

    Oct. 1   Notes Receivable………………………   1,000
                        Accounts Receivable-S. Greene   1,000

3. Nov. 30: Received payment on the $1,000, 60-day, 15% note from S. Greene.
    Nov. 30   Cash…………………………………..   1,025
                      Notes Receivable………………   1,000
                      Interest Revenue……………….   25

4. Dec. 1: Granted a 90-day time extension to J. Smith, who owed $800 on account. Mr. Smith signed a 90-day, 15% note for the amount owed.
    Dec. 1   Notes Receivable……………………….   800
                      Accounts Receivable—J. Smith   800

NOTE: Assume the accounting period ends on December 31. At that time, 30 days of interest have been earned on the note from J. Smith. The matching concept dictates that any interest earned but not received must be recorded through an adjusting entry. Therefore, an adjusting entry would be made to record 30 days of interest on the $800 note.

5. Dec. 31: Record interest earned on the note from J. Smith.
    Dec. 31   Interest Receivable……………………   10
                      Interest Revenue……………….   10

6. Mar 1: Received payment on the $800, 90-day, 15% note from J. Smith.
    Mar. 1   Cash ……………………………………   1,030
                     Notes Receivable………………   1,000
                     Interest Receivable……………   10
                     Interest Revenue………………   20

DEMONSTRATION PROBLEM — Dishonored Note

If the maker of a note fails to pay the note when it is due, the note has been dishonored. The total amount due on the dishonored note is transferred back to the customer's accounts receivable account. This places a record of the dishonored note in the customer's account, making it visible should the customer attempt to purchase additional merchandise on credit.

On October 1, Joy's TV and Electronics accepts a $1,500, 60 day, 10% note from R. Sams as a time extension on an open account. The note is dishonored on its due date, November 30.

Entry to record acceptance of the note on October 1:
    Oct. 1   Notes Receivable………………………   1,500
                      Accounts Receivable—R. Sams   1,500

Entry to record dishonor of the note on November 30:
    Nov. 30   Accounts Receivable—R. Sams………   1,525
                      Notes Receivable……………….   1,500
                      Interest Revenue………………..   25

EXERCISES & PROBLEMS FOR REINFORCEMENT:
- Exercise 8-16   Problem 8-4A   Problem 8-4B
- Exercise 8-17   Problem 8-5A   Problem 8-5B
- Exercise 8-18   Problem 8-6A   Problem 8-6B
- Exercise 8-19
- Exercise 8-20

OBJECTIVE 8 — Prepare the Current Assets presentation of receivables on the balance sheet.

SUGGESTED APPROACH

The group learning activity that follows asks your students to prepare the Current Assets section of a balance sheet. This exercise will review the concepts presented in Chapters 7 and 8.

GROUP LEARNING ACTIVITY – Current Assets on the Balance Sheet

Transparency 8-9 shows information taken from the accounting records of Leder Hardware. Divide your class into small groups and ask them to prepare the Current Assets section of the balance sheet. Emphasize that current assets are normally presented in order of their liquidity on the balance sheet. Transparency 8-10 contains the solution.

EXERCISES & PROBLEMS FOR REINFORCEMENT:
- Exercise 8-21

OBJECTIVE 9 – Compute and interpret the accounts receivable turnover and the number of days' sales in receivables.

KEY TERMS:
Accounts Receivable Turnover

SUGGESTED APPROACH

The ratios to compute accounts receivable turnover and average days' sales in receivables are used to evaluate the efficiency in collecting receivables and managing credit. They provide a method to analyze the accounting data related to receivables. Lecture aids for use in presenting this material follow.

LECTURE AIDS — Financial Ratios Related to Receivables

Accounts receivable turnover measures the efficiency in collecting accounts receivable by comparing a company's average accounts receivable balance to sales. The formula is:

$$\text{Accounts Receivable Turnover} = \frac{\text{Net Sales}}{\text{Average Accounts Receivable}}$$

In effect, this ratio measures how many times during a year a company collects its average outstanding accounts receivable. For example, if a company sold $300 in merchandise during a year and its average accounts receivable balance that year was $100, the company turned over (or collected) its receivables three times ($300/100 = 3). The company sold $100 worth of merchandise and collected its money three times.

The ratio uses average accounts receivable instead of the ending balance of accounts receivable in order to smooth out any seasonal fluctuations in receivables. In determining this average, it is ideal to average accounts receivable at the end of each month for a year. However, in many cases monthly data are not available, so the beginning and end of the year accounts receivable data are averaged.

$$\text{Average Accounts Receivable} = \frac{\text{Beginning Accounts Receivable} + \text{Ending Accounts Receivable}}{2}$$

Number of days' sales in receivables estimates the average time (in days) it takes a company to collect its accounts receivable. This collection time can be compared with the company's standard credit terms to determine whether the credit collection policies are effective in collecting receivables. For example, a number of days' sales in receivables of 45 is not good if the standard credit terms are n/30.

The formula for number of days' sales in receivables is as follows:

$$\text{Number of Days' Sales in Receivables} = \frac{\text{Accts. Receivable Balance, End of Year}}{\text{Average Daily Sales}}$$

where:

$$\text{Average Daily Sales} = \frac{\text{Net Sales}}{365}$$

For example, assume a business sold a total of $839,500 during the current year and its accounts receivable balance at the end of the year was $73,600. The number of days' sales in receivables would be computed as follows:

Average Daily Sales = $2,300 ($839,500/365)
Number of Days' Sales in Receivables = 32 ($73,600/$2,300)

Ask your students to comment on this ratio if the company's standard credit terms ask customers to pay in 30 days.

Assume that same business had $72,000 in accounts receivable on Dec. 31 of the prior year. What was the business' accounts receivable turnover?

Average Accounts Receivable = $72,800 ([$72,000 + $73,600]/2)
Accounts Receivable Turnover = 11.5 ($839,500/72,800)

INTERNET ACTIVITY – Accounts Receivable Turnover

Instruct your students to search the web using "Accounts Receivable Turnover" as their search criteria. At the time this manual was written, the following site offered some interesting information:

>www.webpage.ca/unison/samples.html
>>On this site, Unison Accounts Receivable Assistance provides some of its recommendations to a client regarding Accounts Receivable management.

EXERCISES & PROBLEMS FOR REINFORCEMENT:
>Exercise 8-22
>Exercise 8-23
>Exercise 8-24

APPENDIX – Discounting Notes Receivable

KEY TERMS:
>Contingent Liabilities   Proceeds
>Discount   Protest Fee

SUGGESTED APPROACH

The calculations and entries to record the discount of notes receivable are complex. You will probably want to demonstrate these entries for your class, using the following problems. Then give your students the opportunity to practice with a group learning activity.

DEMONSTRATION PROBLEM — Discounting Notes Receivable

If a company needs cash immediately, one alternative to borrowing is to discount a note receivable. When a note is discounted, it is endorsed and transferred to a bank. The bank pays the maturity value of the note less a fee, known as a discount. In reality, the discount is an interest cost the company pays to a bank in order to receive cash for a note before its due date. Before discounting a note, it is a good idea to determine the cash that will be received from the bank, known as the cash proceeds.

For example, assume that a $2,400, 120-day, 14% note dated March 2 is discounted on April 1 at a rate of 12%. Use the following steps to determine the cash proceeds received from discounting the note.

>Step 1: Determine the interest on the note.
>>Interest = $2,400 x 14% x 120/360 = $112

>Step 2: Determine the maturity value of the note.
>>Maturity Value = $2,400 + $112 = $2,512

Step 3: Determine the discount the bank will charge.

Because 30 days have passed since the note was signed, 90 days remain until the note matures. Therefore, the bank will have to wait 90 days to receive the cash from the note's maker. As a result, the bank will charge the payee interest on the note's maturity value for 90 days.

    Discount = Maturity Value x Discount Rate x Time
    Discount = $2,512 x 12% x 90/360 = $75.36

Step 4: Calculate the cash proceeds.
    Cash Proceeds = Maturity Value - Discount
    Cash Proceeds = $2,512 - $75.36 = $2,436.64

Because the cash proceeds is the actual cash received, it must be entered into the accounting records. The note, which has been transferred to the bank, must be removed from the accounting records. The entry to accomplish this is as follows:

Apr. 1	Cash	2,436.64	
	Notes Receivable		2,400.00
	Interest Revenue		36.64

The interest revenue is the difference between the interest revenue earned on the note and the interest expense (discount) paid to the bank.

Interest earned on the $2,400 note	
(120 days at 14%)	$112.00
Less: Discount paid to the bank	75.36
Interest revenue	$ 36.64

Emphasize that if the discount paid to the bank had been larger than the interest earned on the note, the journal entry on April 1 would have shown an entry to Interest Expense.

GROUP LEARNING ACTIVITY — Discounting Notes Receivable

Transparency 8-11 is a problem that may be assigned as a group learning activity. Divide the class into small groups and ask your students to calculate the cash proceeds from discounting the note and prepare the journal entry to record this event. Transparency 8-12 shows the solution to this problem.

DEMONSTRATION PROBLEM — Dishonor of a Discounted Note

If a note that has been discounted at a bank is dishonored by the note's maker, the company that discounted the note is required to pay the bank. The total amount owed on the note, plus any protest fee charged by the bank, is recorded in the customer's accounts receivable account as a record of the default.

On June 17, Joy's TV and Electronics discounted a $3,000, 90-day, 10% note from NTP Co., dated May 18, at 12%. Cash proceeds of $3,013.50 were received. NTP Co. dishonored the note on August 16. Joy's TV and Electronics paid the full maturity value of the note, $3,075, plus a $15 protest fee.

Entry to record discounting the note on June 17:

June 17	Cash..........................	3,013.50	
	Notes Receivable		3,000.00
	Interest Revenue		13.50

Entry to record dishonor of the note by its maker on August 16 (Maturity Value = $3075; Maturity Value + Protest Fee = $3,090):

Aug. 16	Accounts Receivable—NTP Co.	3,090	
	Cash........................		3,090

EXERCISES & PROBLEMS FOR REINFORCEMENT:
    Exercise 8-25
    Exercise 8-26

Transparency Master 8-1

INTERNAL CONTROLS—RECEIVABLES
Separation of Duties

The following tasks should be separated (performed by two different people):

Task	Reason
1. Accounting for receivables and collecting receivables.	1. The accountant could steal cash collected from customers and hide the theft by modifying the accounting records.
2. Accounting for receivables and granting credit.	2. The accountant might refrain from writing off uncollectible accounts because that might point to poor judgment in granting credit.
3. Granting credit and sales.	3. A salesperson might overlook poor credit risks in an eagerness to get a sale (and commission).
4. Accounting for the accounts receivable subsidiary ledger and the general ledger.	4. Employees would be unable to check for errors by comparing the total of the customer accounts in the subsidiary ledger to the balance of accounts receivable in the general ledger.

In summary, the operations of selling, credit approval, collection of accounts receivable, and accounting for accounts receivable should be performed by different people.

WRITING EXERCISE

Hartwick's of New England is a small custom clothier, specializing in men's and women's career apparel. A customer may apply for an account at Hartwick's by filling out a brief credit application and leaving it with a sales clerk. The store's owner, Jason Hartwick, reviews these applications and approves all new accounts.

Shirley Singleton is responsible for receiving and processing accounts receivable. She opens the mail, records all receipts in the appropriate customer's account, and prepares the deposit slip for the checks received. Mr. Hartwick actually makes the bank deposit in order to keep close tabs on the cash coming into the business. Whenever a customer has a question about his or her account, the customer is referred to Mrs. Singleton, because she is most familiar with the customer accounts.

Are there any internal control weaknesses in the assignment of responsibilities related to accounts receivable? If so, please describe them.

Transparency Master 8-3

JOURNAL ENTRIES FOR UNCOLLECTIBLE ACCOUNTS— ALLOWANCE METHOD

Blocker Company estimates its uncollectible accounts based on an analysis of receivables. On December 31, a junior accountant prepared the following aging schedule for the company's $88,000 in outstanding receivables.

Age Interval	Amount	%	Estimated Uncollectible Accounts Amount
Not due	$58,650	2%	$1,173
1–30 days past due	13,220	4%	529
31–60 days past due	8,930	20%	1,786
61–90 days past due	4,000	30%	1,200
Over 90 days past due	3,200	50%	1,600
	$88,000		$6,288

The Allowance for Doubtful Accounts currently has a $210 debit balance.

1. Prepare the adjusting entry to record the company's estimate of uncollectible accounts.
2. Prepare the journal entry to write off the following accounts:
   - T. Donaldson .... $ 700
   - J. Kyle 450
   - D. Mize 1,000
3. Prepare the journal entry to record receipt of the $450 owed by J. Kyle.
4. Write an answer to the following question: What circumstances would cause the Allowance for Doubtful Accounts to have a debit balance prior to adjustment?

Transparency Master 8-4

JOURNAL ENTRIES FOR UNCOLLECTIBLE ACCOUNTS— ALLOWANCE METHOD

Solution

1. Prepare the adjusting entry to record the company's estimate of uncollectible accounts.

Uncollectible Accounts Expense	6,498	
Allowance for Doubtful Accounts		6,498

2. Prepare the journal entry to write off the following accounts: T. Donaldson, $700; J. Kyle, $450; D. Mize, $1,000

Allowance for Doubtful Accounts	2,150	
Accounts Receivable—T. Donaldson		700
Accounts Receivable—J. Kyle		450
Accounts Receivable—D. Mize		1,000

3. Prepare the journal entry to record receipt of the $450 owed by J. Kyle.

Accounts Receivable—J. Kyle	450	
Allowance for Doubtful Accounts		450
Cash	450	
Accounts Receivable—J. Kyle		450

4. Write an answer to the following question: What circumstances would cause the Allowance for Doubtful Accounts to have a debit balance prior to adjustment?

   The actual amount of uncollectible accounts written off in the prior accounting period was greater than the estimate used to record the adjusting entry for bad debts.

Transparency Master 8-5

JOURNAL ENTRIES FOR UNCOLLECTIBLE ACCOUNTS—DIRECT WRITE-OFF METHOD

1. Richard Ellis purchased $500 in merchandise on account, terms n/30.

2. After 6 months, the Richard Ellis account was written off as uncollectible.

3. David Sans purchased $280 worth of merchandise on account, terms n/30.

4. Received notice that David Sans had filed for bankruptcy; therefore, his account was written off.

5. One year later, received $280 from David Sans as payment on his account.

Transparency Master 8-6

JOURNAL ENTRIES FOR UNCOLLECTIBLE ACCOUNTS—DIRECT WRITE-OFF METHOD

Solution

1. Richard Ellis purchased $500 in merchandise on account, terms n/30.
   Accounts Receivable—R. Ellis 500
      Sales 500

2. After 6 months, the Richard Ellis account was written off as uncollectible.
   Uncollectible Accounts Expense 500
      Accounts Receivable—R. Ellis 500

3. David Sans purchased $280 worth of merchandise on account, terms n/30.
   Accounts Receivable—D. Sans 280
      Sales 280

4. Received notice that David Sans had filed for bankruptcy; therefore, his account was written off.
   Uncollectible Accounts Expense 280
      Accounts Receivable—D. Sans 280

5. One year later, received $280 from David Sans as payment on his account.
   Accounts Receivable—D. Sans 280
      Uncollectible Accounts Expense 280
   Cash 280
      Accounts Receivable—D. Sans 280

Transparency Master 8-7

PROMISSORY NOTES

Calculate the due date, interest, and maturity value for these promissory notes.

Note #1: $5,000, 90-day, 8% promissory note dated September 28

Note #2: $25,000, 180-day, 11% promissory note dated April 2

Transparency Master 8-8

PROMISSORY NOTES
Solution

Note #1: $5,000, 90-day, 8% promissory note dated September 28
Due Date:

Term of the note		90
Days that pass in September:		
Number of days in Sept.	30	
Date on note	28	2
Number of days left		88
Days that pass in October		31
Number of days left		57
Days that pass in November		30
Number of days left		27

Due date is December 27

    Interest: $5,000 × 8% × 90/360 = **$100**
    Maturity Value: $5,000 + $100 = **$5,100**

Note #2: $25,000, 180-day, 11% promissory note dated April 2
Due Date:

Term of the note		180
Days that pass in April:		
Number of days in April.	30	
Date on note	2	28
Number of days left		152
Days that pass in May		31
Number of days left		121
Days that pass in June		30
Number of days left		91
Days that pass in July		31
Number of days left		60
Days that pass in August		31
Number of days left		29

Due date is September 29

    Interest: $25,000 × 11% × 180/360 = **$1,375**
    Maturity Value: $25,000 + $1,375 = **$26,375**

BALANCE SHEET—LEDER HARDWARE

The following information was taken from the accounting records of Leder Hardware on December 31. Prepare the Current Assets section of Leder's balance sheet as of December 31.

1. Leder Hardware has $42,000 in cash in its bank accounts. The company is required to keep a minimum of $10,000 cash in its checking account as a compensating balance on a line of credit.

2. Ledger Hardware has invested $7,000 in a money market fund.

3. Leder Hardware currently has notes receivable totaling $28,000. The company's accounts receivable total $85,000; 2% of that amount will probably not be collected.

4. A total of $700 interest has accrued on notes that have not been collected.

5. Leder Hardware has $110,000 in inventory.

6. Leder Hardware owns office and store equipment costing $78,000.

Leder Hardware
Partial Balance Sheet
December 31, 20–

Current Assets:

Cash and cash equivalents		$ 49,000*
Notes receivable		28,000
Accounts receivable................	$85,000	
Less allowance for doubtful accounts	1,700	83,300
Interest Receivable...................		700
Inventory		110,000
Total current assets		$271,000

*The $10,000 compensating balance requirement must be disclosed in the notes to the financial statements.

DISCOUNTING A NOTE RECEIVABLE

Joy's TV and Electronics had a $5,000, 90-day, 8% note dated September 14. This note was discounted at 12% on September 24.

1. Calculate the cash proceeds from discounting the note.

2. Prepare the journal entry to record this event.

Transparency Master 8-12

DISCOUNTING A NOTE RECEIVABLE

Solution

Discount a $5,000, 90-day, 8% note dated September 14 at 12% on September 24.

1. Calculate the cash proceeds from discounting the note.
   Step 1: Determine the interest on the note.
   Interest = $5,000 × 8% × 90/360 = $100
   Step 2: Determine the maturity value of the note.
   Maturity Value = $5,000 + $100 = $5,100
   Step 3: Determine the discount the bank will charge.
   Because 10 days have passed since the note was signed, there are 80 days in the discount period.
   Discount = Maturity Value × Discount Rate × Time
   Discount = $5,100 × 12% × 80/360 = $136
   Step 4: Calculate the cash proceeds.
   Cash Proceeds = Maturity Value – Discount
   Cash Proceeds = $5,100 – $136 = $4,964

2. Prepare the journal entry to record this event.
   Sept. 24 Cash 4,964
              Interest Expense 36
                 Notes Receivable................................... 5,000

The interest expense is the difference between the interest income earned on the note and the interest expense (discount) paid to the bank.

Interest earned on the $5,000 note (90 days at 8%)...	$100
Less: Discount paid to the bank..............	136
Interest expense..	$ 36

Chapter 9
Inventories

OPENING COMMENTS

Chapter 9 comprehensively covers the topic of inventories, including the effects of inventory errors, internal controls, inventory costing methods, lower-of-cost-or-market adjustments, and estimating inventory.

The inventory costing methods are presented both for the perpetual and periodic inventory systems. Since Chapter 6, "Accounting for Merchandising Businesses," emphasized the perpetual inventory system, you will need to treat this chapter as if it were your students' first significant exposure to the periodic inventory system.

After studying the chapter, your students should be able to:

1. Summarize and provide examples of internal control procedures that apply to inventories.
2. Describe the effect of inventory errors on the financial statements.
3. Describe three inventory cost flow assumptions and how they impact the income statement and balance sheet.
4. Compute the cost of inventory under the perpetual inventory system, using the following costing methods: first-in, first-out; last-in, first-out; and average cost.
5. Compute the cost of inventory under the periodic inventory system, using the following costing methods: first-in, first-out; last-in, first-out; and average cost.
6. Compare and contrast the use of the three inventory costing methods.
7. Compute the proper valuation of inventory at other than cost, using the lower-of-cost-or-market and net realizable value concepts.
8. Prepare a balance sheet presentation of merchandise inventory.
9. Estimate the cost of inventory, using the retail method and the gross profit method.
10. Compute and interpret the inventory turnover ratio and the number of days' sales in inventory.

OBJECTIVE 1 — Summarize and provide examples of internal control procedures that apply to inventories.

KEY TERMS:
    Inventory
    Inventory Ledger
    Physical Inventory

SUGGESTED APPROACH

Internal controls for inventory exist to (1) protect inventory from theft and damage and (2) ensure that inventory is reported accurately in the financial statements. Ask your students to give examples of how retail stores safeguard inventories. Examples might include cameras, locked show cases, and inventory control tags. Ask your students to identify whether each control mentioned is a preventive or detective control. The group activity below will facilitate further discussion of inventory controls.

This objective also covers the procedures for taking a physical inventory. To stimulate interest in this topic, ask your class for real-world examples of how a physical inventory is taken, using the class discussion ideas that follow. As part of this discussion, be sure to remind students of the special attention that must be devoted to merchandise in transit and on consignment to ensure that all valid inventory items are counted.

GROUP LEARNING ACTIVITY — Internal Controls over Inventory

Transparency 9-1 presents a case of poor internal controls over inventory. Divide the class into small groups. Ask your students to read that case, identify the control problems, and suggest how to correct the inappropriate inventory procedures.

CLASS DISCUSSION — Procedures for a Physical Inventory Count

Ask your students to indicate, by a show of hands, whether they have participated in taking a physical inventory count. Next, ask who has participated in an inventory count recently. Call on one or two students to describe the procedures that were used during the inventory count. This will supplement the procedures described in the text with additional, real-world examples. If you have participated in a physical inventory count, you may also want to describe the procedures used.

The following question can be used to stimulate further class discussion: Should warehouse employees be members of the inventory count team? Point out that a warehouse employee could steal inventory and cover up the theft by inflating the physical inventory count if he/she were on the count team.

LECTURE AIDS — Items Included in Ending Inventory

Remind students that all merchandise owned by the business on the physical inventory date should be included in the inventory amount shown on the financial statements. Transparency 9-2 outlines the items included in inventory.

EXERCISES & PROBLEMS FOR REINFORCEMENT:
    Exercise 9-1
    Exercise 9-2
    Exercise 9-3

OBJECTIVE 2 – Describe the effect of inventory errors on the financial statements.

SUGGESTED APPROACH

Objective 2 explains how errors in the physical inventory count effect a company's financial statements. A group learning activity that asks students to analyze inventory errors follows.

LECTURE AIDS — Inventory Errors

Transparency 9-3 emphasizes the importance of accurately counting a business' ending inventory by listing the financial statement items affected by physical inventory errors. In addition to knowing which items are affected, students should be able to analyze whether a particular inventory error will overstate or understate financial statement items.

The physical inventory count is the basis for recording the adjusting entry for inventory shrinkage. Remind students that the adjusting entry to reduce merchandise inventory for shrinkage is:

>   Cost of Merchandise Sold………   XXX
>   Merchandise Inventory…   XXX

If the physical inventory count is understated, too much shrinkage will be recorded. This will understate Merchandise Inventory on the Balance Sheet and overstate Cost of Merchandise Sold on the Income Statement.

If the physical inventory count is overstated, the accountant will not record enough shrinkage. This will overstate Merchandise Inventory on the Balance Sheet and understate Cost of Merchandise Sold.

Remind students that an incorrect value for Cost of Merchandise Sold effects a company's reported net income. If net income is not computed accurately, this incorrect amount will be closed into the owner's capital account, causing owner's equity to be misstated.

The following group learning activity will allow students to analyze the financial effect of inventory errors on the income statement and the balance sheet.

GROUP LEARNING ACTIVITY — Inventory Errors

Transparency 9-4 presents information concerning a business that has made an error in counting its ending inventory. Divide the class into small groups and ask them to determine the effect of this error. Corrected financial statements are shown on Transparency 9-5.

WRITING EXERCISE — Effect of Misstatements of Inventory on Financial Statements

Ask your students to write a response to the following question (also on Transparency 9-6):

> Why is it important to be accurate when taking a physical inventory count?

EXERCISES & PROBLEMS FOR REINFORCEMENT:
    Exercise 9-4
    Exercise 9-5
    Exercise 9-6

OBJECTIVE 3 – Describe three inventory cost flow assumptions and how they impact the income statement and balance sheet.

KEY TERMS:
    Average Cost Method
    First-in, First-out (FIFO) Method
    Last-in, First-out (LIFO) Method

SUGGESTED APPROACH

This objective opens with a quick description of the specific identification inventory method and an explanation of why this method is impractical for most businesses. Next, the text illustrates the FIFO, LIFO, and average cost methods. Use the lecture aids below to supplement the text's presentation.

LECTURE AIDS — Inventory Costing Methods

Remind your class that inventory is shown on the balance sheet at an amount equal to what the merchandise cost. Next, establish the need for inventory costing methods by presenting the following scenario to your class (Transparency 9-7).

> At the beginning of the current year, John Bach opened a music store that sells compact disks of classical music. The store is called Strictly Classical. During the year, Strictly Classical purchased 10,000 compact disks for $7 each. At the end of the year, a physical inventory count revealed that 1,000 of those disks were on hand. What value should be shown for ending inventory on the year-end balance sheet? (Answer: 1,000 x $7 = $7,000).

Next, pose the following question: How realistic is it that every item of merchandise that a business purchases during a year has the same cost?

Transparency 9-8 presents the following scenario:

> Assume instead that Strictly Classical purchased 10,000 compact disks as follows:

Date	No. of Disks Purchased	Cost/Unit	Total Cost
Jan. 1	800	$7.00	$ 5,600
Mar. 8	2,200	$7.50	16,500
June 23	4,000	$7.25	29,000
Sept.15	3,000	$7.40	22,200
Total	10,000		$73,300

If the year-end inventory reveals 1,000 disks on hand, what is the inventory value on the balance sheet? What is the store's cost of merchandise sold?

Explain that you must make an assumption about which disks are the ones in ending inventory and which disks were sold. At this point, introduce the three commonly used inventory methods. Remind your students that the name of the LIFO and FIFO methods describes which inventory items have been sold.

Method	Items Sold (**out** the door)	Items in Ending Inventory
First-in, first-**out**	First items purchased	Last items purchased
Last-in, first-**out**	Last items purchased	First items purchased

Some students find it helpful to attach a mental picture to each inventory method by associating it with a product. The following are examples of products that would be sold in a FIFO, LIFO, or average cost flow.

FIFO — Milk (or any perishable item). When shelves are restocked, the "older" milk is moved to the front, and the "newer" milk is placed in back to encourage customers to buy the older milk first.

LIFO — Packages of nails or screws at a hardware store. When shelves are restocked, the older packages are slid to the back of the shelf or rack and the newer packages placed in front. Customers buy the newest hardware first.

Average — Gasoline. When new gasoline is delivered to a gas station, it is dumped into the tank with any old gas that has not been sold. Therefore, the customer is buying a mixture of old and new gas.

If you do mention these examples, point out that a company's inventory costing method does not have to match how the products are actually sold.

OBJECTIVE 4 — Compute the cost of inventory under the perpetual inventory system, using the following costing methods: first-in, first-out; last-in, first-out; and average cost.

SUGGESTED APPROACH

You can use this objective to review the journal entries under a perpetual inventory system as well as teach the inventory costing methods. It is helpful to present a simple demonstration of each method. Note that the average cost method is not illustrated in the text; however, an example of this method is included below if you wish to illustrate the moving average concept.

DEMONSTRATION PROBLEM — Perpetual Inventory Methods

Obtain two sheets each of blue, green, and yellow 8-1/2" x 11" paper (or any three different colors available). Divide each sheet in half. These half sheets of paper will serve as inventory items, with each color representing a different cost. On each half sheet of blue paper, write $.10. Write $.12 on each green sheet and $.15 on each yellow sheet.

Example #1: FIFO Inventory

Inform your students that they will be recording journal entries for a merchandiser who uses a perpetual inventory system and the FIFO inventory method. For each transaction you cover, they will be given approximately one minute to record the entry. After that time, you will show them the correct entry (using Transparency 9-9). Ask your students to assume that all inventory items are sold for $1.00 each—price increases cannot be passed on to the consumer. After checking each entry, it is helpful to compute the current inventory balance for your students.

Use tape to attach the four $.10 inventory items (blue sheets) to the board. Tell your students that these items were purchased on account on April 1. Ask them to record the journal entry for this purchase. At this point, the inventory on hand is valued at $0.40 (4 x $0.10).

Tell your students that a customer purchased two items for cash on April 3. Ask them to record this sale. Remind them that the perpetual inventory system requires two entries for a sales transaction: one to record sales revenue and one to record the cost of merchandise sold. After the students have completed their entries, remove two of the blue sheets from the board. At this point, the inventory on hand is valued at $0.20 (2 x $0.10).

Next, tape the four $.12 inventory items (green sheets) to the board. These items were purchased on account on April 6. Ask your students to record the purchase. At this point, the inventory on hand is valued at $0.68 [(2 x $0.10) + (4 x $0.12)].

Tell your students that a customer purchased three items for cash on April 12. Ask them to record this sale. Remind them that the company uses the FIFO costing method. After the students have completed their entries, remove the two blue sheets and one green sheet from the board. At this point, the inventory on hand is valued at $0.36 (3 x $0.12).

Tape the four $.15 inventory items (yellow sheets) to the board. These items were purchased on account on April 20. Ask your students to record the purchase. At this point, the inventory on hand is valued at $0.96 [(3 x $0.12) + (4 x $0.15)].

Inform your students that a customer purchased five items for cash on April 27. Ask them to record this sale. After they have completed their entries, remove three green sheets and two yellow sheets from the board.

Ask your students to compute the ending inventory value at the end of April. The correct answer is $0.30 (2 units at $0.15 each).

Example #2: LIFO Inventory

Repeat the previous transactions. Ask your students to record them using the LIFO method. The correct journal entries are listed on Transparency 9-10. The correct ending inventory value is $0.20 (2 units at $0.10 each).

Example #3: Average Cost Inventory

Repeat the same transactions a third time using the average cost method. You will need to remind students that a new average cost must be computed after each purchase. To reinforce this, ask them to compute the new average cost after each purchase is recorded. The correct journal entries are listed on Transparency 9-11. The correct ending inventory value is $0.27 (2 units at $0.134 each).

These simple demonstrations point out how time consuming and costly it would be to maintain a perpetual inventory system without the use of computers. You can also emphasize that, in practice, perpetual inventories are often maintained only in units and then converted to dollars for preparing financial statements at the end of the period.

EXERCISES & PROBLEMS FOR REINFORCEMENT:
    Exercise 9-7   Problem 9-1A   Problem 9-1B
    Exercise 9-8   Problem 9-2A   Problem 9-2B
    Exercise 9-9
    Exercise 9-10
    Exercise 9-11

OBJECTIVE 5 — Compute the cost of inventory under the periodic inventory system, using the following costing methods: first-in, first-out; last-in, first-out; and average cost.

SUGGESTED APPROACH

Although your students were introduced to the periodic inventory system in Chapter 6, you will find it worthwhile to review some basic information. Use transparency 9-12 to overview the accounting procedures in a periodic inventory system.

Chapter 9 does not illustrate the calculation of Cost of Merchandise Purchased or Cost of Merchandise Sold in a periodic inventory system; those calculations were presented in Chapter 6. However, you may want to reinforce those calculations since they are relevant in the gross profit and retail methods of estimating inventory.

After an introduction to the periodic inventory system, ask your students to practice calculating ending inventory and cost of merchandise sold under the LIFO, FIFO, and average cost methods with a group learning activity.

LECTURE AIDS – Cost of Merchandise Sold

In Chapter 6, the lecture aids gave you a "twinkies" story to present the calculation of Cost of Merchandise Sold. Here is a shorter version of this silly story for a quick review.

> Assume your favorite snack to eat while studying are Twinkies. One evening, before a night of heavy studying for an accounting test, you notice that you only have 3 Twinkies in your cupboard. Knowing this will never get you through your intense study session, you go to the grocery and buy a box of 12 Twinkies. The next morning, you wonder how many Twinkies you ate. Since you didn't track of the number of Twinkies consumed as you were eating them, how could you determine the number eaten? Answer: count the Twinkies left. If you only have 5 Twinkies left, you ate 10. (3 + 12 = 15 – 5 =10)

This is the same methodology a merchandiser uses to calculate the cost of merchandise sold.

      Beginning Inventory
+   <u>Cost of Merchandise Purchased</u>
      Merchandise Available for Sale
-   <u>Ending Inventory</u>
      Cost of Merchandise Sold

DEMONSTRATION PROBLEM – Cost of Merchandise Sold

To reinforce this concept, you may want to ask your students to calculate a company's cost of merchandise sold using the following information:

> Beginning Inventory = $5,000
> Purchases = $120,000
> Ending Inventory = $10,000
> Cost of Merchandise Sold = ?   (Answer: $115,000)

Next, give the class the following additional information:

> The same company had purchase returns of $2,000, purchases discounts of $3,500, and transportation costs of $1,500. What did it cost the company to purchase its merchandise, and what is the cost of merchandise sold?
>
> (Answers: Cost of Merchandise Purchases = $116,000
>   Cost of Merchandise Sold = $111,000)

Use Transparency 9-13 to illustrate that cost of merchandise purchased is simply one part of calculating cost of merchandise sold. This amount is also called "net purchases."

GROUP LEARNING ACTIVITY — Inventory Costing Methods

Display the information on inventory purchases made by Strictly Classical (Transparency 9-8). Divide the class into small groups and ask them to determine the value of Strictly Classical's ending inventory and cost of merchandise sold under each of the three inventory costing methods. Emphasize that assumptions concerning which items were sold are not made until the end of the year. Transparency 9-14 provides the solution to this exercise.

EXERCISES & PROBLEMS FOR REINFORCEMENT:
    Exercise 9-12   Problem 9-3A   Problem 9-3B
    Exercise 9-13

OBJECTIVE 6 — Compare and contrast the use of the three inventory costing methods.

SUGGESTED APPROACH

Transparency 9-15 presents information to allow you to compare the advantages and disadvantages of the three inventory methods. Point out that if all units of inventory on hand during a year had the same cost, all three inventory methods would yield the same results.

EXERCISES & PROBLEMS FOR REINFORCEMENT:
    Exercise 9-14

OBJECTIVE 7 — Compute the proper valuation of inventory at other than cost, using the lower-of-cost-or-market and net realizable value concepts.

KEY TERMS:
    Lower-of-Cost-or-Market (LCM) Method
    Net Realizable Value

SUGGESTED APPROACH

Inventory is carried on the financial statements at its cost unless one of the following conditions has occurred:

1. If the current cost to purchase inventory items is lower than the cost recorded in the accounting records, the value of the inventory is reduced to the current replacement cost ("market"). This is the lower-of-cost-or-market principle. The market cost is determined based on normal quantities purchased.
2. If inventory items have been damaged or have become obsolete such that they cannot be sold at normal prices, the value of these items is reduced to their net realizable value. Net realizable value is the estimated selling price less any costs to sell or dispose of the items.

Use the following group learning activity to review these concepts.

GROUP LEARNING ACTIVITY — Valuing Inventory at Other than Cost

Transparency 9-16 presents three inventory items. Divide your class into small groups and ask them to determine the value that each item should carry.

The solutions to this exercise are as follows:

1. DVD Players: 100 units x $125 = $12,500
2. CD Players: 50 units x $75 = $3,750
3. Cassette Players: 25 units x ($50 - $5 - $3.50) = $1,037.50

WRITING EXERCISE — Valuing Inventory at Other than Cost

Ask your students to practice their critical thinking skills by writing a response to the following question (also on Transparency 9-17):

> In Chapter 1, you learned that the cost concept requires accountants to record all items purchased at their cost. In Chapter 9, you have learned that inventory may be written down to its current replacement cost or its net realizable value if these amounts are lower than original cost. Why do you think the accounting profession has decided to violate the cost concept and reduce the value of inventory in these circumstances?

EXERCISES & PROBLEMS FOR REINFORCEMENT:
    Exercise 9-15   Problem 9-4A   Problem 9-4B

OBJECTIVE 8 — Prepare a balance sheet presentation of merchandise inventory.

SUGGESTED APPROACH

Review the following material with your students:

1. Merchandise inventory is reported in the Current Assets section of the balance sheet.
2. The following information must be stated either in parentheses on the balance sheet or in a footnote to the financial statements:
   a. Inventory cost method (LIFO, FIFO, average cost)
   b. Method of valuing inventory (cost or lower-of-cost-or-market)

Use the following group learning activity to review the Current Assets section of the balance sheet.

GROUP LEARNING ACTIVITY — Current Assets Section of the Balance Sheet

Transparency 9-18 presents information to prepare the Current Assets section of the balance sheet for Bostitch Art Supplies. The exercise reviews the information covered in Chapters 7 - 9. Divide your class into small groups and ask them to complete the balance sheet. Transparency 9-19 contains the solution.

EXERCISES & PROBLEMS FOR REINFORCEMENT:
    Exercise 9-16

OBJECTIVE 9 — Estimate the cost of inventory, using the retail method and the gross profit method.

KEY TERMS:
    Gross Profit Method
    Retail Inventory Method

SUGGESTED APPROACH

Begin by reviewing the reasons that a company may need to estimate its inventory. Reasons for estimating inventory include the following:

1. Determining inventory balances for interim financial statements. Businesses using the periodic inventory system may find it too costly to take a physical inventory each month.
2. Determining inventory lost in a disaster, such as a fire, flood, tornado, hurricane, or earthquake.
3. Determining inventory lost due to theft. In this case, a physical inventory count is compared to the inventory that should be on hand according to estimation techniques.

You will also want to demonstrate the two methods for estimating inventory using the following problems. Because the gross profit method requires fewer steps than the retail method, it is preferable to cover it first.

LECTURE AIDS — Gross Profit Method of Estimating Inventory

The gross profit method is based on the following equation.

      Beginning Inventory
+   Cost of Merchandise Purchased
      Merchandise Available for Sale
−   Cost of Merchandise Sold
      Ending Inventory

If you know the beginning inventory, cost of merchandise purchased, and cost of merchandise sold, you can determine the ending inventory that should be on hand. The problem is this: what if you do not know your cost of merchandise sold? For example, cost of merchandise sold is not tracked under the periodic inventory system. If a fire has destroyed your business, you may no longer have the accounting records which showed your cost of merchandise sold. Explain that you can calculate cost of merchandise sold using the following methodology:

    Sales - Gross Profit on Sales = Cost of Merchandise Sold

GROUP LEARNING ACTIVITY — Gross Profit Method of Estimating Inventory

Transparency 9-20 presents information your students can use in solving a gross profit method problem. Divide the class into small groups and ask them to solve this problem using the previous equations. The solution is shown on Transparency 9-21.

After your students have solved this problem, remind them that the gross profit method works best with companies that have a stable markup on merchandise.

DEMONSTRATION PROBLEM — Retail Method of Estimating Inventory

The retail method can be used successfully by merchandisers who do not use a stable gross profit percentage. One step in the retail method is to determine the markup on merchandise by comparing the cost of inventory items to their retail value.

To use the retail method, a merchandiser must track his or her beginning inventory and all inventory purchases, both at their cost and their retail value.

Example: Malarky Enterprises has the following data for the current year of operations. Use these data to estimate Malarky's ending inventory.

	Cost	Retail Value
Beginning inventory	$15,000	$22,400
Merchandise purchases	52,000	77,600
Sales (at retail prices)		68,000

Solution:

	Cost	Retail Value
Beginning inventory	$15,000	$22,400
Merchandise purchases	52,000	77,600
Merchandise available for sale	$67,000	$100,000

Ratio of cost to retail price = 67%

Sales (at retail prices)	68,000
Ending inventory at retail	$32,000
Ratio of cost to retail price	x 67%
Ending inventory at cost	$21,440

You may also want to point out that retailers often take a physical inventory at retail prices and then use the retail method to convert the inventory to its cost.

EXERCISES & PROBLEMS FOR REINFORCEMENT:
    Exercise 9-17   Problem 9-5A   Problem 9-5B
    Exercise 9-18
    Exercise 9-19

OBJECTIVE 10 – Compute and interpret the inventory turnover ratio and the number of days' sales in inventory.

KEY TERMS:
- Inventory Turnover Ratio
- Number of Days' Sales in Inventory

SUGGESTED APPROACH

The following lecture aids will help you in presenting the inventory ratios to your students. Follow that information with a short demonstration problem.

The textbook compares the inventory turnover and number of days' sales in inventory for SUPERVALU and Zale Corporation. Use this text material to stress that the differences in these two retailers can be clearly seen in their inventory ratios.

LECTURE AIDS — Financial Ratios Related to Inventories

Inventory turnover measures the efficiency in managing inventories by comparing a company's average inventory to the total inventory sold. The formula:

$$\text{Inventory Turnover} = \frac{\text{Cost of Merchandise Sold}}{\text{Average Inventory}}$$

In effect, this ratio measures how many times during a year a company purchased and sold its average inventory balance. For example, if a company usually carries an average of $100 in inventory and its sales were $800 during a year, that company sold (or turned over) its average inventory eight times.

The ratio uses average inventory instead of the ending balance in the inventory account in order to smooth out any seasonal fluctuations in inventory balances. In determining this average, it is ideal to average inventory balances at the end of each month for a year. However, in many cases, monthly data are not available, so the beginning and end of the year inventory amounts are averaged.

$$\text{Average Inventory} = \frac{\text{Beginning Inventory} + \text{Ending Inventory}}{2}$$

The number of days' sales in inventory estimates the time (in days) it takes to acquire, sell, and replace inventory. The formula for the number of days' sales in inventory:

$$\text{Number of Days' Sales in Inventory} = \frac{\text{Inventory, end of year}}{\text{Average Daily Cost of Merchandise Sold}}$$

where:

$$\text{Average Daily Cost of Merchandise Sold} = \frac{\text{Cost of Merchandise Sold}}{365}$$

Point out that business' generally work to reduce the amount of inventory they carry. Holding inventory creates many costs, such as costs to store, insure, and move inventory items. These costs can be dramatically reduced by lowering inventory levels. Just-in-time inventory techniques have been adopted by many businesses to combat the problems of carrying too much inventory. Therefore, increases in the inventory turnover ratio and decreases in the number of days' sales in inventory are usually viewed as favorable trends.

DEMONSTRATION PROBLEM – Inventory Ratios

Use the following data to calculate inventory turnover and number of days' sales in inventory:

Cost of Merchandise Sold	$456,250
Inventory, Beginning of Year	65,000
Inventory, End of Year	67,500

The inventory turnover would be computed as follows:

Average Inventory = $66,250 ([$65,000 + $67,500]/2)
Inventory Turnover = 6.9 ($456,250/$66,250)

The number of days' sales in inventory would be computed as follows:

Average Daily Cost of Merchandise Sold = $1,250 ($456,250/365)
Number of Days' Sales in Inventory = 54 ($67,500/$1,250)

INTERNET ACTIVITY – Inventory Turnover

Instruct your students to search the web using "Inventory Turnover" as their search criteria. At the time this manual was written, the following site offered some interesting information:

www.effectiveinventory.com./article2.html
On this site, Effective Inventory Management, Inc. shares insights on the inventory turnover formula.

EXERCISES & PROBLEMS FOR REINFORCEMENT:
Exercise 9-20
Exercise 9-21

Transparency Master 9-1

INTERNAL CONTROLS— INVENTORY

The City of Milford Parks and Recreation operates three community swimming pools. Each pool has a concession stand that sells candy. Each concession stand is staffed with two workers.

To be eligible for volume discounts, the Parks and Recreation department orders the candy for all three pools. Sandy Wells is responsible for ordering the concession stand goodies. Sandy uses a locked closet down the hall from her office at the Parks and Recreation headquarters to store the candy. She checks the closet periodically, and, when supplies seem low, she orders more.

Whenever a concession stand needs to restock inventory, a worker goes to the Parks and Recreation headquarters to get the needed candy. Because Sandy knows all of the concession workers, she usually just hands the worker the key to the candy closet so the worker can get whatever is needed. Sandy has attached a chart to the closet door to keep track of candy withdrawals. On that chart, each worker records the number of boxes of candy that he or she is taking and the pool it is going to.

By the end of the summer, Sandy becomes worried that someone else has a key to the candy closet. The candy seems to be disappearing quicker than it did at the beginning of the summer. For the last month or so, she hasn't found time to compare the withdrawals on her chart with candy purchases, but something just doesn't seem right.

Requirement: Review the candy inventory procedures and suggest any modifications that might be needed.

Transparency Master 9-2

ITEMS INCLUDED IN INVENTORY

All inventory on hand when the physical inventory is taken

+ Merchandise in transit that was purchased FOB Shipping Point

+ Merchandise in transit that was sold FOB Destination

+ Merchandise on consignment in other locations that is still owned by the company taking the inventory count

− Merchandise included in the inventory on hand that belongs to another company but is being held on consignment

---

Inventory shown on the financial statements

Transparency Master 9-3

EFFECT OF ERRORS IN REPORTING INVENTORY

If ending inventory is reported inaccurately, the following financial statement data are incorrect.

On the income statement:
1. Cost of merchandise sold
2. Gross profit
3. Net income

On the balance sheet:
1. Ending inventory
2. Total current assets
3. Total assets
4. Owner's capital (due to the incorrect net income being added to the capital account)

Transparency Master 9-4

INVENTORY ERRORS

Condensed financial statements for Jackson Company are shown below:

Income Statement:

Sales	$37,000
Cost of merchandise sold	19,000
Gross profit on sales	$18,000
Operating expenses	9,000
Net income	$ 9,000

Balance Sheet:

Assets:	
Current assets	$22,000
Fixed assets	38,000
Total assets	$60,000
Liabilities	$41,000
Owner's equity	19,000
Total liabilities & owner's equity	$60,000

After preparing these financial statements, Jackson discovered that the physical inventory count was incorrect, understating the year's ending inventory by $4,000.

Requirement: Prepare corrected financial statements. Next, determine whether each of the following items were overstated or understated on the original financial statements: (1) cost of merchandise sold, (2) gross profit, (3) net income, (4) current assets, (5) total assets, and (6) owner's equity.

Transparency Master 9-5

INVENTORY ERRORS

Corrected Financial Statements for Jackson Company

Income Statement:

Sales	$37,000
Cost of merchandise sold	15,000
Gross profit on sales	$22,000
Operating expenses	9,000
Net income	$13,000

Balance Sheet:

Assets:

Current assets	$26,000
Fixed assets	38,000
Total assets	$64,000
Liabilities	$41,000
Owner's equity	23,000
Total liabilities & owner's equity	$64,000

WRITING EXERCISE

Why is it important to be accurate when taking a physical inventory count?

Transparency Master 9-7

INVENTORY VALUATION

Strictly Classical

At the beginning of the current year, John Bach opened a music store that sells compact disks of classical music. The store is called Strictly Classical. During the year, Strictly Classical purchased 10,000 compact disks for $7 each. At the end of the year, a physical inventory count revealed that 1,000 of those disks were on hand. What value should be shown for ending inventory on the year-end balance sheet?

Transparency Master 9-8

INVENTORY VALUATION

Strictly Classical

Assume that Strictly Classical purchased 10,000 compact disks as follows:

Date	No. of Disks Purchased	Cost/Unit	Total Cost
Jan. 1	800	$7.00	$ 5,600
Mar. 8	2,200	$7.50	16,500
June 23	4,000	$7.25	29,000
Sept. 15	3,000	$7.40	22,200
Total	10,000		$73,300

If the year-end inventory reveals 1,000 disks on hand, what is the inventory value on the balance sheet?

What is the store's cost of merchandise sold?

Transparency Master 9-9

PERPETUAL INVENTORY SYSTEM FIFO METHOD

JOURNAL

DATE	DESCRIPTION	DEBIT	CREDIT
2000 April 1	Merchandise Inventory	.40	
	Accounts Payable		.40
3	Cash	2.00	
	Sales		2.00
	Cost of Merchandise Sold	.20	
	Merchandise Inventory		.20
6	Merchandise Inventory	.48	
	Accounts Payable		.48
12	Cash	3.00	
	Sales		3.00
	Cost of Merchandise Sold	.32	
	Merchandise Inventory		.32
20	Merchandise Inventory	.60	
	Accounts Payable		.60
27	Cash	5.00	
	Sales		5.00
	Cost of Merchandise Sold	.66	
	Merchandise Inventory		.66

PERPETUAL INVENTORY SYSTEM LIFO METHOD

JOURNAL

DATE	DESCRIPTION	DEBIT	CREDIT
2000			
April 1	Merchandise Inventory	.40	
	Accounts Payable		.40
3	Cash	2.00	
	Sales		2.00
	Cost of Merchandise Sold	.20	
	Merchandise Inventory		.20
6	Merchandise Inventory	.48	
	Accounts Payable		.48
12	Cash	3.00	
	Sales		3.00
	Cost of Merchandise Sold	.36	
	Merchandise Inventory		.36
20	Merchandise Inventory	.60	
	Accounts Payable		.60
27	Cash	5.00	
	Sales		5.00
	Cost of Merchandise Sold	.72	
	Merchandise Inventory		.72

PERPETUAL INVENTORY SYSTEM
AVERAGE COST METHOD
JOURNAL

DATE	DESCRIPTION	DEBIT	CREDIT	
2000 April 1	Merchandise Inventory	.40		Average Cost = .10
	Accounts Payable		.40	
3	Cash	2.00		
	Sales		2.00	
	Cost of Merchandise Sold	.20		Average Cost = .10
	Merchandise Inventory		.20	
6	Merchandise Inventory	.48		2 @ .10 = .20
	Accounts Payable		.48	4 @ .12 = .48
				6 = .68
				Average Cost = .113
12	Cash	3.00		
	Sales		3.00	
	Cost of Merchandise Sold	.34		Average Cost = .113
	Merchandise Inventory		.34	
20	Merchandise Inventory	.60		3 @ .113 = .34
	Accounts Payable		.60	4 @ .15 = .60
				7 = .94
				Average Cost = .134
27	Cash	5.00		
	Sales		5.00	
	Cost of Merchandise Sold	.67		
	Merchandise Inventory		.67	

Transparency Master 9-12

PERIODIC INVENTORY SYSTEM

1. When merchandise inventory is purchased, this purchase is recorded in the accounting records.

2. When merchandise inventory is sold, the sales revenue is recorded in the accounting records. However, the cost of merchandise sold is not recorded and the inventory item sold is not removed from the accounting records.

3. Therefore, the accounting records show how much merchandise inventory has been purchased, but they do not show how much inventory is left on hand.

4. A physical inventory is taken to determine the inventory on hand at the end of the accounting period. At that time, the cost of inventory sold is determined.

Cost of Merchandise Sold

Beginning Inventory
+ Cost of Merchandise Purchased ↔
Merchandise Available for Sale
- Ending Inventory
Cost of Merchandise Sold

> Purchases
> - Purchase Returns & Allowances
> - Purchase Discounts
> Net Purchases
> + Transportation In
> Cost of Merchandise Purchased

Transparency Master 9-14

INVENTORY VALUATION
Strictly Classical
Solution

Method	Ending Inventory	Cost of Merchandise Sold
FIFO	1,000 @ $7.40 = $7,400	800 @ $7.00 = $ 5,600 2,200 @ $7.50 = 16,500 4,000 @ $7.25 = 29,000 2,000 @ $7.40 = 14,800 9,000 = $65,900 OR Merchandise available $73,300 − Ending inventory 7,400 $65,900
LIFO	800 @ $7.00 = $5,600 200 @ $7.50 = 1,500 1,000 $7,100	3,000 @ $7.40 = $22,200 4,000 @ $7.25 = 29,000 2,000 @ $7.50 = 15,000 9,000 $66,200 OR Merchandise available $73,300 − Ending inventory 7,100 $66,200
Average Cost	1,000 @ $7.33* = $7,330	9,000 @ $7.33 = $65,970 OR Merchandise available $73,300 − Ending inventory 7,330 $65,970

*Average Cost per Unit = $\dfrac{\$73{,}300}{10{,}000 \text{ units}}$ = $7.33

266

COMPARISON OF INVENTORY METHODS

Method	Advantages	Disadvantages
FIFO	Ending inventory amount on balance sheet approximates current replacement costs	Creates "illusory profits" during times of high inflation
LIFO	Matches current costs against current revenues on income statement During inflationary periods, reduces income taxes	Ending inventory amount on income statement may be substantially different from current replacement cost
Average Cost	Easy to understand Yields same answer whether prices start at $1 and increase to $2 or start at $2 and decrease to $1	Ending inventory amount on income statement may not represent current replacement cost Lose tax advantage available from LIFO when prices are rising

Transparency Master 9-16

INVENTORY VALUATION

State the total value that should be shown for each of the following inventory items in the accounting records of Johnson Electronics.

1. Johnson owns 100 DVD players that were purchased for $180 each. As a result of technological advances, Johnson's supplier has just reduced the cost to purchase these DVD players to $125 each. Johnson can sell the DVD players for $275 each.

2. Johnson owns 50 CD players that were purchased for $75 each. Johnson had been selling these units for $150 each. However, a new electronics store has just opened that sells the same CD player for $130 each. Even though Johnson's supplier is still charging $75 to purchase the units, the store has been forced to lower its retail price to $130, matching the competition.

3. Johnson has 25 cassette tape players that were purchased for $80 each. Because of a severe decline in the market for cassette players, Johnson must drop the retail price of these units to $50 each. Johnson is also offering a free 4-year extended warranty on each cassette player sold. Johnson's cost for this warranty is $5. The store also pays salesclerks a 7% commission on all units sold.

WRITING EXERCISE

In Chapter 1, you learned that the cost concept of accounting requires accountants to record all items purchased at their cost. In Chapter 9, you have learned that inventory may be written down to its current replacement cost or its net realizable value if these amounts are lower than original cost. Why do you think the accounting profession has decided to violate the cost concept and reduce the value of inventory in these circumstances?

BALANCE SHEET PREPARATION

Bostitch Art Supplies

Use the following information to prepare the Current Assets section of the balance sheet for Bostitch Art Supplies on December 31, 20—. Also list any information that should be disclosed in the footnotes accompanying the financial statements.

1. Bostitch currently has $14,000 in a checking account and $3,000 in a money market account. Bostitch must keep $5,000 in its checking account as a compensating balance on a line of credit.

2. Bostitch has $25,000 in accounts receivable and $6,000 in notes receivable. Bostitch estimates that it will not collect $2,000 of its accounts receivable.

3. Bostitch has inventory that cost $47,000 using LIFO inventory methods. The current cost to replace these inventory items would be $54,000, and the retail selling price is estimated to be $78,000.

Transparency Master 9-19

BALANCE SHEET PREPARATION

Solution

Bostitch Art Supplies
Balance Sheet
December 31, 20—

Current assets:		
Cash and cash equivalents		$ 17,000
Accounts receivable	$25,000	
Less allowance for doubtful accounts.................................	2,000	23,000
Notes receivable...........................		6,000
Inventory		47,000
Total current assets.................		$93,000

Required footnote disclosures:

1. $5,000 in cash must be kept in Bostitch's checking account as a compensating balance on a line of credit.

2. Inventory is valued at cost using the LIFO inventory method.

ESTIMATING INVENTORY—GROSS PROFIT METHOD

Use the following data to estimate Gooding Company's ending inventory.

Beginning inventory	$10,000
Merchandise purchased	60,000
Sales	95,000
Gross profit on sales	40%

ESTIMATING INVENTORY—GROSS PROFIT METHOD

Solution

Beginning inventory		$10,000
Merchandise purchased.....................		60,000
Merchandise available for sale.........		$70,000
Sales..	$95,000	
Less gross profit ($95,000 × 40%).....	38,000	
Cost of merchandise sold..................		57,000
Ending inventory................................		$13,000

Chapter 10
Fixed Assets and Intangible Assets

OPENING COMMENTS

Chapter 10 addresses fixed assets, intangible assets, natural resources, and the accounting issues related to these assets.

After studying the chapter, your students should be able to:

1. Define fixed assets and describe the accounting for their cost.
2. Compute depreciation, using the following methods: straight-line method, units-of-production method, and declining-balance method.
3. Classify fixed asset costs as either capital expenditures or revenue expenditures.
4. Journalize entries for the disposal of fixed assets.
5. Define a lease and summarize the accounting rules related to the leasing of fixed assets.
6. Describe internal controls over fixed assets.
7. Compute depletion and journalize the entry for depletion.
8. Describe the accounting for intangible assets, such as patents, copyrights, and goodwill.
9. Describe how depreciation expense is reported in an income statement, and prepare a balance sheet that includes fixed assets and intangible assets.
10. Compute and interpret the ratio of fixed assets to long-term liabilities.

OBJECTIVE 1 — Define fixed assets and describe the accounting for their cost.

KEY TERMS:
    Depreciation
    Fixed assets

SUGGESTED APPROACH

Review the definition of fixed assets. Ask students to give examples of fixed assets, listing them on the board as they are called out.

LECTURE AIDS — Defining Fixed Assets

Fixed assets are long-term (or relatively permanent) assets that can be used in a business. Emphasize that the word "used" is essential in this definition. As long as the asset is capable of being used, it is considered a fixed asset. Therefore, equipment held as back-up in case regular equipment breaks or there is abnormally high volume is a fixed asset. If an asset is being held for sale or future use, but it is not capable of being used in its current condition (such as undeveloped land), it should be classified as an investment, not a fixed asset.

The costs of acquiring fixed assets can be summarized by the following general rule:

> GENERAL RULE: The cost of acquiring a fixed asset includes all costs necessary to get the asset to its place of use and ready for use.

Exhibit 3 in the text lists examples of costs to be included in the total cost capitalized when recording a fixed asset. After referring your students to this exhibit, use Transparencies 10-1 through 10-4 to review specific cost examples with your class.

Transparency 10-3 will provide an opportunity for you to introduce the concept of land improvements. Emphasize that these expenditures are for improvements to land that are neither as permanent as the land nor directly related to a building.

LECTURE AIDS — Nature of Depreciation

The nature of depreciation was explained in Chapter 3. However, a considerable amount of material has been covered since that explanation. You will probably want to explain the nature of depreciation again to ensure that the class is focused on the correct concept before beginning depreciation calculations. In this review, emphasize once again that accounting is concerned only with allocating the cost of an asset to the periods it is used. Accountants do not attempt to track the market value of an asset.

(As an aside, I once heard the following story concerning a history professor. During his first term as a teacher, he spent two class periods in one of his courses discussing the contributions of Martin Luther. At the end of the second class, a group of students asked him when they were going to cover the "I Have a Dream" speech. It dawned on the professor that the whole time he was discussing Martin Luther, his students were picturing the 20th century black civil rights leader Martin Luther King, Jr. You don't want to allocate a class period to depreciation calculations only to find that your students think they are learning how to determine the decrease in market value of an asset.)

Use the following story (Transparency 10-5) to reinforce the concept of depreciation, which was introduced in Chapter 3.

> Assume you have just accepted a job that requires you to do a lot of driving. Because your current car is on its "last leg," you have decided to purchase an automobile. You estimate that you will drive 20,000 miles each year. Since you don't like to deal with major car repairs, you will trade in the car when it reaches 60,000 miles.
>
> You have found two cars that you are considering. One is a new car, and you can purchase it for $18,000. The other is a late-model used car. The used car has 20,000 miles on it, but it is in excellent condition. The price of this used car is $11,000.
>
> Using the criteria outlined, what would be your depreciation cost per year for each car?
>
> Answer: New Car: $18,000/3 = $6,000
>   Used Car: $11,000/2 = $5,500

Point out that when evaluating major purchases, we sometimes compare the cost of an item to the number of years it will be used. In the previous example, we computed a cost per year to compare the two automobiles.

Accounting also recognizes that whenever a long-term asset is purchased, an implicit cost per year is associated with that asset. A $50,000 machine that will last 5 years costs a company $10,000 per year. And this $10,000 cost must be recognized as an expense on each year's income statement. The process of recording this expense is known as depreciation.

Depreciation is required because physical deterioration and/or obsolescence cause all fixed assets, with the exception of land, to lose their usefulness. Therefore, we must show that a portion of these assets is "used up" each year. This is similar to showing that a portion of a company's supplies may be used up by the end of an accounting period. These concepts can be illustrated as follows:

Supplies
  Recorded as an asset   Transferred to an
  when purchased.   expense account as used.
     Supplies ─────────────▶   Supplies Expense

Fixed assets
Example: Machinery
  Recorded as an asset   Transferred to an
  when purchased.   expense account as used.
     Machinery ─────────────▶   Depreciation Expense

REMINDER: The adjusting entry to reduce supplies credits the supplies account, reducing it directly for the amount of supplies that are physically gone. Since depreciation is only an estimate of the usefulness of a long-term asset that has expired, the asset account is not reduced directly. Rather, a contra-account called Accumulated Depreciation is used to reduce the asset. For example, the adjusting entry to record depreciation on a piece of machinery would be:

  Depreciation Expense—Machinery............... XXX
       Accumulated Depreciation—Machinery   XXX

As a final note, stress that depreciation does not provide cash for replacing assets as they wear out. Depreciation only allocates a past cost to current and future periods. A business must separately budget for the replacement of assets.

INTERNET ACTIVITY – Fixed Assets

Instruct your students to search the web using "Fixed Assets" as their search criteria. This search will bring up many web sites promoting fixed asset software packages. Ask your students to pick a software package and describe its capabilities. Best Software has several fixed asset packages. Information can be found at:
  www.best-software.com/products/FixedAssetSystems/FASSuite/index.asp

EXERCISES & PROBLEMS FOR REINFORCEMENT:
    Exercise 10-1   Problem 10-1A   Problem 10-1B
    Exercise 10-2
    Exercise 10-3
    Exercise 10-4

OBJECTIVE 2 — Compute depreciation, using the following methods: straight-line method, units-of-production method, and declining-balance method.

KEY TERMS:
    Accelerated Depreciation Method   Residual Value
    Book Value   Straight-Line Depreciation Method
    Declining-Balance Depreciation Method   Units-of-Production Depreciation Method

SUGGESTED APPROACH

The three factors used in determining depreciation are a fixed asset's (1) initial cost, (2) useful life, and (3) residual value. Review the formulas for each depreciation method, and give your students an opportunity to apply these formulas using a group learning activity.

LECTURE AIDS — Straight-Line and Units-of-Production Methods

The straight-line depreciation method allocates the cost of an asset evenly over the number of years it is used. The formula to calculate the depreciation expense recorded each year is as follows:

    (Cost - Residual Value)/Number of Years of Useful Life

Remind students that under the straight-line method, the depreciation expense recognized is the same each year.

The units-of-production depreciation method allocates depreciation based on an asset's usage. The life of some assets is more easily measured in units, such as miles or hours used, than in years. The units-of-production depreciation method calculates depreciation per unit of usage. The formula for this calculation is:

    (Cost - Residual Value)/Estimated Life in Units of Usage

Once a depreciation rate per unit is established, the yearly depreciation expense is calculated by multiplying this rate by the number of units consumed in a year. For example, assume that a machine had a units-of-production depreciation rate of $2 per operating hour. That machine was used 20,000 hours the first year. Depreciation for that year would be $40,000 ($2/hour x 20,000 hours). The depreciation expense recorded each year will change, based on the asset's actual usage for each year. The units-of-production method is the only method that considers the amount of usage in determining depreciation.

GROUP LEARNING ACTIVITY — Straight-Line and Units-of-Production Depreciation

Transparency 10-6 presents a depreciation exercise to be worked in small groups. The solution is provided on Transparency 10-7.

LECTURE AIDS — Declining-Balance Method

The formula for declining-balance depreciation is as follows:

> (Cost - Accumulated Depreciation) x Declining Balance Rate
> OR
> Book Value x Declining Balance Rate

The declining-balance rate is twice (or double) the depreciation rate that would be used under the straight-line method. Therefore, to solve a declining-balance depreciation problem, use the following steps:

1. Calculate the rate that would be used under straight-line depreciation.

   Example: A $10,000 machine will be used for 5 years. At that time, the machine's salvage value will be $2,000.

   Straight-line rate = 1/5 or 20%.

   Spreading the cost of the asset evenly over 5 years requires 1/5 of the asset to be depreciated each year.

2. Double the straight-line rate to get the declining-balance rate.

   Declining-balance rate = 20% x 2 = 40%.

3. Use the formula to calculate declining-balance depreciation.

   (Cost - Accumulated Depreciation) x Declining Balance Rate

GROUP LEARNING ACTIVITY — Declining Balance Depreciation

Using Transparency 10-8, ask your students to calculate depreciation under the declining-balance method.

Transparency 10-9 contains the solution to this problem. When reviewing the solution, be sure to point out the depreciation calculation for the last year of the asset's life under the declining-balance method. In the last year, simply take whatever depreciation is needed to reduce the book value of the asset to residual value. Because the residual value of the asset is not subtracted out in the depreciation formula, the formula may cause you to over-depreciate (or under-depreciate) the asset in its final year.

LECTURE AIDS — Comparing Depreciation Methods

Point out that the declining-balance method is called an accelerated depreciation method since the depreciation expense is highest in the first year of the asset's life and gradually declines.

The benefits of accelerated depreciation are:

1. Decreasing depreciation charges are matched against increasing repair and maintenance charges.
2. Higher depreciation charges drive net income down in the early years of an asset's life. As a result, accelerated depreciation methods are favored for tax purposes.

LECTURE AIDS — Tax Depreciation

Stress that assets are depreciated for tax purposes using methods prescribed by the Internal Revenue Service (IRS). Therefore, a company may be recording different depreciation for tax and financial accounting purposes.

Assets acquired after 1986 are depreciated using the Modified Accelerated Cost Recovery System (MACRS). MACRS depreciates assets using the declining-balance method at twice the straight-line rate. The table on text page 403 shows the MACRS percentages for 5-year-class assets. Remind students that residual value is ignored in computing MACRS depreciation—the cost of the asset is simply multiplied by the percentage listed in the MACRS table. You will also want to mention that MACRS takes only a half-year depreciation in the first year an asset is placed in service.

LECTURE AIDS — Miscellaneous

In addition to the information above, you may want to stress the following points.

1. Revision of Depreciation — If estimates of a fixed asset's residual value or useful life change, this effects the depreciation calculation. However, depreciation charges are revised only for future periods. No attempt is made to "correct" past depreciation amounts.
2. Subsidiary Ledgers — In order to control the accounting for fixed assets, it is helpful to have a subsidiary ledger showing each asset recorded in the fixed asset accounts.
3. Depreciation on Low-Cost Assets — Assets which have a low cost (i.e. a wastepaper basket, small hand tools, etc.) are not usually depreciated. They are frequently recorded as an expense when they are purchased.

EXERCISES & PROBLEMS FOR REINFORCEMENT:

Exercise 10-5	Exercise 10-10	Problem 10-2A	Problem 10-2B
Exercise 10-6	Exercise 10-11	Problem 10-3A	Problem 10-3B
Exercise 10-7	Exercise 10-12		
Exercise 10-8	Exercise 10-13		
Exercise 10-9			

OBJECTIVE 3 — Classify fixed asset costs as either capital expenditures or revenue expenditures.

KEY TERMS:
- Capital Expenditure
- Component
- Revenue Expenditure

SUGGESTED APPROACH

Review the definitions of capital and revenue expenditures and their accounting treatment using transparencies 10-10 and 10-11. Next, give your students an opportunity to apply these definitions in practice through a group learning activity.

LECTURE AIDS — Capital and Revenue Expenditures

Capital expenditures are expenditures that benefit future operating periods, such as purchasing fixed assets, adding to an existing fixed asset, improving a fixed asset or extending the life of a fixed asset. These expenditures are recorded as an increase in the asset account or a reduction to the accumulated depreciation account. Either way, the book value of the asset is increased.

Revenue expenditures are costs that benefit only the current account period or costs incurred to keep assets in the normal working order. These expenditures are recorded in an expense account.

Transparency 10-10 lists the terms addition, betterment, extraordinary repair and ordinary repair and summarizes their accounting treatment. Please note that these terms have been omitted from the 21st edition of ACCOUNTING. The transparency is provided for instructors who want to expose their classes to this terminology. It will also explain the opening sentences from this objective, which state, "The costs of acquiring fixed assets, adding to a fixed asset, improving a fixed asset, or extending the life of a fixed asset are called capital expenditures. Such expenditures are recorded by either debiting the asset account or its related accumulated depreciation account."

Transparency 10-11 describes capital and revenue expenditures in terms of the stages of acquiring fixed assets: preliminary stage, preacquisition stage, acquisition/construction stage, and the in-service stage.

GROUP LEARNING ACTIVITY — Capital and Revenue Expenditures

Transparency 10-12 lists several expenditures related to fixed assets. Ask your students to classify each as a capital or a revenue expenditure. Also instruct them to name the specific account that would be debited to record each expenditure. Transparency 10-13 presents the correct solution.

EXERCISES & PROBLEMS FOR REINFORCEMENT:
- Exercise 10-14
- Exercise 10-15
- Exercise 10-16
- Exercise 10-17

OBJECTIVE 4 — Journalize entries for the disposal of fixed assets.

KEY TERMS:
- Boot
- Trade-in Allowance

SUGGESTED APPROACH

Whenever a business disposes of a fixed asset, however a business disposes of a fixed asset, both the asset and its accumulated depreciation must be removed from the accounting records. Remind students that depreciation must be brought up to date before recording the disposal of an asset. Use the following notes and demonstration problems to illustrate the discard, sale, and exchange of fixed assets.

Please note that in presenting the journal entries for the exchange of similar assets, I call the value placed on the new assets received in a gain situation a "plug" number. If that overly simplistic approach is offensive, the text presents two methods for calculating the amount to be capitalized on page 409.

LECTURE AIDS — Discarding Fixed Assets

To record a discarded fixed asset:

1. Remove the asset and its accumulated depreciation from the accounting records.
2. If the asset is not fully depreciated, record a loss equal to the book value of the asset.

Ask your students to record in their notes the discard of the following two assets. After a few minutes, review the correct answers.

Machine #1: Original cost, $10,000; accumulated depreciation, $10,000

Entry: Accumulated Depreciation—Machinery   10,000
            Machinery……………………….   10,000

Machine #2: Original cost, $25,000; accumulated depreciation, $20,000

Entry: Accumulated Depreciation—Machinery   20,000
            Loss on Disposal of Fixed Assets……..   5,000
                Machinery……………………….   25,000

LECTURE AIDS — Selling Fixed Assets

To record the sale of a fixed asset:
1. Remove the asset and its accumulated depreciation from the accounting records.
2. Record the cash received.
3. Record any gain or loss. The gain or loss can be determined by comparing the book value of the asset to the cash received.

Ask your students to record in their notes the sale of the following two assets. After a few minutes, review the correct answers.

Machine #1: Original cost, $50,000; accumulated depreciation, $35,000; sold for $18,000

Entry:	Cash...	18,000	
	Accumulated Depreciation—Machinery	35,000	
	Machinery............................		50,000
	Gain on Disposal of Fixed Assets		3,000

Machine #2: Original cost, $75,000; accumulated depreciation, $65,000; sold for $4,000

Entry:	Cash...	4,000	
	Accumulated Depreciation—Machinery	65,000	
	Loss on Disposal of Fixed Assets.........	6,000	
	Machinery............................		75,000

LECTURE AIDS — Exchanging Similar Fixed Assets

To record the exchange of a fixed asset for a similar fixed asset:

1. Remove the old asset and its accumulated depreciation from the accounting records.
2. Record any cash paid.
3. If there is a loss on the exchange, it can be recorded for financial reporting purposes. Gains are NOT recorded.
4. If there is a gain or loss on the exchange that is not recognized, think of the value of the new asset as a "plug" number. If there is a loss that is recognized, record the new asset at its stated cost.

Most exchanges of fixed assets are trade-in arrangements, where an old asset plus some cash is exchanged for a new asset. To determine whether there is a gain or a loss on the trade, you must compare the book value of the old asset to the trade-in allowance granted toward a new asset. For example, if a purchaser is given a $3,000 trade-in allowance on a machine with a book value of $5,000, the purchaser would have a $2,000 loss.

DEMONSTRATION PROBLEM — Exchanging Similar Fixed Assets

A piece of equipment with an original cost of $100,000 and accumulated depreciation of $92,000 is traded in on a new machine with a cost of $150,000. The seller has agreed to take $140,000 cash plus the old equipment in exchange for the new machine. Record this transaction.

Cost of new machine	$150,000
Cash (boot) paid	140,000
Trade-in allowance	$ 10,000

Book value of old machine $ 8,000
Trade-in allowance   10,000
Gain $ 2,000

NOTE: This gain cannot be recognized.

Entry: Accumulated Depreciation—Equipment (old)   92,000
        Equipment (new) **PLUG NUMBER**.....   148,000
                Equipment (old)................   100,000
                Cash............................   140,000

The PLUG NUMBER can be checked as follows:

What was given up to acquire the new machine?
        Cash $140,000
        Old machine—book value   8,000
                                $148,000

A second piece of equipment with an original cost of $270,000 and accumulated depreciation of $250,000 is traded in on a new machine with a cost of $400,000. The seller has agreed to take $385,000 cash plus the old equipment in exchange for the new machine. Record the following transaction.

Cost of new machine $400,000
Cash (boot) paid   385,000
Trade-in allowance $ 15,000

Book value of old machine $ 20,000
Trade-in allowance   15,000
Loss $ 5,000

NOTE: This loss can be recognized for financial reporting purposes.

Entry: Accumulated Depreciation—Equipment (old)   250,000
        Equipment (new).................   400,000
        Loss on Disposal of Fixed Assets...............   5,000
                Equipment (old)........................   270,000
                Cash...................................   385,000

EXERCISES & PROBLEMS FOR REINFORCEMENT:

Exercise 10-18	Exercise 10-22	Problem 10-4A	Problem 10-4B
Exercise 10-19	Exercise 10-23	Problem 10-5A	Problem 10-5B
Exercise 10-20	Exercise 10-24		
Exercise 10-21			

OBJECTIVE 5 — Define a lease and summarize the accounting rules related to the leasing of fixed assets.

KEY TERMS:
    Capital Leases
    Operating Leases

SUGGESTED APPROACH

Use the following scenario (Transparency 10-14) to introduce capital leases.

    Company A : Purchases a $250,000 asset that has an estimated 15-year life, after which time it will have a $10,000 salvage value. The asset is purchased on credit. Therefore, Company A records a $250,000 asset and a $250,000 liability.

    Company B: Leases the same $250,000 asset for 15 years. At the end of the 15 years, the company has the right to purchase the asset for $100. Since Company B does not own the asset, it does not record the asset on its accounting records. In addition, it does not recognize any liability related to the lease.

    Is this a fair accounting treatment?

In 1976, the Financial Accounting Standards Board decided that it was unacceptable for Company B to avoid recording a $250,000 debt on its balance sheet just because it used something legally called a "lease" to obtain use of the asset.

This lease agreement contains a bargain purchase option, which allows Company B to buy the asset for $100 at the end of the 15 years. Since the asset will be worth $10,000 at that point, you can be sure that Company B will exercise the bargain purchase option. Therefore, Company B is really purchasing the asset. This is called a capital lease.

Under a capital lease, the lessee must (1) record the asset in its accounting records at its market value, (2) recognize a liability for the lease payments to be made, and (3) depreciate the asset over the period it is used.

The criteria to determine if a lease is a capital lease are not presented in the text; this is more an intermediate accounting concern. However, in case your students ask, a lease is classified as a capital lease if it meets one of these four criteria:

1. The lease transfers ownership of the asset to the lessee at the end of the lease term.
2. The lease contains an option for a bargain purchase of the asset by the lessee.
3. The lease term covers 75% or more of the economic life of the asset.
4. The lease requires rental payments that compensate the lessor for 90% or more of the fair market value of the asset.

If the lease does not meet any of these criteria, it is classified as an operating lease. Under an operating lease, the lessee records lease payments as rent expense. The asset and the lease obligation are not recorded in the accounting records.

OBJECTIVE 6 — Describe internal controls over fixed assets.

SUGGESTED APPROACH

The group learning activity that follows asks students to apply the concepts of internal control discussed in the text to a specific situation. You may want to review these concepts before assigning the group activity. Alternatively, you may wish to assign this project without an in-class review to see whether students are keeping up with their reading.

GROUP LEARNING ACTIVITY — Internal Control of Fixed Assets

Wilson Insurance has just purchased a lap-top computer for each of its insurance agents. The lap-tops have been programmed with a variety of financial information related to Wilson's insurance policies. The agents will use the computer in making their sales presentations to potential clients, and they are free to use the computers as they wish as long as they are employed by Wilson. Your students' task is to develop internal control procedures for the lap-top computers. Use Transparency 10-15 to assign this task. Transparency 10-16 contains a suggested solution.

CLASS DISCUSSION — Internal Control of Fixed Assets

One control over fixed assets is to physically safeguard them from theft. Ask your students to give examples of how they safeguard their cars from theft. Examples include always locking the car, alarm systems, parking under street lights, and switches that shut off gas to the engine. Emphasize that the same care is needed in protecting a company's assets.

EXERCISES & PROBLEMS FOR REINFORCEMENT:
    Exercise 10-25

OBJECTIVE 7 — Compute depletion and journalize the entry for depletion.

KEY TERMS:
    Depletion

SUGGESTED APPROACH

Mining companies purchase rights to metal ore or mineral deposits. These rights are recorded in an asset account when they are purchased. As the metal ore or minerals are mined, they must be removed from the asset account and shown as an expense. This process is called depletion.

Depletion is always computed using a units-of-production method. Use the demonstration problem that follows to illustrate how depletion is calculated and journalized.

DEMONSTRATION PROBLEM — Depletion

A company purchased the rights to a mineral deposit for $500,000. Engineers estimate that the deposit contains 2 million tons of ore. During the first year of mining operations, 450,000 tons of ore were removed. What depletion expense would be recorded that first year?

$500,000/2 million tons = $0.25/ton
450,000 tons x $0.25/ton = $112,500

Journal Entry: Depletion Expense...............   112,500
                    Accumulated Depletion   112,500

EXERCISES & PROBLEMS FOR REINFORCEMENT:
    Exercise 10-26

OBJECTIVE 8 — Describe the accounting for intangible assess, such as patents, copyrights, and goodwill.

KEY TERMS:
    Amortization   Intangible Assets
    Copyright   Patents
    Goodwill   Trademark

SUGGESTED APPROACH

Intangible assets are long-term assets that have no physical substance but benefit operations. Emphasize that in most cases, intangible assets involve legal rights. For example, a copyright is the legal right to publish and sell printed material.

Begin your coverage of this objective by reviewing the major categories of intangibles (patents, copyrights and trademarks, goodwill) using Transparency 10-17. Transparency 10-18 summarizes the ongoing accounting treatment for intangibles. Emphasize the value of intangibles through the real-world case examples that follows.

Patents and goodwill are two intangibles that merit additional coverage. Use the lecture aids below to explain the differences in costs capitalized for a purchased and an internally developed patent, due to accounting rules regarding the treatment of research and development expenses. Lecture aids are also provided to explain the nature of goodwill. To sum up your coverage of fixed assets, natural resources, and intangible assets, review Transparency 10-19 with your students.

LECTURE AIDS — Patents

If a patent is purchased, the full purchase price is recorded in the patent account. In most cases, the purchase price of the patent would reimburse the seller for research costs in developing the product patented, as well as for the legal costs of filing and defending the patent.

If a patent is developed internally, only the legal costs to file and defend the patent may be recorded in the patent account. All research and development costs to discover and perfect the product or technology must be recorded as expenses as they are incurred. Research and development costs are expensed because a company can never be sure whether or not its projects will lead to marketable products. Once a product is determined to be marketable, it would be difficult to go back and trace all the costs that went into the product—especially since it may have taken several years to develop the product.

As a result, patents that are developed internally will be carried at a substantially lower value than patents that are purchased.

LECTURE AIDS — Goodwill

Let's say that you wanted to open a restaurant that specializes in pizza. You price ovens, refrigerators, tables, chairs, cash registers—all the items you need to open your restaurant. You discover that the needed equipment will cost $75,000.

You also hear that the owner of a local pizzeria wants to sell his business. This business has all of the equipment you had priced for your own store. Although this equipment is used, it is in good working order. The business is in a location equivalent to the one you were considering. This pizzeria has been in business for more than 20 years and has an established clientele. The owner is asking $125,000 for his business.

How can the owner of the established pizzeria justify asking $125,000 for a business, when the same equipment could be purchased new for $75,000?

Whenever a company is purchased at a price higher than the value of its assets, goodwill is recognized. If you were to purchase the established pizzeria, you would record the following entry:

```
    Assets (list actual accounts)   75,000
    Goodwill......................  50,000
        Cash................                    125,000
```

EXERCISES & PROBLEMS FOR REINFORCEMENT:
    Exercise 10-27   Problem 10-6A   Problem 10-6B

OBJECTIVE 9 — Describe how depreciation expense is reported in an income statement, and prepare a balance sheet that includes fixed assets and intangible assets.

SUGGESTED APPROACH

Review the following information regarding income statement and balance sheet disclosures.

Income Statement - must show amount of depreciation and amortization expense, either on the statement or in a footnote. It also must disclose the method used to calculate depreciation.

Balance Sheet - must show the balance of each major class of fixed assets, along with the accumulated depreciation (either by class or in total). Mineral rights and ore deposits (less accumulated depletion) are shown as part of the fixed asset section. Other intangible assets are listed in their own section, net of amortization taken to date, immediately following the fixed assets.

GROUP LEARNING ACTIVITY — Income Statement and Balance Sheet

Using Transparency 10-20, ask your students to prepare the assets section of a balance sheet for Georgia Electronics Co. The solution is presented in Transparency 10-21.

EXERCISES & PROBLEMS FOR REINFORCEMENT:
Exercise 10-28

OBJECTIVE 10 – Compute and interpret the ratio of fixed assets to long-term liabilities.

SUGGESTED APPROACH

Why do financial analysts compare a company's level of fixed assets with long-term debt? Answer: because if the purchase of fixed assets is financed, it is usually financed with long-term debt. Most folks can't pay off a new car in 6 months, so they take out a car loan for a longer period, maybe 4 or 5 years. Therefore, they are paying off the car in about the same number of years they will use their car. When businesses purchase assets they will use for several years, these assets are often financed with a loan that will be repaid over several years.

The ratio of fixed assets to long-term liabilities is computed as follows:

$$\frac{\text{Fixed Assets (net)}}{\text{Long Term Liabilities}}$$

Transparency 10-22 presents the ratio of fixed assets to long-term liabilities for two companies for several years. As you review this transparency, ask your students the following questions:

1. Is it better for the ratio of fixed assets to long-term liabilities to be increasing or decreasing?
2. Which company provides a better margin of safety for its creditors?

3. What advice would you give to Company A? Company B?

EXERCISES & PROBLEMS FOR REINFORCEMENT:
    Exercise 10-29
    Exercise 10-30

APPENDIX — Sum-of-the-Years-Digits Depreciation

SUGGESTED APPROACH

Sum-of-the-years-digits depreciation is a second example of an accelerated depreciation method. In practice, this method is used by less than 2% of the companies surveyed by *Accounting Trends & Techniques*. Therefore, if class time is becoming a scarce resource, you may want to omit covering this appendix. On the other hand, you may want to expose your students to this concept and draw a parallel between sum-of-the-years digits depreciation and the rule of 78's in calculating interest.

LECTURE AIDS — Sum-of-the-Years-Digits Method

The formula for sum-of-the-years-digits-method depreciation is as follows:

    (Cost - Residual Value) x Sum-of-the-Years-Digits Fraction

The sum-of-the-years-digits fraction is determined as follows:

1. The denominator is the sum of all the digits that add up to the number of years in the asset's expected life. The denominator is the same number for each year's depreciation calculation. For example, if an asset is expected to last 4 years, add the digits that count up to 4 (1 + 2 + 3 + 4 = 10)
2. The numerator is the number of years of life remaining at the beginning of each year for which depreciation is being calculated. Therefore, the numerator decreases by one each year. For example, if an asset is expected to last 4 years, the numerator for the first year is 4, the second year is 3, the third year is 2, and the last year is 1.

GROUP LEARNING ACTIVITY — Sum-of-the-Years-Digits Method

Display Transparency 10-8. This transparency was used in Objective 2 to calculate declining-balance depreciation. Instruct your students to use the same information to calculate depreciation using the sum-of-the-years-digits method. The solution is shown on Transparency 10-23.

EXERCISES & PROBLEMS FOR REINFORCEMENT:
    Exercise 10-31
    Exercise 10-32
    Exercise 10-33

COST TO ACQUIRE FIXED ASSETS

Advanced Technology, a computer manufacturer, purchased a machine that applies computer chips to circuit boards, using a process known as Surface Mount Technology (SMT). The costs associated with acquiring the SMT machine are listed below. Where should each cost be recorded in the accounting records?

Purchase price	$150,000
Transportation	1,200
Engineer's fee to set up and adjust the machine to required specifications	2,000
Electrician's fee to install a new power outlet required by the SMT machine	800
Repairs made to wall as a result of damage during installation of the new power outlet	500
Cost of chips and circuit board used to test the new machine before it is used in production	300
Cost of 3-year service contract requiring the manufacturer of the SMT machine to make any repairs needed, at no cost	3,000

Transparency Master 10-2

COST TO ACQUIRE FIXED ASSETS
Solution

Advanced Technology, a computer manufacturer, purchased a machine that applies computer chips to circuit boards, using a process known as Surface Mount Technology (SMT). The costs associated with acquiring the SMT machine are listed below. Where should each cost be recorded in the accounting records?

		Recorded in
Purchase price	$150,000	Equipment
Transportation	1,200	Equipment
Engineer's fee to set up and adjust the machine to required specifications	2,000	Equipment
Electrician's fee to install a new power outlet required by the SMT machine	800	Equipment
Repairs made to wall as a result of damage during installation of the new power outlet	500	Repair Expense
Cost of chips and circuit boards used to test the new machine before it is used in production	300	Equipment
Cost of 3-year service contract requiring the manufacturer of the SMT machine to make any repairs needed, at no cost	3,000	Prepaid Expense

Transparency Master 10-3

COST OF LAND ACQUIRED AS A BUILDING SITE

When land is acquired as a building site, all costs to purchase the land and prepare it for the new building are considered a cost of the land.

Indicate whether the following costs should be recorded in the land, building, or land improvements account.

Cost	Explanation
$200,000	Purchase price paid for land and old warehouse building. The warehouse building will be torn down, and a new manufacturing plant will be erected in its place. The land has an appraised value of $125,000; the warehouse is appraised at $75,000.
5,000	Closing costs associated with purchasing the land and warehouse.
20,000	Cost to tear down and remove old warehouse building.
8,000	Cash received from selling a crane and other salvageable materials from the old warehouse.
11,000	Cost to level the land prior to construction of the new building.
25,000	Cost to excavate land for the foundation of the new building.
60,000	Fees paid to architect to design the new building.
540,000	Fees paid to contractor for erecting the new building.
7,000	Interest paid on construction loan before the building is completed.
5,000	Repair as a result of windstorm damage during construction.
12,000	Cost of parking lot adjacent to the building.
8,000	Cost of landscaping to beautify building and parking lot.

Transparency Master 10-4

COST OF LAND ACQUIRED AS A BUILDING SITE
Solution

Indicate whether the following costs should be recorded in the land, building, or land improvements account.

		Amount Recorded in			
Cost	Explanation	Land	Building	Land Improve.	Expense
$200,000	Purchase price of land and old warehouse.	$200,000			
5,000	Closing costs.	5,000			
20,000	Cost to tear down old warehouse.	20,000			
8,000	Cash received from selling salvageable materials from old warehouse.	(8,000)			
11,000	Cost to level land.	11,000			
25,000	Cost to excavate land for foundation of new building.		$25,000		
60,000	Architect's fees for new building.		60,000		
540,000	Building contractor's fees for new building.		540,000		
7,000	Interest paid on construction loan before the building is completed.		7,000		
5,000	Repair as a result of windstorm damage during construction.				$5,000
12,000	Cost of parking lot.			$12,000	
8,000	Cost of landscaping.			8,000	

Transparency Master 10-5

REVIEW—DEPRECIATION

Assume that you have just accepted a job that requires you to do a lot of driving. Because your current car is on its "last leg," you have decided to purchase another car. You estimate that you will drive 20,000 miles each year. Since you don't like to deal with major car repairs, you will trade in the car when it reaches 60,000 miles.

You have found two cars that you are considering. One is a new car, and you can purchase it for $18,000. The other is a late-model used car. The used car has 20,000 miles on it, but it is in excellent condition. The price of this used car is $11,000.

Using the criteria outlined, what would be your depreciation cost per year for each car?

Transparency Master 10-6

DEPRECIATION CALCULATIONS

STRAIGHT-LINE AND UNITS-OF-PRODUCTION METHODS

Lucianno's Pizza purchased a car to be used in delivering pizzas. The car cost $14,000. It will be used for 5 years, after which its residual value will be about $2,000. In those 5 years, Lucianno's estimates that the car will be driven 80,000 miles.

1. Calculate depreciation for all 5 years, using the straight-line method.

2. Assume that the car was driven 10,000 miles in year 1, 15,000 in year 2, 18,000 in year 3, 20,000 in year 4, and 17,000 in year 5. Calculate depreciation, using the units-of-production method for all 5 years.

Transparency Master 10-7

DEPRECIATION CALCULATIONS

STRAIGHT-LINE AND UNITS-OF-PRODUCTION METHODS

Solution

1. ($14,000 − $2,000)/5 years = $2,400 per year

2. ($14,000 − $2,000)/80,000 miles = $0.15 per mile

   Year 1: 10,000 miles × $0.15 per mile = $ 1,500
   Year 2: 15,000 miles × $0.15 per mile =   2,250
   Year 3: 18,000 miles × $0.15 per mile =   2,700
   Year 4: 20,000 miles × $0.15 per mile =   3,000
   Year 5: 17,000 miles × $0.15 per mile =   2,550
   $12,000

DEPRECIATION CALCULATIONS
DECLINING-BALANCE METHOD

ABC Marketing recently purchased a machine that cost $80,000. The machine is expected to last 4 years and have a residual value of $6,000.

Calculate the depreciation expense to be recorded each year under the declining-balance method.

DEPRECIATION CALCULATIONS
DECLINING-BALANCE METHOD

Solution

Year 1: ($80,000 − $0)   × 50% = $40,000
Year 2: ($80,000 − $40,000) × 50% =   20,000
Year 3: ($80,000 − $60,000) × 50% =   10,000
Year 4: ($74,000 − $70,000)   =   4,000
                                                               $74,000

Transparency Master 10-10

CAPITAL AND REVENUE EXPENDITURES

Type of Expenditure	Capital or Revenue	Accounting Treatment
Addition—enlarging an asset or adding a new feature	Capital	Debit fixed asset account
Betterment—increasing operating efficiency or capacity	Capital	Debit fixed asset account
Extraordinary Repairs—extending the service life of an asset	Capital	Debit accumulated depreciation account
Ordinary Repairs and Maintenance—maintaining an asset in current working condition	Revenue	Debit an expense account

CAPITAL AND REVENUE EXPENDITURES

Stage	Capital or Revenue	Accounting Treatment
Preliminary - studies & analysis before acquiring a fixed asset is probable	Revenue	Debit expense account
Preacquisition – mgmt. has decided to aquire the fixed asset	Capital	Debit fixed asset account
Acquisition or Construction - asset is under construction, but not yet in use	Capital	Debit fixed asset (or Construction in Progress)
In-service – asset is complete & ready for use		
• Add new component	Capital	Debit fixed asset
• Replace component	Capital	Debit fixed asset
• Normal repair	Revenue	Debit expense

CAPITAL AND REVENUE EXPENDITURES

Classify each of the following expenditures as a capital or a revenue expenditure.

Name the specific account that would be debited to record each expenditure.

Expenditure	Classification	Account Debited
1. Purchasing a fax machine		
2. Adding an air purification system to the HVAC system in an office building		
3. Painting the interior walls of an office building		
4. Installing an overhead crane in a warehouse		
5. Replacing the motor of a machine		
6. Paying for a service call to repair photocopy machine		
7. Upgrading the processor on a PC to allow the computer to process data more quickly		

Transparency Master 10-13

CAPITAL AND REVENUE EXPENDITURES
Solution

Classify each of the following expenditures as a capital or a revenue expenditure.

Name the specific account that would be debited to record each expenditure.

Expenditure	Classification	Account Debited
1. Purchasing a fax machine	Capital	Office Equipment
2. Adding an air purification system to the HVAC system in an office building	Capital	HVAC System
3. Painting the interior walls of an office building	Revenue	Maintenance Expense
4. Installing an overhead crane in a warehouse	Capital	Crane
5. Replacing the motor of a machine	Capital	Machinery
6. Paying for a service call to repair photocopy machine	Revenue	Repair Expense
7. Upgrading the processor on a PC to allow the computer to process data more quickly	Capital	Computer Equipment

LEASES

Company A: Purchases a $250,000 asset that has an estimated 15-year life, after which time it will have a $10,000 salvage value. The asset is purchased on credit. Therefore, Company A records a $250,000 asset and a $250,000 liability.

Company B: Leases the same $250,000 asset for 15 years. At the end of the 15 years, the company has the right to purchase the asset for $100. Since Company B does not own the asset, it does not record the asset on its accounting records. In addition, it does not recognize any liability related to the lease.

Is this a fair accounting treatment?

INTERNAL CONTROLS—FIXED ASSETS

Procedures for Lap-Top Computers at Wilson Insurance

Wilson Insurance has just purchased a lap-top computer for each of its insurance agents. The lap-tops have been programmed with a variety of financial information related to Wilson's insurance policies. The agents will use the computers in making their sales presentations to potential clients, and they are free to use the computers as they wish as long as they are employed by Wilson.

Your task is to develop internal control procedures for the lap-top computers. Your procedures should address how the lap-tops should be issued to the salespeople and returned to the company at the end of employment. You may also want to address procedures for repair and replacement of the lap-tops and a periodic inventory of the computers.

INTERNAL CONTROLS—FIXED ASSETS

Suggested Solution

1. When lap-top computers are purchased, they should be tagged with an identification number and recorded in a subsidiary ledger. Until issued, the lap-top computers should be kept in a locked storage facility.

2. The sales manager (or other authorized employee) should be responsible for issuing the computers to the sales agents. A record should be maintained showing who each computer was issued to.

3. When a computer needs repairs, it should be returned to Wilson. Information about the type of repairs made and their cost should be entered into the subsidiary ledger. If the computer shows evidence of abusive treatment, Wilson may require the sales agent to pay for repairs.

4. A manager's authorization is needed before purchasing any new computers or replacing a sales agent's lap-top.

5. Records should be verified once per year by asking all sales agents to bring in their computers for a physical inventory.

6. All sales agents are required to return their computers immediately upon termination of employment. The Payroll Department should be instructed to hold the agent's final paycheck until the sales manager verifies that the computer has been returned in proper working order.

INTANGIBLE ASSETS

	Definition	Legal Life
Patents	Exclusive right to produce and sell a product with one or more unique features	20 years
Copyrights	Exclusive right to publish and sell a literary, artistic, or musical composition	Life of author + 70 years
Trademarks	Exclusive right to use a name, term, or symbol in identifying and marketing a product	Indefinite life; registration renewed every 10 yrs.
Goodwill	Intangible asset that results from superior location, product quality, reputation, or managerial skills; evidenced when a company is purchased at a price that is higher than the market value of its net assets (assets minus liabilities)	Indefinite life

INTANGIBLE ASSETS

Intangible	Accounting Treatment
Patents & Copyrights	Amortized over useful life (not legal life)
Trademarks & Goodwill	Not amortized; value is written down if impaired

Transparency Master 10-19

DEPRECIATION, DEPLETION, AMORTIZATION—THREE WORDS THAT REPRESENT THE SAME CONCEPT

Depreciation, depletion, and amortization all represent the process of allocating the cost of a long-term asset to expense over its useful life.

Applies to	Journal Entry to Record	Methods Used
DEPRECIATION		
Fixed assets (i.e., machinery, buildings)	Depreciation Expense 　Accumulated Depreciation	Straight-line, Units-of-production, Declining-balance
DEPLETION		
Natural resources (i.e., mineral deposits, metal ore)	Depletion Expense 　Accumulated Depletion	Units-of-production
AMORTIZATION		
Intangible assets (patents & copyrights)	Amortization Expense 　Patents or 　Copyrights	Straight-line

Transparency Master 10-20

BALANCE SHEET PREPARATION

Use the following accounts to prepare the Assets section of the balance sheet for Georgia Electronics Co. as of December 31, 20—.

Cash	$105,000
Accounts Receivable	180,000
Allowance for Doubtful Accounts	14,000
Land (where office building is located)	55,000
Merchandise Inventory	260,000
Prepaid Insurance	29,000
Buildings	300,000
Office Equipment	140,000
Patents	75,000
Goodwill	25,000
Accumulated Depreciation—Buildings	115,000
Accumulated Depreciation—Office Equipment	36,000
Undeveloped Land (held for investment purposes)	50,000

BALANCE SHEET PREPARATION
Solution

Georgia Electronics Co.
Partial Balance Sheet
December 31, 20—

Current assets:			
Cash		$ 105,000	
Accounts receivable	$ 180,000		
Less allowance for doubtful accounts	14,000	166,000	
Merchandise inventory		260,000	
Prepaid insurance		29,000	
Total current assets			$ 560,000
Property, plant, and equipment:			
Land		$ 55,000	
Buildings	$ 300,000		
Less accumulated depreciation	115,000	185,000	
Office equipment	$ 140,000		
Less accumulated depreciation	36,000	104,000	
Total property, plant, and equipment			344,000
Intangible assets:			
Patents		$ 75,000	
Goodwill		25,000	
Total intangible assets			100,000
Investments:			
Undeveloped land			50,000
Total assets			$1,054,000

Ratio of Fixed Assets to Long-Term Liabilities

	2000	2001	2003	2004
Company A	2.4	2.4	2.1	2.3
Company B	1.8	1.9	2.4	2.6

DEPRECIATION CALCULATIONS SUM-OF-THE-YEARS-DIGITS METHOD

Solution

Year 1:	($80,000 − $6,000)	× 4/10	=	$29,600
Year 2:	($80,000 − $6,000)	× 3/10	=	22,200
Year 3:	($80,000 − $6,000)	× 2/10	=	14,800
Year 4:	($80,000 − $6,000)	× 1/10	=	7,400
				$74,000

Chapter 11
Current Liabilities

OPENING COMMENTS

Chapter 11 covers a variety of obligations included in the Current Liabilities section of the balance sheet: notes payable, contingent liabilities, payroll, and employee fringe benefits. The quick ratio is introduced in this chapter as a tool to analyze the level of current liabilities held by a business.

After studying the chapter, your students should be able to:

1. Define and give examples of current liabilities.
2. Prepare journalize entries for short-term notes payable and for the disclosure for the current portion of long-term debt.
3. Describe the accounting treatment for contingent liabilities and journalize entries for product warranties.
4. Determine employer liabilities for payroll, including liabilities arising from employee earnings and deductions from earnings.
5. Describe payroll accounting systems that use a payroll register, employee earnings records, and a general journal.
6. Journalize entries for employee fringe benefits, including vacation pay and pensions.
7. Use the quick ratio to analyze the ability of a business to pay its current liabilities.

OBJECTIVE 1 – Define and give examples of current liabilities.

SUGGESTED APPROACH

Transparency 11-1 lists current liability accounts already discussed in previous chapters. Ask your students what these accounts have in common. Hopefully, they will realize that these are all debts which are settled within one year. You may want to add the following new accounts, which are introduced in Chapter 11, to this list:
    Product Warranty Payable
    Social Security Tax Payable
    Medicare Tax Payable
    Employees Federal Income Tax Payable
    State Unemployment Tax Payable
    Federal Unemployment Tax Payable
    Vacation Pay Payable
    Unfunded Pension Liability

EXERCISES & PROBLEMS FOR REINFORCEMENT:
Exercise 11-1

OBJECTIVE 2 — Prepare journal entries for short-term notes payable and disclosure for the current portion of long-term debt.

KEY TERMS:
Discount
Discount Rate
Proceeds

SUGGESTED APPROACH

The entries for notes payable are parallel to the entries discussed in Chapter 8 for notes receivable. Therefore, it is helpful to use this objective to review the entries for notes receivable and show their relationship to notes payable.

Also, remind students that the amount due on installment loans which will be paid over the next 12 months must be classified on the balance sheet as a current liability. Ask your students what amounts would be reported in the current liabilities and long-term liabilities sections of the balance sheet on the following loan: a $3,600 loan to be repaid over the next 3 years by a monthly payment of $100. (Answer: $1,200 in current liabilities and $2,400 in long-term liabilities.)

GROUP LEARNING ACTIVITY — Short-Term Notes Payable

Transparency 11-2 presents three transactions related to a promissory note issued as a time extension on an open account. Ask your class to record these entries on the accounting records of the seller. This will force students to review entries for notes receivable from Chapter 8.

After completing entries for the seller, ask your class to prepare entries for the buyer. You may want to review the accounts used by the buyer to record these transactions. List the accounts used by the seller on the board (accounts receivable, notes receivable, and interest income), and ask your students to name the corresponding accounts on the buyer's accounting records (accounts payable, notes payable, and interest expense).

Transparency 11-3 shows the correct entries for both the buyer and the seller.

DEMONSTRATION PROBLEM — Non-Interest-Bearing Notes Payable

Many of your students will be familiar with the saying, "There's no such thing as a free lunch!" Notes that truly have no interest charged are just as rare. For example, if a company borrows cash from a bank by signing a non-interest-bearing note, the interest is simply deducted from the cash proceeds received on the note. At maturity, only the face value of the note is repaid. Therefore, interest is deducted up front, rather than paid at the end. This is similar to the process of discounting a note receivable, which was presented in the appendix to Chapter 8.

You can explain the steps to account for a non-interest-bearing note as follows:

STEP 1: Calculate the Discount on the Note

The discount on a non-interest-bearing note is computed using the following formula:

   Discount = Face Amount of Note x Discount Rate x Time Period

The discount rate is the interest rate being charged on the note. For example, assume that Wycoff Company borrows $7,500 by signing a 90-day non-interest-bearing note. The bank discounts the note at 12%. (Translation: the bank is charging 12% interest.) The discount on this note is:

   $7,500 x 12% x 90/360 = $225

STEP 2: Calculate the Cash Proceeds Received on the Note

The cash that Wycoff Company will receive is computed by subtracting the discount from the face amount of the note. After the bank deducts the discount, Wycoff Company will receive $7,275 ($7,500 - $225).

STEP 3: Record the Liability Resulting from the Note and the Cash Received

Wycoff must record the note payable at its full face amount, since this is the amount to be repaid in 90 days. The discount retained by the bank is recorded as Interest Expense. The journal entry for this transaction is:

   Cash.........................   7,275
   Interest Expense............   225
         Notes Payable......   7,500

STEP 4: Record Payment when the Note Matures

Wycoff will repay the full $7,500 when the note becomes due. Since the interest on the note has already been recorded, the journal entry at that time is:

   Notes Payable   7,500
         Cash................   7,500

WRITING EXERCISE — Short-Term Notes Payable

Stimulate critical thinking by asking your students to write an answer to the following question (Transparency 11-4):

   Would you rather borrow $10,000 by issuing (a) a 90-day, 15% note or (b) a 90-day, non-interest-bearing note discounted at 15%?

This question will allow you to emphasize that it is better to receive the full $10,000 for 90 days than to receive only $9,625 for the same time period. Either way, the interest cost is $375.

EXERCISES & PROBLEMS FOR REINFORCEMENT:
    Exercise 11-2   Exercise 11-5
    Exercise 11-3   Exercise 11-6
    Exercise 11-4

OBJECTIVE 3 – Describe the accounting treatment for contingent liabilities and journalize entries for product warranties.

SUGGESTED APPROACH

Begin coverage of this objective by defining a contingent liability. A contingent liability is an obligation that (1) resulted from a past transaction but is (2) contingent on a future event. Exhibit 1 shows that contingent liabilities are only recorded in the accounting records if they are probable and the amount can be estimated. Other contingent liabilities are simply disclosed in the financial statements.

Contingent liabilities can be effectively illustrated by looking at product warranties. As the result of a past transaction (a sale to a customer), a future event may create a liability (the product may require warranty repairs). A demonstration problem illustrating the accounting for warranties is included below.

You may want to stress that the matching concept also guides the accounting for warranties. The cost of repairs made under warranties must be recorded as an expense in the same period as the sales revenue is recognized. Since warranty repairs are often not made until months or years after the sale occurs, these potential warranty costs must be estimated and accrued.

DEMONSTRATION PROBLEM — Warranties

Explain that the entry to accrue warranty costs is as follows:

    Product Warranty Expense…………….   XXX
        Product Warranty Payable…….   XXX

Read the following problem to your class. Ask your students to record in their notes the entry to accrue warranty costs. This should be a relatively simple task if you have just reviewed the accounts involved in this entry. Next, ask your students to record the entry to pay warranty costs.

> Jet-Clean sold washing machines totaling $1 million. Each washing machine carries a 3-year warranty. Jet-Clean estimates that warranty repairs on the washing machines will cost 1% of the sales price.
>
> 1. Record the entry to accrue Jet-Clean's warranty costs.

>   Product Warranty Expense………   10,000
>   Product Warranty Payable   10,000

2. Jet-Clean paid $750 for washing machine repairs under warranty. Record this entry.

>   Product Warranty Payable………   750
>   Cash…………………..   750

EXERCISES & PROBLEMS FOR REINFORCEMENT:
   Exercise 11-7   Problem 11-1A   Problem 11-1B
   Exercise 11-8
   Exercise 11-9
   Exercise 11-10

OBJECTIVE 4 — Determine employer liabilities for payroll, including liabilities arising from employee earnings and deductions from earnings.

KEY TERMS:
   FICA Tax   Net Pay
   Gross Pay   Payroll

SUGGESTED APPROACH

Payroll is the largest expense for most service businesses, such as public accounting firms, law firms, and advertising agencies. As a result of jobs they have held, many of your students will be familiar with the calculation of gross pay and the typical payroll deductions. Therefore, it is usually effective to review payroll information simply by asking a few questions.

LECTURE AIDS — Calculation of Gross Pay

The Fair Labor Standards Act specifies that all employers engaged in interstate commerce must pay their workers 1-1/2 times the regular wage rate for all hours worked in excess of 40 per week. Executive, administrative, and certain supervisory positions are exempt from this requirement. As a result, some employers simply refer to a position as "exempt" or "non-exempt." Workers in non-exempt positions can expect to receive time-and-a-half for overtime because they are not exempt from the Fair Labor Standards Act.

Ask students to give examples, from their experiences, of premiums paid for overtime (such as working at night or on holidays).

CLASS DISCUSSION — Gross Pay and Deductions from Gross Pay

Begin by asking your students to define gross pay and state how it is calculated (hours worked x wage rate). Next, ask them to name items that can be deducted from an employee's gross pay. List these items on the board as they are named.

Once the list is compiled, the following items will merit further explanation.

> FICA — Federal Insurance Contributions Act. This represents the amount withheld for social security and Medicare. These tax rates are set by Congress, and they change frequently. The textbook uses a social security rate of 6% on the first $100,000 an employee earns and a Medicare rate of 1.5% on all earnings. (In addition to mentioning the rates used in the text, you may want to announce the current social security and Medicare tax rates.)

> Federal Income Tax — The amount withheld for federal income tax depends on your tax filing status (married, single, etc.) and the number of withholding allowances claimed (one for yourself, one for a spouse, and one for each dependent). The employer gets this information by asking each employee to complete a W-4 form. The Internal Revenue Service (IRS) publishes withholding tables that are used to determine how much tax should be withheld (Publication 15-A). You may want to obtain copies of this publication and have students who are working look up amounts that should be withheld from their payroll checks.

A W-4 form is reproduced in Exhibit 2. Review this form step-by-step with your students so they will understand what they are signing the next time they fill out a W-4.

GROUP LEARNING ACTIVITY — Calculation of Net Pay

Ask your students to determine net pay (or take-home pay) for Blake Edwards, an employee described on Transparency 11-5. They will need to use the federal income tax withholding table included in Exhibit 3 in the textbook. See Transparency 11-6 for the solution.

Once this activity is complete, ask your students to determine Blake's net pay as a percentage of his gross pay. Instruct your students to do the same using their own paychecks. Students are often surprised how large deductions are when expressed as a percent of gross pay.

LECTURE AIDS — Employer's Payroll Taxes

Employers must pay the payroll taxes listed below. These taxes are considered an operating expense. Employer payroll taxes are a significant expense for most businesses.

> FICA Tax — The employer must match the amount paid by the employee for social security and Medicare.

> Federal Unemployment Compensation Tax — The employer pays this tax to cover the cost of unemployment benefits. This tax is paid only by the employer; it is not deducted from the employee's paycheck. The federal tax rate is set by Congress. In homework problems, the text uses a rate of 0.8% (.008) on the first $7,000 an employee earns each year. Within the chapter, the text states that the tax rate is 6.2%. The authors do point out (in a footnote on page 447) that this rate can be reduced to 0.8% for credits for state unemployment compensation tax. It is a good idea to mention this footnote so students understand the difference in rates mentioned in the text and used in the problems.

State Unemployment Compensation Tax — The state unemployment tax rate varies from state to state. As of January 1, 2004, the maximum state rate recognized by the federal unemployment system was 5.4% on the first $7,000 an employee earns each year. This tax is also paid only by the employer. Employers who have stable employment histories are permitted by most states to pay reduced unemployment compensation tax rates.

EXERCISES & PROBLEMS FOR REINFORCEMENT:
    Exercise 11-11
    Exercise 11-12

OBJECTIVE 5 — Describe payroll accounting systems that use a payroll register, employee earnings records, and a general journal.

KEY TERMS:
    Employee's Earnings Record
    Payroll Register

SUGGESTED APPROACH

Review the accounts used in the journal entries to record payroll and payroll taxes. Next, use the group learning activity below to ask your students to complete a payroll register. They will need to follow the example in text Exhibit 5 and the instructions on Transparency 11-7. Using the data from the payroll register, ask your students to prepare payroll journal entries.

Transparency 11-10 presents a Form 941. You may want to show this transparency as an example of the many payroll-related forms that must be filed with federal and state agencies.

This is a good time to point out that the record keeping requirements to maintain payroll data for each pay period and each employee can be burdensome for small businesses. Some small businesses use outside firms to process their payroll data. Another option for small businesses is to purchase a microcomputer accounting package. Most of the popular accounting software packages include a payroll system. In effect, an employer's file of employees' earnings records act as a subsidiary ledger for the payroll expense accounts.

LECTURE AIDS — Journal Entries for Payroll

The journal entry to record employee paychecks is:

Salaries Expense (gross pay)............................	XXX	
Social Security Tax Payable................		XXX
Medicare Tax Payable		XXX
Employees Federal Income Tax Payable		
(and other payable accounts as required		
by the employee's deductions)............		XXX
Salaries Payable (net pay)..................		XXX

The journal entry to record employer payroll taxes is:

Payroll Tax Expense...............................	XXX	
Social Security Tax Payable............		XXX
Medicare Tax Payable		XXX
State Unemployment Tax Payable.....		XXX
Federal Unemployment Tax Payable..		XXX

Note that all employer payroll taxes become liabilities when the payroll is actually paid to the employees, even though it may be some time before those taxes are remitted to the appropriate government agency.

GROUP LEARNING ACTIVITY — Payroll Register

Transparency 11-7 presents information to be used in preparing a payroll register and journal entries for employee paychecks and employer's payroll taxes. The solution is shown on Transparencies 11-8 and 11-9.

CLASS DISCUSSION — Internal Controls over Payroll

Objective 5 also discusses internal controls related to payroll. Transparencies 11-11 and 11-12 summarize internal controls related to payroll. To stimulate class discussion, ask your students to identify the internal control implications of using direct deposits to pay employees through electronic funds transfers.

WRITING EXERCISE — Internal Controls over Payroll

Ask your students to write answers to one or both of the following questions (Transparency 11-13):

1. How might the owner of a construction company determine whether a supervisor who distributes payroll and has authority to hire and fire employees has fictitious employees on the payroll and is cashing the related payroll checks?

2. Why is it desirable to have at least two officials approve pay rate changes?

EXERCISES & PROBLEMS FOR REINFORCEMENT:

Exercise 11-13	Problem 11-2A	Problem 11-2B
Exercise 11-14	Problem 11-3A	Problem 11-3B
Exercise 11-15	Problem 11-4A	Problem 11-4B
Exercise 11-16	Problem 11-5A	Problem 11-5B
Exercise 11-17		

OBJECTIVE 6 — Journalize entries for employee fringe benefits, including vacation pay and pensions.

KEY TERMS:
- Defined Benefit Plan
- Defined Contribution Plan
- Fringe Benefits
- Postretirement Benefits

SUGGESTED APPROACH

When covering this objective, be sure to point out the relationship between the matching concept and accounting requirements for accruing fringe benefits. You may want to spark some interest in the accounting treatment of fringe benefits by asking students to describe the benefits available to them through their jobs.

CLASS DISCUSSION — Fringe Benefits

Begin this discussion by asking your class to name fringe benefits they are eligible for through their jobs. After you have exhausted that list, ask students to name any fringe benefits provided to their family members or friends.

LECTURE AIDS — Journalizing Entries for Vacation Benefits

The matching concept is the key concept directing the accounting entries for fringe benefits. This concept dictates that the cost of providing fringe benefits must be recorded in the same accounting period as they are earned. This may be a different accounting period from the one in which the benefit is actually paid.

For example, a company may have a vacation policy stating that an employee earns one day of vacation for each month worked. If an employee does not take that vacation day in the month it is earned, theoretically it should be accrued. In practice, many companies accrue earned vacation time only at the end of the year, instead of monthly. The journal entry to accrue vacation pay that has been earned by employees, but not yet paid, is as follows:

    Vacation Pay Expense.........   ...   XXX
            Vacation Pay Payable....   XXX

Remind students that it is a good internal control to require employees to take vacations. While the employee is on vacation, another person performs his/her duties, which helps to deter or detect irregularities.

LECTURE AIDS — Journalizing Entries for Pension Benefits

Pensions are another benefit that may be earned and paid at different times. Employees earn their pensions over the period that they work for a company. That pension is not paid until retirement. The matching concept dictates that the cost of pension benefits that will be paid after retirement must be accrued as they are earned.

In a defined contribution plan, the employer has an obligation to make annual payments into a pension fund. This annual payment is the extent of the employer's liability for pensions, since these plans to not make specific promises regarding the pension benefits a retiree will receive. The accounting for a defined contribution plan is straightforward. The annual contribution is shown as an expense as follows:

    Pension Expense............................ XXX
        Cash................................   XXX

Defined benefit plans, on the other hand, promise employees a specified amount of pension payments based on each employee's years of service and salary level. Calculating the cost of the pension benefits to be accrued under a defined benefit plan is a complicated task. It is necessary to project what employees will be earning when they retire, how many years they will receive benefits (life expectancy), and how much income can be earned on pension contributions. The experience of actuaries is used extensively in making these projections. Once this cost is determined, it is recorded as follows:

    Pension Expense........................... XXX
        Cash (for any cash contributions
           to the pension fund).............   XXX
        Unfunded Pension Liability
        (for any portion of the current
        pension cost not funded by
        a contribution to the pension fund)   XXX

Also point out that other postretirement benefits earned by employees as they work (such as health care or life insurance) must be accrued and recorded as an expense over the years the employee is working. This requirement is similar in complexity to the accounting for defined benefit pension plans.

WRITING EXERCISE — Fringe Benefits

Ask your students to respond to the following scenario (see Transparency 11-14).

    ComExpress Airlines provides the following fringe benefits to its employees.

1. Each employee earns 2 days of paid sick leave for each 160 hours he or she works for the company.
2. Each employee is also permitted to fly free of charge on any ComExpress flight that is not fully booked with customers. The employee may take as many flights in the course of a year as he or she wishes.

For each benefit, state whether or not an accounting entry would be needed at the end of the year to accrue the cost of the benefit. State your justification for each answer.

EXERCISES & PROBLEMS FOR REINFORCEMENT:
>   Exercise 11-18   Problem 11-6A   Problem 11-6B
>   Exercise 11-19
>   Exercise 11-20

OBJECTIVE 7 – Use the quick ratio to analyze the ability of a business to pay its current liabilities.

KEY TERMS:
>   Acid-Test Ratio
>   Quick Ratio

SUGGESTED APPROACH

The quick ratio measures the "instant" debt paying ability of a company by comparing quick assets (cash, cash equivalents, and receivables) to current liabilities. Transparency 11-15 presents several questions related to the quick ratio. Use this transparency to initiate a class discussion or ask your students to write responses.

EXERCISES & PROBLEMS FOR REINFORCEMENT:
>   Exercise 11-21
>   Exercise 11-22

Transparency Master 11-1

WHAT DO THESE ACCOUNTS HAVE IN COMMON?

Accounts Payable **Interest Payable**

Unearned Rent **Wages Payable**

Taxes Payable

Transparency Master 11-2

JOURNAL ENTRIES TO RECORD A PROMISSORY NOTE

The following transactions occurred between Spoke Company (the seller) and Bryden Company (the buyer).

Apr. 19 Spoke Co. sold $80,000 in merchandise to Bryden Co. on account, with terms n/30.

May 19 Spoke Co. granted Bryden Co. a 90-day extension on the account receivable. Bryden Co. signed an $80,000, 10%, 90-day note as evidence of the time extension.

Aug. 17 Bryden Co. paid Spoke Co. the amount due on the note.

1. Prepare the journal entries used by Spoke Company to record the sale and the note receivable. Assume that the cost of the merchandise sold to Bryden Company was $50,000.

2. Prepare the journal entries used by Bryden Company to record the purchase and the note payable.

Transparency Master 11-3

JOURNAL ENTRIES TO RECORD A PROMISSORY NOTE

Solution

1. Spoke Co.

Date	Account	Debit	Credit
Apr. 19	Accounts Receivable—Bryden Co.	80,000	
	Sales		80,000
Apr. 19	Cost of Merchandise Sold	50,000	
	Merchandise Inventory		50,000
May 19	Notes Receivable	80,000	
	Accounts Receivable—Bryden Co.		80,000
Aug. 17	Cash	82,000	
	Notes Receivable		80,000
	Interest Revenue		2,000

2. Bryden Co.

Date	Account	Debit	Credit
Apr. 10	Merchandise Inventory	80,000	
	Accounts Payable—Spoke Co.		80,000
May 19	Accounts Payable—Spoke Co.	80,000	
	Notes Payable		80,000
Aug. 17	Notes Payable	80,000	
	Interest Expense	2,000	
	Cash		82,000

WRITING EXERCISE

Would you rather borrow $10,000 by issuing (a) a 90-day, 15% note or (b) a 90-day, non-interest-bearing note discounted at 15%?

Transparency Master 11-5

CALCULATION OF NET PAY

Blake Edwards is single. He claims one withholding allowance. During the week of July 21, he worked 46 hours. Blake is in a non-exempt position. His regular wage rate is $19 per hour. Prior to the week of July 21, Blake has earned $26,100. In addition to social security, Medicare and federal income taxes, withholdings from Blake's check are state and local taxes, $48; United Way contributions, $5; and health insurance contributions, $20. Calculate Blake's net pay.

Transparency Master 11-6

CALCULATION OF NET PAY

Solution

Gross pay:

| 40 hours × $19.00/hour | = $760.00 |
| 6 hours × $28.50/hour | = 171.00 |

$931.00

Deductions:

Federal income tax*	$144.20
Social security tax	55.86
Medicare tax	13.97
State and local tax	48.00
United Way	5.00
Health insurance	20.00
Total deductions	287.03

Net pay **$643.97**

* $931.00 − 354.22 = 576.78 * 25% = $144.20

Transparency Master 11-7

PAYROLL REGISTER AND JOURNAL ENTRIES

On a blank sheet of paper, draw a payroll register, similar to the one in Exhibit 5 in the text. Your register will need the following sections:

1. EARNINGS—to record gross pay. Include the following four columns: Total Hours Worked, Regular Wages, Overtime Wages, and Total Wages.
2. DEDUCTIONS—include the following five columns: Social Security Tax, Medicare Tax, Federal Income Tax, State Income Tax, and Total Deductions.
3. NET PAY

Use your register to record payroll information for the week of December 20, using the following data. All employees are eligible for overtime compensation at 1-1/2 times their regular pay rate. All employees have federal income taxes withheld at the single rate and claim one withholding allowance. All are office employees.

	Earnings Prior to December 20	Hours Worked	Wage Rate	State Taxes
J. Smith	$98,500	40	$50/hour	$100
S. Bratton	$ 6,800	45	$27/hour	$64
D. Houston	$84,000	43	$42/hour	$93

After computing the net and gross pay for each employee, prepare the journal entries to record the employee paychecks and the employer's payroll taxes. Assume that the state unemployment tax rate is 5.4% and federal unemployment tax is 0.8%, both on the first $7,000 of each employee's earnings during a calendar year.

Transparency Master 11-8

Payroll Register and Journal Entries

Solution

EARNINGS

Name	Total Hours Worked	Regular Wages	Overtime Wages	Total Wages
J. Smith	40	2,000.00	0	2,000.00
S. Bratton	45	1,080.00	202.50	1,282.50
S. Houston	43	1,680.00	189.00	1,869.00
		4,760.00	391.50	5,151.50

DEDUCTIONS

Social Security Tax	Medicare Tax	Federal Income Tax	State Income Tax	Total Deductions	Net Pay
90.00	30.00	430.15	100.00	650.15	1,349.85
76.95	19.24	232.07	64.00	392.26	890.24
112.14	28.04	393.47	93.00	626.65	1,242.35
279.09	77.28	1,055.69	257.00	1,669.06	3,482.44

Transparency Master 11-9

PAYROLL REGISTER AND JOURNAL ENTRIES

Solution

To record employee paychecks:

Salaries Expense (gross pay)	5,151.50	
Social Security Tax Payable		279.09
Medicare Tax Payable		77.28
Emp. Federal Income Tax Payable		1,055.69
State Income Tax Payable		257.00
Salaries Payable (net pay)		3,482.44

To record employer's payroll taxes:

Payroll Tax Expense	368.77	
Social Security Tax Payable		279.09
Medicare Tax Payable		77.28
State Unemployment Tax Payable		10.80
Federal Unemployment Tax Payable		1.60

Transparency Master 11-10

Form 941 — Employer's Quarterly Federal Tax Return

(Rev. January 2003) Department of the Treasury, Internal Revenue Service (99)

▶ See separate instructions revised January 2003 for information on completing this return.
Please type or print.

OMB No. 1545-0029

Enter state code for state in which deposits were made **only** if different from state in address to the right ▶ (see page 2 of separate instructions).

- Name (as distinguished from trade name)
- Trade name, if any
- Address (number and street)
- Date quarter ended
- Employer identification number
- City, state, and ZIP code

T / FF / FD / FP / I / T

If address is different from prior return, check here ▶

IRS Use

A If you **do not have to file** returns in the future, check here ▶ ☐ and enter date final wages paid ▶
B If you are a seasonal employer, see **Seasonal employers** on page 1 of the instructions and check here ▶ ☐

1	Number of employees in the pay period that includes March 12th ▶	
2	Total wages and tips, plus other compensation	
3	Total income tax withheld from wages, tips, and sick pay	
4	Adjustment of withheld income tax for preceding quarters of **this calendar year**	
5	Adjusted total of income tax withheld (line 3 as adjusted by line 4)	
6	Taxable social security wages . . . 6a _____ × 12.4% (.124) = 6b	
	Taxable social security tips . . . . 6c _____ × 12.4% (.124) = 6d	
7	Taxable Medicare wages and tips . . 7a _____ × 2.9% (.029) = 7b	
8	Total social security and Medicare taxes (add lines 6b, 6d, and 7b). **Check here if wages are not subject to social security and/or Medicare tax** . . . . ▶ ☐	
9	Adjustment of social security and Medicare taxes (see instructions for required explanation) Sick Pay $_____ ± Fractions of Cents $_____ ± Other $_____ =	
10	Adjusted total of social security and Medicare taxes (line 8 as adjusted by line 9)	
11	**Total taxes** (add lines 5 and 10)	
12	Advance earned income credit (EIC) payments made to employees (see instructions)	
13	Net taxes (subtract line 12 from line 11). **If $2,500 or more, this must equal line 17, column (d) below (or line D of Schedule B (Form 941))**	
14	Total deposits for quarter, including overpayment applied from a prior quarter	
15	Balance due (subtract line 14 from line 13). See instructions	
16	Overpayment. If line 14 is more than line 13, enter excess here ▶ $ _____ and check if to be: ☐ Applied to next return **or** ☐ Refunded.	

- **All filers:** If line 13 is less than $2,500, do not complete line 17 or Schedule B (Form 941).
- **Semiweekly schedule depositors:** Complete Schedule B (Form 941) and check here . . . . ▶ ☐
- **Monthly schedule depositors:** Complete line 17, columns (a) through (d), and check here . . . ▶ ☐

17 Monthly Summary of Federal Tax Liability. (Complete **Schedule B (Form 941)** instead, if you were a semiweekly schedule depositor.)

(a) First month liability	(b) Second month liability	(c) Third month liability	(d) Total liability for quarter

Third Party Designee — Do you want to allow another person to discuss this return with the IRS (see separate instructions)? ☐ Yes. Complete the following. ☐ No
Designee's name ▶   Phone no. ▶ (   )   Personal identification number (PIN) ▶

Sign Here — Under penalties of perjury, I declare that I have examined this return, including accompanying schedules and statements, and to the best of my knowledge and belief, it is true, correct, and complete.
Signature ▶   Print Your Name and Title ▶   Date ▶

For Privacy Act and Paperwork Reduction Act Notice, see back of Payment Voucher.   Cat. No. 17001Z   Form **941** (Rev. 1-2003)

Transparency Master 11-11

INTERNAL CONTROLS—PAYROLL

1. Companies frequently use a special payroll account to write all payroll checks. On payday, a sum of money equal to the total net pay is transferred from the regular bank account to the special account. This eases the bank reconciliation process because the balance in the payroll account will be zero if all employee paychecks are cashed.

2. An appropriate manager should approve the payroll and authorize the transfer of funds from the regular account to the payroll account.

3. If a check-signing machine is used to sign payroll checks, the machine and the blank checks should be locked up when not in use.

(Continued)

INTERNAL CONTROLS PAYROLL
(Concluded)

4. All additions, deletions, or changes in pay rates of employees should be authorized before being entered into the payroll system.

5. Time clocks should be used to record the employee's time on the job. The time clock area should be monitored periodically to ensure that one employee is not clocking in or out for others.

6. Employees should be required to present identification to obtain their paychecks. Or, as an alternative, a periodic audit should be conducted to ensure that all paychecks are going to valid employees.

7. Any changes to a computerized payroll system should be made by someone outside the payroll department and should be authorized by management.

WRITING EXERCISE

1. How might the owner of a construction company determine whether a supervisor who distributes payroll and has authority to hire and fire employees has fictitious employees on the payroll and is cashing the related payroll checks?

2. Why is it desirable to have at least two officials approve pay rate changes?

WRITING EXERCISE

ComExpress Airlines provides the following fringe benefits to its employees.

1. Each employee earns 2 days of paid sick leave for each 160 hours he or she works for the company.

2. Each employee is also permitted to fly free of charge on any ComExpress flight that is not fully booked with customers. The employee may take as many flights in the course of a year as he or she wishes.

For each benefit, state whether or not an accounting entry would be needed at the end of the year to accrue the cost of the benefit. State your justification for each answer.

QUICK RATIO

$$\text{Quick Ratio} = \frac{\text{Quick Assets}}{\text{Current Liabilities}}$$

1. Why do you think cash, cash equivalents, and receivables are called "quick assets"?

2. What is the benefit of comparing quick assets and current liabilities?

3. Ideally, should the quick ratio be greater than or less than 1?

4. What are the implications if a company has a quick ratio less than 1?

Chapter 12
Corporations: Organization, Capital Stock Transactions, and Dividends

OPENING COMMENTS

Chapter 12 begins a three chapter series covering corporations and partnerships. This chapter explains the characteristics of a corporation. It also introduces many of the terms related to stock: common, preferred, par value, stated value, no-par, cumulative, noncumulative, participating, and nonparticipating. Additional topics covered in Chapter 12 are treasury stock (cost method), stock splits, and dividends.

After studying the chapter, your students should be able to:

1. Describe the nature of the corporate form of organization.
2. List the two main sources of stockholders' equity.
3. List the major sources of paid-in capital, including the various classes of stock.
4. Journalize the entries for issuing stock.
5. Journalize the entries for treasury stock transactions.
6. State the effect of stock splits on corporate financial statements.
7. Journalize the entries for cash dividends and stock dividends.
8. Describe and illustrate the reporting of stockholders' equity.
9. Compute and interpret the dividend yield on common stock.

OBJECTIVE 1 — Describe the nature of the corporate form of organization.

KEY TERMS:
   Stock
   Stockholders

SUGGESTED APPROACH

Objective 1 opens with the characteristics of a corporation. Use Transparency 12-1 to review these characteristics. When covering the concept of limited liability, point out that it is common for owners of small private corporations to pledge their personal assets in order to obtain bank loans. Also emphasize the penalty resulting from double taxation of corporate earnings; this is one of the main disadvantages of the corporate form of business.

The following is an interesting real world note you can share with your students. Nonprofit entities often organize as corporations to limit their legal liability and to obtain favorable tax treatment under federal tax laws. Examples of nonprofit corporations include the United Way and The Salvation Army.

This objective also explains the steps necessary to form a corporation and the accounting treatment for the resulting organizational costs. The lecture aids and group learning activity below will help you present this material.

LECTURE AIDS — Organization Costs

To begin the process of forming a corporation, a business must file an application of incorporation with the state. After approving this application, the state grants a charter (or articles of incorporation) which formally creates the corporation.

Organization costs are the costs incurred during the process of incorporating a business. These costs can be significant. They include:

1. Legal fees
2. Taxes
3. State incorporation fees
4. License fees
5. Promotional costs related to sale of stock

Organization costs are recorded as an expense as they are incurred.

GROUP LEARNING ACTIVITY — Organization Costs

Ask your students to record the following entry for Hoover Corporation (see Transparency 12-2). The correct journal entry is listed on Transparency 12-3.

> Hoover Corporation was organized early in 2004. Legal costs and other fees associated with incorporation totaled $3,500.

OBJECTIVE 2 — List the two main sources of stockholders' equity.

KEY TERMS:
 Deficit   Stockholders' Equity
 Retained Earnings   Paid-in Capital

SUGGESTED APPROACH

Ask your class the following question: If you need money, what legal methods can you use to get it? Usually, students' responses will fit into one of the following categories:

1. You can borrow money.
2. You can earn it by getting a job.
3. Someone (such as a parent) can give it to you.

This will allow you to point out that a corporation has the same options to obtain the cash it needs for operations. It can borrow money, creating a liability. This is known as debt financing.

It can also get cash by making a profit from its operations. Finally, it may be given cash by its shareholders as they invest in the corporation by purchasing shares of stock. Funds resulting from a corporation's profits and shareholder investment are known as equity financing.

Therefore, the two sources of owner's equity are as follows:

1. Paid-in capital (also called contributed capital): funds invested by the shareholders
2. Retained earnings: the net income of the corporation less the dividends that have been paid to the shareholders. If the business has sustained net losses, Retained Earnings may have a negative (or deficit) balance.

OBJECTIVE 3 — List the major sources of paid-in capital, including the various classes of stock.

KEY TERMS:
- Common Stock
- Cumulative Preferred Stock
- Nonparticipating Preferred Stock
- Outstanding Stock
- Par
- Preferred Stock
- Stated Value

SUGGESTED APPROACH

As you can see from the list of key terms above, this objective presents a number of definitions. Use the following lecture aids to explain the difference between common and preferred stock. You will also need to reinforce the terms related to preferred stock (cumulative, noncumulative, and nonparticipating) using a demonstration problem.

Other terms which merit special emphasis are legal capital and outstanding shares. Legal capital is the amount invested by shareholders which cannot be returned in the form of dividends. In most states, the par or stated value of the stock establishes legal capital. Legal capital provides protection to creditors because, even in liquidation, it cannot be returned to stockholders until all debts are paid.

Stock that is "issued" has been sold to stockholders. Stock is "outstanding" if it is still owned by stockholders. Stock that has been reacquired by a corporation (introduced in Objective 5 as treasury stock) is issued, but it is not outstanding. This can be expressed through the following equation:

Issued Stock - Stock Reacquired (Treasury Stock) = Outstanding Stock

Ask your students to solve the following problem. XYZ Corporation is authorized to sell 1 million shares of common stock; 750,000 shares have been issued, and 50,000 shares have been reacquired by XYZ. How many shares are outstanding? (Answer: $700,000)

LECTURE AIDS — Classes of Capital Stock

A corporation may have different classes of stockholders. The most common class of stock is called common stock. The major rights usually granted to a common shareholder are:

1. The right to vote in matters concerning the corporation.
2. The right to share in distributions of earnings.
3. The right to share in assets upon liquidation.

A corporation may establish additional classes of stock by granting certain shareholders preferential treatment in one or more of these rights. In many cases, the corporation will issue stock that is given preferential treatment in the area of dividends, called preferred stock. A corporation can even establish more than one class of preferred stock. Ask your students to check the Wall Street Journal and identify corporations that have multiple classes of preferred stock.

LECTURE AIDS — Preferred Stock

Before discussing the dividend characteristics of preferred stock, stress that dividends are not a liability of a corporation until declared by the board of directors. Corporations are not required to pay dividends.

Cumulative vs. Noncumulative Preferred Stock: Although preferred shareholders are "first in line" for dividends, they are not guaranteed dividends. If a corporation determines that it needs to keep its earnings to finance growth, or if earnings are low, the preferred dividend may be passed in one or more years. These passed dividends are called dividends in arrears.

If the preferred stock is cumulative, all dividends in arrears must be paid before any dividends are granted to the common shareholder. If the preferred stock is noncumulative, the preferred stockholder forfeits any passed dividends.

Participating vs. Nonparticipating Preferred Stock: If preferred stock is participating, preferred shareholders may receive more than their regular dividend if the corporation has a large sum of money available to pay dividends. If the preferred stock is nonparticipating, the shareholders will receive only their regular dividend, with all additional dividends going to the common shareholder. Since participating preferred stock is fairly rare, the text illustrates only nonparticipating preferred stock.

Investors in common stock run a greater risk of not receiving dividends than do investors in preferred stock. On the other hand, common stock investors have a greater potential for earning more dividends than do investors in preferred stock.

DEMONSTRATION PROBLEM — Distributing Dividends

Belson Corporation has 10,000 common shareholders and 5,000 preferred shareholders. The preferred stock has a $5 dividend rate. Two years of dividends are currently in arrears.

Assume that the preferred stock is cumulative and nonparticipating. Belson has $155,000 to distribute in the form of dividends. Use this information to calculate the dividends distributed to the preferred and common shareholders.

	Preferred Shareholders	Common Shareholders	Total Distributed
Dividends in arrears (5,000 x $5 x 2)	$50,000		$50,000
Regular dividend	25,000		75,000
Remainder		$80,000	155,000
Total dividends paid	$75,000	$80,000	
Per share dividends	$15	$8	

You may want to illustrate an example of noncumulative preferred stock to emphasize the impact this feature can have on dividend distribution. Use the data above, but assume that the preferred stock is noncumulative and nonparticipating. In this case, dividends would be distributed as follows:

	Preferred Shareholders	Common Shareholders	Total Distributed
Regular dividend	$25,000		25,000
Remainder		$130,000	155,000
Total dividends paid	$25,000	$130,000	
Per share dividends	$5	$13	

GROUP LEARNING ACTIVITY — Distributing Dividends

Ask your students to work in groups to distribute $65,000 of dividends to be paid by Belson Corporation under each of the following assumptions:

1. There is one year of preferred dividends in arrears. The preferred stock is cumulative and nonparticipating.
2. There are three years of preferred dividends in arrears. The preferred stock is noncumulative and nonparticipating.

The solutions are shown on Transparencies 12-4 and 12-5.

WRITING EXERCISE — Characteristics of Preferred Stock

Ask your students to respond to the following question (Transparency 12-6).

Assume that you have decided to invest a portion of your money in the stock market. You ask your broker to recommend a couple of preferred stocks for you to consider as an investment. Your broker recommends the following two companies. Both are start-up corporations, but you agree with your broker that both have excellent potential for the future.

Company A: Noncumulative, nonparticipating, preferred stock with a $4-per-year dividend rate. Each share of this stock will cost you $20.

Company B: Cumulative, nonparticipating, preferred stock with a $4-per-year dividend rate. Each share of this stock will cost you $25.

You have decided to invest in only one of the companies. State which company you would choose and why.

EXERCISES & PROBLEMS FOR REINFORCEMENT:
    Exercise 12-1   Problem 12-1A   Problem 12-1B
    Exercise 12-2

OBJECTIVE 4 — Journalize the entries for issuing stock.

KEY TERMS:
    Discount
    Premium

SUGGESTED APPROACH

Explain the terms par value and stated value. Illustrate how these stock characteristics affect the journal entries for issuing stock using the demonstration problem that follows.

DEMONSTRATION PROBLEM — Entries for Issuance of Capital Stock

Par value is an arbitrary amount assigned to shares of stock. When preferred or common stock is issued, the par value of the stock is credited to the stock account. Any amount received above par (called a premium) is credited to "Paid-in Capital in Excess of Par."

Example: Belson Corporation sold 1,000 shares of $10 par value common stock for $17 per share.

Cash..	17,000	
Common Stock...		10,000
Paid-in Capital in Excess of Par—Common Stock..........		7,000

Ask your students to record the following entry in their notes:

Belson sold 1,000 shares of $25 par value preferred stock for $30 per share.

Cash..	30,000	
Preferred Stock...		25,000
Paid-in Capital in Excess of Par—Preferred Stock..........		5,000

To emphasize that par value is not related to market value, compare the par value of Home Depot's common stock (see Appendix F) to the current selling price from the Wall Street Journal.

No-par stock does not have an assigned par value. Some states require that a stated value be assigned to any no-par stock. If a stock has a stated value, it is treated the same as a par value in recording the stock: the stock account is credited for the stated value, and any premium is recorded in "Paid-in Capital in Excess of Stated Value." If a no-par stock does not have a stated value, the full proceeds from issuing the stock are recorded in the stock account.

Ask your students to record the following entry in their notes:

1. Camden Corp. issued 100 shares of no-par preferred stock for $50 per share.

Cash...	5,000	
Preferred Stock...		5,000

2. Camden Corp. also issued 500 shares of common stock with a stated value of $5 per share for $7 per share.

Cash...	3,500	
Common Stock..		2,500
Paid-in Capital in Excess of Stated Value—Common Stock		1,000

3. Camden Corp. also issued 1,000 shares of $5 stated value common stock in exchange for equipment with a fair market value of $8,500.

Equipment..	8,500	
Common Stock..		5,000
Paid-in Capital in Excess of Stated Value—Common Stock		3,500

You may want to contrast this last entry to the entry in the text for a corporation that receives land in exchange for shares of stock. Point out that the corporation knew the value of its stock, but the value of the land was not given. Therefore, the transaction was recorded at the fair market value of the stock. When stock is exchanged for another asset, use the fair market value that is most easily determined: the value of the asset received or the stock given up.

EXERCISES & PROBLEMS FOR REINFORCEMENT:
    Exercise 12-3   Exercise 12-6   Problem 12-2A   Problem 12-2B
    Exercise 12-4   Exercise 12-7
    Exercise 12-5   Exercise 12-8

OBJECTIVE 5 — Journalize the entries for treasury stock transactions.

KEY TERMS:
    Cost Method   Treasury Stock

SUGGESTED APPROACH

The term "treasury stock" originated because the treasurer's office of a corporation usually has the responsibility for purchasing and maintaining custody of such stock. The text presents the cost method of accounting for treasury stock. The par value method is mentioned only in a footnote. The following demonstration problem presents sample entries that you can review with your class.

You will want to stress that the treasury stock account is a contra equity account, reducing shareholders' equity for the amount returned to shareholders through the purchase of treasury stock. Many students are under the false impression that treasury stock is an asset, because it has a debit balance. Point out that a corporation does not (1) pay dividends on treasury stock, (2) vote treasury stock, or (3) recognize gains or losses if the treasury stock is reissued. Therefore, a corporation does not purchase its own stock as an investment and it is not recorded as an asset.

You should also stress that treasury stock is the only "stock" account that is not recorded at par. The cost of treasury stock, not the par value, is debited to the account.

Before covering the entries for treasury stock, you may want to discuss the reasons that a corporation would purchase shares of its own stock (Transparency 12-7).

DEMONSTRATION PROBLEM — Entries for Treasury Stock

Record the following entries for Lawry Corporation.

Lawry purchased 1,000 shares of $5 par value common stock for $10 per share.

    Treasury Stock... 10,000
        Cash... 10,000

Lawry sold 100 shares of its treasury stock at $12 per share.

    Cash.. 1,200
        Treasury Stock.. 1,000
        Paid-in Capital from Sale of Treasury Stock   200

Emphasize that paid-in capital from the sale of treasury stock is not reported on the income statement. A corporation cannot report a gain as the result of buying and selling its own stock. This would encourage insider trading. Paid-in capital from treasury stock is reported as an increase in owner's equity. When purchasers of treasury stock pay more than the cost of the stock, they have contributed additional capital to the corporation.

Lawry sold 100 shares of its treasury stock at $9 per share.

Cash...	900	
Paid-in Capital from Sale of Treasury Stock..........	100	
Treasury Stock...................................		1,000

After demonstrating these entries, ask your students to record the following three transactions in their notes.

Lawry sold 100 shares of its treasury stock at $14 per share.

Cash...	1,400	
Treasury Stock...................................		1,000
Paid-in Capital from Sale of Treasury Stock		400

Lawry sold 100 shares of its treasury stock at $8 per share.

Cash...	800	
Paid-in Capital from Sale of Treasury Stock.........	200	
Treasury Stock...................................		1,000

Lawry sold 100 shares of its treasury stock at $10 per share.

Cash...	1,000	
Treasury Stock...................................		1,000

WRITING EXERCISE — Treasury Stock

Ask your students to respond to the following (Transparency 12-8).

Name and explain two reasons that a corporation might choose to repurchase its own stock.

EXERCISES & PROBLEMS FOR REINFORCEMENT:
Exercise 12-9

OBJECTIVE 6 — State the effect of stock splits on corporate financial statements

KEY TERMS:
Stock Split

SUGGESTED APPROACH

With a stock split, one share of stock is split into two or more shares. When this occurs, the par value of the stock decreases, and the number of shares increases. The market value of the stock should also fall.

Under this objective, you will need to explain why a corporation would choose to split its stock. Also illustrate the effect of a stock split on the number of shares and par value.

DEMONSTRATION PROBLEM — Stock Splits

Bravara Corp. has 10,000 shares of $20 par-value common stock selling at $100 per share. Determine the new number of shares, par value, and market price under each of the following independent assumptions.

Split	New Par Value (Current Par Value = $20)	New No. of shares (Current No. of shares = 10,000)	"Theoretical" New Market Price (Current Market Price = $100)
2:1	$10	20,000	$50
4:1	$ 5	40,000	$25
10:1	$ 2	100,000	$10
5:2	$ 8	25,000	$40

The new market price is what the stock should sell for in theory after the stock split. However, many other factors other than the split may affect the price of the stock. For example, favorable news about the economy may keep the price of the stock from dropping as low as it should.

Stock splits tend to be very good for shareholders. The split will lower the price, making stock affordable for more investors. More investors will enter the market, creating demand. Additional demand will begin to drive the stock price back up, and the shareholders enjoy the profits resulting from the share appreciation.

Emphasize that no journal entry is required for a stock split.

INTERNET ACTIVITY – Stock Splits

Since stock splits create excitement in the stock market, many investors track which companies have announced stock splits. The following are two web sites which provide a "Stock Split Calendar."

    http://moneycentral.msn.com/investor/calendar/splits/current.asp
    http://money.cnn.com/markets/IRC/

Have your students visit these sites or perform a search on "Stock Splits" for more information.

WRITING EXERCISE — Stock Splits

Ask your students to answer the following question (Transparency 12-9).

    Why would a company choose to split its stock?

EXERCISES & PROBLEMS FOR REINFORCEMENT:
    Exercise 12-12

OBJECTIVE 7 — Journalize the entries for cash dividends and stock dividends.

KEY TERMS:
- Cash Dividend
- Stock Dividend

SUGGESTED APPROACH

Begin this topic by commenting on dividend policies. Point out that some companies make it a policy not to pay dividends at all, plowing all profits back into the company. Stockholders in these corporations count on share appreciation in order to receive a return on their investment. Companies that do pay dividends usually try to maintain a stable regular dividend, generally paid quarterly.

Next, review the entries for cash dividends, stressing the importance of the three dividend dates (declaration, record, and payment). Use the demonstration problem covering cash dividends for this purpose.

When covering stock dividends, it is important to discuss the motivation behind a stock dividend. Hints to lead this discussion are found in the lecture aids that follow. A demonstration problem to use in journalizing stock dividends is also included.

You may also want to illustrate closing entries for a corporation at this point. Although this material is not covered in the text, it emphasizes the final disposition of the cash dividend and stock dividend accounts. It also illustrates how the balance of retained earnings is obtained.

DEMONSTRATION PROBLEM — Cash Dividends

On January 15, the Board of directors of Barns Incorporated declared a $0.25 per-share dividend on its common stock to shareholders of record on January 31, payable on February 15. Barns has 25,000 shares of stock authorized, 10,000 shares issued, and 8,000 shares outstanding.

1. Date of Declaration: Once declared, the dividend becomes a liability of the corporation. Therefore, it is credited to a liability account.

   January 15   Cash Dividends......................   2,000
                    Cash Dividends Payable....   2,000

The cash dividends account is the corporate counterpart to the sole proprietor's drawing account. It is closed to retained earnings at year end.

Also note that the total dollar amount of the dividend is $2,000 (8,000 shares x $0.25). Dividends are not paid on the 2,000 treasury shares.

2. Date of Record: No journal entry is required. This date determines who will receive the dividend. Anyone owning stock in Barns at the close of business that day will receive the dividend.

3. Date of Payment: The liability is paid by mailing the dividend checks.

    February 15   Cash Dividends Payable............ 2,000
                        Cash........................   2,000

LECTURE AIDS — Stock Dividends

When stock dividends are "paid," additional shares of stock are mailed to the shareholders. This allows the corporation to give a return to its shareholders without using any of its cash.

In reality, shareholders own exactly the same portion of the corporation after the stock dividend as they did before the dividend was issued. You can compare the corporation to a pie. Let's say that you cut a pie into six pieces. If you have three pieces, you have half of the pie. If you originally cut that same pie into eight pieces, four pieces equal half the pie. Four pieces may seem like more than three, but because they are smaller pieces, you still get the same amount of dessert (and calories)!

A corporation issuing a stock dividend doesn't get any bigger because the dividend doesn't bring in any new assets. The corporation also doesn't get any smaller because a stock dividend doesn't use up any assets. The corporation is just divided into smaller pieces. All shareholders have more pieces, but they're still getting the same share of the pie.

How do shareholders profit from stock dividends? In theory, a 10% stock dividend should reduce the market price of the stock by 10% since each share represents a 10% smaller piece of the pie. However, in many cases the market price of the stock does not decline the full 10%. Therefore, the total market value of each shareholder's stock increases.

Even if the market price does fall the full 10%, shareholders have more shares on which to realize any future share appreciation. They also have more shares on which to receive any future cash dividend payments.

DEMONSTRATION PROBLEM — Stock Dividends

On June 20, the board of directors of Carlisle Corp. declares a 4% stock dividend on its 50,000 shares of common stock. The shares will be issued on July 14. The par value of the stock is $10 per share; the market value on June 20 is $16 per share.

1. Declaration Date: A liability to distribute the dividends is established with a credit to the stock dividends distributable account.

    June 20   Stock Dividends..................... 32,000
                         Stock Dividends Distributable............   20,000
                         Paid-in Capital in Excess of Par
                             —Common Stock.......................   12,000

Note that the stock dividends account is debited for the market value of the stock (2,000 shares x $16). This is the case for stock dividends declared by most large public corporations; the market price of the stock is easily determined, and the dividend usually does not alter the stock price dramatically. For small, private corporations, stock dividends are usually recorded at the par value of the stock.

The stock dividends account will be closed to Retained Earnings at year end. Therefore, the effect of a stock dividend is to capitalize a portion of the corporation's earnings.

The Stock Dividends Distributable account is credited for the par value of the stock. The balance in this account will be transferred to Common Stock (which is also carried at par) when the shares are distributed. If a balance sheet is prepared before distributing the dividend, Stock Dividends Distributable is listed as part of paid-in capital.

2. Distribution Date: The additional shares are mailed to the shareholders, relieving the corporation's liability. The shares are recorded as outstanding by crediting the common stock account.

July 14	Stock Dividends Distributable...............	20,000	
	Common Stock........................		20,000

It is important to distinguish between a stock dividend and a stock split. A stock dividend is usually small in relation to the total shares outstanding. A stock dividend also transfers an amount from retained earnings to paid-in capital. A stock split applies to all shares (unissued, issued, and treasury) and does not transfer any amounts from retained earnings to paid-in capital.

WRITING EXERCISE — Stock Dividends

Ask your students to explain the following (Transparency 12-10).

> Explain the benefits of a stock dividend both to the corporation issuing the dividend and to the shareholder receiving the dividend.

DEMONSTRATION PROBLEM — Closing Entries for a Corporation

Assume a corporation had the following account balances at the end of a fiscal year. (For simplicity, all expenses are assumed to be recorded in one expense account.)

Revenues	$200,000
Expenses	150,000
Cash Dividends	12,000
Stock Dividends	8,000

Use these accounts to demonstrate closing entries for a corporation. Remind students that (1) revenues and expenses are closed to Income Summary, (2) Income Summary is closed to Retained Earnings, and (3) dividend accounts are closed to Retained Earnings.

Revenues			Expenses	
	Bal. 200,000		Bal. 150,000	
Clos. 200,000				Clos. 150,000

Income Summary	
Clos. 150,000	Clos. 200,000
	Bal. 50,000
Clos. 50,000	
	Bal. 0

Retained Earnings	
	Clos. 50,000
Clos. 12,000	
Clos. 8,000	
	Bal. 30,000 *

*NOTE: The ending balance of Retained Earnings = Net Income - Dividends

Cash Dividends			Stock Dividends	
Bal. 12,000			Bal. 8,000	
	Clos. 12,000			Clos. 8,000

EXERCISES & PROBLEMS FOR REINFORCEMENT:
    Exercise 12-13   Problem 12-3A   Problem 12-3B
    Exercise 12-14   Problem 12-5A   Problem 12-5B
    Exercise 12-15
    Exercise 12-16

OBJECTIVE 8 – Describe and illustrate the reporting of stockholders' equity.

KEY TERMS:
    Restrictions
    Prior Period Adjustment

SUGGESTED APPROACH

This objective covers paid-in capital, retained earnings, and treasury stock on the balance sheet. It also illustrates the retained earnings statement, describes restrictions on retained earnings and describes prior period adjustments. Aids to cover each of these items follow.

LECTURE AIDS – Paid-in Capital on the Balance Sheet

Paid-in capital and retained earnings are the two major sources of stockholders' equity; therefore, they are the two major sections on a corporation's balance sheet.

You will probably need to remind your students that paid-in capital consists of the following accounts:
> Preferred Stock
> Paid-in Capital in Excess of Par—Preferred Stock
> Common Stock
> Paid-in Capital in Excess of Par—Common Stock
> Paid-in Capital from Treasury Stock

Transparency 12-11 lists the stockholders' equity accounts that are reported in the paid-in capital section of the balance sheet.

Refer your students to Exhibit 5 in the text to see two examples of how these accounts are reported. Stress that the second format for Stockholder's Equity summarizes all of the paid-in capital accounts as one total, labeled "Additional Paid-in Capital."

To make sure your students see the "big picture," remind them that the Stockholders' Equity section of the balance sheet consists of the following:
>   Paid-in Capital
> + Retained Earnings
> - Treasury Stock
>   Total Stockholders' Equity

Emphasize that treasury stock is deducted because it is a contra-equity account.

DEMONSTRATION PROBLEM – Retained Earnings Statement

Begin by reviewing the concept of retained earnings. Retained earnings are profits that have been kept (retained) by a corporation. They are profits that have not been returned to shareholders through dividends. Therefore, retained earnings is increased by a corporation's net income and reduced by dividends declared.

Ask your students to compute the retained earnings balance at the end of the year for Parks Corporation, based on the following data:

> Retained Earnings, Jan. 1 $ 50,000
> Net Income $100,000
> Dividends Declared $ 30,000
>
> (Answer: $120,000)

Transparency 12-12 presents a retained earnings statement for Parks Corporation.

LECTURE AIDS – Restrictions on Retained Earnings

Many students have the following misconception: restricting retained earnings sets aside cash for a specific purpose. You must work to dispel the notion that restricting retained earnings affects a corporation's cash.

Use the following story to introduce the concept of restricted retained earnings.

Let's say that you have decided to treat yourself to a nice lunch off campus today. You have $10 in your pocket. When you get to the restaurant where you plan to eat, you notice that your car's gas tank is on empty. You don't have any credit cards with you, and you know you will have to purchase at least $2 in gas. How much can you afford to spend on lunch? Answer: $8.

In your mind, you have just restricted $2 of your money to purchase gas. As a result, you know that you have a maximum of $8 to spend on lunch.

A corporation may find itself in a position in which it needs to restrict a portion of its retained earnings. The retained earnings account shows the profits of a corporation less any profits returned to shareholders in the form of dividends. Under normal conditions, the corporation is free to distribute all of its earnings to its shareholders if it chooses to do so, just as you are free to spend your entire $10 on lunch. However, some conditions limit the earnings that may be returned to the shareholders, just as your need for gas limited what you could spend on lunch.

Restricting retained earnings does not set aside any cash in a special account. For example, assume that a corporation with a net income of $500,000 must restrict $100,000 of retained earnings due to the terms of a bank loan. The restriction informs shareholders that $100,000 in profits are needed to repay the bank loan. However, the corporation must also consciously save $100,000 in cash to make the loan payments. The fact that you restricted $2 for gas doesn't do any good if you spend the $2 on dessert.

Remind students that some states require a corporation to restrict retained earnings for an amount equal to the cost of any treasury stock that has been purchased.

WRITING EXERCISE — Restriction of Retained Earnings

Ask your students to write a response to the following question (Transparency 12-13).

> Technograph Corporation discovered that some hazardous material was buried on a parcel of land currently owned by the corporation. A former owner of the property buried the material. It will cost Technograph $1 million to remove the material and dispose of it properly.
>
> Would it be appropriate for Technograph's board of directors to restrict $1 million for clean up of the hazardous material? If so, what would the restriction accomplish?

DEMONSTRATION PROBLEM — Prior-Period Adjustments

When an error in a prior year's net income is discovered, it is reported as a prior-period adjustment. Prior-period adjustments are shown on the retained earnings statement as a correction to the beginning balance of retained earnings.

The text does not illustrate a retained earnings statement with a prior period adjustment. The following example will help you give a brief practical example of this concept.

At the end of 2004, E & M Corporation discovered that several errors were made in the physical inventory count taken at the end of 2003. As a result, the cost of merchandise sold was understated by $10,000 in 2003, causing income before taxes to be overstated by the same amount. E & M reported $100,000 in retained earnings on December 31, 2003.

E & M made $80,000 of net income after taxes in 2004. The company declared $30,000 in dividends. E & M's tax rate is 40%.

E & M Corporation
Retained Earnings Statement
For the Year Ended December 31, 2004

Retained earnings, January 1, 2004		$100,000
Less prior-period adjustment for 2003 error in calculating cost of merchandise sold, net of $4,000 in taxes		6,000
Corrected retained earnings, January 1, 2004		$ 94,000
Net income for 2004	$80,000	
Less dividends	30,000	
Increase in retained earnings		50,000
Retained earnings, December 31, 2004		$144,000

In practice, only material errors from prior periods are reported as a prior-period adjustment. Errors arising from the use of estimates are never treated as prior-period adjustments.

EXERCISES & PROBLEMS FOR REINFORCEMENT:

Exercise 12-10	Exercise 12-19	Problem 12-4A	Problem 12-4B
Exercise 12-11	Exercise 12-20		
Exercise 12-17	Exercise 12-21		
Exercise 12-18			

OBJECTIVE 9 – Compute and interpret the dividend yield on common stock.

KEY TERMS:
    Dividend Yield

SUGGESTED APPROACH

Transparency 12-14 presents questions related to dividend yield. Use these questions to stimulate a class discussion on dividend policies. In order to answer question #1, your students will need to compute dividend yield. The formula for dividend yield is:

$$\text{Dividend Yield} = \frac{\text{Dividends per Share of Common Stock}}{\text{Market Price per Share of Common Stock}}$$

EXERCISES & PROBLEMS FOR REINFORCEMENT:
    Exercise 12-22
    Exercise 12-23

CHARACTERISTICS OF A CORPORATION

1. Separate legal existence
2. Ownership evidenced by shares of stock
3. Ownership is easily transferred through sale of stock
4. Limited liability
5. Owners elect a board of directors to set corporate policies and select officers to manage the corporation
6. Separate taxable entity (leading to double taxation)
7. Earnings distributed in the form of dividends

Transparency Master 12-2

ORGANIZATION COSTS

Record the following entry for Hoover Corporation.

Hoover Corporation was organized early in 2004. Legal costs and other fees associated with incorporation totaled $3,500.

ORGANIZATION COSTS

Solution

Hoover Corporation was organized early in 2004. Legal costs and other fees associated with incorporation totaled $3,500.

Organization Expenses..............	3,500	
Cash...		3,500

Transparency Master 12-4

DISTRIBUTION OF DIVIDENDS—COMMON AND PREFERRED SHAREHOLDERS

Belson Corporation
Preferred stock is cumulative and nonparticipating.
Dividend = $65,000

	Preferred Shareholders	Common Shareholders	Total Distributed
Dividends in arrears (5,000 × $5 × 1 year)	$25,000		$25,000
Regular dividend (5,000 × $5)	25,000		50,000
Remainder to common		$15,000	65,000
Total dividends paid	$50,000	$15,000	
Per share dividends	$10	$1.50	

DISTRIBUTION OF DIVIDENDS—COMMON AND PREFERRED SHAREHOLDERS

Belson Corporation
Preferred stock is nonparticipating and noncumulative.
Dividend = $65,000

	Preferred Shareholders	Common Shareholders	Total Distributed
Regular dividend (5,000 × $5)	$25,000		$25,000
Remainder to common		$40,000	65,000
Total dividends paid	$25,000	$40,000	
Per share dividends	$5	$4	

Transparency Master 12-6

WRITING EXERCISE

Assume that you have decided to invest a portion of your money in the stock market. You ask your broker to recommend a couple of preferred stocks for you to consider as an investment. Your broker recommends the following two companies. Both are start-up corporations, but you agree with your broker that both have excellent potential for the future.

Company A: Noncumulative, nonparticipating, preferred stock with a $4-per-year dividend rate. Each share of this stock will cost you $20.

Company B: Cumulative, nonparticipating, preferred stock with a $4-per-year dividend rate. Each share of this stock will cost you $25.

You have decided to invest in only one of the companies. State which company you would choose and why.

WHY PURCHASE TREASURY STOCK?

1. To have shares to issue to employees under stock purchase plans

2. To have shares to issue to employees under bonus plans (such as stock options awarded to executives)

3. To create demand for the stock to maintain the stock's price in a down market

4. To return a portion of the company's profits to shareholders who are looking to sell their investment

WRITING EXERCISE

Name and explain two reasons that a corporation might choose to repurchase its own stock.

Transparency Master 12-9

WRITING EXERCISE

Why would a company choose to split its stock?

WRITING EXERCISE

Explain the benefits of a stock dividend, both to the corporation issuing the dividend and to the shareholder receiving the dividend.

STOCKHOLDERS' EQUITY

Paid-in capital:

Preferred Stock (show par value, dividend rate, shares authorized and issued)

Paid-In Capital in Excess of Par—Preferred

Common Stock (show par value, shares authorized, and shares issued)

Paid-In Capital in Excess of Par—Common

Paid-In Capital from Treasury Stock

RETAINED EARNINGS STATEMENT

Parks Corporation
Retained Earnings Statement
For the Year Ended Dec. 31

Retained earnings, Jan. 1		$ 50,000
Net income	$100,000	
Less dividends declared	30,000	
Increase in retained earnings		70,000
Retained earnings, Dec. 31		$120,000

Transparency Master 12-13

WRITING EXERCISE

Technograph Corporation discovered that some hazardous material was buried on a parcel of land currently owned by the corporation. A former owner of the property buried the material. It will cost Technograph $1 million to remove the material and dispose of it properly.

Would it be appropriate for Technograph's board of directors to restrict $1 million for cleanup of the hazardous material? If so, what would the restriction accomplish?

Transparency Master 12-14

Dividend Yield

1. Considering only dividend payments, which of the following companies appears to be a better investment?

	Co. A	Co. B
Dividend/Share	$ .80	$ 3.00
Market Price/Share	$16.00	$90.00

2. Assume a company has a dividend yield on its common stock of 2%. Is it a poor choice to invest in this company's stock? Why or why not?

Chapter 13
Partnerships and Limited Liability Corporations

OPENING COMMENTS

This chapter compares and contrasts proprietorships, corporations, partnerships, and limited liability corporations. After reviewing the characteristics and equity reporting of these business forms, the chapter focuses on partnerships and limited liability corporations. The topics covered include partnership formation, dissolution, and liquidation. The chapter also discusses arrangements for distributing partnership income and loss.

After studying the chapter, your students should be able to:

1. Describe the basic characteristics of proprietorships, corporations, partnerships, and limited liability corporations.
2. Describe and illustrate the equity reporting for proprietorships, corporations, partnerships, and limited liability corporations.
3. Describe and illustrate the accounting for forming a partnership.
4. Describe and illustrate the accounting for dividing the net income and net loss of a partnership.
5. Describe and illustrate the accounting for dissolution of a partnership.
6. Describe and illustrate the accounting for liquidating a partnership.
7. Describe the lifecycle of a business, including the role of venture capitalists, initial public offerings, and underwriters.

OBJECTIVE 1 -- Describe the basic characteristics of proprietorships, corporations, partnerships, and limited liability corporations.

KEY TERMS:
    Limited liability corporation   Partnership
    Limited partnership   Partnership agreement
    Operating agreement   S Corporation

SUGGESTED APPROACH

The proprietorship and corporate form of business have been covered in previous chapters. In this objective, you will need to introduce your students to partnerships and limited liability corporations. Ask for volunteers to describe the partnership form of organizing a business. Next, ask your class to identify characteristics of partnerships. Write your students' ideas on the board. Use Transparency 13-1 to review any partnership characteristics not identified by your class.

Emphasize that the same journals, ledgers, and procedures to record transactions described in previous chapters are used by partnerships. The only change is in the owner's equity accounts. Each partner will have his or her own capital and drawing accounts.

The limited liability corporation is a relatively new business form that is a hybrid between a partnership and a corporation. Use Transparency 13-2 to explain the characteristics of the limited liability corporation. Finally, use text Exhibit 1 to compare all of the organizational forms presented in the textbook.

OBJECTIVE 2 – Describe and illustrate the equity reporting for proprietorships, corporations, partnerships, and limited liability corporations.

KEY TERMS:
- Statement of members' equity
- Statement of owner's capital
- Statement of partnership capital
- Statement of stockholders' equity

SUGGESTED APPROACH

Transparency 13-3 lists the names of the equity reports for each form of business. In reality, the equity reports for proprietorships, partnerships, and limited liability corporations (LLC's) are all build on the basic structure (Transparency 13-4):

    Capital, beginning of the year
+ Investments (also called "Capital Additions")
+ Net Income (or – Net Loss)
- <u>Withdrawals</u>
    Capital, end of the year

Use the group learning activity below to review the equity reports for proprietorships, partnerships, and LLC's. A second group learning activity is provided to cover the Statement of Stockholders' Equity.

GROUP LEARNING ACTIVITY – Equity Reports for Proprietorships, Partnerships, and LLC's

Handout 13-1 presents a Statement of Owner's Equity for Vince Gray, owner of Woodhaven Spas. Divide your students into groups and ask them to complete the handout. This handout will instruct them to modify the Statement of Owner's Equity assuming Vince has a partner. Next the handout will instruct them to modify the Statement of Partnership Capital assuming the business is organized as an LLC. The goal of this activity is to point out the similarity in equity reporting for proprietorships, partnerships, and LLC's.

GROUP LEARNING ACTIVITY — Statement of Stockholders' Equity

The statement of stockholders' equity reports the changes in a corporation's equity accounts. The following group learning activity will give your students an opportunity to prepare this statement. Transparency 13-5 presents the equity accounts of Teldar Corporation. Divide your class into small groups and ask them to prepare Teldar's statement of stockholders' equity.

Instruct your students to prepare this statement in a columnar format (see text Exhibit 2). In this format, the equity accounts are listed across the page, with each account as a separate column. The beginning balance of each equity account is written at the top of the column. (You may want to warn your students that they will need a column for Paid-In Capital from Treasury Stock.) Next, transactions affecting the equity accounts are listed down the page, and the dollar impact of these transactions is shown in the appropriate account columns. After all equity transactions have been listed, the accounts are totaled to determine ending balances.

The correct solution to this activity is displayed on Transparency 13-6.

EXERCISES & PROBLEMS FOR REINFORCEMENT:
    Exercise 13-1

OBJECTIVE 3 – Describe and illustrate the accounting for forming a partnerships.

SUGGESTED APPROACH

Each partner usually contributes cash and/or other assets to form a partnership. Remind students that the following rules are used in recording each partner's contribution.

    Noncash Assets: recorded at their current market value.

    Receivables: Any receivable that will not likely be collected is written off. The remaining receivables are recorded at their face amount. An allowance for uncollectible accounts is established for the possibility of bad debts that cannot be detected when the partnership is formed.

    Liabilities: Any liabilities assumed by the partnership are credited to the appropriate liability account.

    Capital: Each partner's capital account is credited for the net amount of his/her contribution.

Remind students that contributions from members of an LLC are recorded using the same rules. The only difference is the name of the equity account credited. In an LLC, the equity account is called "Member Equity" instead of "Capital."

DEMONSTRATION PROBLEM -- Journal Entry for Partnership Formation

Willis Gibs and George Reed each own a landscape business. They decide to combine their resources and form a partnership.

Just before the partnership is formed, the trial balance of Gibs Landscaping (Transparency 13-7) is as follows:

Cash	$8,500	
Accounts Receivable	12,000	
Inventory	4,000	
Equipment	43,000	
Accumulated Depreciation-Equipment		$17,500
Accounts Payable		5,800
Willis Gibs, Capital		44,200
	$67,500	$67,500

All of Gibs' assets and liabilities will be contributed to the partnership. Although all of the receivables appear to be collectible at this time, the partners agree to a $1,000 allowance for doubtful accounts. The partners also agree that the current market value of the equipment is $24,000.

The partnership's entry to record Gibs' contribution is:

Cash	8,500	
Accounts Receivable	12,000	
Inventory	4,000	
Equipment	24,000	
Allowance for Doubtful Accounts		1,000
Accounts Payable		5,800
Willis Gibs, Capital		41,700

Just before the partnership is formed, the trial balance of Reed Landscaping (Transparency 13-8) is as follows:

Cash	$14,000	
Accounts Receivable	20,000	
Allowance for Doubtful Accounts		$3,400
Inventory	5,200	
Equipment	28,000	
Accumulated Depreciation--Equipment		14,000
Accounts Payable		11,300
George Reed, Capital		38,500
	$67,200	$67,200

Reed has agreed to transfer all of his business assets and liabilities, except $4,000 of his cash. The partners agree that Reed's equipment has a current market value of $17,000. In addition, it is agreed that $2,000 of Reed's accounts receivable should be written off as uncollectible, and a $1,600 allowance for doubtful accounts will be sufficient for future bad debts.

The partnership's entry to record Reed's contribution is:

Cash	10,000	
Accounts Receivable	18,000	
Inventory	5,200	
Equipment	17,000	
Allowance for Doubtful Accounts		1,600
Accounts Payable		11,300
George Reed, Capital		37,300

The entries for both partners' contributions are found on Transparency 13-9. You could use a transparency marker to change the partners' capital account titles to "Member Equity" to reinforce the accounting treatment for LLC's.

EXERCISES & PROBLEMS FOR REINFORCEMENT:
Exercise 13-2

OBJECTIVE 4 – Describe and illustrate the accounting for dividing the net income and net loss of a partnership.

SUGGESTED APPROACH

Use Transparency 13-10 to explain the steps in allocating partnership income/loss. Following that explanation, use the demonstration problems below to show one or more examples of how partnership income is allocated.

DEMONSTRATION PROBLEM -- Division of Net Income/Net Loss

The partnership agreement of Gibs and Reed Landscaping provides an $18,000 salary allowance to Willis Gibs and a $24,000 salary allowance to George Reed. Both partners are given 10% interest on their capital balances at the beginning of the year. The beginning capital balance for Gibs was $41,700 and for Reed, $37,300. Any remaining income or loss is shared equally. Assume that the business had net income of $56,000 during its first year of operations. Calculate the net income distributed to each partner.

	Gibs	Reed	Total
Salary allowance	$18,000	$24,000	$42,000
Interest allowance	4,170	3,730	7,900
Subtotal			$49,900
Remainder = $6,100			
($56,000 - $49,900)	3,050	3,050	6,100
	$25,220	$30,780	$56,000

You may want to point out that allocating a portion of the partnership income as interest on each partner's capital account provides an incentive for partners to retain investments in the business. Ask your class if it is more equitable to allocate interest on the partners' beginning capital balances, end-of-year balances, or the average balances throughout the year. Answer: using an average balance is more equitable. This prevents a partner from withdrawing capital immediately after the beginning of the year or investing additional funds just prior to the end of the year in order to increase his/her interest allowance.

Assume that the business formed by Gibs and Reed had net income of $40,000 during its first year of operations. Calculate the net income distributed to each partner.

	Gibs	Reed	Total
Salary allowance	$18,000	$24,000	$42,000
Interest allowance	4,170	3,730	7,900
Subtotal			$49,900
Remainder = -$9,900			
($40,000 - $49,900)	- 4,950	- 4,950	- 9,900
	$17,220	$22,780	$40,000

Assume that the Gibs/Reed partnership agreement has the following provisions:

1. Salary allowances are $20,000 for Gibs and $30,000 for Reed.
2. No interest is given on the partners' capital balances.
3. Any income/loss greater than the salary allowances is divided using a 2:3 ratio.

Net income for the first year of operations was $68,000.

	Gibs	Reed	Total
Salary allowance	$20,000	$30,000	$50,000
Remainder = $18,000			
($68,000 - $50,000)			
Split 2:3 ratio			
Gibs gets 2/5	7,200		
Reed gets 3/5		10,800	18,000
	$27,200	$40,800	$68,000

A couple of points regarding the division of income need special emphasis. First, if there is no partnership agreement or the agreement does not address division of income, partnership profits or losses are divided evenly among the partners. Second, partners are not employees of the partnership, but owners. When profits are divided between the partners, this is not considered a salary expense. Any profits taken out of the business are recorded in the appropriate partner's drawing account. A partner's withdrawals usually do not equal his/her share of the partnership income.

GROUP LEARNING ACTIVITY -- Closing Entries for a Partnership

Divide your class into small groups. Instruct them to prepare the entry to close the income summary account for Gibs and Reed Landscaping under each of the preceding scenarios. The correct closing entries are illustrated on Transparency 13-11.

LECTURE AIDS -- Partnership Financial Statements

The textbook illustrates that the division of net income may be reported at the bottom of the partnership income statement. Otherwise, there are no differences between the income statements for a partnership and a sole proprietorship. The differences between the statement of owner's capital and the statement of partnership capital were explained in learning objective 2.

You may also want to discuss the differences in the balance sheet. The asset and liability sections of the balance sheet are identical for a partnership and a proprietorship. In the owners' equity section, generally each of the partner's capital accounts is listed. However, some large partnerships may report partners' capital as a total amount, rather than reporting each individual partner's capital account balance.

EXERCISES & PROBLEMS FOR REINFORCEMENT:

Exercise 13-3	Exercise 13-7	Problem 13-1A	Problem 13-1B
Exercise 13-4	Exercise 13-8	Problem 13-2A	Problem 13-2B
Exercise 13-5	Exercise 13-9	Problem 13-3A	Problem 13-3B
Exercise 13-6	Exercises 13-10		

OBJECTIVE 5 – Describe and illustrate the accounting for the dissolution of a partnership.

SUGGESTED APPROACH

The dissolution of a partnership can be very complex. Whenever a partner is admitted by contributing new assets to a partnership or leaves by selling his or her interest in the partnership, the partnership's assets must be revalued. These procedures and the related accounting entries can be illustrated using the demonstration problems that follows.

LECTURE AIDS -- Admission of a New Partner

A partnership is dissolved whenever there is any change in the ownership of a partnership. When a partner leaves the firm or a new partner is added, legally the former partnership is dissolved and a new partnership must be formed.

From an accounting perspective, however, the change in ownership is recorded simply as a change in the capital accounts. This change may involve the capital accounts of the partners currently involved in the business as well as the partner(s) who are entering or leaving the business.

Transparencies 13-12 and 13-13 outline the two methods for admitting a new partner: (1) purchase of a partnership interest from one or more of the current partners and (2) contribution of new assets to the partnership.

The purchase of a partnership interest from current partners is a transaction between the new partner and existing partners acting as individuals. It is not a transaction between the new partner and the partnership. As a result, the total assets and total equity of the partnership are not affected. The amount paid for the partnership interest does not impact the entry to record the new partner's capital.

Admission of a new partner who contributes new assets to the partnership, however, is a transaction between the new partner and the partnership. The demonstration problem below illustrates this more complex situation.

DEMONSTRATION PROBLEM -- Admission of a New Partner through Contribution of New Assets

Melanie Sherby and Nancy Libby operate a partnership. Sherby's capital account balance is $47,000 and Libby's is $36,000. Sherby and Libby have decided to admit a new partner to their business--Jim Fittro.

Fittro will contribute $20,000 cash to receive a one-third interest in the partnership. Prior to admitting Fittro, Sherby and Libby hired a certified public accountant to determine the current market values of the partnership assets. The CPA determined that the building owned by the partnership has a market value $15,000 greater that the book value shown on the financial statements. In addition, the partnership's inventory is undervalued by $2,000 in the accounting records. Sherby and Libby share any income/loss equally.

a. Revalue the partnership assets.

Building	15,000	
Merchandise Inventory	2,000	
Sherby, Capital		8,500
Libby, Capital		8,500

b. Determine the total equity of the partnership after the new partner is admitted.

Sherby, capital ($47,000 + $8,500)	$ 55,500
Libby, capital ($36,000 + $8,500)	44,500
Fittro's contribution	20,000
Total	$120,000

c. Determine the new partner's share of the total equity.

Total equity	$120,000
New partner's share	x 1/3
	$ 40,000

d. Compare the new partner's equity to his contribution.

Fittro's equity in the partnership	$40,000
Fittro's contribution	20,000
Bonus paid to Fittro	$20,000

Entry to record admission:

Cash	20,000	
Sherby, Capital	10,000	
Libby, Capital	10,000	
Fittro, Capital		40,000

Instead, assume that Fittro had contributed $80,000 to join the partnership.

a. Revalue the partnership assets.

Building	15,000	
Merchandise Inventory	2,000	
Sherby, Capital		8,500
Libby, Capital		8,500

b. Determine the total equity of the partnership after the new partner is admitted.

Sherby, capital ($47,000 + $8,500)	$ 55,500
Libby, capital ($36,000 + $8,500)	44,500
Fittro's contribution	80,000
Total	$180,000

c. Determine the new partner's share of the total equity.

Total equity	$180,000
	x 1/3
New partner's share	$ 60,000

d. Compare the new partner's equity to his contribution.

Fittro's equity in the partnership	$60,000
Fittro's contribution	80,000
Bonus paid to Sherby and Libby	$20,000

Entry to record admission:

Cash	80,000	
Sherby, Capital		10,000
Libby, Capital		10,000
Fittro, Capital		60,000

Note that the bonus is distributed to Sherby and Libby based on the income-sharing ratio.

WRITING EXERCISE -- Admission of a Partner

To stimulate critical thinking, ask your students to write answers to the following questions (Transparency 13-14):

1. Why are the assets contributed by each partner recorded at their current market values?
2. In what circumstances would existing partners be willing to pay a bonus to a new partner?

DEMONSTRATION PROBLEM -- Withdrawal of a Partner

When a partner wishes to withdraw from a partnership, he or she may either sell his or her interest in the partnership to another individual or sell the interest directly to the partnership.

For example, assume Bruce Jordan, Ken Kohlenberg, and Dan Greene are partners in a music publishing business with capital accounts of $28,000, $42,000, and $35,000, respectively. Jordan has decided to retire. Prepare the journal entry to record Jordan's retirement under the three independent assumptions which follow.

1. Jordan sells half of his interest to Kohlenberg and half to Greene. Each partner pays $10,000.

Jordan, Capital	28,000	
Kohlenberg, Capital		14,000
Greene, Capital		14,000

2. Jordan sells his entire interest in the partnership to Bob Ruckman for $25,000.

Jordan, Capital	28,000	
Ruckman, Capital		28,000

3. Jordan sells his interest directly to the partnership. Jordan will receive cash equal to the value of his capital account after all partnership assets are adjusted to their current market values. If the partnership does not have sufficient cash to pay Jordan, the partnership agreement states that the partnership can sign a one-year note for the difference.

The partnership currently has $17,000 in cash. The book value of its inventory is $5,000 below the current market value. The book value of its equipment is $8,000 greater than the current market value. The three partners split income or losses equally.

To revalue the partnership assets:

Inventory	5,000	
Jordan, Capital	1,000	
Kohlenberg, Capital	1,000	
Greene, Capital	1,000	
Equipment		8,000

To record Jordan's withdrawal:

Jordan, Capital ($28,000 - $1,000)	27,000	
Cash		17,000
Notes Payable		10,000

EXERCISES & PROBLEMS FOR REINFORCEMENT:

Exercise 13-11	Exercise 13-15	Problem 13-4A	Problem 13-4B
Exercise 13-12	Exercise 13-16		
Exercise 13-13	Exercise 13-17		
Exercise 13-14	Exercise 13-18		

OBJECTIVE 6 – Describe and illustrate the accounting for liquidating a partnership.

KEY TERMS:
- Deficiency
- Liquidation
- Realization

SUGGESTED APPROACH

There are two basic scenarios when partnerships are liquidated: (1) all partners end up with a positive capital balance and receive cash or (2) one or more of the partners ends up with a negative capital balance. If a partner has a negative capital balance, that partner should contribute cash to the partnership equal to his or her deficit so that the remaining partners may receive the cash they are due. If the partner is unwilling or unable to make up this deficit, his or her deficit must be allocated to the remaining partners.

Use Transparency 13-15 to review the steps in liquidating a partnership, and use the following demonstration problem to illustrate liquidation.

DEMONSTRATION PROBLEM -- Partnership Liquidation

Mary Hills, Beth Smith, and Kathy Grove are partners in HSG Pharmaceutical Company. They decide to liquidate their partnership when the partners have capital balances of $45,000, $48,000, and $22,000, respectively. The partnership has $13,000 in cash, $128,000 of noncash assets, and $26,000 in liabilities. The noncash assets are sold for $78,000. The partners split all income/losses using a 4:3:3 ratio. (Note: all gains and losses in liquidation are split using the partners' income-sharing ratio.)

	Cash	Noncash Assets	Liabilities	Capital Hills	Capital Smith	Capital Grove
Beginning balance	13,000	128,000	26,000	45,000	48,000	22,000
Assets sold	+78,000	-128,000		-20,000	-15,000	-15,000
Balance	91,000	0	26,000	25,000	33,000	7,000
Pay liabilities	-26,000		-26,000			
Balance	65,000	0	0	25,000	33,000	7,000

In this case, all three partners end up with a positive balance in their capital accounts. All partners will receive cash equal to their capital balances.

What if the noncash assets of HSG Pharmaceutical Company were sold for $48,000?

	Cash	Noncash Assets	Liabilities	Capital Hills	Smith	Grove
Beginning balance	13,000	128,000	26,000	45,000	48,000	22,000
Assets sold	+48,000	-128,000		-32,000	-24,000	-24,000
Balance	61,000	0	26,000	13,000	24,000	-2,000
Pay liabilities	-26,000		-26,000			
Balance	35,000	0	0	13,000	24,000	-2,000

In this case, Grove has a deficit in her capital balance. If Grove will contribute the $2,000 needed to make up her capital deficiency, the partnership will have $37,000 in cash, of which $13,000 will be distributed to Hills and $24,000 to Smith. If Grove will not contribute an additional $2,000 to the partnership, her deficit must be split between Hills and Smith in their 4:3 ratio, as follows:

	Cash	Noncash Assets	Liabilities	Capital Hills	Smith	Grove
Beginning balance	13,000	128,000	26,000	45,000	48,000	22,000
Assets sold	+48,000	-128,000		-32,000	-24,000	-24,000
Balance	61,000	0	26,000	13,000	24,000	-2,000
Pay liabilities	-26,000		-26,000			
Balance	35,000	0	0	13,000	24,000	-2,000
Deficit allocated				-1,143	-857	2,000
Balance	35,000	0	0	11,857	23,143	0

In this case, the $35,000 cash is distributed to Hills and Smith based on their capital balances after Grove's deficit is allocated. Point out that the most common error in partnership liquidation is the improper distribution of cash to partners. It is wise to always double-check these calculations and compare them to any liquidation procedures outlined in the partnership agreement.

After completing this explanation, ask your students to journalize the accounting entries to record this third scenario (noncash assets sold for $48,000; Grove does not contribute cash to make up her deficit).

EXERCISES & PROBLEMS FOR REINFORCEMENT:
Exercise 13-19   Exercise 13-23   Problem 13-5A   Problem 13-5B
Exercise 13-20   Exercise 13-24   Problem 13-6A   Problem 13-6B
Exercise 13-21   Exercise 13-25
Exercise 13-22

OBJECTIVE 7 – Describe the lifecycle of a business, including the role of venture capitalists, initial public offerings, and underwriters.

KEY TERMS:
    Initial public offering (IPO)
    Underwriting firms
    Venture capitalist

SUGGESTED APPROACH

The text presents a good story about Della's Delights, a candy store which moves through several changes in business form during its lifecycle. The progression is as follows:

    Proprietorship
      …to Partnership
        …to Limited Liability Corporation
          …to regular Corporation
            …and finally the corporation is purchased by a bigger corporation.

Ask your students to share stories about businesses that have moved through one or more changes in entity form.

INTERNET ACTIVITY – Establishing a Limited Liability Corporation

If your students do an internet search on "Limited Liability Corporation," the search will return several websites sponsored by companies that help businesses set up a limited liability corporations. One site which presents a good overview of the pros and cons of limited liability corporations and the steps to establish them is www.bizfilings.com.

Handout 13-1

Woodhaven Spas

Statement of Owner's Capital

For the year ended December 31, 2004

	Vince Gray, Capital		
Balance, Jan. 1	$120,000		
Investments	$15,000		
Net Income	$87,000		
Less: Withdrawals	($61,000)		
Balance, Dec. 31	$161,000		

Instructions:

1. Modify the above report assuming Woodhaven Spas is organized as a partnership. Vince's partner is Anita Carnes. Anita's capital balance on January 1 was $75,000. During the year, she invested an additional $7,000 and made withdrawals of $13,000. The total company's income was $109,000; Anita's share was $22,000. If possible, make all of these changes in pencil.
2. Next, modify the above report assuming Woodhaven Spas is organized as a limited liability corporation. If possible, make these changes in pen.

CHARACTERISTICS OF A PARTNERSHIP

1. Limited life
2. Unlimited liability
3. Co-ownership of partnership property
4. Mutual agency
5. Participation in income
6. Non-taxable entity
7. Created by contract (partnership agreement or articles of partnership)

Transparency Master 13-2

Limited Liability Corporation

Characteristics similar to partnerships:

1. Multiple owners, called "members"
2. Members create an operating agreement
3. May elect for income to pass through to members' individual tax returns
4. Usually have a limited life
5. Mutual agency if member managed

Characteristics similar to corporations:

1. Limited liability
2. Must file articles of organization with state government authorities
3. If manager managed, only authorized members may legally bind the company

Transparency Master 13-3

EQUITY REPORTING

Business form	Report
Proprietorship	Statement of Owner's Capital
Corporation	Statement of Stockholders' Equity
Partnership	Statement of Partnership Capital
Limited Liability Corporation	Statement of Members' Equity

REPORTING CHANGES IN OWNERS' CAPITAL

Capital, beginning of the year

+   Investments (also called "Capital Additions")

+   Net Income (or – Net Loss)

–   <u>Withdrawals</u>

Capital, end of the year

STATEMENT OF STOCKHOLDERS' EQUITY—TELDAR CORPORATION

The January 1, 2004 balances of Teldar Corporation's equity accounts are listed below:

Preferred Stock	$300,000
Common Stock	$800,000
Paid-In Capital—Common Stock	$ 50,000
Retained Earnings	$240,000

During 2004, the following transactions affected Teldar's equity accounts:

1. 1,000 shares of $10 par value common stock were sold for $12 per share.
2. 500 shares of common stock were repurchased to be held as treasury stock. The cost to repurchase these shares was $6,000.
3. Treasury shares costing $1,500 were reissued for $2,000.
4. 2004 net income was $170,000.
5. Dividends totaling $30,000 were declared and paid to preferred stockholders; common dividends were $50,000.

STATEMENT OF STOCKHOLDERS' EQUITY

Solution

Teldar Corporation
Statement of Stockholders' Equity
For the Year Ended December 31, 2004

	Preferred Stock	Common Stock	Paid-In Capital—Common Stock	Paid-In Capital—Treasury Stock	Retained Earnings	Treasury Stock
Balance, January 1	$300,000	$800,000	$50,000	$0	$240,000	$0
Issued common stock		10,000	2,000			
Purchased treasury stock						(6,000)
Reissued treasury stock				500		1,500
Net income					170,000	
Preferred dividends					(30,000)	
Common dividends					(50,000)	
Balance, December 31	$300,000	$810,000	$52,000	$500	$330,000	($4,500)

Transparency Master 13-6

Transparency Master 13-7

PARTNERSHIP FORMATION

Gibs Landscaping
Trial Balance

Cash	$ 8,500	
Accounts Receivable	12,000	
Inventory	4,000	
Equipment	43,000	
Accum. Deprec.-Equip.		$17,500
Accounts Payable		5,800
Willis Gibs, Capital		44,200
	$67,500	$67,500

All of Gibs' assets and liabilities will be contributed to the partnership. Although all of the receivables appear to be collectible at this time, the partners agree to a $1,000 allowance for doubtful accounts. The partners also agree that the current market value of equipment is $24,000.

PARTNERSHIP FORMATION

Reed Landscaping
Trial Balance

Cash	$14,000	
Accounts Receivable	20,000	
Allow.-Doubtful Accts.		$3,400
Inventory	5,200	
Equipment	28,000	
Accum. Deprec.-Equip.		14,000
Accounts Payable		11,300
Willis Gibs, Capital		38,500
	$67,200	$67,200

Reed has agreed to transfer all of his business assets and liabilities, except $4,000 of his cash. The partners agree that Reed's equipment has a current market value of $17,000. In addition, it is agreed that $2,000 of Reed's accounts receivables should be written off as uncollectible and a $1,600 allowance for doubtful accounts will be sufficient for future bad debts.

PARTNERSHIP FORMATION

Journal Entries

Cash	8,500	
Accounts Receivable	12,000	
Inventory	4,000	
Equipment	24,000	
Allow. For Doubtful Accts.		1,000
Accounts Payable		5,800
Willis Gibs, Capital		41,700

Cash	10,000	
Accounts Receivable	18,000	
Inventory	5,200	
Equipment	17,000	
Allow. For Doubtful Accts.		1,600
Accounts Payable		11,300
George Reed, Capital		37,300

Transparency Master 13-10

DIVIDING PARTNERSHIP NET INCOME OR NET LOSS

1. Give each partner his or her salary allowance.

2. Give each partner interest on his or her capital account balance.

3. Divide any remainder according to the ratio in the partnership agreement. Divide the remainder evenly if the partnership agreement does note state how it should be divided.

    NOTE: the remainder may be a negative amount.

PARTNERSHIP CLOSING ENTRIES

Scenario #1: Net income = $56,000

Income Summary	56,000	
Willis Gibs, Capital		25,220
George Reed, Capital		30,780

Scenario #2: Net income = $40,000

Income Summary	40,000	
Willis Gibs, Capital		17,220
George Reed, Capital		22,780

Scenario #3: Net income = $68,000

Income Summary	68,000	
Willis Gibs, Capital		27,200
George Reed, Capital		40,800

Transparency Master 13-12

ADMISSION OF A NEW PARTNER

Steps if new partner purchases an interest from one or more of the current partners.

1. The partnership interest that is purchased is transferred from the capital account of the selling partner(s) to the purchasing partner(s).

2. The amount paid for the partnership interest is irrelevant as far as the accounting records are concerned.

ADMISSION OF A NEW PARTNER

Steps if new partner contributes assets to the partnership.

1. The partnership assets are revalued to their current market value prior to recording the new partner's contribution. This will increase or decrease the current partner's capital accounts.

2. Determine the total equity of the partnership after admission of the new partner by adding the new partner's contribution to the current partner's equity.

3. Determine the new partner's share of the total equity by multiplying the ownership percentage of the new partner by the total equity in the partnership.

4. Compare the new partner's equity value to the amount of his or her contribution.
    a. If the contribution is greater than the new partner's equity, the current partners get a bonus.
    b. If the contribution is less than the new partner's equity, the new partner gets a bonus.

WRITING EXERCISE

1. Why are the assets contributed by each partner recorded at their current market values?

2. In what circumstances would existing partners be willing to pay a bonus to a new partner?

STEPS IN LIQUIDATING A PARTNERSHIP

1. Any non-cash assets are sold, and the resulting gains or losses are allocated to the partners' capital accounts.

2. The partnership liabilities are paid.

3. The remaining cash is distributed to the partners based on the balances in their capital accounts.

If a partner has a deficit (debit balance) in his or her capital account, one of the following occurs:

1. The partner may pay the deficiency to the partnership, allowing the other partners to receive cash equal to their capital balances.

OR

2. The deficit balance may be allocated to the other partners, reducing their capital balances and the amount of cash they will receive.

Chapter 14
Income Taxes, Unusual Income Items, and Investments in Stocks

OPENING COMMENTS

Chapter 14 discusses unusual items that affect income statements and illustrates how these items are reported. In addition, the chapter discusses other specialized accounting and reporting topics, including accounting for income taxes, earnings per share, and comprehensive income.

Chapter 14 also presents the accounting treatment for both short-term and long-term investments. Next, students receive their first exposure to accounting for mergers and acquisitions, including a brief overview of the consolidation process. The chapter ends with the price-earnings ratio.

After studying the chapter, your students should be able to:

1. Journalize the entries for corporate income taxes, including deferred income taxes.
2. Prepare an income statement reporting the following unusual items: fixed asset impairments, restructuring charges, discontinued operations, extraordinary items, and cumulative changes in accounting principles.
3. Prepare an income statement reporting earnings per share data.
4. Describe the concept and the reporting of comprehensive income.
5. Describe the accounting for investments in stocks.
6. Describe alternative methods of combining businesses and how consolidated financial statements are prepared.
7. Compute and interpret the price-earnings ratio.

OBJECTIVE 1 — Journalize the entries for corporate income taxes, including deferred income taxes.

KEY TERMS:
　　Permanent Differences
　　Taxable Income
　　Temporary Differences

SUGGESTED APPROACH

This objective covers estimated income tax payments, deferred income taxes, and the presentation of income taxes on the corporate income statement. The demonstration problem and the lecture aids will help you present this material to your students.

DEMONSTRATION PROBLEM — Estimated Income Tax Payments

Companies must estimate their tax liability based on projections of sales and expenses. Taxes are paid through four quarterly installments, due on April 15, June 15, September 15, and January 15.

For example, Bravara Corporation has made the following projections for 2004:

Sales	$1,000,000
Expenses	850,000
Taxable Income	$ 150,000

Tax rate = 40%

Ask your students to calculate the amount of taxes that Bravara will have to pay for 2004 based on the corporation's projections. (Answer: $60,000).

Next, ask your students to calculate the amount that Bravara will pay in each quarterly installment. (Answer: $15,000). Instruct them to prepare the journal entry to record a quarterly tax payment in their notes.

> Income Tax Expense........ 15,000
>   Cash..................   15,000

Assume that Bravara actually has $180,000 in taxable income at the end of 2004. Ask your students to calculate Bravara's total tax liability using a 40% tax rate. (Answer: $72,000). Next, instruct them to record any taxes that Bravara owes in addition to the amounts paid through quarterly installments. Tell your students to assume that Bravara will not pay these taxes immediately, but will wait until they are due to pay them.

> Income Tax Expense........ 12,000
>   Income Tax Payable   12,000

A portion of Bravara's income statement is shown on Transparency 14-1. Ask your students to complete the income statement, starting with "Income before income taxes". (To assist you in checking their work, net income is $108,000).

LECTURE AIDS — Temporary Differences and Deferred Taxes

Certain revenues and expenses may be recorded differently on a corporation's financial statements than on its tax return. These differences occur because of the following reasons:

1. Sometimes companies will elect to use different accounting methods for financial accounting and tax purposes. For example, a company may use straight-line depreciation for financial accounting and an accelerated method for taxes.
2. Sometimes the tax laws require a company to report a transaction in a way that violates accepted financial accounting principles. For example, cash payments received from

customers that have not been earned cannot be recorded as revenue under accrual accounting. However, the Internal Revenue Code mandates that these payments be included in taxable revenues when preparing the tax return.

Ask your class the following question: Would a company attempt to prepare its tax return using accounting methods that would result in a taxable income that is higher or lower than income on the financial statements? (Answer: a lower taxable income).

When revenues or expenses are recognized in one period for financial accounting purposes and another for tax purposes, they create a temporary difference that either delays or accelerates the payment of taxes. Temporary differences do not change the total amount of taxes paid. They only affect the timing of when taxes are paid.

Stress that most companies seek to defer payment of taxes by selecting appropriate accounting methods (such as accelerated depreciation methods). This allows companies to invest tax savings from deferred taxes in current operations. A newly organized corporation, on the other hand, may want to select accounting methods that do not defer taxes if the company has little or no income in the current period.

GROUP LEARNING ACTIVITY — Temporary Differences and Deferred Taxes

Transparency 14-2 presents an income statement for Gibson Corporation and information on two temporary differences. Ask your students to answer the questions regarding Gibson's net income and taxable income listed on the transparency. A solution to this activity is provided in Transparency 14-3.

EXERCISES & PROBLEMS FOR REINFORCEMENT:
    Exercise 14-1   Problem 14-1A   Problem 14-1B
    Exercise 14-2

OBJECTIVE 2 — Prepare an income statement reporting the following unusual items: fixed asset impairments, restructuring charges, discontinued operations, extraordinary items, and cumulative changes in accounting principles.

KEY TERMS:
    Above-the-line   Extraordinary Items
    Below-the-line   Fixed Asset Impairment
    Discontinued Operations   Restructuring Charges

SUGGESTED APPROACH

Transparency 14-4 shows the basic outline of an income statement with the following unusual items: restructuring charge, fixed asset impairment, discounted operations, extraordinary items, and cumulative change in accounting principle. Use a colored transparency marker to draw a line after Income from Continuing Operations. This will illustrate the concept of above-the-line and below-the-line items.

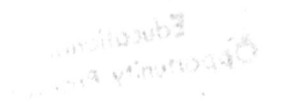

LECTURE AIDS — Unusual Income Statement Items

1. Fixed Asset Impairments: A fixed asset impairment occurs when the carrying amount (book value) of a fixed asset exceeds its fair market value. The asset account is reduced to its fair value and the charge is debited to Loss on Fixed Asset Impairment.

2. Restructuring Charges: These are costs associated with involuntarily terminating employees, terminating contracts, consolidating facilities, or relocating employees. For example, assume a restaurant chain decides to close several of its unprofitable locations. Closing the restaurants may create the following costs: severance packages for managers, fees associated with breaking a lease, or fees paid to an employment agency to help workers find other jobs. The company may be willing to incur these costs because the short-term restructuring costs are less than the long-term costs of running unprofitable restaurants.

Ask you students if they have ever incurred a fee for early termination of a contract, such as on a cell phone or home alarm system. Ask if they would mind sharing the amount of the fee and why they chose to terminate the contract and pay the fee.

Since employee termination benefits are normally the most significant restructuring charge, ask your students to share examples of benefits they or a friend may have received when loosing a job due to the closing or relocation of their company.

3. Discontinued Operations: This section contains information concerning any segment of a business (such as a division, department, or product line) that is sold or closed during the year. The amount displayed in this section is calculated as follows:

+/-	Profits or losses from operating the segment before it is disposed of
+/-	<u>Gains or losses from the act of selling or closing the business</u>
	Net gain or loss on discontinued operations before taxes
-/+	<u>Taxes paid on a net gain or taxes saved on a net loss</u>
	Net gain or loss on discontinued operations

Note that a net gain on the discontinued segment creates taxable income, which causes the corporation to incur an additional tax expense. A net loss on the discontinued segment creates a tax deduction, which allows the corporation to reduce its tax expense.

4. Extraordinary Items: These are revenues or expenses that result from events that are "unusual and infrequent." Examples include natural disasters (flood, earthquake, fire) and condemnation of land or buildings. Extraordinary items must be shown net of tax. An extraordinary gain is reduced by taxes paid; an extraordinary loss is reduced by taxes saved.

5. Changes in Accounting Principles: This section shows the effect of changing from one accepted accounting principle to another. For example, a corporation might choose to change its depreciation method from the straight-line to the declining-balance method. That corporation would need to recompute depreciation for all of its assets under the new method (declining-balance) for any prior years. The amount needed to bring the accumulated depreciation account

up to the balance it would have if the declining-balance method had been used in past years is shown as the cumulative effect of a change in accounting principle. This amount is also shown net of tax.

GROUP LEARNING ACTIVITY — Change in Accounting Principle

Transparency 14-5 presents information concerning a corporation that owns one asset. That corporation decides to switch from straight-line to declining-balance depreciation. Your students are asked to compute depreciation for the asset under these two methods, determine the cumulative effect of the change, and show how this change is reported on the income statement.

Check figures for this exercise are:

1. Straight-line depreciation for 3 years = $60,000.
2. Declining-balance depreciation for 3 years = $78,400.
3. Additional depreciation to be recorded = $18,400.
4. Reported on the income statement as follows:
    Cumulative Effect of a Change in Depreciation
    Methods, net of $7,360 in tax savings = ($11,040).
5. Current year's depreciation expense = $8,640.

Remind students that in the real world, companies have more than one asset. Changing depreciation methods forces the company to recompute depreciation on all assets for all years they have been in use under the new depreciation method. This can be a cumbersome task.

GROUP LEARNING ACTIVITY — Preparing an Income Statement

Transparency 14-6 contains instructions for completing an income statement that contains several below-the-line items. You may want your students to practice preparing an income statement with these unusual items since they must be shown net of tax. Ask students to work in small groups to complete this exercise. The solution to this activity is shown in Transparency 14-7.

Remind students that the unusual items discussed in this learning objective are events which are not likely to recur. Since investors use past income statements to predict future performance, they need to see these items highlighted separately from the results of continuing operations.

WRITING EXERCISE — Below-the-Line Items Reported on the Income Statement

Ask your students to write a response to the following questions (Transparency 14-8).

1. Why are the results of discontinued operations, extraordinary items, and changes in accounting principles shown in separate sections at the bottom of the income statement?
2. Why are discontinued operations, extraordinary items, and changes in accounting principles shown net of tax?

EXERCISES & PROBLEMS FOR REINFORCEMENT:
- Exercise 14-3
- Exercise 14-4
- Exercise 14-5
- Exercise 14-6
- Exercise 14-7
- Exercise 14-8
- Exercise 14-9
- Exercise 14-10
- Exercise 14-11

OBJECTIVE 3 — Prepare an income statement reporting earnings per share data.

KEY TERMS:
  Earnings Per Share (EPS)

SUGGESTED APPROACH

Explain the significance of earnings per share data and present the formula for basic earnings per share. Refer to Transparency 14-4 to show which income statement items are shown on a per-share basis. A group learning activity is included so students can practice this calculation.

LECTURE AIDS — Earnings Per Share

Assume that two couples residing in the same city each have combined incomes of $70,000. Would you expect both couples to have about the same life-style? If you knew that one of those couples had no children and the other couple had seven children, would you still expect both couples to have the same life-style? In this case, the per-person income of the two families is dramatically different.

Couple A—No Children
Earnings per person = $70,000 / 2 = $35,000

Couple B—Seven Children
Earnings per person = $70,000 / 9 = $7,778

This same concept can be applied to corporations. Assume that two corporations both made $100,000 of net income last year. Corporation A has 1,000 shares of stock, and Corporation B has 100,000 shares. Would you rather have a share of stock in Corporation A or B? Corporation A has more income for each share of stock.

Corporation A
Earnings per share = $100,000 / 1,000 = $100

Corporation B
Earnings per share = $100,000 / 100,000 = $1

The formula for earnings per share is as follows:

$$\text{Earnings per share} = \frac{\text{Net Income - Preferred Dividends}}{\text{\# of Common Shares Outstanding}}$$

Remind your students that, if a company has no preferred stock, earnings per share is simply:

$$\text{Earnings per share} = \frac{\text{Net Income}}{\text{\# of Common Shares Outstanding}}$$

Earnings per share data are reported for the following income statement items:

1. Income from continuing operations.
2. Gains or losses on discontinued operations.
3. Income before extraordinary items and the cumulative effect of a change in accounting principle.
4. Extraordinary items.
5. Cumulative effect of a change in accounting principle.
6. Net income.

Earnings per share for income from continuing operations and net income must be presented on the company's income statement. Earnings per share data for the other items may be presented on the income statement or in the notes to the financial statements.

Stress that earnings per share does not normally represent the amount that stockholders can expect to receive in dividends. It would only represent this amount if the corporation paid out all its earnings in dividends.

GROUP LEARNING ACTIVITY — Earnings Per Share

Ask your class to use the income statement for Sigma Shoes, Inc. (prepared under Objective 2) to calculate and report earnings-per-share data. Assume that Sigma has 15,000 shares of $4 preferred stock and 100,000 shares of common stock outstanding. The company chooses to report all earnings per share data on the face of the income statement. The solution is shown in Transparency 14-9.

EXERCISES & PROBLEMS FOR REINFORCEMENT:
Exercise 14-12   Problem 14-2A   Problem 14-2B
Exercise 14-13   Problem 14-3A   Problem 14-3B
Exercise 14-14

OBJECTIVE 4 — Describe the concept and the reporting of comprehensive income.

KEY TERMS:
   Comprehensive Income

SUGGESTED APPROACH

Describing comprehensive income is a challenge, since it encompasses so many advanced accounting topics. However, it is important to address this accounting measure. In 1997, the

Financial Accounting Standards Board issued a statement requiring companies to report comprehensive income.

LECTURE AIDS – Comprehensive Income

The easiest way to explain comprehensive income adjustments is in the context of unrealized gains and losses on investments. Therefore, you may want to cover this objective after discussing investments in stocks (Objective 5).

First, it is important to explain the difference between a realized and unrealized gain. Assume an investor purchases a share of Provident Corp. stock for $10. Next, assume the market price of the stock goes up to $15. If the investor sells the stock for $15, he has a *realized* gain of $5. If the investor doesn't sell the stock, he has an *unrealized* gain of $5. Whether or not the investor sells the share of stock, his net worth is increased as the value of the stock he owns increases.

Traditionally, only *realized* gains on investments are reported as income on a company's income statement. Under this conservative approach, net income is only increased for gains actually "in hand" as a result of selling the investment. However, unrealized gains on certain investments are recorded as an increase in owner's equity to reflect the increase in the business' net worth. For a company with unrealized gains on investments, comprehensive income would be reported as follows:

    Traditional Net Income
  + <u>Unrealized Gain on Investments</u>
    Comprehensive Income

Remind your students that there are other items which effect comprehensive income; however, it is best to discuss these items (such as foreign currency items and pension liability adjustments) in advanced accounting courses.

In summary, comprehensive income is

    Traditional Net Income
  + All Changes in   _____   *except* those resulting from
     <u>Stockholders' Equity</u>   dividends & stockholder investments
    Comprehensive Income

EXERCISES & PROBLEMS FOR REINFORCEMENT:
    Exercise 14-15

OBJECTIVE 5 — Describe the accounting for investments in stocks.

KEY TERMS:
    Available-for-Sale Securities   Marketable Securities
    Cost Method   Temporary Investments
    Equity Method   Trading Securities

Equity Securities — Unrealized Holding Gain or Loss

SUGGESTED APPROACH

Remind students that businesses invest in equity securities for one of the following reasons:

1. To receive a return on excess cash
2. To develop or maintain a business relationship with another company
3. To gain control of another company.

Businesses invest in equity securities by buying stocks either directly from the issuing corporation or from other investors. Purchases from other investors occur through organized stock exchanges (such as the New York Stock Exchange) or over the counter. Use the brainstorming activity below to explore the reasons a business would want to acquire control of another business.

Securities purchased by a business are classified as trading securities or available-for-sale securities. The text illustrates the accounting for available-for-sale securities.

After covering the accounting for short-term and long-term investments, remind students that the sale of stock investments is treated the same in all cases. The difference between the carrying value of the investment and the cash proceeds (sales price less commissions and other selling costs) is recorded as a gain or loss and is included in determining net income.

BRAINSTORMING ACTIVITY — Reasons for Investing in Another Company

Ask your students to brainstorm reasons that a business would want to gain control of another company. This will give you the opportunity to discuss the concepts of horizontal and vertical integration.

DEMONSTRATION PROBLEM — Short-Term Investments

First, cover the difference between a short-term and a long-term investment in stocks. An investment can be considered short-term (a temporary investment) if two conditions are met: (1) the securities are readily marketable and can be sold for cash at any time and (2) management intends to sell the securities when the business needs cash for operations.

Your students will need to know how to record the purchase of short-term stock investments and the receipt of dividends. Before presenting the journal entries, ask your students to use their accounting knowledge to "guess" how the following transactions would be journalized.

Jordan Corporation purchased 1,000 shares of ATE Inc. common stock as a temporary investment on June 1 for a total cost of $38,500.

    Correct answer:

June 1   Marketable Securities............   38,500
                      Cash.....................   38,500

Stress that an investment in equity securities is recorded at cost, including any broker's commissions.

Next, ask your students to record the following transaction in their notes.

On September 30, Jordan received a $1 per share cash dividend on its ATE Inc. common stock. This dividend was declared on August 15.

Correct answer:

Sept. 30   Cash.............................   1,000
                        Dividend Revenue......   1,000

GROUP LEARNING ACTIVITY – Short-Term Investments

Once temporary investments have been purchased, they are reported on the balance sheet at their fair market value, net of any applicable income taxes. Transparency 14-10 provides information about the cost and market value of a portfolio of marketable securities. From this information, ask your students to determine the carrying value that would be shown for the securities on the balance sheet. In order to determine this amount, they will need to compute the unrealized gain or loss and subtract the income taxes related to the gain or loss. Remind students that this unrealized gain or loss, net of tax, is reported under owner's equity on the balance sheet and is included in comprehensive income. The solution is shown on Transparency 14-11.

DEMONSTRATION PROBLEM – Long-Term Investments: no significant influence

The accounting for long-term investments in stocks depends on whether the investor has "significant influence" over the investee. The equity method is used whenever an investor has significant influence over the operating and financing activities of another company. The general guideline to determine whether an investor has a significant influence is the 20% rule. If an investor owns 20% or more of a company's stock, it is presumed that the investor has significant influence. The extent of intercompany transactions and the interchange of managerial personnel can also be factors in determining significant influence.

If the investor does not have significant influence (owns less than 20% of a company's stock), the investment is treated as available-for-sale securities. Similar to short term investments, these stocks are reported on the balance sheet at their market value. To revalue the securities at market, investments are reported on the balance sheet at their cost plus or minus the amount of unrealized gain or loss, net of any tax applicable income taxes.

The journal entries for these long-term investments look very similar to the entries for temporary investments. For example, assume that on Sept. 1, Jordan Corporation purchased 1,000 shares of Cumberland, Inc. as a long-term investment at $15 per share plus a brokerage fee of $60. Jordan's purchase represents less than 20% of the shares of Cumberland, Inc. In addition, there are no other factors which would suggest Jordan had a significant influence over Cumberland. On Oct. 18, Jordan received a $.50 per share dividend. The journal entries for these events are:

Sept. 1	Investment in Cumberland, Inc. Stock	15,060	
	Cash.............................		15,060
Oct. 18	Cash...	500	
	Dividend Revenue..............		500

Point out that, on Sept. 1, "Investment in Cumberland, Inc. Stock" was debited. For short-term investments, the account debited is "Marketable Securities."

DEMONSTRATION PROBLEM – Long-Term Investments: Equity Method

Under the equity method, the investor records a portion of the investee's net income as an increase to the investment account. This increase is also recorded as income to the investor. As a result, cash dividends can be viewed as the receipt of the income previously recorded.

For example, assume that Jordan Corporation purchased a 30% interest in Mini-Marts Inc. for $500,000. For the year ended December 31, Mini-Marts reported net income totaling $100,000. On January 18, Mini-Marts paid a $40,000 cash dividend.

Entry to record the purchase of Mini-Marts Inc. stock:

Investment in Mini-Marts Inc. Stock	500,000	
Cash.......................................		500,000

Note that the initial investment is recorded the same whether or not the investor has significant influence over the investee.

Entry to record 30% of Mini-Marts' net income:

Investment in Mini-Marts Inc. Stock	30,000	
Income of Mini Marts Inc............		30,000

Entry to record receipt of 30% of Mini-Marts' cash dividend:

Cash..	12,000	
Investment in Mini-Marts Inc. Stock..		12,000

EXERCISES & PROBLEMS FOR REINFORCEMENT:

Exercise 14-16	Exercise 14-20	Problem 14-4A	Problem 14-4B
Exercise 14-17	Exercise 14-21		
Exercise 14-18	Exercise 14-22		
Exercise 14-19	Exercise 14-23		

OBJECTIVE 6 — Describe alternative methods of combining businesses and how consolidated financial statements are prepared.

KEY TERMS:
- Consolidated Statements
- Consolidation
- Goodwill
- Merger
- Minority Interest
- Parent Company
- Purchase Method
- Subsidiary Company

SUGGESTED APPROACH

Transparency 14-12 lists the three methods used to combine businesses. Review this transparency with your class. Explain that parent-subsidiary relationships are accounted for under the purchase method. This method accounts for the purchase of a subsidiary company similar to the purchase of other types of assets. The subsidiary's net assets are reported in the consolidated balance sheet at their fair market values at the time of purchase. If the parent pays more than the fair value of the subsidiary's net assets, the difference is recorded as Goodwill.

Remind students that consolidated financial statements combine the income statements, balance sheets, and other financial reports of a parent company and its subsidiaries into one set of financial statements. The combined financial statements are more meaningful because, in reality, the parent company controls the subsidiary companies. A parent accounts for its ownership in a subsidiary using the equity method.

Also remind students that intercompany transactions must be eliminated when the financial statements are combined. For example, if the parent company has loaned cash to a subsidiary, the consolidated balance sheet should not show the parent's receivable or the subsidiary's payable.

Transparency 14-13 summarizes the steps to consolidate the income statements of two companies. The demonstration problem below can be used to illustrate consolidated income statements.

DEMONSTRATION PROBLEM — Consolidated Income Statements

Transparency 14-14 presents the income statements for two companies. The goal is to consolidate the statements by eliminating an intercompany sale. The transparency is set up in a slightly different format from Exhibits 6 and 7 in the text. Transparency 14-14 includes a column to show the adjustments needed to eliminate the intercompany sale. The solution is found on Transparency 14-15.

OBJECTIVE 7 — Compute and interpret the price-earnings ratio.

KEY TERMS:
    Price-Earnings Ratio

SUGGESTED APPROACH

Present the following scenario to your class. Two companies (company A and company B) both had earnings per share of $10 this past year. The stock of company A is selling for $20 per share and the stock of company B is selling for $50. Why are investors willing to pay more for B's stock if that company is earning the same profits per share as company A?

Point out that investors buy stock based on how they believe the company will perform in the future. Therefore, investors must believe company B has better prospects for future earnings.

The price-earnings ratio (P/E ratio) measures the spread between earnings and stock price. It is calculated as follows:

$$\frac{\text{Market Price per Share of Common Stock}}{\text{Earnings per Share of Common Stock}} = \text{P/E Ratio}$$

The P/E ratio for company A is 2; company B's ratio is 5. The higher ratio indicates greater optimism regarding a company's growth potential.

INTERNET ACTIVITY – P/E Ratio

At that time this manual was written, the following web site provided a very comprehensive overview of the P/E Ratio: http://www.investopedia.com/terms/p/price-earningsratio.asp.

You may also want to instruct your students to use the internet to search for information about an alternative to the P/E Ratio which is growing in popularity: the price-earnings growth ratio or PEG ratio.

EXERCISES & PROBLEMS FOR REINFORCEMENT:
    Exercise 14-24
    Exercise 14-25

Bravara Corporation

Income Statement
For the Year Ended December 31, 2004

Net Sales...		$1,200,000
Cost of merchandise sold..........		410,000
Gross profit		$ 790,000
Operating expenses:		
Salaries expense	$300,000	
Utilities expense	170,000	
Advertising expense	60,000	
Depreciation expense	43,000	
Miscellaneous expense	37,000	610,000
Income before income tax		$ 180,000

Transparency Master 14-2

NET INCOME VS. TAXABLE INCOME

The income statement for Gibson Corporation's year ended December 31, 2004, is as follows:

Net Sales		$500,000
Cost of merchandise sold		200,000
Gross profit		$300,000
Operating expenses:		
Salaries expense	$75,000	
Utilities expense	30,000	
Warranty expense	10,000	
Depreciation expense	15,000	
Other expense	8,000	138,000
Income before income tax		$162,000

Gibson has the following temporary differences:

1. Straight-line depreciation is used when preparing financial statements. Accelerated depreciation is used for tax purposes. Gibson's depreciation expense for the year under accelerated methods is $27,000.
2. The amount shown on the financial statements for warranty expense is the estimated cost of warranty repairs that will be made on all units sold this year. However, Gibson spent only $6,000 on warranty repairs this year. Warranty expenses must be paid in order to deduct them when preparing a tax return.

Required:

1. Calculate the amount of taxable income that will be reported on Gibson's tax return.
2. Assume that Gibson's tax rate is 40%. Calculate the income taxes that will be paid now, based on Gibson's taxable income.
3. Calculate the income taxes that Gibson would have paid if the amount shown as "Income before Income Tax" on the financial statements was the amount on which Gibson was taxed.
4. Compute the taxes that Gibson has deferred to future years. This is the difference between the numbers you calculated in #2 and #3.
5. Prepare the journal entry to record Gibson's income taxes (you may want to refer to the example in the text).
6. Complete Gibson's 2004 income statement, starting with Income before Income Tax.

Transparency Master 14-3

NET INCOME VS. TAXABLE INCOME

Solution

1. Net income per accounting records $162,000
   Additional depreciation under accelerated depreciation ($27,000 – $15,000) .... (12,000)
   Warranty expense accrued but not paid ($10,000 – $6,000) 4,000
   Net income per tax return $154,000

2. $154,000 × 40% = $61,600

3. $162,000 × 40% = $64,800

4. $64,800 – $61,600 = $3,200

5. Income Tax Expense 64,800
      Income Tax Payable 61,600
      Deferred Income Tax Payable 3,200

6. Net income before income tax $162,000
   Income tax expense 64,800
   Net income .... $ 97,200

Transparency Master 14-4

INCOME STATEMENT

    Net Sales
− **Cost of Merchandise Sold**
    Gross profit
− **Operating Expenses (Selling and Administrative)**
− **Restructuring Charge**
− **Loss from Asset Impairment**
    Income from Continuing Operations before Tax
− **Income Tax Expense**
    Income from Continuing Operations*
+/− **Gain or Loss on Discontinued Operations (net of tax)***
+/− **Extraordinary Items (net of tax)***
+/− **Cumulative Effect of a Change in Accounting Principle (net of tax)***
    Net Income*

*Must show earnings per share data.

Transparency Master 14-5

CHANGE IN ACCOUNTING PRINCIPLE

A corporation has one asset that originally cost $100,000. That asset has a 5-year expected life. As of the beginning of 2004, 3 years of depreciation had been recorded on the asset.

This corporation has decided to change from straight-line to declining-balance depreciation beginning in 2004. The corporation's tax rate is 40%.

1. Choose two group members to compute the depreciation that was recorded in the first 3 years using straight-line depreciation.

2. The remaining group members need to compute the depreciation that would have been recorded in the first 3 years if declining-balance depreciation had been used.

3. Compare depreciation totals from #1 and #2 to determine how much additional depreciation needs to be recorded to bring the accumulated depreciation account up to the balance it should have under the declining-balance method.

4. Show how this additional depreciation will be reported on an income statement.

5. What amount will be shown for the current year's depreciation expense on the income statement?

Transparency Master 14-6

PREPARATION OF AN INCOME STATEMENT

Starting with the subtotal "Income from Continuing Operations before Income Tax," complete the income statement for Sigma Shoes, Inc. using the following information.

1. Sigma's income from continuing operations before income tax is $1.65 million.

2. Sigma's income tax rate is 40%.

3. During the year, Sigma sold its casual shoe division so that the company could concentrate on athletic shoes. The casual shoe division had a $30,000 net loss for the year prior to its sale. Sigma realized a $195,000 gain on the sale of the division.

4. A flash flood destroyed $70,000 worth of inventory in one of Sigma's warehouses.

5. Sigma decided to change from straight-line to declining-balance depreciation. If declining-balance depreciation had been used in prior years, Sigma would have recorded an additional $280,000 in accumulated depreciation.

PREPARATION OF AN INCOME STATEMENT

Sigma Shoes, Inc.
Income Statement
For the Year Ended December 31, 20—

Income from continuing operations before income tax...	$1,650,000
Income tax expense ($1,650,000 × 40%)....	660,000
Income from continuing operations	$ 990,000
Gain on discontinued operations, net of $66,000 in income taxes	99,000
Income before extraordinary item and the cumulative effect of a change in accounting principle	$1,089,000
Extraordinary item: Loss due to flood, net of $28,000 in income tax savings ...	(42,000)
Cumulative effect of changing to a different depreciation method, net of $112,000 in income tax savings........	(168,000)
Net income...	$ 879,000

WRITING EXERCISE

1. Why are the results of discontinued operations, extraordinary items, and changes in accounting principles shown in separate sections at the bottom of the income statement?

2. Why are discontinued operations, extraordinary items, and changes in accounting principles shown net of tax?

Transparency Master 14-9

EARNINGS PER SHARE DATA FOR SIGMA SHOES, INC.

Income from continuing operations
  ($990,000 – $60,000) / 100,000……………….… $ 9.30

Gain on discontinued operations
  ($99,000 / 100,000)……………………..……….. .99

Income before extraordinary item and
  the cumulative effect of a change in
  accounting principle…………………………… $ 10.29

Extraordinary item……………………………….. (.42)

Cumulative effect of a change in
  accounting principle…………………………… (1.68)

Net income ($879,000 - $60,000) / 100,000…….. $ 8.19

TEMPORARY INVESTMENTS

Portfolio of Temporary Investments	Cost	Market Value	Unrealized Gain(Loss)
Security A	$10,000	$10,000	$
Security B	22,000	21,900	
Security C	8,000	9,500	
Total	$40,000	$41,400	

Cost............................ $40,000

Unrealized Gain/(Loss)..................

40% Income Tax Paid/(Savings)...............

Value Reported on Balance Sheet...............

Transparency Master 14-11

TEMPORARY INVESTMENTS
Solution

Portfolio of Temporary Investments	Cost	Market Value	Unrealized Gain(Loss)
Security A	$10,000	$10,000	$ 0
Security B	22,000	21,900	(100)
Security C	8,000	9,500	1,500
Total	$40,000	$41,400	$1,400

Cost………………………. $40,000

Unrealized Gain/(Loss)……………… $1,400

40% Income Tax (Paid)/Savings………….. ($560)

Value Reported on Balance Sheet………….. $40,840

BUSINESS COMBINATIONS

Three methods are used to combine businesses, as follows:

1. <u>Merger</u>—One company purchases the assets and liabilities of another company. The acquired company is dissolved.

2. <u>Consolidation</u>—Two companies transfer their assets and liabilities to a new corporation. Both of the original companies are dissolved.

3. <u>Parent-Subsidiary Relationship</u>—One company purchases a controlling interest in another company by acquiring shares of its voting stock. Neither company is dissolved.

STEPS TO CONSOLIDATE INCOME STATEMENTS

1. Eliminate any revenues and expenses resulting from intercompany transactions, including the following:

    a. Revenues on intercompany sales
    b. Cost of merchandise sold resulting from intercompany purchases
    c. Interest income or expense on intercompany loans
    d. Management fees or other costs charged by the parent and paid by the subsidiary

2. Combine the remaining amounts for all revenue and expense accounts.

CONSOLIDATED INCOME STATEMENTS

P Corp. sold merchandise to S Corp. for $1,000. The merchandise cost P Corp. $400. S Corp. sold the merchandise to a customer for $1,500.

	P Corp.	S Corp.	Elimination Entry	Consolidated Income Statement
Sales	$100,000	$20,000		
Cost of Merch. Sold	30,000	6,000		
Gross Profit	$ 70,000	$14,000		
Operating Expenses	50,000	10,000		
Net Income	$ 20,000	$ 4,000		

CONSOLIDATED INCOME STATEMENTS
Solution

	P Corp.	S Corp.	Elimination Entry	Consolidated Income Statement
Sales	$100,000	$20,000	-$1,000	$119,000
Cost of Merch. Sold	30,000	6,000	-$1,000	35,000
Gross Profit	$ 70,000	$14,000		$ 84,000
Operating Expenses	50,000	10,000		60,000
Net Income	$ 20,000	$ 4,000		$ 24,000

Chapter 15
Bonds Payable and Investments in Bonds

OPENING COMMENTS

The subject of bonds is a challenge for most students. This chapter requires students to apply difficult concepts that most of them have not encountered before: for example, present value and amortization of bond discounts and premiums.

Before attacking bond problems that require the use of present-value tables, take the time to explain this new concept thoroughly and to demonstrate several applications of present-value techniques. This will make present value meaningful and will ease its application to bonds.

After studying the chapter, your students should be able to:

1. Compute the potential impact of long-term borrowing on the earnings per share of a corporation.
2. Describe the characteristics of bonds.
3. Compute the present value of bonds payable.
4. Journalize entries for bonds payable.
5. Describe bond sinking funds.
6. Journalize entries for bond redemptions.
7. Journalize entries for the purchase, interest, discount and premium amortization, and sale of bond investments.
8. Prepare a corporation balance sheet.
9. Compute and interpret the number of times interest charges earned.

OBJECTIVE 1 — Compute the potential impact of long-term borrowing on the earnings per share of a corporation.

KEY TERMS:
    Bond

SUGGESTED APPROACH

In this objective, you need to sensitize students to the trade-offs between equity and debt financing. Notes to assist you with this discussion are included below.

It is also very useful to examine the financial impact of financing with debt and equity. The textbook presents two exhibits (Exhibits 1 & 2) that compare three alternative financing plans under two different income levels ($800,000 and $440,000). These exhibits are designed to illustrate the effect of leverage. To expand this illustration, four additional exhibits examining income levels of $200,000, $300,000, $1 million, and $1.5 million are included in this manual

(Transparencies 15-1 through 15-4). These should give your students a more complete picture of the power of leverage to magnify financial returns as profits increase, and the risk of leverage as profits decrease.

In addition to risk factors, corporations consider interest rates and stock prices when determining whether to raise funds through debt or equity financing. For example, corporations often issue new stock to finance operations when stock prices are high, and debt securities when interest rates are low.

Point out that the U.S. Government uses bonds to finance its operations. U.S. Treasury and U.S. Savings bonds are debt securities issued by our government.

LECTURE AIDS — Risk and Return

Ask students the following questions to introduce the relationship between risk and return.

> How many of you buy lottery tickets? Why do you buy them? By a show of hands, how many of you would buy a $1 lottery ticket if the jackpot were $1 million? How many of you would buy a $1 lottery ticket if the jackpot were $10 million? How many of you would buy a $1 lottery ticket if the jackpot were $50 million? How many of you would buy a $1 lottery ticket if the jackpot were $1.04? (You should get some strange looks, but no takers.)
>
> Why wouldn't you buy the lottery ticket that pays $1.04? That's a 4% return on your money if you win. Some folks keep money in savings accounts that earn less than 4%.

Hopefully, your students will point out that interest earned on a savings account is a sure bet, whereas winning the lottery is a long shot. This story illustrates the relationship between risk and reward. The riskier an investment, the greater the reward an investor expects if his or her investment pays off.

When a company is considering whether to raise funds by selling stock (equity) or issuing bonds (debt), it must balance the following information:

1. Debt funding is cheaper than equity funding. Because shareholders accept more risk than creditors do, they demand a greater return. The shareholders will want a return on their investment through dividends and share appreciation that is greater than the interest rate paid to bondholders.

2. Debt funding uses leverage to increase shareholder returns. Purchasing additional assets through debt allows a company to expand its operations and generate more profits. Creditors must be paid interest for the use of their money out of those profits, but anything left goes to the shareholders.

3. Debt funding is riskier than equity funding. When sales and profits drop, a corporation can cease paying dividends. However, it cannot cease its debt payments.

EXERCISES & PROBLEMS FOR REINFORCEMENT:
  Exercise 15-1   Problem 15-1A   Problem 15-1B
  Exercise 15-2
  Exercise 15-3

OBJECTIVE 2 — Describe the characteristics of bonds.

KEY TERMS:
  Bond Indenture   Debenture Bonds
  Callable Bonds   Serial Bonds
  Convertible Bonds   Term Bonds

SUGGESTED APPROACH

Use Transparencies 15-5 and 15-6 to review the characteristics of bonds and the types of bonds that may be issued. After reviewing Transparency 15-6 and the following information concerning callable and convertible bonds, ask your class to identify bond characteristics that increase the risk assumed by the bondholder and those that reduce the bondholder's risk.

  Characteristics that increase   Characteristics that decrease
  the bondholder's risk: the bondholder's risk:
    Term bonds   Serial bonds
    Callable bonds   Convertible bonds
    Debenture bonds   Secured bonds

Bonds may be guaranteed against default by the purchase of insurance by the issuing entity. Municipal governments sometimes insure their bonds against default to reduce the risk to the investor and increase the proceeds from issuing the bonds.

Many of your students will have heard the term "junk bonds." Junk bonds are bonds issued by a corporation to finance the takeover of another company. They are secured by the assets and expected profits of the company targeted for takeover, and they offer a high interest rate to make them attractive.

LECTURE AIDS — Convertible and Callable Bonds

Convertible bonds give the bondholder the right to exchange his or her bonds for shares of stock if certain conditions exist. However, the bondholder chooses whether or not to convert. Bondholders convert bonds only if it is to their benefit.

Callable bonds may be redeemed by the corporation at its option. Therefore, the corporation will redeem bonds only if it will benefit the corporation. For example, if interest rates drop, the corporation may pay off bonds that carry a high interest rate and issue bonds with a low rate. This hurts the bondholder because he or she must turn in a bond that is paying a high interest rate and invest in a bond with a lower interest rate. As a result, callable bonds are riskier for the investor.

OBJECTIVE 3 — Compute the present value of bonds payable.

KEY TERMS:
    Annuity   Market (Effective) Rate of Interest
    Contract (Coupon) Rate   Premium
    Discount   Present Value
    Future Value   Present Value of an Annuity

SUGGESTED APPROACH

This objective introduces students to present-value concepts. This concept is new to most accounting principles students, and many find it very difficult. Therefore, you may want to spend time discussing present value in general before applying this concept to bonds.

A series of questions follow, which you can ask your class to lead into a discussion of present value. Several demonstration problems showing the use of present value outside the area of bonds are also presented. To give your students a chance to practice these concepts, assign Handout 15-1 as a group learning activity or as homework. The solution to this handout is found on Transparency 15-7.

LECTURE AIDS — Introduction to Present Value

Present the following scenario to your class.

> If I told you that I would give you $100 today or $100 one year from now, how many of you would want the money today? What if I told you that I would give you $100 today or $105 one year from now? How many of you would wait one year to get an extra $5? If I offered to pay $110 one year from now, how many would wait one year for an extra $10? What about $125 in one year? What about $150 in one year?

Ask a student who did not raise his or her hand when you offered $105 why he or she was not willing to wait one year for the extra $5. Next, ask a student who did raise his or her hand when you offered $125 or $150 why he or she was willing to wait one year to receive an extra $25 or $50.

Your students' comments should provide a good lead-in to a discussion of time value of money.

DEMONSTRATION PROBLEMS — Present Value of a Single Sum

One hundred dollars today is more valuable than $100 in the future. You can invest the $100 you have today and end up with more than $100 in the future.

Ask your students to calculate how much money they would have in one year if they invested $100 and earned 7% interest on their money (Answer: $107).

Look at this same concept from the reverse perspective. How much money do you need to invest today to have $100 in one year if interest rates are 7%? Show your students how to solve this problem with an algebraic equation.

let X = $ to be invested today

X + .07X = $100
1.07X = $100
X = $100/1.07
X = $93.46

$93.46 is the present value of receiving $100 in one year if interest rates are 7%.

Next, ask your students to write down the equation to determine how much they would need to invest to have $100 in 2 years, assuming a 7% interest rate. After a minute, show them the correct formula.

X + .07X = 1.07X (what you will have at the end of year 1)
1.07X + .07(1.07X) = 1.1449X (the amount at the end of year 2)

Therefore,
1.145X = $100
X = $87.34

This calculation gets fairly complex after just 2 years because of the compounding of interest. Present-value tables, such as the one in Exhibit 3 in the text, were developed as a shortcut. To calculate the amount needed today to accumulate $100 in 2 years at 7%, the present-value factor from the table for two periods at 7% is multiplied by $100.

$100 x 0.87344 = $87.34.

Ask your students to use the table to find the present value of receiving $100,000 ten years from now at 7%.

$100,000 x 0.50835 = $50,835

In simple terms, this means that $50,835 invested at 7% will grow to $100,000 in 10 years.

Finally, ask your students to answer the following question (Transparency 15-8).

Assume that you have a rich uncle who dies. In his will, he leaves you with the following option: You can have $100,000 today or $200,000 in 10 years. Interest rates are 10% Which should you choose?

$200,000 x 0.38554 = $77,108
$100,000 > $77,108, so take the $100,000 now

DEMONSTRATION PROBLEMS — Present Value of an Annuity

Begin by defining an annuity. An annuity is a series of equal payments at equal intervals (for example, $100 per year for 5 years). Ask students for examples of annuities. Examples include insurance and pension annuities.

Demonstrate the need to calculate the present value of an annuity through the following scenario.

> Assume that you have won a sweepstakes with a $5 million grand prize. Now you have to choose how to take your winnings: $500,000 per year for 10 years or $3 million now. If interest rates are 11%, which would you choose?

To solve this problem, you need to compare the $3 million that could be yours today with what receiving the money over 10 years is worth today. In other words, you need to compute the present value of an annuity using the table in text Exhibit 4.

To calculate the present value of an annuity:

Annuity Amount x Factor from PV Table for Annuities (Exhibit 4)

$500,000 x 5.88923 = $2,944,615
$3,000,000 > $2,944,615, so take the $3 million today

Next, ask your students to determine whether they would want the sweepstakes prize today or over 10 years if they could earn only 6% interest on investments.

$500,000 x 7.36009 = $3,680,045
$3,000,000 < $3,680,045, so take payments over 10 years

GROUP LEARNING ACTIVITY — Present Value of an Annuity

Transparency 15-9 contains additional annuity problems to be solved with present-value concepts. One of these problems requires students to use present value interest factors for a 20 year period. These factors can be found on the expanded present value tables included in Appendix A of the text.

Ask your students to solve the present value problems in small groups. Transparency 15-10 presents the solutions.

EXERCISES & PROBLEMS FOR REINFORCEMENT:
    Exercise 15-4
    Exercise 15-5
    Exercise 15-6
    Exercise 15-7

OBJECTIVE 4 — Journalize entries for bonds payable.

KEY TERMS:
    Effective Interest Rate Method
    Zero-Coupon Bonds

SUGGESTED APPROACH

Transparency 15-11 details the steps that a corporation uses in issuing bonds. It also points out the problem with interest rate fluctuations when issuing a bond.

After reviewing this information, use the following lecture aids and problems to demonstrate calculations to determine the issue price of a bond.

LECTURE AIDS — Issuance of a Bond

Pose the following question to your class:

> Assume that your bond has an interest rate of 10% when other bonds are paying 12%. Investors will not want to buy your bond if they can earn 12% elsewhere. What can you do to get investors to buy your 10% bond? Answer: lower the price.
>
> You will need to drop the price of your bond so the investors are really getting a 12% return. In other words, you need to drop the price to the present value of the bond using a 12% interest rate. You will need to sell the bond at a discount.

The selling price of a bond is determined by the relationship between the bond's contract interest rate and the market interest rate when the bond is sold.

> If contract rate = market rate, bond sells at face value.
> If contract rate > market rate, bond sells at a premium.
> If contract rate < market rate, bond sells at a discount.

When determining the present value of a bond, the following two components must be viewed separately:

1. Principal, repaid when bond matures (a single payment). Use Exhibit 3 to determine the present value.
2. Interest payments, usually made semiannually (an annuity). Use Exhibit 4 to determine the present value.

DEMONSTRATION PROBLEM — Issuance of a Bond

On January 1, a corporation issued a $1 million, 5-year, 10% bond that pays interest semiannually. The market interest rate on January 1 was 12%.

Principal = $1,000,000
Interest payments = $50,000 ([$1,000,000 x 10%] /2)

NOTE: Stress that interest payments are based on the bond's contract interest rate.

1. PV of principal, i = 6%, n = 10
   Stress that a 6% interest rate is used because the bond pays interest semiannually. Therefore, the 12% annual rate must be divided by 2 to get a 6% semiannual rate.

   $1,000,000 x 0.55840 .... $558,400

2. PV of interest payments, i = 6%, n = 10

   $50,000 x 7.36009 .... $368,005

   Selling price of bond $926,405

Always do a reasonableness check: Market interest rate is greater than contract rate, so the bond should sell at a discount. The calculation appears OK because $926,405 is less than the face value of $1 million.

The journal entry to record issuing the bond is:

Cash...................................	926,405	
Discount on Bonds Payable.........	73,595	
Bonds Payable..............		1,000,000

Emphasize that the Discount on Bonds Payable is a contra account which reduces the Bonds Payable account on the balance sheet. The normal balance of Discount on Bonds Payable is a debit.

GROUP LEARNING ACTIVITY — Issuance of a Bond

Ask your students to work in groups to determine the selling price (present value) of the bonds listed on Transparency 15-12. The correct solutions are displayed on Transparencies 15-13 and 15-14. Remind students that they may need to use the expanded present value tables in Appendix A.

LECTURE AIDS — Amortizing a Bond Discount using the Straight-Line Method

Refer to the previous demonstration problem in which the $1 million, 5-year, 10% bond that paid interest semiannually was sold for $926,405 to yield the market interest rate of 12%. In the case of that bond, the following statements are true:
1. The investor loans the company $926,405 by buying the bond.
2. At the end of the 5 years, the company repays the investor $1 million.

3. Therefore, the investor gets $73,595 more at maturity than he or she paid for the bonds. The $73,595 discount is really just extra interest that is paid in one lump sum at maturity. It's the extra interest needed to bring the bond up to a 12% interest rate.
4. Because the $73,595 discount is really just extra interest, it must be recorded as interest expense. This interest must be spread across the 5-year term of the bond. The process of recognizing a portion of the discount as interest each time an interest payment is made to the bondholder is called amortizing the discount.

Straight-line amortization of a bond discount is similar to straight-line depreciation. The discount is amortized evenly over the bond's life. The bond mentioned previously has a life of 5 years or a total of 10 semiannual interest payments. If the discount is spread over the 10 semiannual interest payments, $7,359.50 of the discount is amortized on each payment date ($73,595/10). Since the discount is additional interest, the interest expense recognized is greater than the amount of interest paid.

The journal entry to record the interest payment and discount amortization is:

    Interest Expense...................... 57,359.50
        Discount on Bonds Payable   7,359.50
        Cash ($1,000,000 x 5%)...   50,000.00

LECTURE AIDS — Zero-Coupon Bonds

A corporation issuing zero-coupon bonds does not make periodic interest payments on its bonds. The corporation's only payment is to repay the face amount of the bonds at maturity.

As a result, zero-coupon bonds sell at a substantial discount. The bondholder's interest is the difference between the purchase price of the bond and the face amount at maturity. The purchase price of zero-coupon bonds is determined by computing the present value of the face amount at the market interest rate.

Ask your students to identify zero-coupon bonds by consulting the Wall Street Journal. Note that the Wall Street Journal identifies zero-coupon bonds with a "z" in the quotation.

DEMONSTRATION PROBLEM — Zero-Coupon Bonds

A corporation issues $50,000 in zero-coupon bonds due in 5 years. Assume that the market interest rate is 10%, compounded semiannually.

    Principal = $50,000
    Interest payments = 0

    PV of principal, i = 5%, n = 10
        $50,000 x 0.61391 = $30,696

Therefore, the selling price of the bonds is $30,696. The journal entry to record the issuance of the bond is:

Cash.................................	30,696	
Discount on Bonds Payable.......	19,304	
Bonds Payable.............		50,000

The $19,304 discount is amortized as interest expense over the life of the bond.

EXERCISES & PROBLEMS FOR REINFORCEMENT:
Exercise 15-8	Problem 15-2A	Problem 15-2B
Exercise 15-9	Problem 15-3A	Problem 15-3B
Exercise 15-10		
Exercise 15-11		
Exercise 15-12		
Exercise 15-13		

OBJECTIVE 5 — Describe bond sinking funds.

KEY TERMS:
    Sinking Fund

SUGGESTED APPROACH

A bond agreement may require the issuing corporation to make periodic deposits in a sinking fund. These deposits may be invested in other securities to accumulate the cash needed to repay the principal on the bonds at maturity. As an alternative, sinking fund deposits may be used to repurchase corporate bonds, so that some of the debt from a bond issue is retired each year. Either way, bond sinking funds reduce risks to the bondholder by increasing the probability that the bond principal will be repaid on or before maturity.

Transparency 15-15 lists the accounts used to record entries for a bond sinking fund.

OBJECTIVE 6 — Journalize entries for bond redemptions.

KEY TERMS:
    Carrying Amount

SUGGESTED APPROACH

Begin coverage of Objective 6 by stating that the redemption of bonds refers to the retirement of bonds before they mature. Bonds can be retired before they mature by: (1) exercising a call feature or (2) purchasing the bonds on the open market. In either case, it is likely that the company will incur a gain or a loss on the transaction.

Use the following demonstration problem to illustrate the redemption of bonds. Remind students that any gain or loss on the early retirement of bonds is reported in the extraordinary items section of the income statement.

DEMONSTRATION PROBLEM — Entries for Bond Redemptions

When redeeming a bond, compare the bond's carrying value to the price paid to redeem the bonds.

If carrying value > the cost to redeem, a gain is recognized.
If carrying value < the cost to redeem, a loss is recognized.

Assume that a $500,000 bond with a $7,000 premium is called for redemption at 102.

Bonds Payable...............................	500,000	
Premium on Bonds Payable................	7,000	
Loss on Redemption of Bonds............	3,000	
Cash...................................		510,000

Ask students to record the entry to call the bonds at 101 in their notes. The correct answer:

Bonds Payable............................	500,000	
Premium on Bonds Payable.............	7,000	
Cash..............................		505,000
Gain on Redemption of Bonds		2,000

EXERCISES & PROBLEMS FOR REINFORCEMENT:
   Exercise 15-14   Problem 15-4A   Problem 15-4B
   Exercise 15-15

OBJECTIVE 7 — Journalize entries for the purchase, interest, discount and premium amortization, and sale of bond investments.

SUGGESTED APPROACH

When a bond is purchased as an investment, it is recorded in Investment in Bonds, an asset account. Interest received is recognized as interest revenue. Any premium or discount on the bond purchase must be amortized. Use Transparency 15-16 to contrast the effect of amortizing a premium or discount on bond investments and bonds payable. Use the following demonstration problems to illustrate journal entries for bond investments.

DEMONSTRATION PROBLEM — Investment in Bonds

Smyth Co. purchased a $1,000 bond of the Whitney Corporation on March 1 at 84 plus a $15 brokerage fee and accrued interest. The bond pays 12% interest semiannually, on December 31 and June 30.

Accrued Interest: Assuming that Smyth still owns the bond on June 30, it will receive a $60 check from Whitney Corporation for 6 months' interest. However, Smyth owned the bond for only 4 months (March to June). The first 2 months' interest should go to the person who owned the bond before Smyth.

To solve this problem, Smyth will pay the previous owner for 2 months of interest ($20) when purchasing the bond. When Smyth receives the full 6-month interest payment at the end of June, the company will be reimbursed for the 2 months of interest paid to the previous bond owner.

The journal entry to record this bond purchase:

    Investment in Bonds ($840 + $15).......   855
    Interest Revenue...........................   20
        Cash.................................   875

The journal entry to record receipt of the first interest payment:

    Cash.......................................   60
        Interest Revenue...................   60

The accrued interest paid to the previous bondholder was debited to the interest revenue account, establishing a negative balance in that account. The entire 6-month interest payment was credited to the interest revenue account when it was received. This leaves an account balance of $40, the 4 months of interest that Smyth earned by holding the bond March 1 through June 30.

Interest Revenue	
Interest paid to previous owner 20	
	60 6-month interest payment
	40 4-months' interest earned by Smyth

Amortization of the Discount: Smyth purchased the Whitney Corporation bond at a discount. Even though Smyth paid only $840 for the bond, the company will receive the full $1,000 face value if the bond is held to maturity. Therefore, the $160 discount actually represents additional interest that Smyth will earn over the term of the bond. Therefore, Smyth must amortize the discount as additional interest revenue.

Point out that discounts (and premiums) on bonds held as investments are not recorded in separate discount or premium accounts. They are included in the investment account. In addition, most companies amortize any discount or premium on bonds held as investments at the end of the year rather than when interest payments are received.

Assume that Smyth determines it should amortize $33 of the bond discount at the end of the first year.

The journal entry to amortize the discount:

> Investment in Bonds............................. 33
>   Interest Revenue......................   33

Notice that the amortization of the discount increases both the investment in bonds and interest revenue accounts. The balance in the investment in bonds account after amortization of the discount is $888, as illustrated below.

Investment in Bonds	
Beginning balance	855
Discount amortized	33
Ending balance	888

When the discount is fully amortized, the balance in the Investment in Bonds account will be $1,000. This is the amount of principal which will be paid to Smyth at maturity.

Ask your students the following question. Does the amortization of a premium on a bond investment increase or decrease interest income? Answer: decrease.

DEMONSTRATION PROBLEM — Sale of a Bond Investment

Assume that Smyth holds the bond purchased in the previous problem for 3 years. At the end of the third year, the bond is sold for $1,150 plus accrued interest of $50. The carrying value of the bond (including amortization of the premium) is $968. Note that the amortization of bond premium or discount should be brought up to date before recording the sale of a bond investment.

The journal entry to record the sale:
> Cash.. 1,200
>   Interest Revenue................   50
>   Investment in Bonds............   968
>   Gain on Sale of Investments...   182

INTERNET ACTIVITY – Investing in Bonds

After learning all the intricacies of accounting for bonds, your students may enjoy learning about opportunities to invest in bonds. You may want to refer them to the following websites:
> http://moneycentral.msn.com/content/Investing/Buyingbonds/Buyingbonds.asp
> http://www.investinginbonds.com/
> http://www.fool.com/FoolFAQ/FoolFAQ0010.htm

EXERCISES & PROBLEMS FOR REINFORCEMENT:
> Exercise 15-17   Problem 15-5A   Problem 15-5B
> Exercise 15-18
> Exercise 15-19

OBJECTIVE 8 — Prepare a corporation balance sheet.

KEY TERMS:
  Held-to-Maturity Securities

SUGGESTED APPROACH

Use the following notes to review the presentation of bonds payable and investments in bonds. Refer your students to Exhibit 5 in the text for an example of a consolidated balance sheet which illustrates many of the accounting practices covered in Chapters 7 through 15.

LECTURE AIDS — Balance Sheet Presentation of Bonds Payable

Ask your students where bonds payable are reported on a balance sheet. Unless bonds are due to mature within the next year, they are listed in the Long-Term Liabilities section of the balance sheet. Bonds to be paid from a sinking fund are always reported as a noncurrent liability even if they will be paid within one year. This treatment is required since the sinking fund from which the bonds will be paid is listed as a noncurrent asset.

Next, ask students to write in their notes how a $100,000 bond with a $7,000 unamortized discount should appear on the balance sheet of the issuing company. After a minute, review the following solution with your students:

Long-term liabilities:
  Bond payable $100,000
  Less discount   7,000 $93,000

Remind your students that a premium is added to the bond payable account.

Review the following list of information which must be disclosed in the financial statements or accompanying notes of any company that has issued bonds:

1. Description of bond, including
    a. Term
    b. Security (collateral)
    c. Due date
    d. Effective interest rate
2. Maturities and/or sinking fund requirements for each of the next 5 years
3. Fair market value of the bonds

LECTURE AIDS — Balance Sheet Presentation of Investment in Bonds

Investments in Bonds are reported in the Assets section of the Balance Sheet under the caption Investments. The value reported is the cost of the investment less any amortized premium or plus any amortized discount. The fair market value of the investment also must be disclosed.

EXERCISES & PROBLEMS FOR REINFORCEMENT:
    Exercise 15-16

OBJECTIVE 9 – Compute and interpret the number of times interest charges earned.

SUGGESTED APPROACH

The number of times interest charges earned compares the "pool" of money available for interest payments to a company's interest expense. The larger the "pool," the easier it is for a company to meet its interest payments. The group learning activity below will help your students master this concept.

GROUP LEARNING ACTIVITY – Number of Times Interest Charges Earned

Transparency 15-17 lists revenue and expense data for Bates Corporation. Ask your students, working in small groups, to compute the amount of funds available to pay interest charges. The correct answer is $10,000. This amount is obtained by subtracting the operating expenses from the revenues. If any of your groups answer $6,000, they have deducted income taxes. Point out that interest is a tax-deductible expense; therefore, it is paid out of before tax earnings. Bates' income before taxes is $9,000.

Next, present the formula for number of times interest charges earned:

$$\frac{\text{Income before income tax + Interest expense}}{\text{Interest expense}}$$

Ask your students to calculate Bates' number of times interest charges earned. The answer is:

$$\text{Number of times interest charges earned} = \frac{\$9,000 + \$1,000}{\$1,000} = \frac{\$10,000}{\$1,000} = 10$$

The funds available to pay interest is 10 times larger than the required interest payments. Remind your students that the number of times interest charges earned should be compared to prior years' data and industry averages for a thorough assessment. A number of times interest charges earned of 10 seems to be adequate, but if that ratio has been steadily declining or is below the ratio for other companies in the same industry, investors could become concerned.

EXERCISES & PROBLEMS FOR REINFORCEMENT:
    Exercise 15-20

APPENDIX — Effective Interest Rate Method of Amortization

SUGGESTED APPROACH

Two demonstration problems to help you introduce effective interest amortization are included below. Stress that this method reports a constant rate of interest. Interest expense reported on the income statement is always the same percentage of the beginning carrying value of any bonds. That percentage is the market rate of interest on the date bonds were issued.

This following comparison of the straight-line and effective interest amortization methods will help your students distinguish between the two methods.

Straight-Line Method ———————— Constant Amount of Interest

Effective Interest Rate Method ————— Constant Rate of Interest

Stress that the effective interest method of amortization is required by generally accepted accounting principles. The straight-line method can only be used if the results are not materially different from the effective interest method.

DEMONSTRATION PROBLEM — Amortizing a Bond Discount Using the Effective Interest Method

The easiest way to amortize a bond discount correctly is to set up an amortization table with the following headings:

Interest Payment	Interest Paid (based on the contract rate)	Interest Expense (based on the market rate)	Discount Amortization	Unamortized Discount	Bond Carrying Amount

For example, assume a $100,000, 2-year, 11% bond that makes semiannual interest payments is sold for $96,574 when the market interest rate is 13%. Prepare an amortization table for your students illustrating all four interest payments. Show each calculation as you step through this table. In addition, make the journal entries to record the first two interest payments.

Interest Payment	5.5% Interest Paid	6.5% Interest Expense	Discount Amortization	Unamortized Discount	Bond Carrying Amount
				3,426	96,574
1	5,500	6,277	777	2,649	97,351
2	5,500	6,328	828	1,821	98,179
3	5,500	6,382	882	939	99,061
4	5,500	6,439	939	0	100,000

Journal entries:

1st payment:	Interest Expense............................	6,277	
	Discount on Bonds Payable........		777
	Cash..................................		5,500
2nd payment:	Interest Expense............................	6,328	
	Discount on Bonds Payable........		828
	Cash..................................		5,500

Your students may find the following hints helpful:

1. Write the interest rate used to determine the interest expense above the column. For a bond that pays interest semiannually, this will be one-half the effective interest rate.
2. When amortizing a discount, make sure that the carrying value of the bond increases after each interest payment. The carrying value must be raised up to the face value by the last interest payment.
3. When recording the last interest payment, any remaining discount must be amortized.

Point out that interest expense reported on the income statement increases each year as you amortize the bond discount. This occurs because the bond's carrying value is increasing.

You may also want to illustrate the journal entry to repay the bond at maturity.

Bonds Payable..	100,000	
Cash		100,000

There is no entry to the discount on bonds payable account because it has been amortized to zero.

DEMONSTRATION PROBLEM — Amortizing a Bond Premium

The easiest way to amortize a bond premium correctly is to set up an amortization table with the following headings:

Interest Payment	Interest Paid (based on the contract rate)	Interest Expense (based on the market rate)	Premium Amortization	Unamortized Premium	Bond Carrying Amount

For example, assume a $250,000, 3-year, 13% bond that makes semiannual interest payments is sold for $269,035 when the market interest rate is 10%. Start the following amortization table by computing the premium amortized with the first two interest payments. Also make the journal entries to record the first two interest payments. Ask your students to complete the amortization table on their own.

Interest Payment	6.5% Interest Paid	5% Interest Expense	Premium Amortization	Unamortized Premium	Bond Carrying Amount
				19,035	269,035
1	16,250	13,452	2,798	16,237	266,237
2	16,250	13,312	2,938	13,299	263,299
3	16,250	13,165	3,085	10,214	260,214
4	16,250	13,011	3,239	6,975	256,975
5	16,250	12,849	3,401	3,574	253,574
6	16,250	12,676	3,574	0	250,000

Journal entries:

    1st payment: Interest Expense....................... 13,452
                        Premium on Bonds Payable........... 2,798
                        Cash............................   16,250

    2nd payment: Interest Expense....................... 13,312
                        Premium on Bonds Payable........... 2,938
                        Cash............................   16,250

When amortizing a premium, stress that the carrying value of a bond must decrease after each interest payment. This will drive the carrying value down to the bond's face value. The amount of interest expense reported on the income statement decreases each year as the premium is amortized. The interest expense is driven downward because the bond's carrying value is decreased each year.

EXERCISES & PROBLEMS FOR REINFORCEMENT:
    Exercise 15-21   Problem 15-6A   Problem 15-6B
    Exercise 15-22   Problem 15-7A   Problem 15-7B
    Exercise 15-23
    Exercise 15-24

Handout 15-1

PRESENT-VALUE PROBLEMS

1. Compute the present value of $80,000, to be received in 10 years, if the interest rate is 12%.

2. You've just accepted a contract to provide services for a client for 7 years at a fee of $6,000 per year. Find the present value of this contract assuming that interest rates are 11%.

3. Ellen Saber is contemplating paying several years' rent on her business office in advance. By paying in advance, she can avoid a rent increase that goes into effect the first of next year. Ellen's rent payment is $4,800 per year. Calculate the sum that Ellen would have to pay now in order to prepay 5 years of rent. Interest rates are 7%.

4. Craig Jones owns a computer sales and repair business. He has decided to sell maintenance contracts with new computers that cover all repairs needed within 3 years of purchase. On average, each new computer needs $100 in repairs and maintenance per year during the first 3 years it is operated. (The $100 is the customer's cost for maintenance, including parts, labor, and Craig's profit.) How much should Craig charge for a maintenance contract if interest rates are 13%?

5. You have just won the Florida lottery, and the jackpot was $10 million!! Your first major decision is how to take your prize winnings. You can choose $1 million a year for 10 years or $5.65 million now. Which would you choose if you believe you can earn 10% interest on money you invest?

Transparency Master 15-1

FINANCIAL IMPACT OF LONG-TERM BORROWING

	Plan 1	Plan 2	Plan 3
12% bonds	—	—	$2,000,000
Preferred 9% stock, $50 par	—	$2,000,000	1,000,000
Common stock, $10 par	$4,000,000	2,000,000	1,000,000
Total	$4,000,000	$4,000,000	$4,000,000
Earnings before interest and income tax	$1,000,000	$1,000,000	$1,000,000
Deduct interest on bonds	—	—	240,000
Income before income tax	$1,000,000	$1,000,000	$760,000
Deduct income tax	400,000	400,000	304,000
Net income	$600,000	$600,000	$456,000
Dividends on preferred stock	—	180,000	90,000
Available for dividends on common stock	$600,000	$420,000	$366,000
Shares of common stock	÷ 400,000	÷ 200,000	÷ 100,000
Earnings per share on common stock	$1.50	$2.10	$3.66

FINANCIAL IMPACT OF LONG-TERM BORROWING

	Plan 1	Plan 2	Plan 3
12% bonds	—	—	$2,000,000
Preferred 9% stock, $50 par	—	$2,000,000	1,000,000
Common stock, $10 par	$4,000,000	2,000,000	1,000,000
Total	$4,000,000	$4,000,000	$4,000,000
Earnings before interest and income tax	$1,500,000	$1,500,000	$1,500,000
Deduct interest on bonds	—	—	240,000
Income before income tax	$1,500,000	$1,500,000	$1,260,000
Deduct income tax	600,000	600,000	504,000
Net income	$ 900,000	$ 900,000	$ 756,000
Dividends on preferred stock	—	180,000	90,000
Available for dividends on common stock	$ 900,000	$ 720,000	$ 666,000
Shares of common stock	÷ 400,000	÷ 200,000	÷ 100,000
Earnings per share on common stock	$ 2.25	$ 3.60	$ 6.66

FINANCIAL IMPACT OF LONG-TERM BORROWING

	Plan 1	Plan 2	Plan 3
12% bonds	—	—	$2,000,000
Preferred 9% stock, $50 par	—	$2,000,000	1,000,000
Common stock, $10 par	$4,000,000	2,000,000	1,000,000
Total	$4,000,000	$4,000,000	$4,000,000
Earnings before interest and income tax	$300,000	$300,000	$300,000
Deduct interest on bonds	—	—	240,000
Income before income tax	$300,000	$300,000	$60,000
Deduct income tax	120,000	120,000	24,000
Net income	$180,000	$180,000	$36,000
Dividends on preferred stock	—	180,000	90,000
Available for dividends on common stock	$180,000	$0	$(54,000)
Shares of common stock	÷ 400,000	÷ 200,000	÷ 100,000
Earnings per share on common stock	$0.45	$0.00	$(0.54)

Transparency Master 15-4

FINANCIAL IMPACT OF LONG-TERM BORROWING

	Plan 1	Plan 2	Plan 3
12% bonds	—	—	$2,000,000
Preferred 9% stock, $50 par	—	$2,000,000	1,000,000
Common stock, $10 par	$4,000,000	2,000,000	1,000,000
Total	$4,000,000	$4,000,000	$4,000,000
Earnings before interest and income tax	$ 200,000	$ 200,000	$ 200,000
Deduct interest on bonds	—	—	240,000
Income before income tax	$ 200,000	$ 200,000	$ (40,000)
Deduct income tax (tax savings)	80,000	80,000	(16,000)
Net income	$ 120,000	$ 120,000	$ (24,000)
Dividends on preferred stock	—	180,000	90,000
Available for dividends on common stock	$ 120,000	$ (60,000)	$ (114,000)
Shares of common stock	÷ 400,000	÷ 200,000	÷ 100,000
Earnings per share on common stock	$ 0.30	$ (0.30)	$ (1.14)

CHARACTERISTICS OF BONDS

1. Issued with face values of $1,000 (or multiples of $1,000)
2. Usually pay interest semiannually
3. Prices quoted as a percentage of face value

Transparency Master 15-6

TYPES OF BONDS

1. **Term Bonds**—All bonds of an issue mature at the same time. As a result, the entire principal received from the issue must be paid at once.

2. **Serial Bonds**—Maturity of the bonds in an issue is spread over several dates. In effect, this staggers the repayment of principal over several years.

3. **Convertible Bonds**—May be exchanged for shares of stock or other securities under certain conditions.

4. **Callable Bonds**—The issuing corporation has the right to pay off the bonds before maturity.

5. **Secured Bonds**—Assets are pledged as collateral on the bond. This gives the bondholder a claim on specified assets if the company fails to make bond payments.

6. **Debenture Bonds**—Have no collateral attached. The bonds are backed only by the credit of the issuing corporation.

Transparency Master 15-7

SOLUTION TO HANDOUT 15-1

1. $80,000 × 0.32197 = $25,757.60
2. $6,000 × 4.71220 = $28,273.20
3. $4,800 × 4.10020 = $19,680.96
4. $100 × 2.36115 = $236.12
5. $1,000,000 × 6.14457 = $6,144,570

    Take $1 million per year for 10 years.

Transparency Master 15-8

PRESENT VALUE

Assume that you have a rich uncle who dies. In his will, he leaves you with the following option: You can have $100,000 today or $200,000 in 10 years. Interest rates are 10%. Which should you choose?

Transparency Master 15-9

PRESENT VALUE—ANNUITIES

1. A health club currently charges $150 for a one-year membership. This club has decided to raise its one-year membership charge to $200.

   The owner of the club wants to offer a 5-year membership contract to current members. If a member signs this 5-year contract, he or she can continue to pay only $150 per year to use the club facilities. The owner also wants to offer members the option of paying for all 5 years when the contract is signed. What should the club charge if the customer chooses to purchase the 5-year membership with one payment? Assume that interest rates are 7%.

2. The owner of a hair styling salon is considering buying a tanning bed. She estimates that a tanning bed will bring in an extra $1,000 per year in profit (after deducting costs for electricity, replacement bulbs, etc.). A good quality tanning bed will last for 6 years; however, it will not have any resale value.

   The owner has not priced tanning beds. Calculate the maximum price that the owner should pay for a tanning bed if she wants to get a 10% return on any money invested in the salon.

3. Your Aunt Sally is looking forward to retirement, but she is concerned about having enough money to enjoy her golden years. Sally wants to be sure that before she retires, she has saved enough money to cover her expenses for the rest of her life.

   Sally estimates that after retirement, she will spend $20,000 per year. Based on average life expectancies, she will probably live 15 years past retirement, but, as a margin of safety, Sally wants to have enough money for 20 years.

   What sum of money will Sally need at her retirement to cover her financial needs for the rest of her life? Assume that Sally can earn 6% interest on her money.

Transparency Master 15-10

PRESENT VALUE—ANNUITIES
Solution

1. Calculate the present value of a $150 annuity for 5 years at 7%.

   $150 × 4.10020 = $615.03

2. Calculate the present value of a $1,000 annuity for 6 years at 10%.

   $1,000 × 4.35526 = $4,355.26

3. Calculate the present value of a $20,000 annuity for 20 years at 6%.

   $20,000 × 11.4699 = $229,398

STEPS TO ISSUE A BOND

1. The corporation's board of directors approves a bond issue, specifying the amount of bonds that will be issued, the maturity date, the interest rate, and any special bond characteristics (i.e., conversion features, call features, collateral attached).

2. The company prepares a prospectus, which gives information about the company and the bond issue. This prospectus is filed with the Securities and Exchange Commission (SEC). The SEC reviews the prospectus to see that it provides investors with the information they will need to evaluate the bond issue. If the prospectus contains the appropriate information, the SEC approves the issue. (SEC approval doesn't mean that the bond is a good investment, only that the company has disclosed adequate information for a knowledgeable investor to determine whether it is a good investment.)

3. An underwriter is contracted.

4. The bonds are sold.

But what happens if the interest rates have changed from those specified by the board of directors?

Transparency Master 15-12

ISSUANCE OF A BOND

Determine the selling price (present value) for the following bonds, and make the journal entry to record each bond's issuance.

1. A $10,000, 5-year, 11% bond is sold when interest rates are 12%. The bond pays interest semiannually.

2. A $50,000, 8-year, 14% bond is sold when market interest rates are 13%. The bond pays interest semiannually.

Transparency Master 15-13

ISSUANCE OF A BOND

Solution

1. A $10,000, 5-year, 11% bond is sold when interest rates are 12%. The bond pays interest semiannually.

   Principal = $10,000
   Interest payments = $550 [($10,000 × 11%)/2]

   PV of principal, i = 6%, n = 10
   $10,000 × 0.55840 .... $5,584

   PV of interest payments, i = 6%, n = 10
   $550 × 7.36009 4,048

   Selling price of bond $9,632

   Reasonableness Check—Market interest rate > contract rate, so the bond should sell at a discount.

   Journal entry:
   Cash... 9,632
   Discount on Bonds Payable .   368
       Bonds Payable   10,000

Transparency Master 15-14

ISSUANCE OF A BOND

Solution

2. A $50,000, 8-year, 14% bond is sold when interest rates are 13%. The bond pays interest semiannually.

   Principal = $50,000
   Interest payments = $3,500 [($50,000 × 14%)/2]

   PV of principal, i = 6.5%, n = 16

   $50,000 × 0.36510 .... $18,255

   PV of interest payments, i = 6.5%, n = 16

   $3,500 × 9.76776 .... <u>34,187</u>
   Selling price of bond .... <u>$52,442</u>

   Reasonableness Check—Market interest rate < contract rate, so the bond should sell at a premium.

   Journal entry:
   Cash... 52,442
      Bonds Payable 50,000
      Premium on Bonds Payable 2,442

BOND SINKING FUNDS

Accounts used to record sinking fund transactions are as follows:

	Classification	Normal Balance	Purpose
Sinking Fund Cash.............	Asset	Debit	Used to record cash deposited into a sinking fund
Sinking Fund Investments ..	Asset	Debit	Used to record securities purchased with sinking fund cash that will be held as investments
Sinking Fund Revenue	Other Income	Credit	Used to record interest earned on sinking fund investments

AMORTIZATION OF A BOND DISCOUNT/PREMIUM

	Effect of Amortization	Reason
Discount:		
Bond is a debt instrument.	Increases interest expense.	Discount represents extra interest paid to bondholders to bring the bond's stated interest rate up to a higher market interest rate.
Bond is an investment.	Increases interest income.	
Premium:		
Bond is a debt instrument.	Reduces interest expense.	Premium represents a reduction in interest to bring the bond's stated interest rate down to a lower market interest rate.
Bond is an investment.	Reduces interest income.	

Transparency Master 15-17

NUMBER OF TIMES INTEREST CHARGES EARNED

The following data was taken from the accounting records of Bates Corporation:

Revenues		$50,000
Salaries Expense	$20,000	
Rent Expense	8,000	
Utilities Expense	5,000	
Supplies Expense	4,000	
Depreciation Expense	1,000	
Miscellaneous Expense	2,000	

Bates income tax rate is 40%.

1. Based on this data, what amount of funds are available to make Bates' interest payments, which total $1,000?
2. What is Bates' income before taxes?

Chapter 16
Statement of Cash Flows

OPENING COMMENTS

This chapter demonstrates that the statement of cash flows is necessary for a complete picture of a company's financial condition. Both the direct and indirect methods of preparing a statement of cash flows are presented.

If course timing is restrictive, you may want to cover only one of the two methods of preparing the statement of cash flows. The indirect method is the most commonly used method for reporting cash flows. The text points out that 99% of the companies surveyed for the 2002 edition of *Accounting Trends & Techniques* used the indirect method for reporting cash flows. It is very easy to cover only this method since the entire statement of cash flows (including operating, investing, and financing activities) is presented in Objective 2.

The direct method reports each of the major categories of operating cash receipts and cash payments. If you choose to cover only the direct method, be aware that Objective 3 only illustrates the operating activities section of the statement of cash flows. You will still need to refer students to the information on financing and investing activities in Objective 2.

After studying the chapter, your students should be able to:

1. Summarize the types of cash flow activities reported in the statement of cash flows.
2. Prepare a statement of cash flows, using the indirect method.
3. Prepare a statement of cash flows, using the direct method.
4. Calculate and interpret the free cash flow.

OBJECTIVE 1 — Summarize the types of cash flow activities reported in the statement of cash flows.

KEY TERMS:
    Cash Flows from Financing Activities   Direct Method
    Cash Flows from Investing Activities   Indirect Method
    Cash Flows from Operating Activities   Statement of Cash Flows

SUGGESTED APPROACH

Below, you will find a writing exercise to introduce the Statement of Cash Flows. The exercise asks your students to evaluate financial data from two companies. The goal is to point out that a firm's profits do not paint a total picture of its operations; cash flow data is also needed. Follow the writing exercise (Transparency 16-1) by reviewing Transparency 16-2, which lists the benefits of a statement of cash flows. Lecture aids are also provided for reviewing the content of each section of the cash flow statement.

WRITING EXERCISE — Importance of the Statement of Cash Flows

Transparency 16-1 presents financial information taken from the accounting records of two companies. These companies have the same net incomes, but very different cash flows. Even though both companies have the same sales, Company B did not collect as much cash from its customers. In addition, Company B did not invest as much cash in fixed assets; this could inhibit future growth.

Show this data to your students and ask them to comment, in writing, on any strengths or weaknesses they see in the two companies. After giving them a few minutes to study the information and write their comments, review their responses.

LECTURE AIDS

Transparencies 16-3 and 16-4 list the three sections of the statement of cash flows and the transactions included in each section. Transparency 16-5 defines the content of the schedule of noncash investing and financing activities.

After reviewing these transparencies, you may want to discuss the treatment of interest on debt and interest/dividends on investments in the statement of cash flows. These transactions can be called the "three foolers" because students typically want to identify them as financing and investing activities instead of operating activities. Use Transparency 16-6 for this purpose.

Have students identify cash flows from operating, investing, and financing activities from their personal experiences. Some examples are listed below.

> Operating Activities: Cash inflows from a job, cash outflows for food or rent
>
> Financing Activities: Cash inflow from a student loan.
>
> Investing Activities: Cash outflow for an automobile, cash inflow from selling a motorcycle.

EXERCISES & PROBLEMS FOR REINFORCEMENT:
Exercise 16-1
Exercise 16-2
Exercise 16-3

OBJECTIVE 2 — Prepare a statement of cash flows, using the indirect method.

SUGGESTED APPROACH

Open your discussion of the indirect method with a basic outline of the reconciliation prepared in the operating activities section. Transparency 16-7 presents an overview of the reconciliation process.

You will also want to illustrate this process by preparing a statement of cash flows as a demonstration problem.

LECTURE AIDS — Indirect Method

During your discussion of Transparency 16-7 (the reconciliation of net income to net cash flows from operating activities), stress the following points:

1. Noncash expenses must be added to remove these expenses from net income. They must be removed from net income because they did not cause cash to be paid out.

Ask your students to identify examples of noncash items reported on the income statement and whether they would be added to or deducted from net income to determine cash flows from operating activities. Several examples are listed below.

Noncash Item	Treatment
Depreciation	Added to net income
Amortization of bond discount	Added to net income
Amortization of bond premium	Deducted from net income
Amortization of patents	Added to net income
Depletion expense	Added to net income

2. Any gains or losses on investing and financing activities affect the amount of cash that was received from selling investments, or the amount of cash paid when settling debts. Because these activities are reported in the investing and financing sections of the statement of cash flows, the gain or loss included in the calculation of net income must be removed to isolate operating cash flows.

For example, a building with a $50,000 book value is sold for $125,000—a $75,000 gain. The $75,000 gain must be removed from net income because it does not represent cash received from operations (buying and selling merchandise). The entire $125,000 cash proceeds from the building (which includes the gain) will be disclosed in the investing activities section.

Remind students that losses are added and gains are subtracted to remove them from the net income.

3. Changes in current assets and current liability accounts related to operating activities must be considered to remove the effects of accrual accounting from net income and return to a cash-basis measure of operations. Emphasize that net cash flow from operating activities is different

from net income because the income statement is based on the accrual basis of accounting. The statement of cash flows presents cash basis accounting.

DEMONSTRATION PROBLEM — Preparing a Statement of Cash Flows: Indirect Method

Because of the amount of data required to prepare a statement of cash flows, it is appropriate to use a problem from the text to demonstrate the preparation of the statement of cash flows. If you plan to cover the direct method of reporting cash flows, use Problem 16-1A or 16-1B to demonstrate the indirect method. Next, use problems 16-5A or 16-5B to illustrate the operating activities section on a direct method statement of cash flows. Problems 16-5A and 16-5B provide the additional information needed to do a direct statement for the same company in 16-1A and 16-1B. Therefore, you can save class time by doing the entire statement under the indirect method, but only the operating activities section under the direct method.

Instruct your students to complete a couple of preparatory steps before attacking a cash flow problem. First, ask them to calculate the increase or decrease for every account on the balance sheet and write it in the margin of the text. When working through a demonstration problem, give them a few minutes of class time to complete this step on their own.

You may want to use the following algebraic proof to demonstrate why students need to calculate the amount by which each account on the balance sheet has increased or decreased.

$$\text{Assets} = \text{Liabilities} + \text{Owner's Equity}$$
$$\text{Cash} + \text{Other Assets} = \text{Liabilities} + \text{Owner's Equity}$$

Therefore,

$$\text{Change in Cash} + \text{Change in Other Assets} = \text{Change in Liabilities} + \text{Change in Owner's Equity}$$

...or

$$\text{Change in Cash} = \text{Change in Liabilities} + \text{Change in Owner's Equity} - \text{Change in Other Assets}$$

If you can explain what caused your noncash assets, liabilities, and owner's equity account balances to change, you have explained what caused the cash account balance to change.

The second preparatory step is to go through the balance sheet accounts and note where the change in each account balance will be reported (O for operating activities, I for investing activities, and F for financing activities). A few accounts, namely retained earnings and accumulated depreciation, must be considered when preparing two sections of the statement of cash flows.

You will probably want to lead the class through this step, instructing them to place an O, I, or A by each account title in the example problem. The accounts in Problem 16-1A or 16-1B would be coded as follows:

Cash (no code—this is the number we are trying to explain)
Accounts receivable—O

Inventories—O
Investments—I
Land—I
Equipment—I
Accumulated Depreciation—O and I
Accounts Payable—O
Accrued Expenses—O
Dividends Payable—F
Common Stock—F
Paid-in Capital—F
Retained Earnings—O and F

Now your students are ready to attack the problem, beginning with the operating activities section. Students should be encouraged to use a "check-off" method in completing the statement of cash flows. The basics of the check-off method are as follows: when the total change in an account has been explained, check it off. Once an account has been checked off, you don't need to look at it again.

For example, the first step in the operating activities section is to show the amount of net income. This information is obtained from the income statement or, in accounting class, from the "additional information" accompanying the problem. Net income is closed to the retained earnings account; however, in Problem 16-1A, retained earnings increased by $124,600, even though net income was $180,600. Some other transaction must be affecting the account. Because the change in the account balance has not been fully explained, the account cannot be checked off. As the coding system shows, students must look at retained earnings again when preparing the financing activities section.

The next step in the operating activities section is to add back any depreciation, amortization, or depletion. What account on the balance sheet would contain the depreciation for the year? Answer: Accumulated Depreciation. However, that account is also affected by entries to remove fixed assets when sold or discarded. In Problem 16-1A, we are told that there were no disposals of equipment. Therefore, the only entry in the accumulated depreciation account would be the adjusting entry for the year's depreciation expense. The $26,000 change in this account is the depreciation expense to be added to net income. Because the change in the account balance has been fully explained, the accumulated depreciation account can be checked off. Those are the basic steps in the check-off method.

At this time, instruct your students to review the additional information given with the problem to look for any gains and losses on investing and financing activities. Remind them that gains and losses occur only when assets are sold and liabilities settled. Problem 16-1A has a $12,000 gain on the sale of investments that must be deducted from net income.

Ask your students to answer the following questions. (1) If there had been a loss of $20,000 on the sale of investments, how would this be reported on the operating activities section of the statement of cash flows? Answer: the loss would be added to net income. (2) If fully depreciated equipment had been sold for $2,000, how would this be reported on the operating activities section of the statement of cash flows? Answer: The $2,000 gain would be deducted from net income.

Now it is time to look at the current assets and current liabilities related to operations. Instruct your students to go through the accounts coded with O's and write down whether each account increased or decreased, and by what amount. Then, ask your students to determine whether the change had a positive or negative effect on cash. Many students want to cling to text Exhibit 4 to assist with this task, so try to give them a logical approach to determine how account changes affect cash.

The suggested explanations are overly simplified and, therefore, not "totally" accurate. However, most of your students will find them useful. For example, accounts receivable in Problems 16-1A and 16-1B increased. A simplified explanation of how this effects cash flows:

> If accounts receivable went up, did you sell more or less on credit? More. If you sold more on credit, did you sell more or less for cash? Less. If you sold less on cash, what was the effect on the cash account? It decreased. Therefore, the change in accounts receivable is subtracted.

Now, in reality, accounts receivable may have increased because customers are paying more slowly. Accounts receivable also may have increased simply because total sales increased without a corresponding increase in cash sales. When insightful students bring up these arguments, agree with them. Point out that the original explanation is useful because it is simple and tends to make sense to most students.

When accounts receivable decrease, your explanation is the inverse: The company sold less on credit, so it sold more for cash and the cash account is increased. Explanations for changes in other accounts follow.

> Increase in Inventory: The company bought more inventory, so it has to pay for more inventory. Cash is decreased.

> Decrease in Inventory: The company bought less inventory, so it doesn't have to pay for as much inventory. Cash is increased.

> Increase in Prepaid Expense: The company has prepaid more expenses, using its cash. Cash is decreased.

> Decrease in Prepaid Expense: The company has prepaid fewer expenses, saving its cash. Cash is increased.

> Increase in Accounts Payable: The company has bought more on credit, so it has bought less with cash. Cash is increased.

> Decrease in Accounts Payable: The company has bought less on credit, so it is buying more with cash. Cash is decreased.

Once all accounts marked O have been checked off, it is time to move on to the investing and financing accounts. Work through these accounts one by one, using the additional information to determine what caused the accounts to change. List the transactions and amounts on the statement of cash flows, checking accounts off as the change in their balances are explained.

GROUP LEARNING ACTIVITY — Indirect Method

Instruct your students to turn to text Exhibit 3. Ask them to describe whether the changes in the balance sheet accounts listed will have the effect of increasing or decreasing cash.

EXERCISES & PROBLEMS FOR REINFORCEMENT:

Exercise 16-4	Exercise 16-11	Problem 16-1A	Problem 16-1B
Exercise 16-5	Exercise 16-12	Problem 16-2A	Problem 16-2B
Exercise 16-6	Exercise 16-13	Problem 16-3A	Problem 16-3B
Exercise 16-7	Exercise 16-14		
Exercise 16-8	Exercise 16-15		
Exercise 16-9	Exercise 16-21		
Exercise 16-10	Exercise 16-22		

OBJECTIVE 3 — Prepare a statement of cash flows, using the direct method.

SUGGESTED APPROACH

The direct method of preparing a statement of cash flows is another topic that can be presented effectively through a demonstration problem. If you have already covered the indirect method, you only need to illustrate the operating activities section.

Prior to beginning the demonstration problem, stress that the operating activities section is the only portion of the statement of cash flows that varies between the direct and indirect methods. The direct and indirect methods will report the same amount of net cash flows from operating activities, but the information is presented in a different format.

When a company chooses to prepare the direct statement of cash flows, it must present the reconciliation of net income to net cash flows from operating activities (the heart of the indirect method) in a supporting schedule. Therefore, the election to prepare a direct statement of cash flows really obligates a company to prepare the operating activities section under both methods. As a result, most companies use the indirect method for cash flow reporting.

DEMONSTRATION PROBLEM — Preparation of a Statement of Cash Flows: Direct Method

The direct method presents the major classes of cash receipts and payments from operating activities. To prepare a direct statement of cash flows, an income statement is needed in addition to comparative balance sheets. Problems 16-5A and 16-5B repeat the information presented in Problems 16-1A and 16-1B plus give an income statement.

When completing a direct statement of cash flows, ask your students complete the same preparatory steps discussed in Objective 3—computing changes in account balances and coding accounts with an O, I, or F (for operating, investing, or financing). The check-off method described previously is also appropriate when preparing a direct statement of cash flows.

Transparency 16-8 presents the major classes of cash receipts and payments that are typically identified in a direct statement. The transparency also presents formulas for computing each cash flow item. In reality, the formulas on Transparency 16-8 are a shortcut approach. Students usually need a complete explanation of the calculations for cash received from customers and cash paid for purchases in order to understand these shortcuts.

For example, Problem 16-5A presents the following data:

Sales $1,580,500	Beg. accounts receivable	$145,700
	End accounts receivable	163,200
	Net change	$ 17,500

Under the direct method, you must determine the cash collected from customers. The sales reported on the income statement does not represent cash collections for two reasons: (1) the sales figure includes credit sales that have not been collected and (2) the sales figure does not include collections on last year's credit sales made during the current year. Therefore, sales must be adjusted as follows:

Sales	$1,580,500
- Credit sales not yet collected (ending balance of accts. receivable) (163,200)	
+ Collections on last year's credit sales (beginning balance of accts. receivable)	145,700
	$1,563,000

OR

Sales	$1,580,500
- Change in accounts receivable	(17,500)
	$1,563,000

Again, discourage your students from trying to memorize rules on whether to add or subtract changes in accounts receivable. Give them a methodology to think through the changes.

The methodology presented under Objective 2 will also work in the direct method. The previous calculation could be explained as follows:

Accounts receivable increased, so the company is selling more on credit and selling less for cash. Therefore, the effect on cash receipts is negative.

OR

Accounts receivable increased, indicating that credit sales on account were $17,500 more than cash collections. Therefore, the increase must be subtracted from sales to get cash receipts.

Under the direct method, you must also determine the cash paid for purchases. Before you can determine cash paid for purchases, you must know the cost of merchandise purchased. The income statement in Problem 16-5A doesn't show the detailed calculation of cost of merchandise sold; therefore, the cost of merchandise purchased cannot be determined just by looking at the income statement. However, it can be determined as follows:

    Beginning Inventory
  + Cost of Merchandise Purchased
  - Ending Inventory
    Cost of Goods Sold

Therefore,
    Cost of Goods Sold
  - Beginning Inventory
  + Ending Inventory
    Cost of Merchandise Purchased

Using data from Problem 16-5A:

    Cost of Merchandise Purchased = $957,300 - 367,900 + 395,000
    Cost of Merchandise Purchased = $984,400

The cost of merchandise purchased must be adjusted to determine cash payments for purchases, as follows:

Cost of merchandise purchased	$984,400
- Credit purchases not yet paid for (ending balance of accounts payable)	(228,700)
+ Payments on last year's credit purchases (beginning balance of accounts payable)	210,500
	$966,200

OR (Combining both of these calculations into one formula)

Cost of merchandise sold	$957,300
+ Change in inventories	27,100
- Change in account payable	(18,200)
Cash payments for purchases	$966,200

Explain that the increase in inventories can be interpreted as increasing cash payments because more inventory was purchased. The increase in accounts payable can be interpreted as decreasing cash payments because the company made more purchases on account.

Continue with the problem, demonstrating the calculations of cash paid for operating expenses and cash paid for income taxes. When you have completed the operating activities section, remind students that the net cash flow is the same number as computed under the indirect method.

EXERCISES & PROBLEMS FOR REINFORCEMENT:

Exercise 16-16	Exercise 16-19	Problem 16-4A	Problem 16-4B
Exercise 16-17	Exercise 16-20	Problem 16-5A	Problem 16-5B
Exercise 16-18			

OBJECTIVE 4 – Calculate and interpret the free cash flow.

KEY TERMS:
    Free Cash Flow

SUGGESTED APPROACH

After explaining the concept of free cash flow, calculate free cash flow for Problem 16-1A (or the problem you used to demonstrate preparing the statement of cash flows.)

DEMONSTRATION PROBLEM – Free Cash Flow

Free cash flow is the amount of operating cash flows left after paying dividends and paying for assets needed to maintain productive capacity. Free cash flow recognizes that operations must generate sufficient cash to replace assets used in operations. It also recognizes that shareholders want to see companies maintain steady dividend payments. The formula for free cash flow is:

    Cash flow from operations
 - Cash used to purchase fixed assets needed to maintain productive capacity
 - Cash used for dividends
    Free Cash Flow

If the calculation of free cash flow yields a negative number, a company's operations cannot support asset replacement and dividends.

Ask your students to review the data given in Problem 16-1A and the completed statement of cash flows (which should be in their notes) to answer the following questions:

1. What is Winner's Edge cash flow from operating activities for 2006? (Answer: $163,300)
2. What much cash was used to pay dividends in 2006? (Answer: $52,000)
3. What amount of cash was paid to purchase equipment? (Answer: $120,000)
4. Can we assume all of the equipment purchases were to maintain productive capacity? (Answer: No.)

Ask your students to assume that 20% of the asset purchases were to maintain productive capacity; the remaining purchases were made to expand operations. Also, ask your students to assume that the purchase of land was made to expand operations. Based on these assumptions, free cash flow would be calculated as follows:

Cash flow from operations		$163,300
Less: Cash invested in equipment to maintain productive capacity	$24,000	
Cash used for dividends	52,000	
		76,000
Free cash flow		$ 87,300

Winner's Edge operations in 2006 did generate sufficient cash flow to pay dividends and maintain productive capacity.

EXERCISES & PROBLEMS FOR REINFORCEMENT:
    Exercise 16-23
    Exercise 16-24

APPENDIX: Work Sheet for Statement of Cash Flows

SUGGESTED APPROACH

A work sheet is a tool which can be used to gather data for preparing a statement of cash flows. It is an alternative to the "check-off" method presented under Objectives 2 and 3.

The work sheet also lends itself to an in-class demonstration. Choose one of the cash flow problems at the end of the text (such as Problem 16-5A or 16-5B) and ask your students to bring the working papers for that problem to class. The working papers include a cash flow work sheet. Demonstrate completion of that work sheet using the steps outlined in the chapter appendix.

Emphasize that entries recorded on a cash flow work sheet are not recorded as journal entries or posted to the ledger. These entries are made to analyze past transactions and provide data for preparing a statement of cash flows.

Transparency Master 16-1

WRITING EXERCISE

Review the following financial data from two companies in the same industry. Comment on any strengths or weaknesses you notice.

Income statements:	Company A	Company B
Sales	$500,000	$500,000
Expenses	425,000	425,000
Net income	$ 75,000	$ 75,000
Cash held:		
Beginning of year	$ 25,000	$ 25,000
End of year	25,000	25,000
Increase in cash	$ 0	$ 0

A detailed analysis of the cash account reveals the following cash receipts and payments:

	Company A	Company B
Cash received:		
from customers	$450,000	$350,000
from sale of fixed assets	5,000	60,000
Total cash received	$455,000	$410,000
Cash paid:		
to suppliers	$380,000	$400,000
for purchase of fixed assets	70,000	10,000
for purchase of investments	5,000	0
Total cash paid	$455,000	$410,000
Increase in cash	$ 0	$ 0

Transparency Master 16-2

WHY ARE CASH FLOWS IMPORTANT?

Cash is what pays the bills.

You must sell your product and collect cash from your customers in time to:

1. **Pay suppliers for merchandise purchases.**

2. **Pay the bank on any loans.**

3. **Pay employees their wages.**

4. **Pay taxes.**

5. **Purchase new equipment as needed.**

Analyzing where a company's cash is coming from and where it is being spent may assist in detecting future profit potential and/or future financial problems.

SECTIONS OF THE STATEMENT OF CASH FLOWS

Cash Flows from Operating Activities—Report cash received and paid in the daily operations of the business, including:

1. Cash received from customers
2. Cash paid to suppliers

Cash Flows from Investing Activities—Report cash received and paid as a result of the sale and purchase of investments. The investments reported in this section can be divided into two categories:

1. Investments in YOURSELF, for example:
   a. Purchase of fixed assets
   b. Sale of fixed assets
2. Investments in OTHERS, for example:
   a. Purchase of equity or debt securities of another corporation
   b. Sale of equity or debt securities held as investments
   c. Making of a loan to another company
   d. Collection of principal payments on a loan made to another company

(Continued)

SECTIONS OF THE STATEMENT OF CASH FLOWS

(Concluded)

<u>Cash Flows from Financing Activities</u>—Report cash received and paid as a result of the activities to obtain and repay funds used to finance the operations of a company. Financing activities can be divided into two categories:

1. **EQUITY financing:**
   a. Issuing shares of stock
   b. Retiring shares of stock
   c. Purchasing shares of treasury stock
   d. Selling shares of treasury stock
   e. Paying cash dividends on stock
2. **DEBT financing:**
   a. Borrowing cash
   b. Repaying principal on a loan

Transparency Master 16-5

STATEMENT OF CASH FLOWS

Schedule of Noncash Investing and Financing Activities

Used to report transactions that are investing and/or financing activities but do not bring in or use up any cash. These transactions need to be reported because they will affect cash flows in the future. Examples include the following:

1. Purchasing fixed assets by signing a note payable
2. Purchasing a building through a mortgage loan
3. Exchanging stock for fixed assets
4. Issuing stock to retire debt
5. Converting preferred stock to common stock

Transparency Master 16-6

STATEMENT OF CASH FLOWS

Three "Foolers"

The following transactions are reported in the operating activities section of the statement of cash flows:

1. Interest paid on debt

   Justification: The decision to finance the business through debt is a financing activity. Once that decision has been made, the cash to pay for the interest on debt must come from operating activities.

2. Interest received on investments

3. Dividends received on investments

   Justification: The decision to use cash to purchase equity or debt securities is an investment decision. Once that decision has been made, the cash received from interest or dividends is used to operate the business.

CASH FLOWS FROM OPERATING ACTIVITIES—INDIRECT METHOD

(Also Known as the "Reconciliation Method")

	Net income (from income statement)..........	$ XXX
+	Noncash expenses (depreciation, amortization, and depletion).....................	XXX
+/–	Losses or gains on investing or financing activities...................................	XXX
+/–	Changes in current asset and current liability accounts related to operating activities..	XXX
	Net cash flows from operating activities....	$ XXX

STATEMENT OF CASH FLOWS FROM OPERATING ACTIVITIES—DIRECT METHOD

Cash received from customers:
Sales +/– Change in Accounts Receivable

Cash payments for purchases:
Cost of Merchandise Sold +/– Change in Inventories +/– Change in Accounts Payable

Cash payments for operating expenses:
Operating Expenses +/– Change in Prepaid Expenses +/– Change in Accrued Expenses

Cash payments for interest:
Interest Expense +/– Change in Interest Payable

Cash payment for income taxes:
Income Tax Expense +/– Change in Income Taxes Payable

Chapter 17
Financial Statement Analysis

OPENING COMMENTS

This chapter presents techniques for analyzing financial statements and the contents of annual reports. The techniques for analyzing financial statements include horizontal analysis, vertical analysis, and ratio analysis. Since an analytical technique has been presented at the end of each chapter, some of the material presented in Chapter 17 will be a review.

When covering this chapter, you should guard against getting bogged down in the calculations surrounding ratio analysis. Try to spend at least as much class time interpreting ratios as calculating them.

After studying the chapter, your students should be able to:

1. List basic financial statement analytical procedures.
2. Apply financial statement analysis to assess the solvency of a business.
3. Apply financial statement analysis to assess the profitability of a business.
4. Summarize the uses and limitations of analytical measures.
5. Describe the contents of corporate annual reports.

OBJECTIVE 1 — List basic financial statement analytical procedures.

KEY TERMS:
   Common-Size Statements
   Horizontal Analysis
   Vertical Analysis

SUGGESTED APPROACH

The basic financial statement analytical procedures are horizontal analysis, vertical analysis, and ratio analysis. Ratio analysis is covered under Objectives 2 and 3.

DEMONSTRATION PROBLEM — Horizontal Analysis

Ask your students to turn to the annual report for Home Depot in Appendix E at the end of text. Specifically, direct them to the Consolidated Statements of Earnings. Ask your students to compute the dollar increase in net sales between fiscal year 2001 and fiscal year 2002. (Answer: $4,694 million or $4,694,000,000). You will need to point out that fiscal year 2002 ended on February 2, 2003 and fiscal year 2001 ended on February 3, 2002.

Next, ask your students to calculate the percentage increase in net sales from 2001 to 2002. The correct answer is 8.8%, calculated as follows:

$$\frac{\text{Increase in Net Sales between 2001 and 2002}}{\text{Net Sales in 2001 (base year)}} = \frac{\$4,694 \text{ million}}{\$53,553 \text{ million}} = 8.8\%$$

Most likely, a few students will have 8.1% as an answer. These students have compared the $4,694 million increase in net sales to sales in fiscal year 2002. Remind them that a percentage change in a financial statement item is computed by comparing the change in dollars to the base year amount. The base year is the starting point—fiscal year 2001 in this case.

Ask your students to calculate the percentage increase in net sales from 2000 to 2001. The answer is as follows:

$$2000 \text{ to } 2001: \frac{\$7,815 \text{ million}}{\$45,738 \text{ million}} = 17.1\%$$

Remind students that this analytical technique is called horizontal analysis (or trend analysis). It is used to compare changes in operating results from year to year.

GROUP LEARNING ACTIVITY — Horizontal Analysis

Divide your class into small groups. Ask them to perform the horizontal analysis requested on Transparency 17-1 using the financial statements. The correct answers are displayed on Transparency 17-2.

GROUP LEARNING ACTIVITY — Vertical Analysis

Under vertical analysis, all financial statement items are shown as a percentage of a significant total on the statement. On an income statement, all items are shown as a percentage of net sales. On a balance sheet, all items are shown as a percentage of total assets.

Divide your class into small groups. Ask each group to perform vertical analysis on Home Depot's 2002 income statement (called the Consolidated Statement of Earnings), showing each item through Operating Income as a percentage of net sales. Suggest that percentages be rounded to one decimal place. The correct solution is shown on Transparency 17-3.

Emphasize that Transparency 17-3 shows common-size income statements. Common-size statements use vertical analysis to show all items as percentages. Expressing financial statements as percentages is useful when comparing one company with another or with industry averages. Common-size income statements for Home Depot for three fiscal years are shown on the second page of the annual report.

EXERCISES & PROBLEMS FOR REINFORCEMENT:
    Exercise 17-1   Exercise 17-4   Problem 17-1A   Problem 17-1B
    Exercise 17-2   Exercise 17-5   Problem 17-2A   Problem 17-2B
    Exercise 17-3

OBJECTIVE 2 — Apply financial statement analysis to assess the solvency of a business.

KEY TERMS:
    Acid-Test Ratio
    Accounts Receivable Turnover
    Current Ratio
    Inventory Turnover
    Number of Days' Sales in Inventory
    Number of Days' Sales in Receivables
    Number of Times Interest Charges Earned
    Profitability
    Quick Assets
    Ratio of Fixed Assets to Long-Term Liabilities
    Ratio of Liabilities to Stockholders' Equity
    Solvency
    Working Capital

SUGGESTED APPROACH

Solvency, which is a company's ability to pay debts as they become due, is assessed through ratio analysis. Transparency 17-4 lists the ratios that measure a firm's solvency.

Use the following group learning activities to give your students the opportunity to practice ratio analysis as it relates to solvency.

GROUP LEARNING ACTIVITY — Computing Solvency Measures

The ratios that assess solvency are listed in the text in the first section of Exhibit 10. Calculating these ratios using real-life financial statements is a challenge for most students due to the differences in terminology used by companies. For example, a company may use the term "plant assets" or "property, plant, and equipment" instead of fixed assets. Of course, students need to become proficient at recognizing different terms for the concepts they have learned in this course. You can help your students make these connections by calculating ratios using financial statements of real companies.

The textbook includes a Home Depot, Inc. Financial Statement Analysis problem immediately following the series B problems. Ask your students to calculate each of the solvency ratios in this problem (items a through h). Remind your students to assume that all of Home Depot's sales were on account. The solution to this problem is found in the Instructor's Solutions Manual and on the Solutions Transparencies.

You may also want to ask your students to describe, in their own words, what each ratio measures.

GROUP LEARNING ACTIVITY — Analyzing Solvency Measures

Transparency 17-5 shows solvency ratios for Ace Company over a 2-year period. The transparency also presents industry averages for the solvency ratios.

Ask your students to analyze the data related to Ace Company and comment on its performance. Specifically, ask them to answer the following questions:

1. For each solvency ratio, state whether or not Ace has improved from the prior year.

2. For each solvency ratio, state whether Ace compares favorably or unfavorably with the industry average.
3. Comment on any significant items noticed when reviewing the solvency ratios and Ace's overall solvency.

EXERCISES & PROBLEMS FOR REINFORCEMENT:

Exercise 17-6	Exercise 17-11	Problem 17-3A	Problem 17-3B
Exercise 17-7	Exercise 17-12		
Exercise 17-8	Exercise 17-13		
Exercise 17-9	Exercise 17-14		
Exercise 17-10	Exercise 17-15		

OBJECTIVE 3 — Apply financial statement analysis to assess the profitability of a business.

KEY TERMS:
Dividends per Share
Dividend Yield
Earnings per Share on Common Stock
Leverage
Price-Earnings (P/E) Ratio

Rate Earned on Common Stockholders' Equity
Rate Earned on Stockholders' Equity
Rate Earned on Total Assets
Ratio of Net Sales to Assets

SUGGESTED APPROACH

Profitability, which is a company's ability to earn income, is also assessed through ratio analysis. Transparency 17-6 lists the ratios that measure a firm's profitability.

Use the group learning activities that follow to give your students the opportunity to practice ratio analysis as it relates to profitability.

GROUP LEARNING ACTIVITY — Computing Profitability Measures

The ratios that assess profitability are listed in the text in the second part of Exhibit 10. Ask your students to calculate each of the profitability ratios (items i through m) for the Home Depot, Inc. Financial Statement Analysis problem in the text. You will also want to emphasize that earnings per share (called "Basic Earnings per Share") are reported on Home Depot's income statement; therefore, students do not need to calculate these amounts. The solution to this problem can be found in the Instructor's Solutions Manual and on the Solutions Transparencies.

Again, you may want to ask your students to describe, in their own words, what each ratio measures.

GROUP LEARNING ACTIVITY — Analyzing Profitability Measures

Transparency 17-7 shows profitability ratios for Ace Company over a 2-year period. The transparency also presents industry averages for the profitability ratios.

Ask your students to analyze the data related to Ace Company and comment on its performance. Specifically, ask them to answer the following questions:

1. For each profitability ratio, state whether or not Ace has improved from the prior year.
2. For each profitability ratio, state whether Ace compares favorably or unfavorably with the industry average.
3. Comment on any significant items noticed when reviewing the profitability ratios and Ace's overall profitability.

EXERCISES & PROBLEMS FOR REINFORCEMENT:

Exercise 17-16	Exercise 17-20	Problem 17-4A	Problem 17-4B
Exercise 17-17	Exercise 17-21	Problem 17-5A	Problem 17-5B
Exercise 17-18	Exercise 17-22		
Exercise 17-19	Exercise 17-23		

OBJECTIVE 4 — Summarize the uses and limitations of analytical measures.

SUGGESTED APPROACH

Emphasize that computing ratios is only the starting point for assessing the performance of a business. To be meaningful, current-year ratios must be compared with ratios from prior years and the ratios of other companies in the same industry. The influence of the general economic and business environment should be considered. Finally, sound financial judgment should be applied.

OBJECTIVE 5 — Describe the contents of corporate annual reports.

SUGGESTED APPROACH

The text presents information on the Management Discussion and Analysis section of the annual report plus the Independent Auditor's Report. You may want to briefly mention other components of the annual report. Transparency 17-8 lists several sections typically included in a corporate annual report. Briefly review these sections and their content with your students, using the notes below.

1. Financial Highlights - presents selected financial data that summarize operations for the past year or two.
2. President's Letter - highlights the company's goals and accomplishments in narrative form.
3. Financial Statements
4. Notes to the Financial Statements - presents supplemental information needed to interpret the financial statements (such as the accounting method selected for recording depreciation, and valuing inventory).
5. Management's Discussion and Analysis - presents management's assessment of their company's operating results and financial condition as reported in the financial statements.

6. <u>Management Report</u> – affirms management's responsibility for internal controls and the accuracy of financial statements; usually signed by the company's CFO
7. <u>Independent Auditors' Report</u> - prepared by the independent auditor; presents the auditors' opinion as to the fairness of the financial statements.
8. <u>Historical Summary</u> - presents key financial data for the past 5 to 10 years.

Ask your students to look through the financial statements of Home Depot and locate as many of these sections as possible.

Use the following group learning activity to cover the independent auditors' report and the management report in more detail.

GROUP LEARNING ACTIVITY — Independent Auditors' Report

Obtain copies of several different annual reports. Divide the class into small groups; give each group an annual report. Ask each group to locate the independent auditors' report.

Next, instruct the groups to outline the auditors' report by briefly describing the main point(s) in each paragraph. You may want to give each group a blank overhead transparency and a pen to record their answers. Ask two or more groups to share their outlines with the class. Note how closely these student outlines follow the outline of a standard audit report (Transparency 17-9).

You may also want to use a similar exercise to review the management report. The management reports will show much greater variation than the highly standardized audit report. However, the basic message of each management report should revolve around management's responsibility for establishing strong internal controls and preparing financial statements that adhere to generally accepted accounting principles.

INTERNET ACTIVITY – Annual Reports

It is possible to find the annual reports of many companies by searching the internet. Ask your students to locate the annual report for a corporation and list the main sections that appear in that report. As an alternative, have them print out a section of the annual report, such as the Management Report. Ask them to compare and contrast their company's Management Report with the one for Home Depot in Appendix E.

WRITING EXERCISE — Historical Summary

Ask your students to write an answer to the following question (Transparency 17-10).

> Many annual reports include a Historical Summary section, which shows key financial data for the past 5 to 10 years. Why would information that is 5- to 10-years old be presented in an annual report?

Transparency Master 17-1

HORIZONTAL ANALYSIS

Using the income statement for Home Depot, compute the percentage change for the following items:

	Percentage Change	
	2001-2002	2000-2001*
Net sales		
Cost of merchandise sold		
Selling & store operating		
Total operating expenses		
Net earnings		

* Fiscal year 2002 ended February 2, 2003
  Fiscal year 2001 ended February 3, 2002
  Fiscal year 2000 ended January 28, 2001

Transparency Master 17-2

HORIZONTAL ANALYSIS

Solution

Using the income statement for Home Depot, compute the percentage change for the following items:

	Percentage Change	
	2001-2002	2000-2001*
Net sales	8.8	17.1
Cost of merchandise sold	7.3	16.7
Selling & store operating	10.0	19.4
Total operating expenses	9.5	18.2
Net earnings	20.4	17.9

* Fiscal year 2002 ended February 2, 2003
  Fiscal year 2001 ended February 3, 2002
  Fiscal year 2000 ended January 28, 2001

Transparency Master 17-3

VERTICAL ANALYSIS

Home Depot, Inc. & Subsidiaries
Consolidated Statement of Earnings
For the Year Ended February 2, 2003

Net sales	**100.0%**
Cost of merchandise sold	**68.9%**
GROSS PROFIT	**31.1%**
Operating expenses:	
Selling & store operating	**19.2%**
Pre-opening	**0.2%**
General & administrative	**1.7%**
Total operating expenses	**21.1%**
OPERATING INCOME	**10.0%**

SOLVENCY MEASURES

1. Current Position Analysis
   a. Working capital
   b. Current ratio
   c. Quick ratio

2. Accounts Receivable Analysis
   a. Accounts receivable turnover
   b. Number of days' sales in receivables

3. Inventory Analysis
   a. Inventory turnover
   b. Number of days' sales in inventory

4. Ratio of Fixed Assets to Long-Term Liabilities

5. Ratio of Liabilities to Stockholders' Equity

6. Number of Times Interest Charges Earned

SOLVENCY MEASURES

	Ace Co. Current Year	Ace Co. Prior Year	Industry Average
Current ratio	2.5	2.4	2.2
Quick ratio	1.2	1.2	1.0
Accounts receivable turnover	7.6	7.9	10.1
Number of days' sales in receivables	48	46	36
Inventory turnover	4.7	4.6	4.3
Number of days' sales in inventory	77	79	85
Ratio of fixed assets to long-term liabilities	3.6	3.6	3.7
Ratio of liabilities to stockholders' equity	0.6	0.7	0.9
Number of times interest charges earned	8.2	8.0	9.5

PROFITABILITY MEASURES

1. Ratio of net sales to assets

2. Rate earned on total assets

3. Rate earned on stockholders' equity

4. Rate earned on common stockholders' equity

5. Earnings per share on common stock

6. Price-earnings ratio

7. Dividends per share

8. Dividend yield

PROFITABILITY MEASURES

	Ace Co. Current Year	Ace Co. Prior Year	Industry Average
Ratio of net sales to assets	1.4	1.3	1.1
Rate earned on total assets	12%	12%	11%
Rate earned on stockholders' equity	18%	17%	15%
Earnings per share on common stock	$1.80	$1.72	
Price-earnings ratio	10.2	10.5	12.4
Dividend yield	4%	4%	3%

SECTIONS OF A CORPORATE ANNUAL REPORT

1. Financial highlights

2. President's letter

3. Financial statements

4. Notes to the financial statements

5. Management's discussion and analysis

6. Management report

7. Independent auditors' report

8. Historical summary

INDEPENDENT AUDITORS' REPORT

1. **Introductory Paragraph**

   Lists the financial statements that were audited. States that management has overall responsibility for the financial statements; the auditors' responsibility is simply to express an opinion on the statements prepared by management.

2. **Scope Paragraph**

   Describes the nature of the audit process. States that audits are conducted in accordance with generally accepted auditing standards and include tests needed to obtain "reasonable assurance" that financial statements do not include material misstatements.

3. **Opinion Paragraph**

   Gives the auditors' opinion on the financial statements. In an unqualified opinion, the auditor affirms that the financial statements present fairly, in all material respects, a company's financial position, results of operations, and cash flows in conformity with generally accepted accounting principles.

WRITING EXERCISE

Many annual reports include a Historical Summary section, which shows key financial data for the past 5 to 10 years. Why would information that is 5- to 10-years old be presented in an annual report?

Section III
Using the Power Accounting System Software (P.A.S.S.)

HOW TO USE THE P.A.S.S. INSPECTOR CD
(Student Solution Checker)

A program called the *Inspector 4e* is available to assist you in checking your students' work. The software will compare student data files (stored on floppy disks or in folders on a hard disk or network) to solution files provided with the *Inspector 4e*. You can check an individual student file against the solution file or you can check a group of student files all at once against a solution file. You can direct the computer to check: (1) just the current folder, or (2) the current folders and all subfolders. By setting the current folder as the root and choosing option 2, you can check the entire hard drive or network.

The *Inspector 4e* software checks the following items:

Accounting System: Business organization, type of business, departmental code, type of accounting system, required accounts, appropriation accounts, current account balances, previous year account balances, department numbers, vendor account balances, customer account balances, missing or extraneous accounts, missing or extraneous vendors, and missing or extraneous customers.

Fixed Assets: Missing and extraneous assets; and for each asset, purchase date, depreciation method, useful life, costs, salvage value, and general ledger account numbers.

Payroll: Missing and extraneous employees; and for each employee, the social security number, number of pay periods, marital status, withholding allowances, general ledger account number, salary amount, hourly rate, piece rate, and commission. For each payroll transaction: transaction date, gross pay, federal income tax, state income tax, Social Security withheld, Medicare withheld, deduction one, deduction two, deduction three, regular hours worked, overtime hours worked, number of pieces produced, and commission sales.

Inventory: Missing or extraneous inventory items. For each item; the units of measure, reorder point, quantity on hand, quantity on order, yearly quantity sold, yearly dollars sold, retail price, and last cost are checked.

INSPECTOR 4e START-UP

To begin working with the *Inspector 4e*:
1. Open the *Inspector 4e* by choosing the Power Accounting System Software Version 4 group from the Start button and then selecting Accounting 21ed Inspector.
2. After the *Inspector 4e* software loads into your computer's memory, a copyright information window will appear. Click on Continue to proceed, or click on Exit to end the program.

INSPECTOR 4e PASSWORD WINDOW

To prevent unauthorized access to the Inspector solution checking software, password protection is provided. The password is established by you the first time the software is run after installation. Thereafter, each time the *Inspector 4e* program is run, the password dialog box shown in Figure 1 will appear and the password you assigned must be entered. Type the password and click on the >Next button.

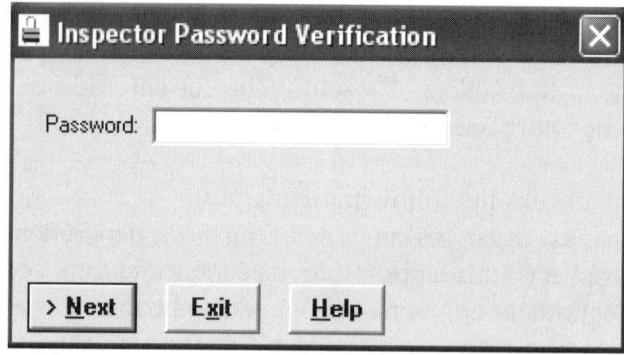

Figure 1 *Inspector 4e* Password Dialog Box

SELECT ANSWER KEY

The Select the Answer Key window shown in Figure 2 is used to select the name of the file you wish to use as the answer key in checking student files. Each file has a prefix that identifies the product, the word KEY to identify it as an answer key file, and the problem number (e.g., 01-5A KEY). Some files have a suffix of P which stands for "post closing". These files should be checked against student files saved after period-end closing has been performed. The Key file without the P suffix contains the solution file created before closing. Checking solutions saved before period-end closing has been performed is preferable to checking solutions after period-end closing. Since the temporary income statement accounts are all closed during period-end closing, there is little left to check after period-end closing.

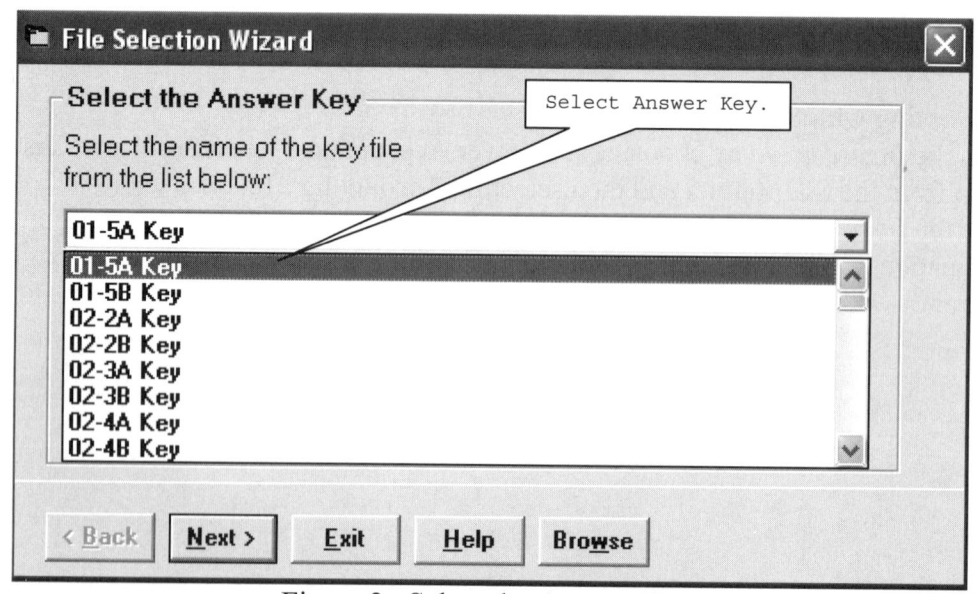

Figure 2 Select the Answer Key

To Select an Answer Key File:
1. Select the desired key file from the drop-down list.
2. Click on the Next> command button to proceed.

SELECT FILES TO CHECK
The Inspector File Selection Wizard window, shown in Figure 3, is used to specify whether an individual student solution files or a group of student solution files are to be checked against the current Key file.

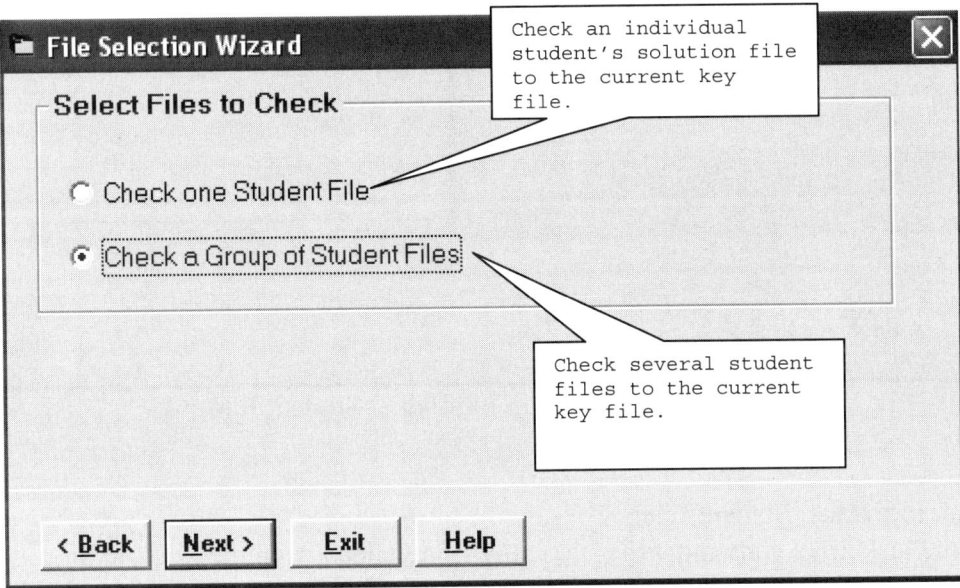

Figure 3   Select Files to Check

To Select Files to Check:
1. Click on the Check One Student File option button if you want to check an individual student's solution file to the current Key file, then click on the Next> command button to proceed.
2. Click on the Check a Group of Student Files option button if you want to check several student files to the current key file, then click on the Next> command button to proceed.

CHECK ONE STUDENT FILE
If the *Check One Student File* option button is selected (see Figure 3), the Select a Folder or File window shown in Figure 4 will appear when the Next> button is clicked. The purpose of this window is to select the disk drive, folder, and individual student file to be checked against the current Key file.

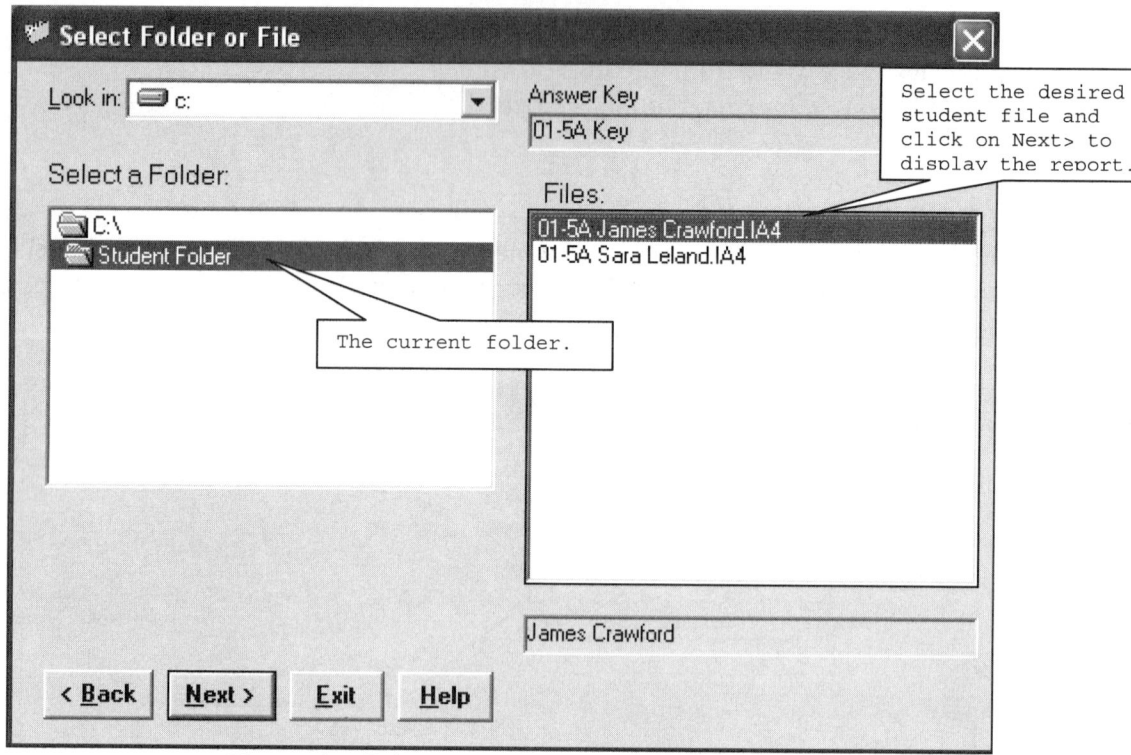

Figure 4 Select an Individual Student File

To Select an Individual Student File:
1. Select the disk drive containing the file you wish to check from the Look in drop-down list. Once the desired disk drive is selected, the names of all the folders stored on the disk drive will appear in the Select a Folder list box. **Note:** If the selected disk does not contain any folders, the names of all the files stored on the disk will appear in the Files list box. Proceed to Step 3.
2. Select the folder containing the file you wish to open from the Select a Folder drop-down list. Once the desired folder is selected, the names of all the files stored in the folder will appear in the Files list box.
3. Click on the student file you wish to check in the Files list box. If the file you wish to check does not appear in the Files list box, check to make sure you selected the correct disk drive and/or folder.
4. Click on the <Next> command button. The detailed report for the selected student will be displayed.

CHECK A GROUP OF STUDENT FILES

If the ***Check a Group of Student Files*** is selected (see Figure 3), the Select a Folder or File window shown in Figure 5 will appear when the Next> button is clicked. The purpose of this window is to select the disk drive, folder, and all the student files that are to be checked against the current Key file.

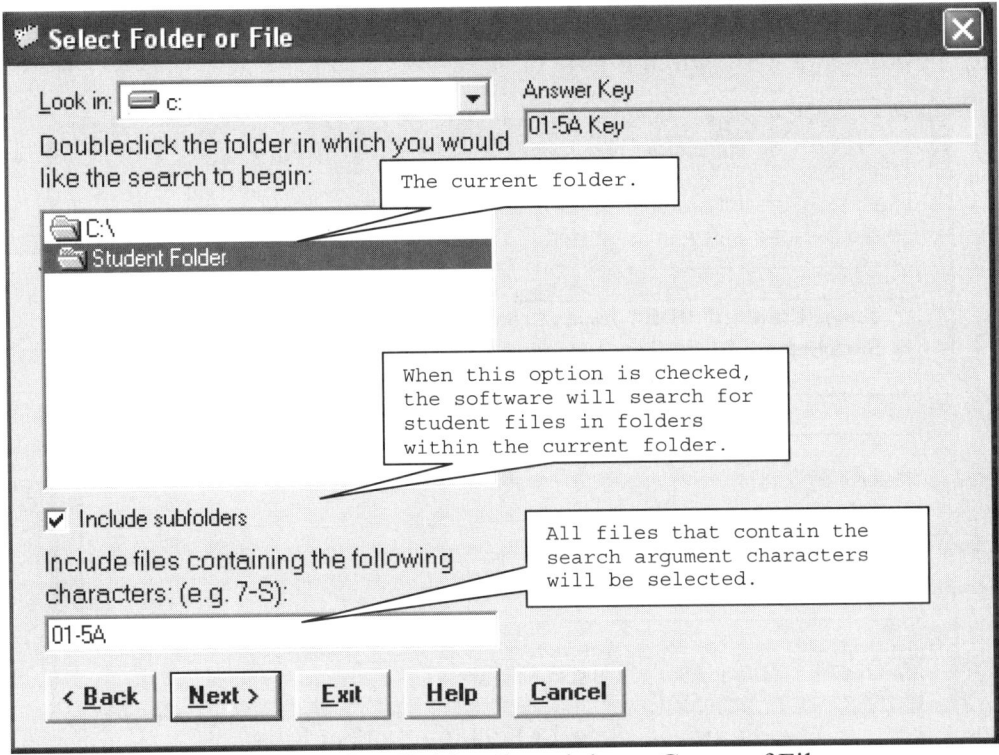

Figure 5 Select Folder Containing a Group of Files

To Select a Group of Student Files:
1. Select the disk drive containing the file you wish to check from the Look in drop-down list. Once the desired disk drive is selected, the names of all the folders stored on the disk drive will appear in the Select a Folder list box. Note, if the selected disk does not contain any folders, proceed to Step 3.
2. Select the folder containing the file you wish to open from the drop-down list under the Double-click the folder in which you would like the search to begin statement.
3. Click on the Include Subfolders check box to instruct the Inspector software to search for student files in folders within the current selected folder. This check box determines the scope of the search for matching student files. You can search just the current folder (when the check box is Off) or the current folder and all subfolders (when the check box is On). If the current folder is set to the root directory of your hard drive, the entire hard drive will be searched.
4. Enter a search argument in the Include Files Containing the Following Characters text box (e.g., 01-5A). The search argument should contain common characters that identify files for all students who have completed the problem of the current key file you previously selected (see Figure 2). Key the string of characters contained within the file names you wish to locate. For example, key 01-5A if you wish to search for all files that contain the characters, 01-5A.

5. Click on the Next> command button to proceed. All matching files will appear in the Select Files window shown in Figure 6.

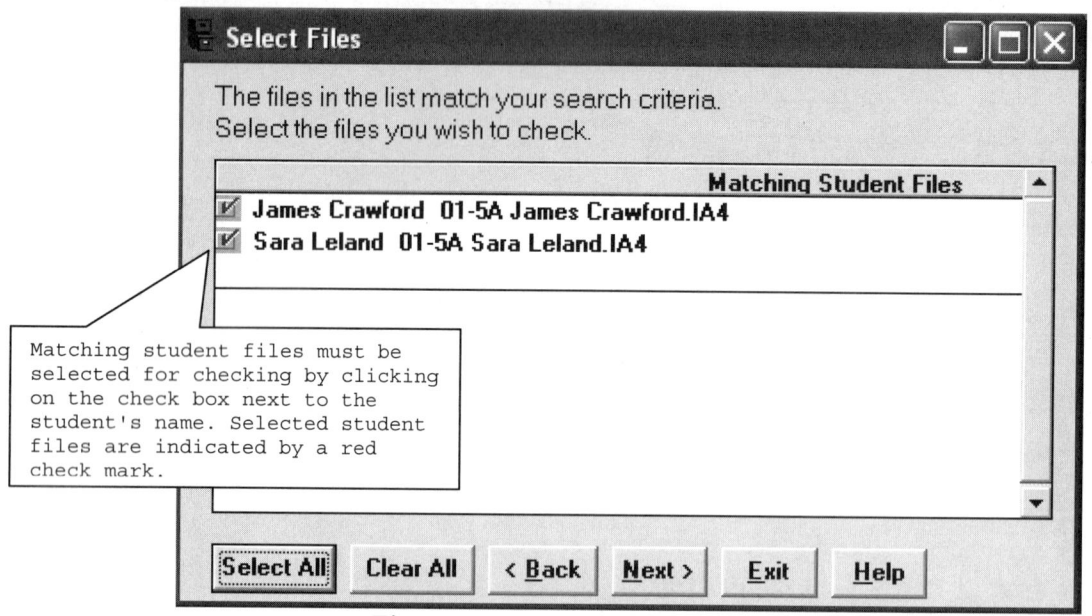

```
Matching student files must be
selected for checking by clicking
on the check box next to the
student's name. Selected student
files are indicated by a red
check mark.
```

Figure 6   Select Matching Student Files

6. Select from the Matching Student Files list those files that you would like the software to check. If the Matching Student Files list is blank, check to make sure you selected the correct disk drive and/or folder and entered a valid search argument.
7. Click on the Next> command button to proceed.
   The Select Report Type window is shown in Figure 7.

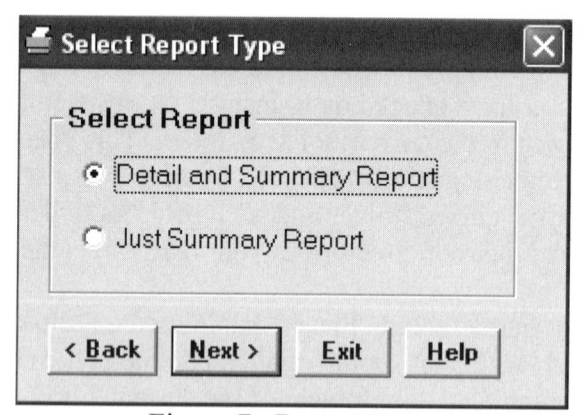

Figure 7   Report Type

8. Click on the Detail and Summary Report option button if you would like a detailed report for each student followed by a summary report of all selected students. Click on the Just Summary Report option button if you want only a single report listing all students and their scores.

9. Click on the Next> command button to display the report.

DETAIL REPORT

The detail report identifies any discrepancies between the answer key and the student's file. For each incorrect item, the correct item is also shown. An example of a detail report is shown in Figure 8.

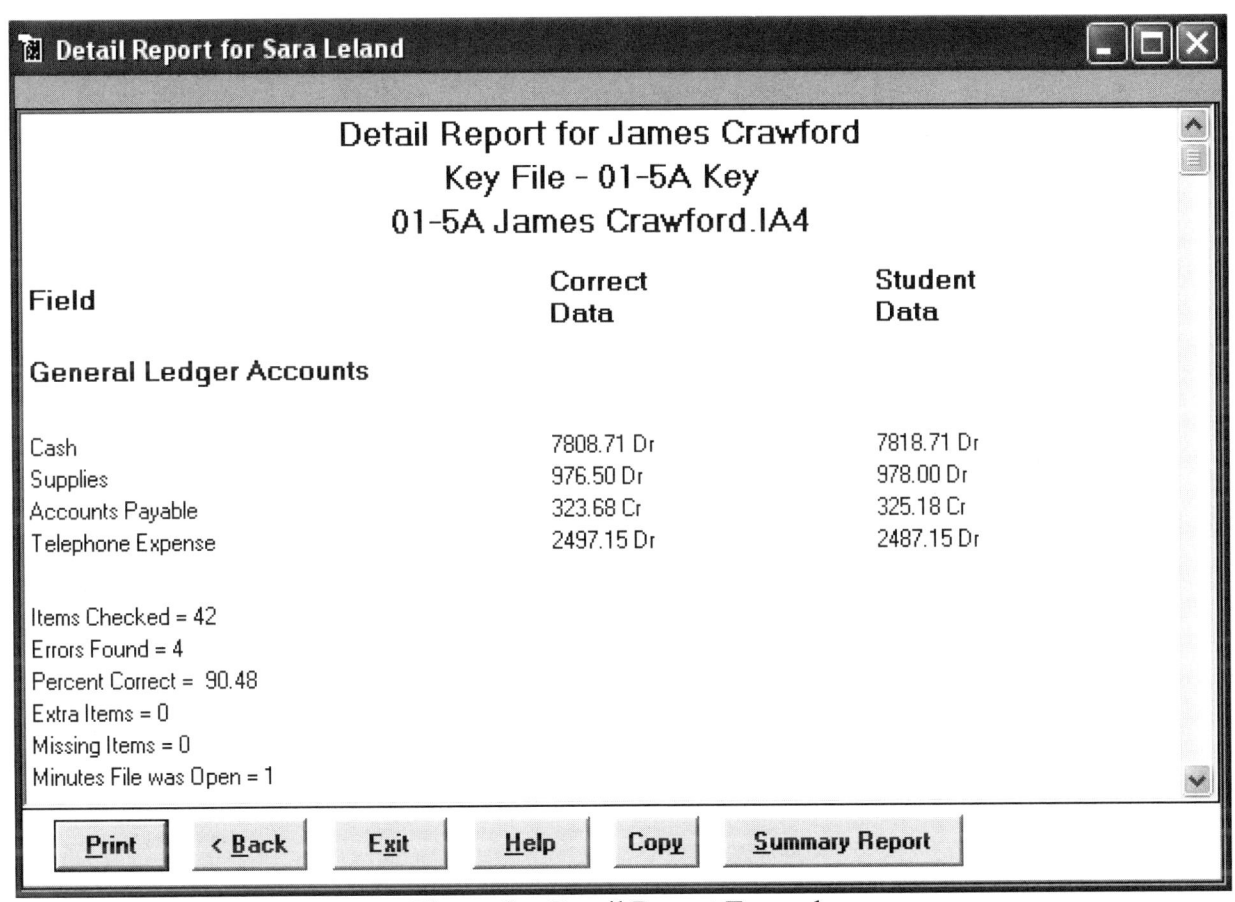

```
Detail Report for James Crawford
        Key File - 01-5A Key
      01-5A James Crawford.IA4

Field                    Correct Data      Student Data

General Ledger Accounts

Cash                     7808.71 Dr        7818.71 Dr
Supplies                 976.50 Dr         978.00 Dr
Accounts Payable         323.68 Cr         325.18 Cr
Telephone Expense        2497.15 Dr        2487.15 Dr

Items Checked = 42
Errors Found = 4
Percent Correct = 90.48
Extra Items = 0
Missing Items = 0
Minutes File was Open = 1
```

Figure 8   Detail Report Example

SUMMARY REPORT

    The summary report lists each student's score based on items checked, errors found, and extraneous items. In addition, the number of minutes it took the student to complete the problem is shown. An example of a summary report is shown in Figure 9.

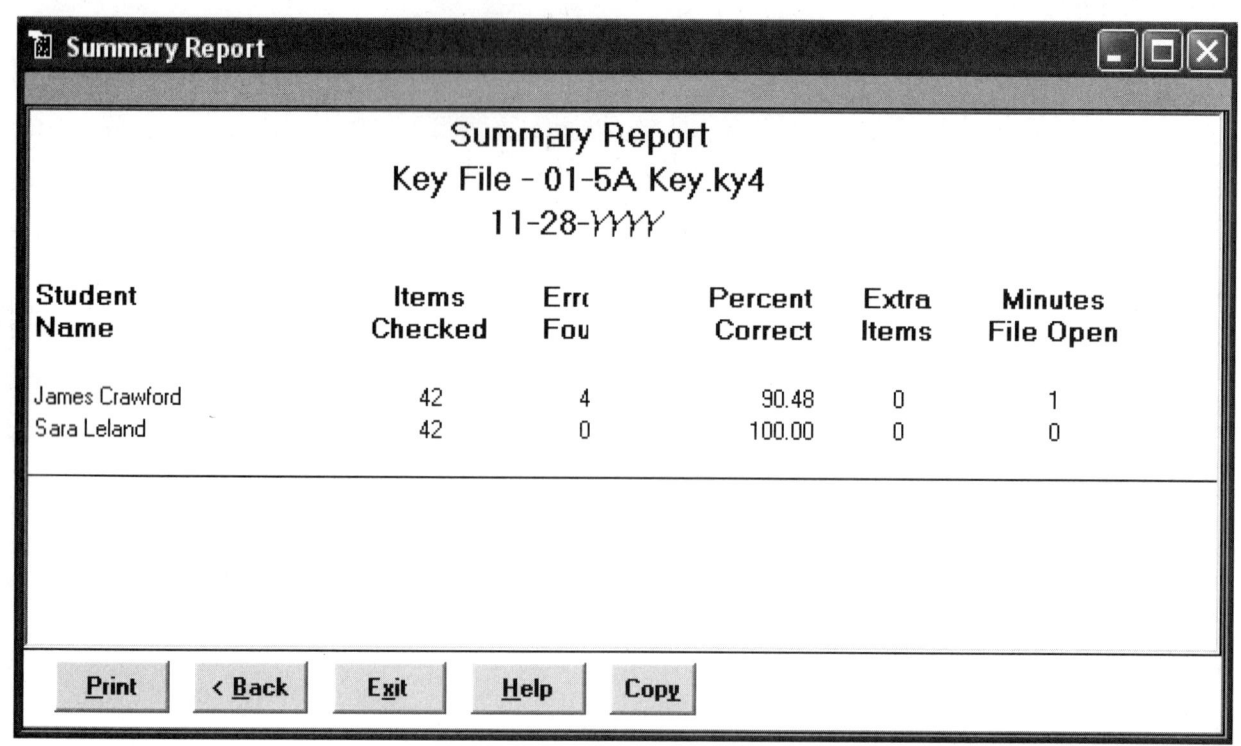

Student Name	Items Checked	Errors Found	Percent Correct	Extra Items	Minutes File Open
James Crawford	42	4	90.48	0	1
Sara Leland	42	0	100.00	0	0

Figure 9   Summary Report Example

POWER ACCOUNTING SYSTEM SOFTWARE (P.A.S.S.) SETUP

P.A.S.S. (Power Accounting System Software) is an accounting package designed to accommodate a wide variety of user needs. It is able to handle various types of businesses, such as proprietorships, partnerships, and corporations for both service and merchandising firms. The software provides opening balance files for selected problems from the text. It also can be used with problems that you or your students wish to create. The following instructions should be provided to students who use the software to create opening balance files for problems that are not in the text.

INTRODUCTION

To solve problems provided with PASS, you have loaded opening balance files for accounting systems that were already established. Another capability of the software is that you can design and create your own accounting data files. *There are two methods that may be used to accomplish this task. The first method is to simply load an existing opening balance file into the PASS software that is similar to what you wish to create, use the software features to modify the data as desired, and then follow the step-by-step instructions provided in the PASS startup group's Readme file. The second method (detailed in the following material) permits you to create the opening balance files from your own data.* In the material that follows, you will learn how to set up opening balance data for Kendell Corporation. Kendell Corporation is a merchandising wholesale business (with Cost of Goods Sold) organized as a corporation. Kendell Corporation wholesales power tools to retail stores.

PLANNING

Prior to setting up a computerized accounting system, you must carefully plan, design, and gather data. For example, account numbers must be assigned to each account to identify it as an asset, liability, equity, revenue, or expense account. Account balances must match the totals of related subsidiary ledgers and assets, liabilities, and equity account balances must be current. Total debit balances must equal total credit balances prior to entering data into the computer.

New

The **New command** in the File menu clears any existing data from memory in preparation for setting up a new accounting system. If you have data in memory, you should save it before you choose New. You will be asked to enter your name in the User Name text box so that the computer can associate your name with the newly created file.

Customize Accounting System

The Customize Accounting System window is used to provide setup company information to PASS. It can be accessed by choosing Customize Accounting System from the Data menu or by clicking on the Custom toolbar button. Each of the five tabs in this window is used to tailor the accounting system to the needs of the business being established. Each is discussed below.

Company Information

The Customize Accounting System, window with the Company Info. tab illustrating setup data for Kendell Corporation, is shown in Figure 1. The purpose and function of each text box, check box, and option button in the Company Info. tab is described in Table 1.

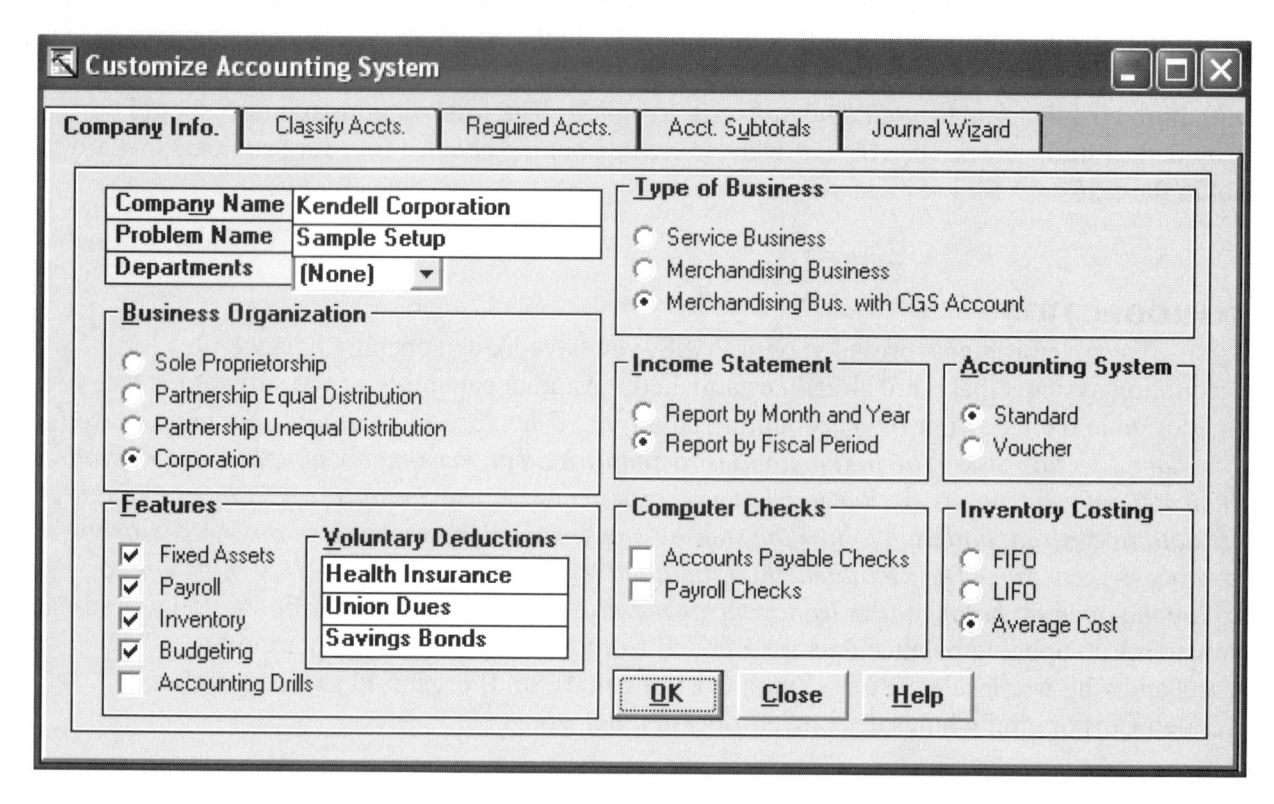

Figure 1   Company Information

Option	Description
Company Name	The name of the company is displayed and printed as part of the heading for each report.
Problem Name	The problem name is printed at the top of the report along with the student name. The problem name also appears in the upper right corner of the PASS application window as a reminder of the problem currently in computer memory.
Departments	This drop-down list allows you to select from three options: None, 2, or 3.
Business Organization	The business organization option is used by the software during financial statement preparation and period-end closing.
Features	A check box is provided for each type of accounting system to be included during setup. Appropriate windows, reports, data entry tabs, etc. are automatically activated based upon the features selected. For example, when the Payroll check box is selected, an Employees tab appears in the Account maintenance window to permit employee maintenance. A Payroll tab appears in the Other window to permit entry of payroll transactions, and a Payroll reports option appears in the Reports window that enables the user to display and print various payroll reports. When the Payroll feature is checked, a Voluntary Deductions group box will appear permitting the user to enter the names of up to three different voluntary deductions that are to be withheld from the employees' pay.

Type of Business	The type of business option is used by the software to determine the format of the income statement. If the Merchandising Business option is chosen, the income statement contains a Cost of Goods Sold section where the cost of goods sold is worked up based on beginning inventory, purchases, and ending inventory and requires an inventory adjusting entry. If the Merchandising Business with CGS option is chosen, the income statement expects that there will be a Cost of Goods Sold account instead of a Purchases account. In this case, it simply uses the Cost of Goods Sold account. In addition, the Sales Invoice entry will generate a journal entry that not only records the sale at retail, but also debits Cost of Merchandise Sold and credits Merchandise Inventory at COST based on the inventory costing method selected (LIFO, FIFO, or Average). The journal entry generated by a Purchase Invoice will debit Merchandise Inventory rather than Purchases.
Income Statement	If this option is set to Month & Year, the income statement will include a column for the current month and another column for the current year. Also included for each column is the percent of each amount in relation to the total operating revenue. If this option is set to Fiscal Period, only the amount column and percent of total operating revenue is included on the income statement representing the current fiscal period.
Accounting System	This option allows you to specify whether or not a voucher system is being used.
Computer Checks	If the Accounts Payable Checks option is set On, accounts payable checks will be created each time a cash payment that involves a vendor is entered into the computer. If the Payroll Checks option is set On, pay checks will be created each time an employee's payroll transaction is entered.
Inventory Costing	This option allows you to specify the method of inventory valuation to be used by the computer during processing of a perpetual inventory system. The Inventory Costing option will appear only if both the Inventory feature and the Merchandising Business with CGS account options have been selected.

Table 1 Company Information Text Boxes and Option Settings

When the Company Information tab is active, enter the Company Name, Problem Name, and click on the Departments drop-down list to select the number of departments (if any). Select the appropriate Business Organization and click on each Feature check box to indicate the accounting system setup data that is to be included in setup. **Note:** If the Payroll feature is selected, the Voluntary Deductions group box will appear. Enter the names of up to three different voluntary deductions that are to be withheld from the employee's pay. Next, select the appropriate type of business, income statement, and accounting system. Click on the appropriate Computer Checks box to indicate if the computer is to generate payable and/or payroll checks. If neither of the check boxes is checked, the computer assumes that checks are written manually. Finally, and if both the Inventory feature and the Merchandising Business with CGS (Cost of Goods Sold) Account features have been selected, select the method of inventory valuation to be used by the computer during processing.

Classify Accounts

The **classify accounts** feature allows you to classify the accounts based on account number ranges. The example shown in Figure 2 contains the account number ranges for Kendell Corporation. In order to perform financial statement analysis, the computer needs to know the range of account numbers for long-term assets and long-term liabilities. These data are provided in the Extended Classification section of the window.

From	To	Account Classification
1000	1999	Assets
2000	2999	Liabilities
3000	3999	Equity
4000	4999	Revenue
5000	5999	Cost
6000	6999	Expenses
7000	7999	Other Revenue
8000	8999	Other Expenses
9000	9999	Corporate Income Tax

From	To	Extended Classification
1500	1999	Long-Term Assets
2500	2999	Long-Term Liabilities

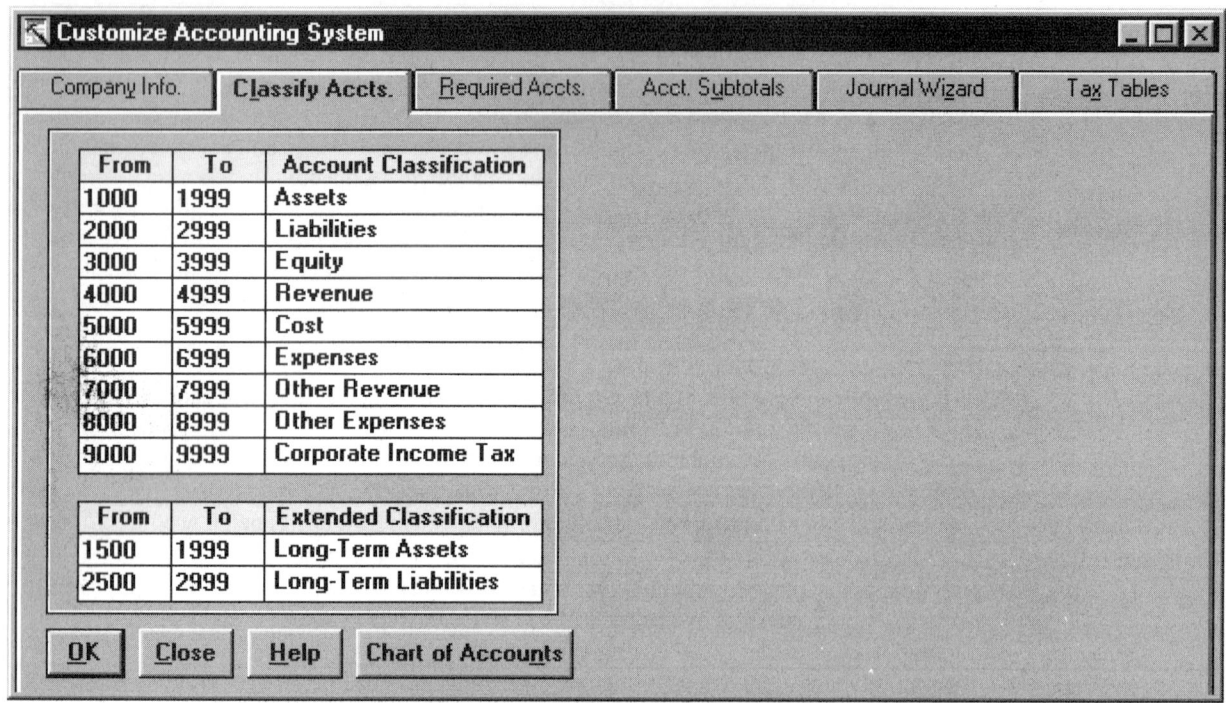

Figure 2   Classify Accounts

The account classifications shown in Figure 2 are also the default classifications used by the PASS system. Unless the account classification numbering scheme is different, it will not be necessary to change the account ranges. If they must be changed, do *not* enter the actual range of account numbers: enter the *potential* range. For example, if your chart of accounts currently has five assets ranging from account number 1110 to 1150, you should not specify the actual range, 1110 to 1150. Specify the potential range, such as 1000 to 1999, so that asset accounts added later will be included in the assets classification automatically. If your chart of accounts does not include a certain classification, enter the anticipated account number range for that classification. For example, if your chart of accounts does not include Other Expenses, include a range of account numbers that are to be reserved for Other Expenses in case they are added to the chart of accounts at a later date.

To enter account classifications, click on the Classify Accts. tab. If the account classifications are different than those shown, enter the account number range for each of the classes of accounts. You may click on the Chart of Accounts button to select an account from the chart of accounts list window.

Required Accounts

Because you have a great deal of flexibility in assigning account numbers and titles, you must provide the computer with specific **required accounts** -- that is, the account numbers that you have assigned to certain key accounts. The computer needs this information to prepare financial statements, carry out integration among the systems (i.e., payroll, purchase order processing, sales order processing), and to complete period-end closing tasks. The Required Accounts tab showing a partial list of required accounts for Kendell Corporation is illustrated in Figure 3.

Customize Accounting System

Tabs: Company Info. | Classify Accts. | **Required Accts.** | Acct. Subtotals | Journal Wizard | Tax Tables

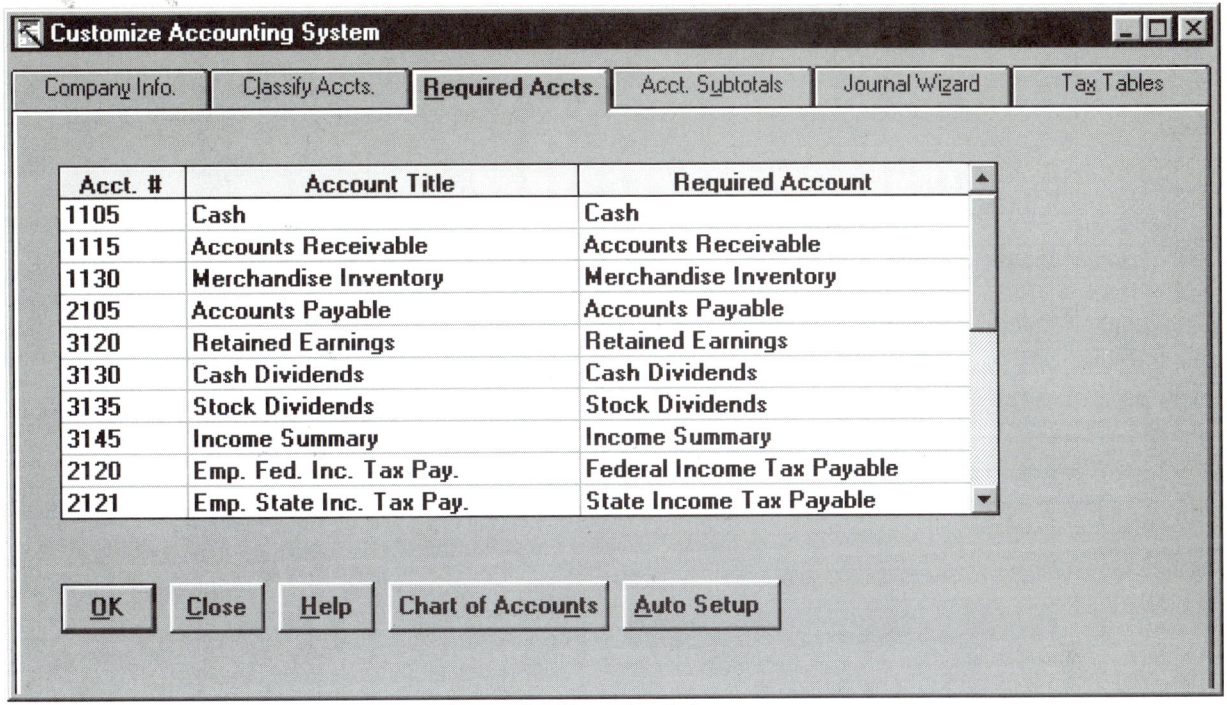

Acct. #	Account Title	Required Account
1105	Cash	Cash
1115	Accounts Receivable	Accounts Receivable
1130	Merchandise Inventory	Merchandise Inventory
2105	Accounts Payable	Accounts Payable
3120	Retained Earnings	Retained Earnings
3130	Cash Dividends	Cash Dividends
3135	Stock Dividends	Stock Dividends
3145	Income Summary	Income Summary
2120	Emp. Fed. Inc. Tax Pay.	Federal Income Tax Payable
2121	Emp. State Inc. Tax Pay.	State Income Tax Payable

Buttons: OK | Close | Help | Chart of Accounts | Auto Setup

Figure 3   Required Accounts

Based upon the departmentalization, business organization, features, and type of business settings in the Company Info. tab, the computer will automatically determine and list the accounts it requires. For example, if the type of business is a service business, no merchandise inventory accounts are required. For a merchandising business, a Merchandise Inventory and an Income Summary account are required for each department. For a proprietorship and a partnership, capital account(s) are listed. For a corporation, a Stock Dividends account is required. If the corporation does not have stock dividends, enter the account number for the Cash Dividends account number.

To specify the required accounts, click on the Required Accts. tab., and then click on the Auto Setup button. The computer will search the newly entered chart of accounts and attempt to match the required accounts to the account titles. All matching accounts are displayed. Enter the account number for each of the unmatched accounts. You may click on the Chart of Accounts button to select an account from the chart of accounts list window.

Account Subtotals

The purpose of the **account subtotals** feature is to allow you to specify where subtotals are to be printed on the financial statements. For example, you may wish to tailor the balance sheet so that a subtotal prints after current assets and another after plant assets. To set up subtotals, enter the account number range of the accounts to be included in the subtotal and the title to be printed on the subtotal line. The account number ranges need not reference actual accounts. Instead, the potential range should be entered so that it will not be necessary to modify the account number range as accounts are added to the chart of accounts. The Account Subtotals for Kendell Corporation are shown in Figure 4.

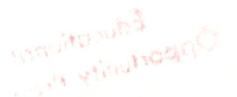

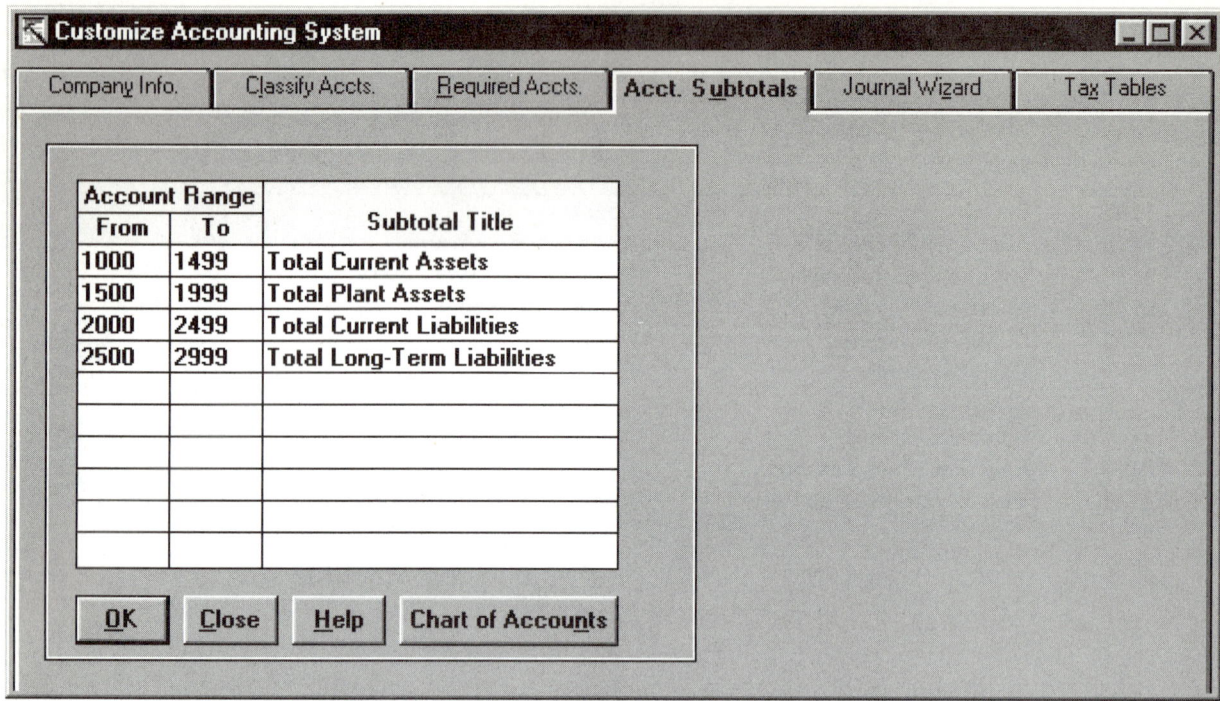

Figure 4   Account Subtotals

To establish account subtotals on financial statements, click on the Acct. Subtotals tab. Enter the account number range and title for each of the subtotals. You may click on the Chart of Accounts button to view a chart of accounts list.

Journal Wizard

The **journal wizard**, shown in Figure 5, can be used to create special general, purchases, cash payments, sales, and cash receipts journals. Using special journals simplifies the process of entering transaction data into the computer. Basic default journals are automatically provided when a new business is established. The Journal wizard may be used to expand these default journals to better meet the needs of the business being established. New journals will be saved to disk along with your data and will be used when entering future transaction data. The journal wizard may also be used with an ongoing automated system to create special journals to more efficiently handle data entry activities. The following procedures and examples shown in Figures 5 through 8 were used to create the special cash payments journal shown in Figure 9.

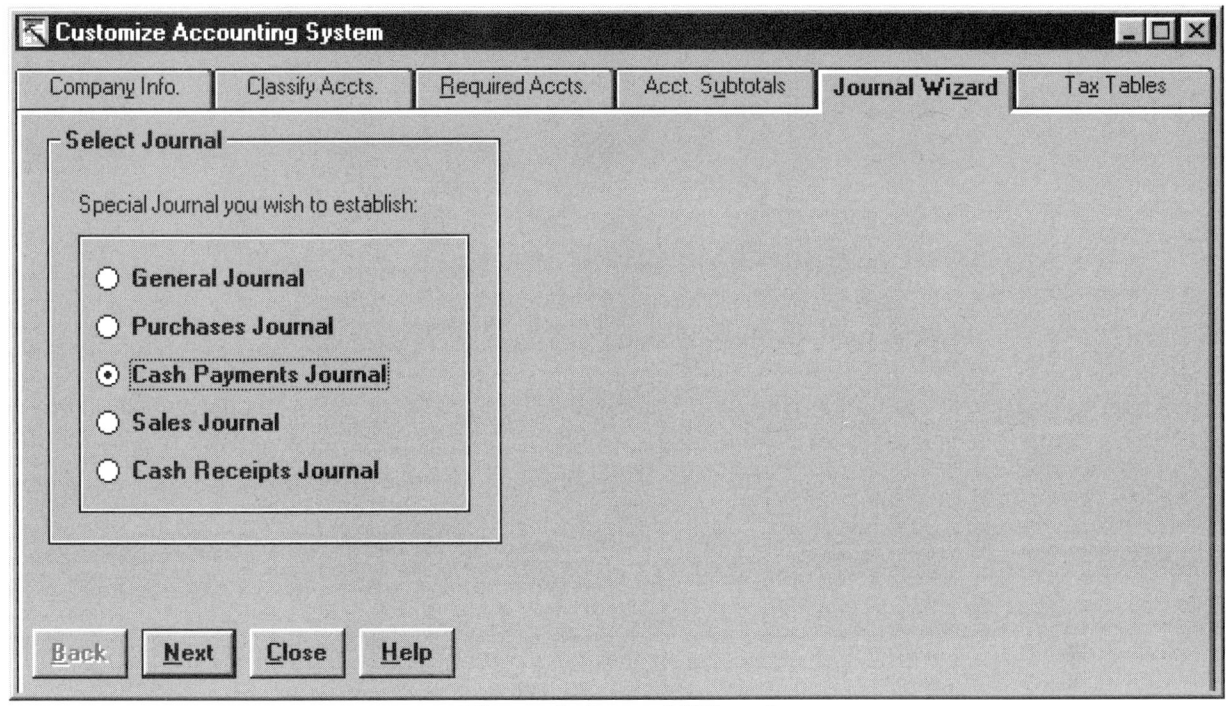

Figure 5 Journal Wizard

Click on the Journal Wizard tab and select the journal to be created (Cash Payments). Click on the *Next* button to continue. The dialog window shown in Figure 6 will appear.

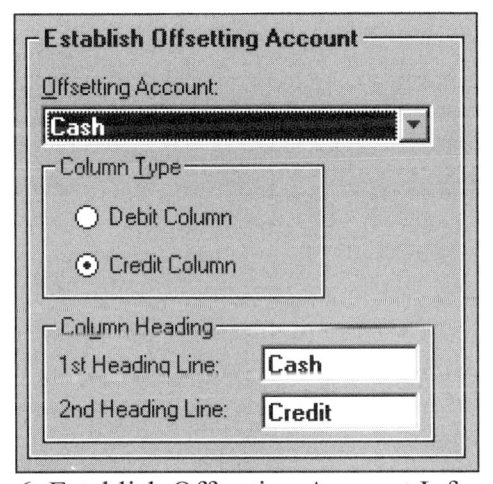

Figure 6 Establish Offsetting Account Information

Click on the drop-down text box to select the offsetting account (Cash), then click on the appropriate Debit or Credit column (offsetting Cash account will be Credited). Enter a one- to two-line heading to identify the offsetting account column on the journal (Cash Credit). Click on *Next* to continue. The dialog window shown in Figure 7 will appear.

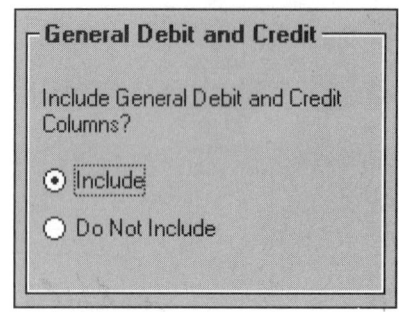

Figure 7 General Debit and Credit Column Dialog Box

Click on the Include or Do Not Include button to indicate if general debit and credit columns should be in the journal (Include). Click on *Next* to continue. The dialog box shown in Figure 8 will appear.

Figure 8 Special Journal Columns

Use the Account drop-down list to select the account to be included in the journal, enter the first and second header to identify the account column in the journal, then click on the Debit or Credit check box to indicate if the account is to be treated as a debit or credit amount. Repeat this procedure for each column to be added to the journal, and then click on *Finish*.

Click on the appropriate tab in the Journal Entries window and verify that the newly created journal is correct (see Figure 9).

General Journal	Purchases	Cash Payments	Sales	Cash Receipts

Date	Refer.	Acct. No.	Debit	Credit	A.P. Debit	Mrch. Inv. Cr.	Cash Credit	Vendor
02/01/--								

Figure 9 Journal Wizard Created Cash Payments Journal

The Date and Refer. column will also be included as the left-most columns in the journal. A Vendor or Customer column will also be automatically added as the right-most column to the appropriate journal if the computer detects that vendor or customer data exist.

Tax Tables

There are three sections in the **tax table** dialog box. The Federal Tax Brackets section contains the federal withholding rates. You may update these rates by referring to IRS Circular E (Employer's Tax Guide), Table 7 (Annual Payroll). The State Tax Brackets section contains the state withholding rates used by the software. Like the Federal rates, the State rates may be updated by referring to your state's Employer's Tax Guide. The Rates and Limits section contains the various tax rates, upper limits, and allowance amounts required by the software to calculate employee and employer payroll taxes. The new rates will be saved to disk along with your data and will be used to compute withholding rates for future payrolls.

It is recommended that you <u>not</u> change these rates (unless instructed to do so) when working with payroll problems. If the brackets, rates, or percentages are changed, the calculated withholding amounts will no longer match the solutions provided to your instructor. The Tax Table tab is shown in Figure 10.

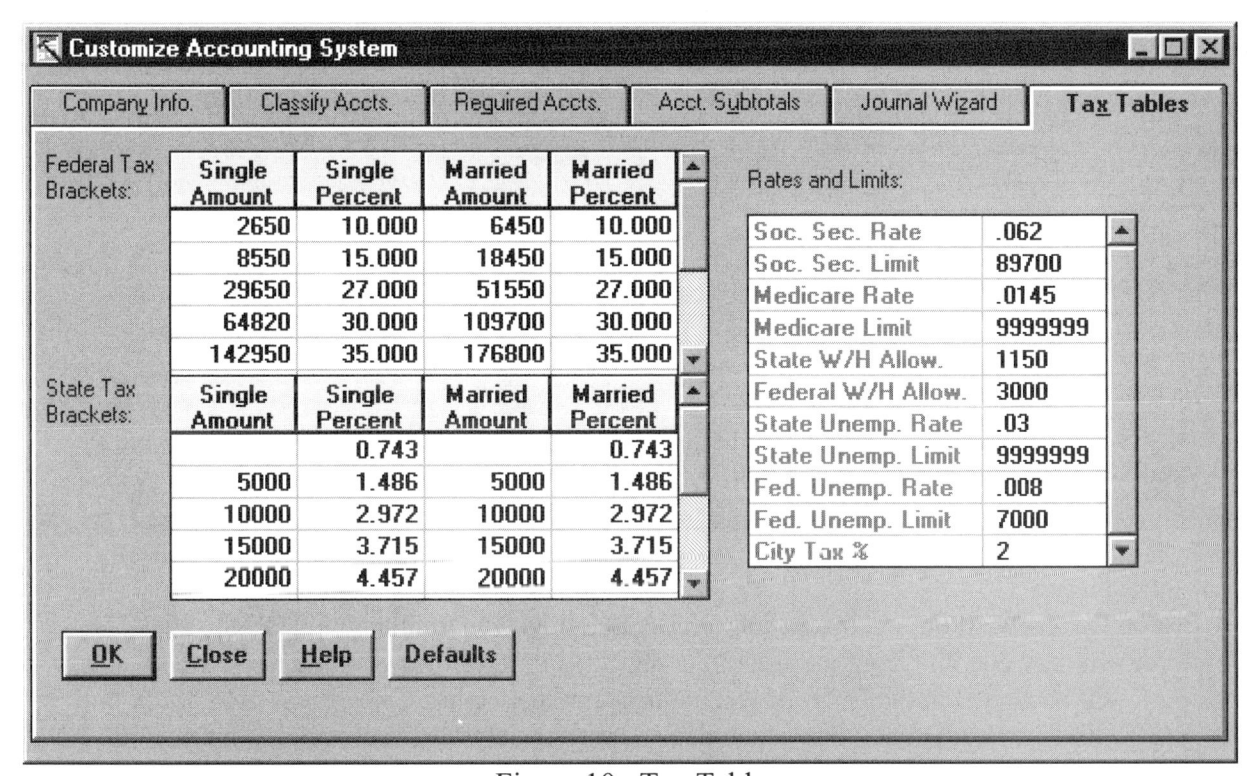

Federal Tax Brackets:	Single Amount	Single Percent	Married Amount	Married Percent
	2650	10.000	6450	10.000
	8550	15.000	18450	15.000
	29650	27.000	51550	27.000
	64820	30.000	109700	30.000
	142950	35.000	176800	35.000

State Tax Brackets:	Single Amount	Single Percent	Married Amount	Married Percent
		0.743		0.743
	5000	1.486	5000	1.486
	10000	2.972	10000	2.972
	15000	3.715	15000	3.715
	20000	4.457	20000	4.457

Rates and Limits:	
Soc. Sec. Rate	.062
Soc. Sec. Limit	89700
Medicare Rate	.0145
Medicare Limit	9999999
State W/H Allow.	1150
Federal W/H Allow.	3000
State Unemp. Rate	.03
State Unemp. Limit	9999999
Fed. Unemp. Rate	.008
Fed. Unemp. Limit	7000
City Tax %	2

Figure 10   Tax Table

To modify the tax table data, click on the Tax Table tab, then click on the appropriate field and enter the change(s) to the amounts and percentages. Click on the Defaults button to restore previously changed rates, limits, etc. to the withholding rates provided with the software.

SYSTEM SETUP DATA

Once the Company Information has been entered, key the accounts and account titles into the Chart of Accounts Maintenance window. If vendors and/or customers are used, key the vendor and/or customer name into the Vendor and/or Customer Maintenance windows. Key the fixed assets, payroll and inventory data into the Account Maintenance window, if needed. Other setup features are discussed below.

Accounts Pick List

As an alternative to entering the chart of accounts entries, you can use the accounts Pick List button located at the bottom of the Chart of Accounts to select accounts from a master chart of accounts list. You should use the Chart of Accounts window to enter accounts that do not appear in the pick list, or to change the account titles as desired. The Chart of Accounts with Pick List is shown in Figure 11.

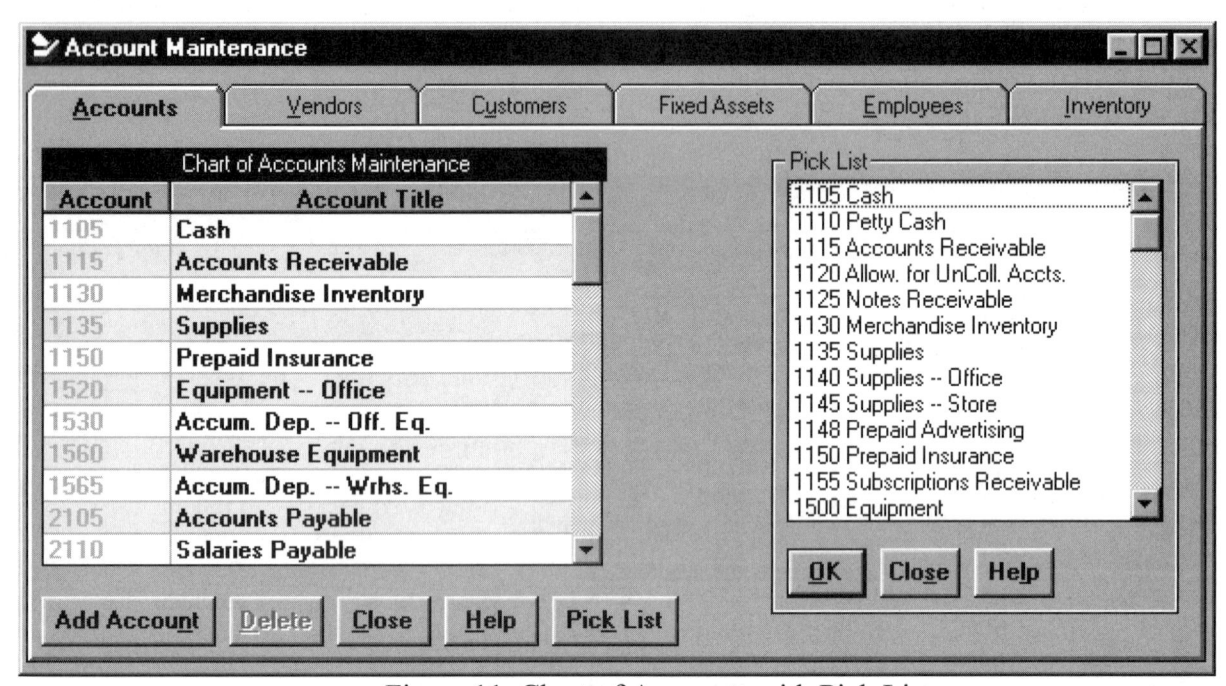

Figure 11 Chart of Accounts with Pick List

Click on the *Accts.* toolbar button, click on the Accounts tab, and then click on the *Pick List* button. Select an account from the Accounts Pick List column and click on *OK*. The selected account will be placed in the Chart of Accounts Maintenance list. Click the *Add Account* button (or strike the Enter key) to add the selected account to the chart of accounts. The selected account will be added to the chart of accounts in account number sequence and will appear in the Chart of Accounts column. To remove an account from the chart of accounts, select the desired account and click on the *Delete* button.

Opening Balances

General ledger opening balance data are entered into the computer via the general journal you used when entering general journal entries in earlier chapters. Each opening balance is posted as a separate general journal entry. Likewise, each customer account balance must be entered as a separate entry.

If the accounting system setup *does not* include inventory, the total of the balances for all the customers will be the balance of the Accounts Receivable general ledger account. Also, each vendor account balance must be entered as a separate entry. Again, the total of the balances for all the vendors will be the balance of the Accounts Payable general ledger account.

As opening balance data are entered, the debit and credit totals will not be equal; however, you should post each transaction anyway. By entering *BALANCE* in the reference grid cells, the computer will know that the entry is an opening balance and will therefore not display the error message warning you that the entry is not in balance. After all data have been entered, you should verify the accuracy of your input by making sure that the debit and credit totals shown on the trial balance are equal.

Fixed Assets

Use the Fixed Assets tab of the Account Maintenance window to enter each of the fixed assets.

Employees

Each of the employees must be entered into the computer. If the accounting system is being established at a time other than the beginning of a new year, you must establish the quarterly and yearly earnings and withholdings for each employee. Quarterly and yearly balances are established by either of two methods: (1) by running simulated payrolls for each pay period up to the desired date, or (2) by entering one payroll transaction for each employee for each quarter that represents the sum of that employee's earnings and withholdings for the quarter. In either case, since the payroll is date-sensitive, be sure to use the appropriate pay-period or end-of-quarter dates. Since the accounting system for Kendell Corporation is being established on February 1, and each employee is paid once each month, one simulated payroll can be run for the month of January to bring the quarterly and yearly balances up to date.

Inventory

Two tasks are required to set up an inventory system: (1) data for each stock item must be entered, and (2) enter purchase order, purchase invoice, and sales invoice historical data. After the company's stock items have been entered, the historical data may be entered.

When purchase orders, and the voucher (purchase invoices) historical data are entered, the computer will perform system integration. Therefore, the accounts payable, merchandise inventory, and vendor account balances will be updated automatically. Likewise, when the sales invoices historical data is entered, the computer will perform system integration. Therefore, the accounts receivable, revenue, merchandise inventory, cost, and customer account balances will be updated automatically.